FISHES OF THE GREAT BASIN

MAX C. FLEISCHMANN SERIES
IN GREAT BASIN NATURAL HISTORY

FISHES OF THE GREAT BASIN

A NATURAL HISTORY

WILLIAM F. SIGLER
and JOHN W. SIGLER

ILLUSTRATED BY SOPHIE SHEPPARD
AND JIM MORGAN

RENO : UNIVERSITY OF NEVADA PRESS : 1987

Table 5.1 is taken from *Biology of Fishes* by Carl E. Bond. Copyright © 1979 by Saunders College Publishing/Holt, Rinehart and Winston. Reprinted by permission of Holt, Rinehart and Winston, CBS College Publishing.

GREAT BASIN SERIES EDITOR: JOHN F. STETTER
COPYRIGHT © 1987 UNIVERSITY OF NEVADA PRESS
ALL RIGHTS RESERVED
COMPOSED AND PRINTED IN THE UNITED STATES
OF AMERICA
DESIGNED BY DAVID COMSTOCK

LIBRARY OF CONGRESS CATALOGING-IN-PUBLICATION DATA

Sigler, William F.
Fishes of the Great Basin.

(Max C. Fleischmann series in Great Basin natural history)
Bibliography: p.
Includes index.
1. Fishes—Great Basin.   I. Sigler, John W., 1946–   .
II. Title.   III. Series.
QL628.G73S54   1986   597.092'979   86-7082
ISBN 0-87417-116-4 (alk. paper)

TO
IRA LA RIVERS
SCHOLAR, TEACHER,
NATURALIST, FRIEND

Angling itself was of great antiquity, and a perfect art, and an art not easily attained to . . . is it not an art to deceive a Trout with an artificial fly? No life, my honest scholar, no life so happy and so pleasant as the life of a well-governed angler . . . then we sit on cowslip banks, hear the birds sing, and possess ourselves in as much quietness as these silent silver streams, which we now see glide so quietly by us . . . if I might be judge, God never did make a more calm, quiet, innocent recreation than angling.

—Izaak Walton, *The Compleat Angler*

There are those that can live without wild things and those that cannot.

—Aldo Leopold, *Sand County Almanac*

CONTENTS

PREFACE

THIS TEXT IS FOR fishermen, naturalists, ichthyologists, fishery biologists, pet owners, and people who just want to know about fish. Families are presented in phylogenetic order; that is, from the least to the most specialized. Within families, species are listed alphabetically, first by genera, then under genera by species.

The text, written in present tense for easy readability, is in two sections. The first is general, covering the characteristics, behavior, and values of fish, and the second covers life histories of fishes of the Great Basin. Each species is discussed under nine subheadings. Species are generally discussed in the singular; that is, as a species rather than a group of individuals.

The amount of space used for each fish life history depends on the economic and ecological importance of the species rather than the amount of literature available. For example, if two species occur in the same geographic area but one occurs in 80 percent of the waters and the other in only 2 percent, then the fish that is more prevalent is more extensively discussed. Of course we have taken into account each fish's palatability, attractiveness to the fishing public, and ecological importance and special considerations such as species uniqueness or threatened/endangered status. The exception to this is when there is relatively little information.

The annotated checklist has a brief statement about each species that may or may not be established in the Great Basin. Appendix 1 lists established fishes of the Great Basin. With a few exceptions, only subspecies of cutthroat trout are listed, although it is recognized that there are many other important subspecies, especially among the native minnows and killifishes. Appendix 2 lists fishes mentioned in the text that do not appear in Appendix 1 or the annotated checklist.

The Great Basin is defined as that area of the United States draining internally in the states of Utah, Wyoming, Idaho, Nevada, California, and Oregon, excluding the Salton Sea. The White River drainage above the lower end of Pahranagat Valley (near Lower Pahranagat Lake) is considered part of the Great Basin. The Northwest system excludes the Goose Lake and Klamath drainages (Hubbs and Miller 1948; King 1982).

The term "fisherman" has no sexist connotation; it means anyone who fishes.

ACKNOWLEDGMENTS

THE LINE DRAWINGS are by Sophie Sheppard, Cedarville, California and Jim Morgan, Mendon, Utah. The map of the Great Basin is after Hubbs and Miller 1948 and King 1982. The key to fishes of the Great Basin and drawings are by Gerald R. Smith. John F. Stetter, editor of the Great Basin Series and director of the University of Nevada Press, was of inestimable help at all times. Mary Hill was of extraordinary help in editing, organizing, and finding small but embarrassing errors.

The following people have aided greatly in the preparation of the manuscript:

Cal Allan, regional fisheries assistant (retired), Nevada Department of Wildlife, Las Vegas.

Don Andriano, chief of fisheries (retired), Utah Division of Wildlife Resources, Salt Lake City.

Robert J. Behnke, professor, Department of Fisheries and Wildlife Biology, Colorado State University, Fort Collins.

David H. Bennett, associate professor of fisheries and wildlife resources, University of Idaho, Moscow.

Carl E. Bond, professor emeritus of fisheries, Oregon State University, Corvallis.

Ross V. Bulkley, leader, Cooperative Fisheries Research Unit, and professor of fisheries and wildlife (deceased), Utah State University, Logan.

Don Chapman, Chapman Consultants, Inc., McCall, Idaho.

Patrick Coffin, chief of fisheries, Nevada Department of Wildlife, Reno.

Jim Curran, regional fisheries supervisor, Nevada Department of Wildlife, Fallon.

Glen Davis, fisheries program coordinator, Utah Division of Wildlife Resources, Salt Lake City.

Gretchen P. Davis, secretary, Logan, Utah.

James E. Deacon, professor of biology, University of Nevada, Las Vegas.

Jack Dieringer, chief of fisheries (retired), Nevada Department of Wildlife, Reno.

Lois Gunnell, secretary, Logan, Utah.

Thomas Hardy, aquatic biologist, Logan, Utah.

William T. Helm, associate professor of fisheries and wildlife, Utah State University, Logan.

Dale K. Hepworth, regional fisheries manager, Utah Division of Wildlife Resources, Cedar City.

James Johnson, fishery biologist, Utah Divison of Wildlife Resources, Salt Lake City.

John King, fishery biologist, Nevada Department of Wildlife, Reno.

John L. Leppink, fish culture coordinator, Utah Division of Wildlife Resources, Salt Lake City.

Peter B. Moyle, associate professor and chair, Department of Wildlife and Fisheries Biology, University of California, Davis.

John M. Neuhold, professor, department of fisheries and wildlife, and assistant dean, College of Natural Resources, Utah State University, Logan.

E. P. Pister, associate fishery biologist, California Department of Fish and Game, Bishop.

Randy Radant, fishery biologist, Utah Division of Wildlife Resources, Salt Lake City.

Edwin V. Rawley, planner, Utah Division of Wildlife Resources, Salt Lake City.

David K. Rice, chief of information and education, Nevada Department of Wildlife, Reno.

Bruce E. Rieman, fishery biologist, Idaho Fish and Game Department, Coeur d'Alene.

Don Sada, biologist, U.S. Fish and Wildlife Service, Reno, Nevada.

Margaret B. Sigler, editor, secretary, Logan, Utah.

Gerald R. Smith, associate curator, Museum of Zoology, University of Michigan, Ann Arbor.

Phillip W. Smith, head of faunistic surveys and insect identification (Emeritus), Illinois State Natural History Survey, Urbana.

Thomas J. Trelease, chief of fisheries (retired), Nevada Department of Wildlife, Reno.

Steven Vigg, biologist, U.S. Fish and Wildlife Service, Cook, Washington.

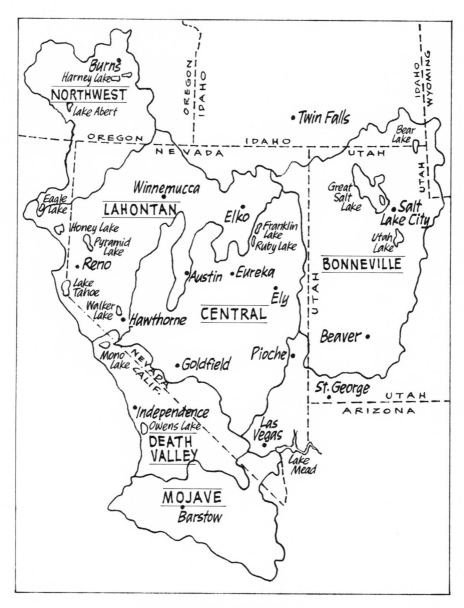

Basins and principal features.

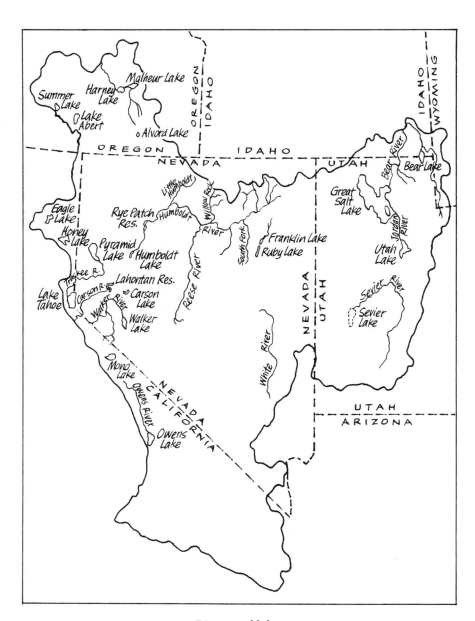

Rivers and lakes.

1

~~~~~~~~~~

Introduction

Aɴʏ ᴅɪsᴄᴜssɪoɴ ᴏғ ғɪsʜ must begin with generalities, but fish, quaint creatures that they are, more often than not are exceptions to any rule. Species of fish vary from one another in almost every conceivable way. What makes them so interesting also makes understanding them more difficult. Their ways of living, growing, reproducing, and even playing are far from simple. Fish provide us with food, sport, entertainment, and satisfaction in just knowing they are there. Many are so adaptable they respond to a wide range of adverse conditions; others die of shock from simply being handled.

How do you go about understanding these variable and intricate creatures? Where do you begin? As in any other science, learning should be taken one step at a time and the start need not be with the most primitive fishes. It can be anywhere along evolutionary or geologic lines. A good rule is to study first those fish that you find most intriguing. Trout fishermen want to know where the fish are and when; later they may want to know why they are there and in what numbers. Non-fishermen may want to know what species occur in what areas or bodies of water. As interest widens, the scope of study spreads accordingly. All fish have three prime motivations: feeding, reproducing, and surviving. If they are feeding, the next question is, "Why is the food there?" This means a look at the environment or ecosystem. Within certain limits, fish follow whatever they are feeding on. For example, in Pyramid Lake, Nevada cutthroat trout feed largely on tui chub, which tend to tolerate and concentrate in warmer water than the trout. This means the trout, which move offshore into the deeper, colder water as summer approaches, must then feed on those less abundant chub scattered throughout deep water. As winter approaches, the trout move inshore and feed there on chub until summer. Part of the inshore population of chub tends to move offshore in winter, but large numbers remain in relatively shallow water. The trout therefore do not feed where the food is most abundant all the time; in summer they must retreat to cold water. Although food is available for chub throughout the lake, it is most abundant in shallow water, where sunlight penetrates to the bottom.

Breeding migrations of fish may be only a few yards or hundreds of miles. Very few Pacific salmon are caught until they move nearer shore and into the estuaries and streams. Here, availability of food has nothing to do with locating fish; movement to acceptable spawning grounds is the governing factor.

Certainly we study fish for many reasons other than wanting to catch them. Pet fish, in a more or less natural setting with plants and cover, provide opportunities to study behavior and mating or to just enjoy their activities. Fish watching in the wild has its limitations, but at spawning time, when fish lose much of their wariness, they can often be observed. Patience and quiet is about all that is required. Common carp spawn generally at twilight in the weedy or rocky areas of shallow water. They race about, splashing and chasing each other, often with their backs out of water. Kokanee, a landlocked form of sockeye salmon, move out of lakes into small streams to spawn. They are more visible than most fish because just before the spawning run they turn a bright red. This, coupled with the hooked jaws of the males and the infighting, makes their breeding activities an interesting spectacle.

Suppose you want to neither catch nor watch fish. What is left? There are several periodicals, hundreds of books, and hundreds of thousands of articles on fish. Many are written so laymen can understand them. You may want to get a book that consists primarily of pictures of fishes. There are several very good ones, but do not expect to see large numbers of Great Basin fishes. The most colorful fishes inhabit tropical reefs and these are what you see most. There the colors are so varied they defy imagination (Herald 1961; Frank 1969).

Male freshwater fishes are almost invariably more colorful than females. Breeding males attract and court females, fertilize the eggs externally (except in livebearers), and may guard the eggs and young. Breeding behavior is most interesting to watch because the fish are more colorful, more aggressive, and less wary. Male green sunfish, for example, will establish territories even in an aquarium. They try to dominate their area by flaring the gill covers so they appear larger and by darting, butting, and nipping. Extreme behavior by male fish is rare, but sometimes serious injuries occur. Black bullheads with broken backs often wash up on one section of beach during the spawning season in Spirit Lake, Iowa.

How do you go about studying fish? The best way is to decide in advance what you would like to know. Consider the questions, preferably in writing, that you will address. Where are the fish? What is the description of their environment? What are they doing? How old are they? Determining a fish's age takes expensive equipment and experience; try consulting the literature. In observing breeding behavior try concentrating on one male or one location. A review of literature before going afield is time well spent. Take copious notes and review them later; actions not understood in the field may later have meaning. Minimum equipment consists of field clothing, pocket thermometer, Polaroid glasses, and notebook and pencil.

2

The Great Basin Drainages

THE GREAT BASIN is a vast area of mountains and deserts located generally between the western ridges of the Rocky Mountains and the eastern edge of the Sierra Nevada. It is south of the Columbia River basin and north of the Colorado River basin (Houghton 1976). It is the largest inland drainage in North America. The Great Basin, contrary to its name, is not made up of just one large inland area with no drainage to the sea. Rather, it is comprised of numerous (over two hundred) drainages that at one time had individual integrity. A three-dimensional map of Utah or, more dramatically, Nevada reveals innumerable geologic folds in which water was trapped in recent geologic times. There were two great lakes in the basin, Lake Bonneville and Lake Lahontan, and each covered thousands of square miles and were many hundreds of feet deep. The discussion presented here deals with the Lake Lahontan basin, the Central basin (both mainly in Nevada but also in California and Oregon), the Northwest Desert basin, the Northwest Oregon Lakes region, the Mojave–Death Valley region, and the Lake Bonneville basin (largely in Utah, but also in Wyoming, Idaho, and Nevada). Also included is the relict portion of the White River that in years of normal precipitation is no longer connected to the Colorado River. The Salton Sea basin is not included.

Smith (1978), in discussing intermountain fishes, concludes that the genus *Salmo* was in the region by Pliocene times (1.8 to 5 million years ago) and possibly then in the area presently occupied. While Pliocene forms are specifically different from recent forms, usually

Pleistocene forms are not (i.e., *Prosopium*, *Salvelinus*, *Gila*, *Richard-sonius*, *Catostomus*, *Chasmistes*, and *Cottus*).

The affinities of the upper Snake River and the Bonneville basin proper indicate that five species of fish (mountain whitefish, cutthroat trout, Utah sucker, longnose dace, and mottled sculpin) entered Lake Bonneville from the Snake River (Miller 1958). Bear River at one time flowed into the Snake. The Lahontan relationships of fish (principally *Chasmistes* and the species of *Catostomus* that were formerly *Pantosteus*) indicate an earlier connection, probably of Pliocene or early Pleistocene epoch, between the Bonneville and Lahontan basins.

THE LAKE LAHONTAN BASIN

The Lake Lahontan basin, fed by the waters of the Truckee, Susan, Carson, and Walker rivers, lies in a wedge approximately 150 to 160 miles wide in a northeasterly direction and extends from Lake Tahoe on the California-Nevada border to the border between Oregon, Idaho, and Nevada on the east.

The Truckee River originates at Lake Tahoe near the Nevada-California border at an altitude of 6,228 feet. As it flows generally north-northeast, several small streams are tributary, including the Little Truckee River, which contributes the largest volume. The Truckee River drains an area of 790 square miles in California and 1,340 square miles in Nevada, traveling 120 miles from origin to mouth and dropping approximately 2,432 feet (Houghton 1976). Near the river's terminus in Pyramid Lake, ancient Lake Lahontan extended to a site at Lagomarsino Canyon at an elevation of 4,380 feet about 65,000 years ago (Morrison 1964). At least one other lake existed in the Truckee River basin upstream from Pyramid Lake at 6,000 feet. The river eventually wore down the basalt dam near Boca and this lake ceased to exist. The Truckee River, teeming with fish (Lahontan cutthroat trout) in the time of John Charles Frémont (1844), was mistaken by him as the mythical Buenaventura River, which was supposed to flow across the continent to the Pacific Ocean.

Tributaries of the Carson River arise along approximately 50 miles of the Sierra crest. The east fork, the principal tributary, originates under Sonora Peak at an altitude of approximately 11,400 feet. In recent geologic time, the Carson River Sink was connected to Lake Lahontan and the largest areal extent of that lake was in the Carson Desert, where approximately 30 percent of the surface area existed.

The two main forks of the Walker River arise in springs and lakes of the Sierra crest under peaks at elevations from 10,000 to 12,000 feet.

The West Walker arises in lakes just below the drainage separation between the Walker River and the western drainages of the Sierra Nevada
in Yosemite National Park. The only pluvial lake known to have been
formed in the Walker River drainage was in Smith Valley, across the
state line into Nevada. Ancient Lake Wellington covered 90 square
miles to a depth of 300 feet, but did not restrain the river's rush to Lake
Lahontan (Houghton 1976). The East Walker flow is now regulated by a
reservoir at Bridgeport, but the old flow continued past this point and
was fed by Sweetwater, Rough, and Bodie creeks. The two forks con-
verge near Yerington and flow approximately 50 miles to the north end
of Walker Lake, which is supplied significant quantities of water only
from the river. Walker Lake is about one-half the size of Pyramid Lake—
18 miles long and 5 to 6 miles wide. It is sufficiently shallow and may
desiccate during very extended dry spells.

THE CENTRAL BASIN

The Central basin, as defined here, is a vast area of eastern-central
Nevada east of the Lahontan basin bounded on the south by the Colorado River drainage of the White and Virgin rivers. King (1982) includes
the White River above Warm Springs Valley in the Great Basin, but we
have drawn the separation line at Lower Pahranagat Lake based on current hydrologic patterns. This area is unique in that it contains no
streams of any size (with the exception of the Humboldt River) with
permanent flow. It does have numerous small sections of streams and
several small lakes and marshes.

The Humboldt River is presently 100 miles longer than it was
60,000 years ago, having cut a new channel from Red House as historic
Lake Lahontan receded (Houghton 1976). The main stem of the river,
which originates in the low hills northeast of Wells, flows only about
300 miles, but has almost 1,000 meandering miles, making it one of the
longest and most important river drainages in the Great Basin (Bradley
et al. 1980). The flow of the Reese River, which heads in the Shoshone
Mountains to the south, does not always reach the main stem Humboldt River. There are four other streams that do reach the Humboldt
River: the Marys River heads to the northeast near the Snake River divide, the South Fork of the Humboldt River heads in the Ruby Mountains, and the North and South forks of the Little Humboldt River head
near the Snake River divide.

NORTHWEST DESERT BASIN

The Quinn and the Kings rivers originate in the mountains of northwestern Nevada and the southern tip of Oregon. Both rivers are short and terminate in sinks in the northwestern corner of Nevada.

NORTHWEST OREGON LAKES REGION

The Northwest Oregon Lakes region lies in the states of California, Nevada, and Oregon with the largest land area in Oregon. In its northern extremity, Silver and Silvies creeks and the Blitzen River drain to Malheur and Harney lakes. The western edge of the area in Oregon contains Paulina Marsh, Silver Lake, Summer Lake, Lake Albert, and the Chewaucan Marsh. The Warner Valley lies north above the border between California and Nevada and contains the Warner Lakes, remnants of pluvial Lake Warner. High Rock Lake and Summit Lake lie in northwestern Nevada while Eagle Lake and Horse Lake lie on the southern edge of this drainage in California (Houghton 1976). Goose Lake, which straddles the Oregon-California border, is not included in this text.

MOJAVE—DEATH VALLEY REGION

The Owens River rises in the snow-fed lakes along the Sierra escarpment and receives water from Glass Creek, Deadman Creek, Hot Creek, and others before it flows into Lake Crowley. Below Lake Crowley the flow of the river is diverted to serve power stations in Owens Gorge. Below Bishop, California the Owens River is fed by numerous streams and creeks. The Owens River channel terminates at Owens Lake, now dry because of diversions for power and agricultural uses (Houghton 1976).

Mono Lake is in the extreme northern portion of this region. It is a remnant of a large water body that today is so salty (borax, sodium chloride, and calcium carbonate) that it supports no fish life (Houghton 1976).

The Death Valley trough lies along the California-Nevada border but is entirely in California. It presently receives water only from the Amargosa River (*amargo* is a Spanish word meaning "bitter"). The Amargosa rises in Nevada along the Pahute Mesa and flows south and southeast, crossing the state line 110 miles from its origin. In California it turns northward near Tecopa and continues to its terminus in Death Valley. At intervals it is fed by warm springs, the most notable being Saratoga Springs and Devil's Hole in Ash Meadows, which contains an endangered fish, the Devils Hole pupfish. Much of the area in the lower two-thirds of Death Valley was previously occupied by Pleistocene Lake Manly (Houghton 1976).

The Mojave River rises on the northern slopes of the San Bernardino Range in southern California and is the shortest of the permanent streams in the Death Valley system. The river follows a winding course northward and eastward into the desert, where it sinks into the sands. Its length, approximately 100 miles, varies with the water year (Houghton 1976).

THE LAKE BONNEVILLE BASIN

The area covered by ancient Lake Bonneville was tremendous (nearly 20,000 square miles in Pleistocene). The basin includes areas of Wyoming, Idaho, Nevada, and the northwestern half of Utah and is defined on the east by the Wasatch Mountain Range and the western end of the Uintah Mountains, on the north by the Snake River basin, on the south by the Colorado Plateau, and on the west by the Central and Lake Lahontan basins. The major rivers of the Bonneville system include the Bear, Provo, Ogden, Weber, Jordan, and Sevier, all with numerous tributaries.

The 325-mile-long Sevier River rises on the Markagunt and Paunsaugunt plateaus and drains northward as the East and Main forks (Bradley et al. 1980). The river continues north toward the town of Gunnison and is joined by the San Pitch River there. At this point the river turns west and south and submerges in the desert 140 miles from its sources. Sevier Lake, when it was mapped in 1872, had a surface area of 188 square miles (Houghton 1976). It exists today only after substantial precipitation, such as in 1983–84. It dries up completely most hot summers.

The Bear River arises in Utah on the north slopes of the Uintah Mountains in Amethyst and McPheters lakes and flows northward into Wyoming, crisscrossing the Utah-Wyoming border. It flows into Idaho and near Soda Springs turns west and then south to enter Utah again. As it flows south into Utah, the tributaries of the Cub, Logan, Blacksmith, and Little Bear rivers join before the Bear enters Bear River Bay then Great Salt Lake below Brigham City. The Bear, like the Sevier River in the southwestern corner of the state, travels many miles but has its origin only a short distance from its discharge point. The Bear River flows about 350 miles, with origin and mouth only about 90 miles apart (Bradley et al. 1980). The Blacksmith and Little Bear rivers arise in northern Utah. The Logan River originates in southeastern Idaho. All of these rivers receive tributary streams from the mountains of the Wasatch Front before joining the larger Bear River in Cache Valley. The Bear River at one time connected directly to Ancient Bear

Lake and repeatedly changed its course during Pleistocene due to fault blocking and volcanism (Morrison 1965). It flowed north to the Portneuf River and then into the Snake River more than 34,000 years ago (Minckley, Hendrickson, and Bond 1984). It is not presently connected to Bear Lake naturally; rather, it has been channeled through Dingle Swamp to provide irrigation and power storage for Utah and Idaho.

The fishes of Bear Lake belong to the Bonneville fauna and show considerable local differentiation. In particular, the peaknose cisco that is now confined to Bear Lake (until recent transplant efforts of unknown success) and presents an important faunal geographic record. The Bear River contributes more than 50 percent of the annual flow into Great Salt Lake.

The Provo, Ogden, and Weber rivers have their origins on the west slope of the Rockies in the canyons of the area known as the Wasatch Front. The headwaters of all three rivers are near the drainage divide of the Bear River. The Provo River traverses some 35 miles before emptying into Utah Lake near Provo. It has been extensively diverted for irrigation since the mid 1850s. The Ogden River originates as three separate forks in the canyons east of Ogden, Utah. It traverses 50 miles in the canyons and across the face of the Wasatch Front before joining the Weber River near the Great Salt Lake. The Weber River originates against the west slope of the Uintah Mountains and travels north and west. Its tributary streams of Beaver, Chalk, and Silver creeks join the river in the 50 miles before it approaches the town of Morgan. Beyond Morgan, the river travels another 30 miles northwest and enters the Great Salt Lake west of the town of Ogden. Its major tributary is the Ogden River. The Weber River contributes approximately 25 percent of the annual flow into Great Salt Lake.

The Jordan River originates at the north end of Utah Lake near Provo. It travels approximately 35 miles north and enters the Great Salt Lake on the southern shore. Historically, this river contained Utah cutthroat trout. Since the coming of the white man it has been used for irrigation diversions and to regulate the level of Utah Lake.

THE FLOODS OF 1983−84

In the winter of 1983 it became obvious that water levels of the Great Salt Lake were headed for record highs. In February 1983 Great Salt Lake was 4,202.1 feet above sea level. The potential for flood damage to transportation facilities, shore-based industry, wildlife refuges, and recreational facilities was evident (*Utah Waterline and Landline*, February 16, 1983). In March 1983 some recreational facilities around

Utah Lake were closed because of flood waters and proposals for lowering the level of Great Salt Lake were being studied.

On March 31, 1983 Great Salt Lake broke a 55-year-old elevation record at 4,203.2 feet. March had shown a one-month near-record increase in lake elevation. In May 1983, with Great Salt Lake at 4,203.7 feet, the National Weather Service revised its prediction on how high Great Salt Lake would rise. It peaked in June at 4,204.0 feet. The Jordan, Weber, and Bear rivers were flowing at close to 100-year highs. Precipitation for the Great Basin area of Utah was an average of 123 percent above normal (*Utah Waterline and Landline*, May 11, May 25, 1983).

The largest rise in Great Salt Lake water level in recorded history (5.1 feet) occurred between September 15, 1982 and July 1, 1983. Property damage exceeded $115 million. The June 30, 1983 level of the lake, highest in 59 years, was 4,205 feet (*Utah Waterline and Landline*, July 20, 1983; *Utah Waterline*, August 3, 1983). By October of 1983 it was obvious that Great Salt Lake was not going to drop the expected average 1.7 feet from evaporation during the summer, but rather had decreased only about 3.6 inches by August 15 and then had begun to rise again (*Utah Waterline*, October 12, 1983).

The early part of the winter of 1983 did nothing to alleviate fears of a second straight record-water year. The opening of the 1983 duck hunt was delayed in Utah by one week to allow late-hatching birds to mature (egg laying had been affected by the high water). The resorts along the Wasatch Front reported record snowfalls in November and early December, in one case breaking a historic record for November snowfall by 30 inches. In June and again in December 1983 water levels were so high that water flowed across the main access road to the Bear River Migratory Bird Refuge west of Brigham City, Utah in two places, and as much as 1.5 miles of road were threatened by high water. By late December 1983 the water level was still threatening property and no letup to winter precipitation was evident.

The 1983 high-water year produced many dramatic floods and mud slides, not the least of which was the creation of what became known temporarily as Thistle Lake in Spanish Fork Canyon, Utah. A 174.5-foot-high mud slide, triggered by saturated soils, closed both the highway and the railroad, and created a 62,000—acre-foot lake which inundated the small town of Thistle.

In 1984 Great Salt Lake rose to a level of 4,209.25 feet, the highest since 1878. Utah Lake, which feeds into Great Salt Lake, rose to 5.43 feet above flood stage.

A panel of experts meeting in Salt Lake City, Utah in early spring of 1985 noted the level of Great Salt Lake was 4,208 feet above sea level. The majority agreed it probably would not rise above 4,218 feet, a level that has been reached in the past 5,000 years. The panel did feel the lake level would exceed 4,212 feet in the next few years. This is the highest level it has reached in the 140 years of record keeping (*Salt Lake Tribune*, March 29, 1985).

The dramatic increase in Great Salt Lake levels does not directly affect fish life because no fish species inhabits the saline water (23 to 27 percent in 1982) of the lake. In Utah Lake flood levels of more than 7 feet may be beneficial to fish life, increasing breeding and feeding areas in shallow water and aiding primary productivity. In the rivers and streams that feed Great Salt Lake flood waters are probably detrimental to fish. Increased flood flows in the spring and continued high flows in summer months destroy fish redds, reducing or eliminating natural reproduction. High waters tend to carry an increased silt load, which abrades gill tissue and covers (in areas of reduced flow) spawning and food-producing areas. High water also substantially reduces fisherman success. The floods of 1983 and 1984 may affect fish populations in the Great Basin in ways yet to be discovered.

3

History of Fishing in the Great Basin States of Utah and Nevada

HISTORIC PERSPECTIVE

THE EARLIEST FISHERMEN to exploit waters in the Great Basin area were probably wandering bands of Asians who crossed the Bering Strait to Alaskan shores and eventually inhabited a vast portion of what is now the western United States. These people were most likely present on the shores of ancient lakes Bonneville and Lahontan 8,000 to 10,000 years ago. Recent archaeological evidence indicates, however, that these Asians were not the direct ancestors of the Pyramid Lake Paiute Indians who now inhabit the area surrounding Pyramid Lake (the remains of ancient Lake Lahontan) nor of the Indians found near Great Salt Lake by explorers in the early 1800s. These Indian tribes had been preceded by people of the Desert Culture as early as 10,000 B.P. (Houghton 1976).

Evidence found in archaeological sites near Pyramid Lake indicates that a cultural group termed the Lovelock Culture inhabited the Pyramid Lake basin from approximately 4,000 years ago until around 1844. They undoubtedly used the resources available in and around the lake for food, clothing, and shelter. Approximately 500 years ago, the nomadic Paiute Indians invaded the Pyramid Lake basin and conquered the tribes existing on the shores of Pyramid Lake, possibly to gain access to the Great Basin's most bountiful fishery. Similar changes in peoples occurred near the Great Salt Lake in Utah prior to the white man's entry into the area in the late 1700s (Houghton 1976). In the case of Pyramid Lake, the presence of two or more cultures is supported by two facts. Archaeological evidence presented by Follett (1977) indicates that specimens found in a cave along the eastern shore of Pyramid Lake are cui-ui and Tahoe sucker. Apparently the cui-ui were approximately 19 to 20 inches long and weighed 3 to 6 pounds. These fish had been decapitated and skinned (which would reduce the weight substantially), implying that they had been carried from a point of capture on the lower Truckee River. Since this practice of decapitating and skinning cui-ui is not in agreement with the practices of the historic northern Paiutes, who normally split and dried cui-ui, it indicates the presence of a previous culture. Additionally, John Charles Frémont, the first white man to visit Pyramid Lake, described "poor looking" Indians along the eastern shore of the lake and stated that they were of a different tribe from the Paiutes living near the mouth of the Truckee River. These poor-looking Indians may have been survivors of the Lovelock Culture (Wheeler 1974).

In January of 1844, Captain Frémont arrived at the northern end of Pyramid Lake with his exploration party. During his trip around the lake, Frémont was approached by a poor-looking Indian who informed him that a large river entered the south end of the lake. At the south end of the lake, Frémont's group found the river inlet and were then approached by a number of Indians whom they presumed to be from a different tribe. The Indians brought a large fish to trade. Frémont's group determined that it was a "salmon-trout," and when they indicated interest in having more of them, the Indians quickly brought the fish in numbers and soon had the camp well stocked. Frémont indicates that the fish were of extraordinary size, about as large as the Columbia River salmon, generally 2 to 4 feet in length (Wheeler 1974). This is the first historical record of the famous Pyramid Lake Lahontan cutthroat trout.

During the mid to late 1840s (white man's record) and possibly for as many as 500 years previously, the Pyramid Lake area was inhabited by the northern Paiute Indian tribe. These Indians were known as Kuyuidikado, which means "cui-ui eaters" or "fish eaters." This fish, a member of the sucker family, has, in combination with the Lahontan cutthroat trout, evidently sustained Indian tribes around Pyramid Lake for centuries (Wheeler 1974).

PYRAMID LAKE—TRUCKEE RIVER FISHERY: 1844 TO PRESENT

During the time shortly after Frémont's discovery of Pyramid Lake, relatively few immigrants traversed the trail near Pyramid Lake on their way to California. These travelers traded for trout with the Indians near the lake. Presumably, these fish had been caught using the Indians' customary methods of harpoons, set lines, and nets with and without weirs. Between 1845 and 1859, the number of travelers increased significantly due to the opening of the Comstock Lode in the nearby Sierra Nevada in 1859. In the following ten years, white settlements developed principally at Truckee Meadows and Wadsworth. Fish from Pyramid Lake and the Truckee River undoubtedly formed an integral part of the diet for both the permanent residents and the travelers. By 1868, when the railroad had been completed to the Wadsworth area, the vast food source present in the lake had been recognized. The winter spawning run up the Truckee River allowed fish to be captured in large numbers and shipped with minimal spoilage anywhere in western Nevada and the surrounding states. The trout became familiar delicacies from Ogden, Utah to San Francisco, California.

In the mid and late 1860s, upstream logging and diversion dams to provide waterpower for sawmills denied fish access to certain spawning grounds. Dams in the headwaters and near Reno presented additional impediments to spawning passage. By 1889 the Reno City Power Company and the Reno Reduction Works had added other dams and effectively blocked the river in most years. In 1884, no fewer than eleven dams existed on the Truckee River, and only two of them had fish ladders that functioned at all (Townley 1980).

In addition to the commercial fishing that developed during the 1860s, pollution from the increased population and from the developing industrial base (timber mills and paper plants) began to affect the Truckee River and subsequently Pyramid Lake. By 1900 efforts to require cleanup of the most prolific pollution sources on the river had been successful, and the trout were no longer threatened by this particular hazard. Dams erected for irrigation, both by individuals and ditch associations, as well as industrial water users provided the next obstacle to fish passage to the spawning grounds of the Truckee River. Not only did these dams present an impediment to the fish (although the trout could easily jump most of the less permanent dams), they forced the fish to congregate in specific areas, thus making them extremely vulnerable to commercial fishermen. Between 1860 and 1900, Townley (1980) estimates that from 60,000 to 200,000 pounds of trout were harvested and shipped annually. These are estimates only and do not include sport fish, fish not shipped from the immediate area of Pyramid Lake, or fish lost to pollution or to instream obstacles. Several times during the later decades of the nineteenth century commercial non-Indian fishermen were warned off the reservation or arrested for taking fish. These measures did not, however, slow the commercial taking of cutthroat. Harvesting methods during this time were aimed at obtaining the maximum numbers of fish with the least effort. Dynamite, poison, traps, nets, and grabhooks were used to collect the cutthroat. A single stick of dynamite thrown into a swarming mass of migrating spawners yielded hundreds of pounds of trout with no effort (Townley 1980).

Behnke (1974) estimates at least 1,000,000 pounds of cutthroat trout could have been harvested annually between 1860 and 1920 and that with all factors considered, approximately 500,000 or more pounds of trout were harvested annually from 1888 to 1890. Despite this extraordinary harvest, the fish population did not appear to be damaged.

Snyder (1918) indicates that in the early 1900s such large numbers of cui-ui appeared in the mouth of the Truckee River that many were crowded out of the water in shallow places, actually having dammed the water with their bodies. The coming of the cui-ui was of great importance to the local Indians as well as to the Paiutes to the south, who traveled many miles to fish for this abundant source of food.

In 1875, the mill in Verdi, Nevada was constructed, and its associated dam became the optimum location above Wadsworth to take cutthroat. Tons of fish were taken from the river here and at Wadsworth. By 1885 the cutthroat trout of Pyramid Lake had been restricted to Pyramid Lake and the river below Reno. By 1900 the trout and some other native fish had been eliminated from 80 percent of the Truckee basin (Townley 1980). All contributors to the changes that occurred from 1844 to 1900 must share the blame for depleting the once magnificent fishery of Pyramid Lake. Industrial pollution, habitat modification and degradation, failure of the federal government to act to preserve the fishery, as well as overfishing promoted the decline of the Lahontan cutthroat trout after 1890. While the fish still existed in numbers, it had been severely depleted.

During the late 1880s and 1890s sport fishermen, greatly agitated by the declining numbers of fish and habitat, loosely organized themselves and began lobbying both Nevada and California legislatures to act before the cutthroat were lost. Heavy sport fishing probably did not start until sometime in the late 1800s. Prior to the coming of large numbers of white men and the organization of communities, fishing was done on a necessity basis. Fishing for sport probably became popular after the development of communities. Their inhabitants had leisure time and could afford the luxury of fishing for reasons other than providing food.

The completion of Derby Dam in 1905 presented fish with an impassable barrier. It, as time demonstrated, helped initiate the demise of the original population of Lahontan cutthroat trout in Pyramid Lake. In 1904, when the diversion dam was being constructed and the water had been diverted around the work area, thousands of trout piled up below the dam while attempting to reach their historic spawning grounds. True to their nature, commercial fishermen by the dozens lined up to capture these trapped fish in what may have been the last great run of spawners. The temporary dam was removed in June of 1905 and a few fish, for a very short time, were once again able to reach their spawning grounds, although thousands died when the water was shut off in the temporary channel. Although Derby Dam was constructed with a fish ladder, the ladder never functioned properly and was swept away in the high waters of 1907. In 1909, some 10 tons of fish were caught below Derby Dam, dramatizing the ineffectiveness of the rebuilt fish ladder. Sport fishermen by that time had become more organized and complained bitterly to the U.S. Reclamation Department, which answered that the water was for irrigation, not for fish and that at any rate "there are enough fish in Pyramid Lake to supply this whole state with fish." Derby Dam was an insurmountable obstacle for the migrating cutthroat trout. It also accomplished what no other dam had: the river below it was dry in many years and flow was severely reduced in all but high-water years.

In 1914 the hydroelectric-irrigation Lahontan Reservoir on the Carson River was completed and water diversion on a year-round basis was started. This depleted the water supply at times other than summer (May to September), the pattern when diversions were for irrigation only. Other circumstances continued to restrict the ability of the trout to reproduce, not the least of which was the development of an often impassable delta at the mouth of the river. The delta was formed as a result of reduced river flows and dropping lake levels. During this time, efforts were made to collect spawn from the trout each year. Due to bickering and interagency rivalries, only limited amounts of spawn were collected in any one year. In 1930, probably the last year there was a productive spawning run, the State Fish and Game Commission was prevented from taking spawn, while the U.S. Bureau of Fisheries (predecessor of the U.S. Fish and Wildlife Service) was allowed to continue taking spawn. The federal agency terminated its hatchery operation in 1932. Thus, years of drought, which precluded fish from crossing the river delta to spawning areas, pollution, and exploitation led to the demise of the Pyramid Lake population of Lahontan cutthroat trout (Townley 1980). Most of them were gone after 1938; a few may have survived until 1943.

In retrospect, many factions and groups can be blamed for the demise of this great population of fish. The white men and, to some extent, the Indians fished the waters and sold fish when the population was in decline, speeding that decline. Pollution from the cities of Sparks and Reno contaminated the Truckee for fifty years before the Lahontan was lost. Upstream logging and milling practices further polluted the stream and clogged spawning grounds, killing fry and adults alike. Derby Dam eliminated most of the water from the historic river channel in the late 1920s and early 1930s, causing the formation of an impassable delta at the mouth of the river, thereby sealing the doom of the cutthroat. Channel modifications and alterations also promoted loss of habitat and warming of the river to the detriment of the cold-water Lahontans. Differences and disagreements among agencies resulted in inaction and conflicting actions, all of which were largely uncoordinated, despite the manifest need for a concerted, coordinated effort.

UTAH LAKE COMMERCIAL FISHERY

Like Pyramid Lake in Nevada, today's large bodies of water in Utah had been preceded by an immense prehistoric lake, Lake Bonneville. Lake Bonneville covered the western portion of Utah almost to the southern state line and its drainage area extended into parts of Nevada, Wyoming, and Idaho. Bear Lake, though not actually part of Lake Bonneville, was at times indirectly connected to it through the Bear River.

Humans occupied the shores of Lake Bonneville as it was receding some 10,000 to 11,000 years ago. These inhabitants were nomadic and did not dwell long in any location. Food may not have been available from Bonneville even at this time, since it was receding across previously established salt flats (Houghton 1976). Findings in archaeological locations on the shores of ancient Lake Bonneville document not the presence of fish but rather of such animals as the horse, camel, and giant sloth, indicating that fishing was not a means of sustenance.

At some point in history, far preceding the coming of the white man, Great Salt Lake had become too salty to sustain a diverse fauna.

Remnants of Lake Bonneville that support fisheries today are limited to Utah Lake near Provo, the streams associated with the Bonneville drainage, and Bear Lake, which was not directly connected to historic Lake Bonneville.

Houghton (1976) mentions that "the Paiutes along the Sevier River were hunted by the Utes in the spring when they were weak and helpless after a long and hungry winter," indicating that these Indians were not availing themselves of the fish in the rivers, Utah Lake, or Sevier Lake.

White men of Father Escalante's party camping on the shores of Utah Lake as early as 1776 recorded that trout were very abundant and that the Indians living around the lake relied very heavily upon them and the other fish for food (Hickman 1978; Carter 1969). Carter notes that in 1813 and again in 1824 Spanish explorers, mountainmen, and trappers probably made some use of the fish in Utah Lake, but the fish were not of great importance to them. The explorers, and later the settlers who entered the Great Basin in the mid 1800s, encountered only one species of trout in most of the Rocky Mountains. This species, observed in both streams and lakes and with a variety of color patterns, was given many names. It is now recognized that all of these variations are one fish species: cutthroat trout. It is a matter of record that sizable migrations of this species occurred in the tributaries of Utah Lake each year and that populations existed in the Bear and Sevier rivers (Cope 1955). Carter states that prehistoric Indians had, for an indeterminate number of years, fished Utah Lake with some sort of small, crude craft. There is no definite indication of how this fishery occurred, but certainly the Indians must have used spears, arrows, basket traps, and snag lines. The Indians who lived near the lake probably formed the first commercial fishery. They caught fish, smoked and dried them, and traded with other Indians from the surrounding areas.

Archaeological finds in a cave in the area of Provo, Utah have been dated between A.D. 800 and 1300. Fish bones identified as Utah chub, native to Utah Lake, were discovered in the excavation. Evidence found in the cave indicates that hunting and fishing were very important to the economy of these prehistoric Indians and that, when the first white man came into the valley, the Indians were depending very heavily upon the lake's fish for food (Carter 1969). The lake was filled with several species. These Indians were known to the Yutas Sabuaganes as fish eaters.

In 1847, Brigham Young and the first Mormon pioneers reached Great Salt Lake valley and began their settlements. Two years later they

had spread some 100 miles from Salt Lake City and had begun extensive agricultural development. Somewhat later, but prior to large-scale
expansion by the Mormons, correspondence from people in the area indicated that Indians were catching fish by the thousands from Utah
Lake. Other statements mention that Indians came to Utah Lake from
as far away as the Uinta basin and south-central Utah to get fish (Carter 1969).

Much of the fishing in these early days was in the rivers (presumably the Provo to the greatest extent) during the spawning migration.
The fish were so thick they packed the bottom of the river and were
easy prey for the Indians. This was an ideal time to catch a maximum
number of fish with very little effort (Carter 1969).

Besides the cutthroat trout, at least one and probably two species
of suckers were abundant. Both Yarrow (1874) and Madsen (1910) mention a "mullet" in Utah Lake and indicate that it was captured along
with the trout. This fish was probably the Utah sucker. Also captured
at various times were June suckers, which, with the cui-ui of Pyramid
Lake and a third species in Oregon, represent the only living members
of this genus (*Chasmistes*) in the world.

In the late spring and early summer of 1849 visitors to the Provo
River described how "the Indians stood in the eddies and when fish approached would slide their hands under water with the ends of their fin-
gers touching the belly of the fish which is magnetized by the touch
and caught" (Carter 1969). Other methods of catching fish included
funnel-type willow traps, which were sometimes baited, or a basket
trap set above a small crude dam constructed in the tributaries. When
the fish jumped over the dam they were caught in the basket. Bow and
arrows as well as spears were also used. The Indians preserved by drying what fish they didn't eat (Carter 1969). The Indians apparently did
not use salt brine to preserve fish, although salt from Great Salt Lake
must have been available.

White men first tried to fish Utah Lake commercially in 1847.
Parley P. Pratt and a group of pioneers from Salt Lake City ventured
onto Utah Lake in December with a boat and fishnet. They had only
poor success but did catch a few "mountain trout" and other fish. In
January of 1849 the Mormon church sent an exploration party to Utah
Valley with a mandate to establish the first commercial fishery on the
lake and supply the market. Prices for the fish caught at this time were
7 to 8 cents per pound.

For at least several years following the arrival of white men, Indians were able to fish unrestricted on Utah Lake and its tributaries as

well as all other Utah waters, taking as many fish as they desired for their own subsistence. The white man's Indian allowance law was repealed about 1890, however, to accommodate the increase in white population. As fish availability decreased, the white man changed the laws in his favor.

In 1850 and 1851 additional settlements were established in the general vicinity of Utah Lake and in the surrounding valleys. These new settlers provided a larger market for Utah Lake fish and stimulated growth of the commercial fishery. In 1851 a 100-foot seine was completed by residents of Lehi; with a skiff and this net they caught enough fish to satisfy their needs. When the settlers caught more than they required or than could be disposed of locally, the fish were transported to other Utah settlements as far away as Tooele. Three species of fish were harvested commercially: lake trout (Utah cutthroat), suckers (probably Utah sucker and June sucker), and the Utah chub (Carter 1969).

Carter (1969) describes rapid increases in fishing activity from 1854 to 1858. He attributes them to increased immigration, the drought and grasshopper invasions of 1855 and 1856, and the invasion of Johnston's Army, sent to put down the "Mormon Rebellion." The population of Utah Territory jumped from 6,000 in 1849 to 20,000 in 1852 and to almost 40,000 by 1858. This expanding population created an ever-expanding market for Utah Lake fish. The "mullet," or sucker, played an important role in the survival of the pioneers at this time. John Henry Smith went so far as to say that the fish was as worthy of historical record as the seagulls and the sego lilies. In September of 1856 the hungry settlers camped along the lower Provo River and waited to be supplied with fish. Peter Madsen (1910) reports that "with help sent by the Bishop of Provo, fishing went on twenty-four hours a day for several weeks, harvesting thousands of fish," possibly depleting the resource to a limited extent. Carter (1969) reports that after this record fishing activity through approximately 1858 the amount of legal fishing on the lake leveled off.

Regulation of the Fisheries

The first fish-harvest control measure was passed in 1857 by the county (Utah) court. It stated that all persons were prohibited from placing dams or obstructions that would prevent fish from passing up and down the Jordan River. Permission to place traps in the river would be granted only by the court. In 1862 the territorial legislature took over the management of the Jordan River and passed a law that forbade the use of fish traps. Obviously, this hurt commercial fishing on the Jordan. It was probably the first instance of regulation of the fishery by other than local government entities. In late 1866 Peter Madsen petitioned the Provo City Council (which controlled the Provo River) for a fishery. He was eventually granted all fisheries at the mouth of the Provo River, providing him with a virtual monopoloy of the commercial fishing on the lower Provo and its mouth in Utah Lake. In 1870 an ordinance was passed by the Provo City Council stipulating that all fish traps had to be set with the permission of the council and under the direction of the watermaster. Fish caught in these traps were not to be subjected to waste and traps were to be constructed in such a fashion that fish would be able to pass through them when they were not in use. In 1872 the county court issued another regulatory order. Peter Madsen had appeared and asked the court to make regulations controlling the size of seine mesh allowable on Utah Lake. This ordinance said in essence that within 1 mile of the shore of Utah Lake, seine mesh size could not be less than 1.5 inches square. Seines or nets could not exceed 50 yards of the allowed size and meshes of the remainder of any net could not be less than 2 inches square. By 1872 decreases in the catch had become obvious. Whereas in 1864 3,500 to 3,700 pounds could be harvested per seine haul, the average in 1872 was closer to 500 pounds. Size of the fish had also decreased.

The territorial legislature became involved in the Utah Lake fishery in 1876, banning all types of fishing on the lake except hook and line. It also made in-stream dams without a fishway illegal. Specifications were given. In 1880 the legislature required that entrances to irrigation ditches be screened, a regulation largely ignored (Carter 1969). In the next year, a position of county fish and game commissioner was authorized and a regulation pertaining to seine size, modified frequently, was passed.

David Starr Jordan, a noted ichthyologist of the late 1800s, visited Utah Lake in 1880 and commented on the number of suckers, trouts, and chub present. He referred to the chub and trout as being abundant, but the number of suckers in the lake, he said, "was simply enormous." Jordan visited the lake again in 1889 and made a seine haul with Peter Madsen in which the number of trout caught was evidently down sharply from the previous occasion. Based on this and other information, Carter (1969) concludes that the decline of the trout was progressing rapidly.

Various changes in the fishing regulations occurred over the years. Eventually, commercial fishermen were required to be bonded and to maintain catch records. Royalties were charged on fish landed. The fees were prohibitively high and caused some fishermen to quit the business.

Period of Decreasing Abundance

From 1876 to 1896 the trout population in Utah Lake rapidly declined. Carter (1969) notes five reasons behind the general decline of the Utah Lake commercial fishery to the point that it was no longer profitable. They are (1) the fishing methods used, (2) the lack of regulation and enforcement, (3) the development of irrigation and its resulting practices, (4) chemical changes in the lake water, and (5) the introduction of exotic species. Underlying the entire situation was the reasoning that since there were so many fish the population could not be damaged. A brief presentation of each of the above factors is in order.

Early fishing methods were unnecessarily destructive. Small mesh seines were used that landed small fish before they had an opportunity to reproduce. The lake and spawning streams were fished year-round. Gill nets and explosives, which were not selective for size, were used (Carter 1969).

Early legal regulation of the fishery was inadequate. No fishing seasons were established and no regulation of minimum size existed. What regulations did exist were irregularly enforced, and persons or groups of people who had no legal fishing privileges regularly fished the lake. Court regulations concerning mesh sizes were ignored (Carter 1969). Yarrow (1874), reporting on the "speckled trout" of Utah Lake (calling it *Salmo virginalis*), notes that it was a cheap article of diet. He adds that the fish were numerous and easy to capture and wasteful methods of fishing were used.

The settlers' irrigation practices and the Utah Lake fishery were immediately in conflict. Utah Lake was used as a reservoir, and inflowing tributaries were largely diverted above the lake. Lake water levels were controlled after 1872 by a dam on the Jordan River. Small fluctuations in water level exposed large areas of shoreline and bottom due to the gradual slopes of the lake bed. This often destroyed aquatic vegetation and reduced rearing and spawning grounds. Early in the spring little irrigation water was diverted from the tributaries, allowing fish to spawn in large areas of the streams. By the time fry emerged and migrated, however, the water was being used for irrigation and thousands or millions of fry were stranded in fields or ditches (Carter 1969).

The chemical makeup of Utah Lake was gradually changed from a sulphate type to a saline type because of the irrigation practices, which diverted water from the tributaries and leached salts from the land and transported them to the lake (Carter 1969). This change adversely impacted the lake's plant community and subsequently the fish populations.

Introduction of exotic (non-native) fish species into Utah waters and into Utah Lake in particular began in the late 1880s. (A section dealing with the development of hatcheries in the states of Utah and Nevada is presented below.) Common carp, introduced in small numbers (fewer than thirty) in small farm ponds near Utah Lake multiplied and eventually found their way into the lake. By approximately 1890 carp were appearing in the seine hauls of the commercial fishermen and soon were the most common catch. These fish competed indirectly with the trout by clouding the water and eating the same food as some native fish. They had detrimental effects upon the ecology of the lake. Popov and Low (1950) state that the first carp were planted in Utah in 1881, when 130 fish were distributed among 5 counties. Two hundred fish were planted in 1882, and by 1886 large numbers of carp were being planted each year. By 1890 it was noted that the carp were established and reproducing, providing a potential food source for the increasing human population. Introductions of carp were therefore continued until 1903. In 1914 it was discovered that carp could be fed to poultry without adversely affecting flavors of either the eggs or the flesh of the birds. Largemouth bass were introduced in 1890 and by 1894 were being taken in the Utah Lake fishery. Several other species were introduced into Utah Lake around the turn of the century, placing an additional strain on the ability of the native fishes to survive. Many of these introductions did not become established, but the planting reflects the philosophy of the times.

Recent Activity in the Utah Lake Fishery

Changes in the food preferences of the American public, the cost of various food items, and the availability of other foods have affected the Utah Lake commercial fishery since the turn of the century. During the 1917 severe food shortage, Utahns as well as other Americans were asked to conserve food. The state then hired seiners to provide Utah residents with fish obtained from Utah Lake that sold for 5 cents per pound.

During the 1930s the market for carp as chicken feed began to fail, principally due to the availability of other feeds and the problems associated with having large amounts of fish on hand all year. About the time the chicken feed market failed, mink farmers started to require quantities of fish as food. A little earlier, around 1928, Utah began to experiment with using processed carp as a food for the state's developing fish hatcheries. In subsequent years the state processed and canned over a quarter-million pounds of carp annually to feed hatchery fish. The advent of manufactured dry pelleted trout food in the 1960s ended the state's dependence on fish and again reduced the market for carp.

As of 1968 only one commercial seiner was operating on Utah Lake. All of his catch was then being transported to private hatcheries in the area around Hagerman, Idaho as food for commercially reared rainbow trout. By 1983 this commercial seiner had an average annual catch of a half-million pounds, on which royalties were still charged. White bass, introduced in the 1950s, is now the dominant fish in Utah Lake.

OTHER GREAT BASIN FISHERIES

McConnell, Clark, and Sigler (1957) report that during the first quarter of this century a fairly substantial commercial fishery operated on Bear Lake, Utah-Idaho. At first, fish were caught by set lines, seines, and large-mesh gill nets. When Lewis Peterson, a fisherman from Sweden, moved to Bear Lake, he initiated more effective methods of catching smaller fish, particularly the Bonneville cisco, in both summer and winter by using small-mesh nets. Mr. Peterson obtained these nets from his native country and effectively fished the cisco and other whitefishes. After the advent of Peterson's methods, the Bonneville cisco became an important item both as bait for the trout fishery and for human consumption.

Commercial fishermen also harvested large numbers of suckers from Bear Lake during the spawning runs in the spring. They took many cutthroat trout as well and sold them in markets as far away as the state of Washington. As recently as 1950 there were people in Logan, Utah who remembered springboard wagons, piled high with both suckers and trout, coming to town from Bear Lake.

Legislative action in Utah and Idaho in the early 1920s terminated the commercial fishing in Bear Lake (McConnell, Clark, and Sigler 1957). For many years thereafter, sport fishing was confined to the general open season for trout. In 1952 the lake was opened to year-round fishing and remains so today.

Sport fishing in Bear Lake still attracts large numbers of fishermen from nearby Wasatch Front towns and from outside the Utah-Idaho area. Lake trout, a species native to the Great Lakes region, was introduced into Bear Lake in 1911 (Popov and Low 1950). It was also introduced into Utah Lake in 1894 by the territorial fish and game warden. One hundred thousand eggs were received, hatched, and released initially in Utah Lake. No record of the success of this introduction is available. Lake trout was also planted in Fish Lake. By 1905 reports that the fish was doing well in Fish Lake but had not been seen in Utah Lake prompted additional plantings in the waters of the state where the earlier plants showed promise.

Bear Lake's winter dip-net fishery for Bonneville cisco is unique in western waters. No other established populations of cisco presently exist, although efforts to establish it in Flaming Gorge Dam and other locations are underway. Cisco were planted in Lake Tahoe, California-Nevada but were never successfully established. This small fish provides a novel fishery primarily on the eastern shores of Bear Lake, attracting thousands of fishermen each winter. Presently, the daily limit is 30 fish and gear is restricted to dip nets with hoops 16 inches or less in diameter.

Juday (1907) reports catches in Lake Tahoe, California-Nevada of the "Lake Tahoe trout" (probably Lahontan cutthroat trout), silver trout, and occasionally mackinaw (lake trout), which had been introduced in 1885. All of the fishing on Lake Tahoe was done by angling, utilizing an egg-shaped metal spoon. The spoon was of generous proportions and of burnished copper or nickel plate. A large hook was baited with worms or minnows and the gear trolled at depths of 50 to 75 feet early in June and at depths of 200 feet or more later in the season. Juday reports shipments of trout from the Lake Tahoe area ranging from 58,667 pounds in 1900 (a year of high harvest) to 7,982 pounds in 1902 (a year of low harvest). In 1904 fishermen received about 30 cents per pound, the fish retailing in San Francisco for 50 to 75 cents per pound. Ninety percent of the fish shipped were Lahontan cutthroat trout. The extinction of native cutthroat from Lake Tahoe was undoubtedly influenced by fishing in the Truckee River and destruction of habitat as well as by limitations in spawning access for the Lahontans that spawned in Lake Tahoe tributaries.

INTRODUCED SPECIES

Numerous species of cold- and warmwater fish have been stocked in the waters of all Great Basin states. Many of these such as rainbow trout, lake trout, and largemouth bass have become established and now provide recreational sport fishing opportunities. Other introductions such as carp were more successful than present-day managers appreciate. Many species introduced one or more times did not become estab-

Table 3.1. Fish Species Introduced in Utah and Nevada

Species	UTAH Year First Stocked	UTAH Location First Stocked	NEVADA Year First Stocked	NEVADA Location First Stocked	Established in Great Basin
American eel	1872	SLC/ponds	—	—	No
American shad	1871	Weber R.	1877	L. Tahoe	No
Lake whitefish	1873	SLC/streams	1939	Lahontan Res.	No
Chum salmon	1939	Strawberry Res., Fish L.	1913	Truckee R.	No
Coho salmon	1925	Strawberry Res., Fish L.	1936	Lahontan Res.	No
Kokanee	1922	Bear L., Strawberry Res.	1879	Lahontan Bas.	Yes
Chinook	1873	Jordan R.	1881	L. Tahoe	No
Sebago salmon	1873	—		L. Tahoe	No
Golden trout	1936	Uinta Mts.	1918	Truckee R.	Yes
Rainbow trout	1883	SLC/streams	1879	Carson R.	Yes
Steelhead trout	prior 1900		1904	—	No
Brown trout	1894	Provo R.	1895	Truckee R.	Yes
Lake trout	1875	Utah L.	1885	L. Tahoe	Yes
Brook trout	1899	SLC/streams	1875	Truckee R.	Yes
Arctic grayling		SLC/streams	1941	Ruby Valley	Yes
Delta smelt	1982	Willard Bay		—	—
Northern pike		Redmond L.		—	Yes
Goldfish	1881	Jordan R.	1884?	unk	Yes
Carp	1881	5 counties		—	Yes
Grass carp		—		—	Yes
Tench		—	1885	Virginia City	No
Golden shiner	1969	Utah L.	1950	Colo. R.	Yes

Species	Date	Locality	Date	Locality	Established
Spottail shiner	1982	Willard Bay	—	—	Yes
Fathead minnow	1969	Utah L.	—	—	Yes
Sacramento blackfish	—	—	1939	Carson R.	Yes
Bullhead minnow	1969	—	—	—	—
White catfish	—	—	1877	Humboldt R.	Yes
Black bullhead	1871	Jordan R.	1887?	Humboldt R.; Truckee R.; Carson R.	Yes
Brown bullhead	—	—	1877?	Humboldt R.; Truckee R.; Carson R.	Yes
Channel catfish	1888	Utah L.	1892	Colo. R.	Yes
Mosquitofish	1931	—	1934	Carson R.	Yes
Guppy	1950	Utah L.	—	Sheldon Natl. Wild. Ref.	Yes
White bass	1896	Bear R.	—	—	Yes
Rock bass	1880s	Cutler Res.	—	—	No
Sacramento perch	1890	Weber R., Utah L.	1877	Washoe L.	Yes
Green sunfish	—	—	1939	—	Yes
Pumpkinseed	1890	Weber R., Utah L.	—	Sheldon Natl. Wild. Ref.	Yes
Bluegill	1912	Utah L.	1909	Near Ely	Yes
Smallmouth bass	1890	Weber R., Utah L.	1888	Carson R.	Yes
Largemouth bass	—	—	1887	Carson R.	Yes
White crappie		—	—	—	Yes
Black crappie	1890	Weber R., Utah L.	1930?	Carson R.?	Yes
Yellow perch	1890	Weber R., Utah L.	1930	W. Carson R.	Yes
Walleye	1952	Utah L.	—	—	Yes

Source: For Utah, Popov and Low 1950; Sigler and Miller 1963; Heckman, Thompson, and White 1981. For Nevada, Miller and Alcorn 1946; La Rivers 1962. For both states, personal communication, Utah and Nevada resource agencies, 1983.

SLC: Salt Lake City.

lished. Table 3.1 lists the species introduced in both Utah and Nevada and their current status. The table indicates the year and location of the first introduction (regardless of whether or not it was in the Great Basin) and whether or not the species is now present within the Great Basin. A species may now be established in waters other than where it was originally stocked.

HATCHERIES AND THE STOCKING OF NON-NATIVE FISH SPECIES

Prior to the entry of white people into the Great Basin, fish populations, both trout and other species, were exploited only by the Indians. These harvests did not endanger the survival of any species. Climatic and hydrologic cycles probably had more severe impacts upon the fish populations than did the harvesting efforts of the Native Americans. The evolution over thousands of years of these species in the drainages of the Great Basin had prepared them to survive the vagaries of nature but not the onslaught of the white invaders.

In the 1800s white settlers modified the amount and methods of the fish harvest and the rivers and lakes themselves. Their excessive harvests, coupled with destruction of habitat and changes in flow patterns in tributaries and main stem rivers, had decimated many of the native fish populations near settlements by the 1890s. Private individuals and public officials who were concerned about the decline of the native populations instituted efforts to reverse the loss of fishing potentials both by hatchery rearing of native stocks and by massive (for that period) stockings of exotic species. Introductions of exotic fishes in Utah and Nevada were primarily for the purpose of increasing the food supply in these states. The wide and somewhat unstructured program consisted of stocking whatever species were available. Initially, fish were stocked from buckboards and pack animals at accessible sites along rivers and streams near population centers and near railroad lines from specially constructed railcars.

Among the most frequently introduced fish was the carp. It was brought to the United States in 1876 by Rudolph Hessel (Hessel 1878). H. G. Parker, the first fish commissioner of Nevada, in his biennial report to the governor in 1878 expressed his intent to stock the waters of that state with this "superior food fish." The stocking of carp in Nevada was continued only until 1889, when George Mills, the third fish commissioner, made public his sentiment concerning carp in his report to the governor, stating:

> Several years ago, during the carp furor, the general government, while not entirely to blame, was "particept criminis" in foisting

upon this state and in polluting our waters, with that undesirable fish, the carp. True, application for some were made by many of our citizens ignorant of the qualities and habits of the fish and unsuspecting as to the ruin their introduction would bring. Time has now established their worthlessness, and our waters are suffering their presence. As a food fish they are regarded inferior to the native chub and sucker, while their tenacity to life and everlasting hunger gives them a reputation for "stayers and feeders" unheard of in any fish reports I have seen to date. A resident of Humboldt, an "old Humboldter" informs me they have not only devoured all the fish food in the Humboldt River, but also the duck food and a band of sheep ranging along the bank.

Utah received its first shipment of carp from the Washington, D.C. U.S. Fish Station in 1881, at which time 130 adult carp were distributed among 5 Utah counties. During the next several years, thousands of carp were planted in streams in Utah (and Nevada), sometimes as many as 17,000 in one year. Shipment of carp into Utah continued until 1903 and stocking from intrastate populations continued for several more years. Carp are now present at lower elevations in all the major drainages in Utah and Nevada (Popov and Low 1950; Sigler and Miller 1963; Miller and Alcorn 1946; La Rivers 1962).

Around the turn of the century thousands of brook trout were planted in suitable waters in both Utah and Nevada. These fish were used to replace the native trouts, whose populations had been decimated, likely encouraged to some extent by the brook trout stocking. Populations of the brook trout were also established in waters that had been previously fishless.

Other fish species stocked in this period include Sacramento perch, McCloud River chinook salmon, Schykill River catfish, Lake Michigan whitefish, American shad, chinook salmon, sebago salmon, rainbow trout, brown trout, Montana grayling, American eel, channel catfish, black bullhead, yellow perch, largemouth bass, rock bass, black crappie, green sunfish, and bluegill. The majority of these fish were obtained as either adults or smaller fish and were stocked as they arrived. In the early stages of the stocking effort only small numbers of fry or eggs were stocked, principally due to problems in handling these life stages.

The need for more fish in Utah and Nevada than could be obtained by stocking adults only led to the shipment of eggs from the eastern United States. Two concepts were originally utilized. "Hatching houses" were the forerunners of today's egg-incubation and fry-rearing facilities and, although primitive, were successful. These houses were used to hatch thousands of fry that could be conveniently stocked into accessible waters. In Nevada in 1878 Commissioner Parker utilized the hatching house concept to process some 250,000 McCloud River salmon eggs as well as other species over a number of years. The hatching houses eventually evolved into more elaborate hatching systems with troughs and trays and then rearing ponds.

The other concept utilized in early days, principally in Utah, was the reservation of natural stream channels as rearing areas for various species of fish. Streams, generally one in each county, were closed to accommodate the planting and propagating of trout with which to stock other waters. Utah had, in 1897, reserved ten streams in different parts of the state. Each stream was closed for varying periods of time, generally three or four years. The fish commissioners in both states remarked throughout this period about the need to establish a state hatchery system. Their argument was that insufficient fish could be handled and/or reared in the absence of such a system to adequately stock all the waters.

The First Hatcheries

The Utah state fish commissioner's third biennial report to the governor, dated 1900, reported the enactment of legislation for the establishment and maintenance of a state fish hatchery. The commissioner was charged with obtaining fry and/or ova in such variety as he deemed most suitable for the waters of the state and distributing them to the waters in an approved and equitable manner. Sites for the first hatchery in Utah were examined in Cache, Box Elder, Weber, Morgan, Summit, Juab, Utah, and Salt Lake counties. A site in Salt Lake County, 1.5 miles east of Murray, was selected on the basis of its quantity and quality of water, having a constant temperature of 50° F and being free from all foreign matter. The site also provided access to additional spring or creek water for rearing ponds. The land was obtained for $1,000 and a hatchery was constructed at a cost of $922. It began operation on December 30, 1889. The facilities consisted of 1 hatchery building, approximately 24 by 61 feet, with 18 hatching troughs. Each trough had a hatching capacity of 50,000 eggs. An additional 122,000 eggs could be held in the auxiliary system, bringing the operating capacity of the hatchery to the desired 1,000,000 eggs. The first year's egg hatch included lake trout, brook trout, landlocked (kokanee) salmon, grayling, and trout (steelhead). Additional eggs were obtained from native Bonneville cutthroat trout from Big Cottonwood Creek near the hatchery. Survivability of the eggs for the several hatches varied from 97 to 98 percent down to 10 or 15 percent, with a total production of 1,146,000 fry.

Nevada's hatching facilities were, until 1888, the property of the individual fish commissioners and were generally maintained on their private property. Because this created problems when the commissioners left office, W. N. Carey, fish commissioner in 1885, proposed the construction of a state-owned and -controlled facility. Estimated cost for the facility was $500. The first hatchery was built in Carson City and served the state for many years. (Hatcheries at this time consisted mainly of facilites for hatching eggs and to a lesser extent for rearing fry. They were indeed "hatcheries" and were not the complex fish-rearing stations now present in both Utah and Nevada.)

In 1892 Fish Commissioner George Mills attempted to establish a system of branch hatcheries in suitable locations throughout the state. The first was to be near Elko, but Mills had doubts about the water quality at the location and therefore placed the eggs originally designated for the facility in the Humboldt River.

During the 1890s, the state of Nevada was providing eyed ova to private hatcheries in White Pine and other counties. These eggs were hatched by private individuals and the fry subsequently stocked in nearby streams, generally on property controlled by the individual. The success of this operation prompted Mills to recommend more of these "home places" for hatching eggs in smaller and less accessible streams. This policy resulted in the stocking of thousands of trout (mostly brook) in both private and public waters. Individuals were provided eggs with the understanding that the state retained access rights to the ponds and reservoirs where these fish were reared and held, so the state could take eggs and fry. Additionally, the natural discharges of the waters to public waterways could not be inhibited.

In 1907 ground was obtained near Verdi, Nevada and construction of the Verdi Hatchery was completed in 1909. At this time the state of Nevada hired its first Fish and Game employee to operate this facility. Eggs from the Carson City house were transferred to the new facility and the Carson City facility was used only to eye eggs. Soon afterward the Carson City hatchery was closed as an economic measure.

Utah was also stocking large numbers of brook trout at this time. These fish were extremely successful in many streams, particularly the Logan River, and in lakes in Big Cottonwood Canyon, which produced 7-pound fish in 6 years.

The use of hatching or rearing ponds began in 1902 in Utah when land north of Nephi was donated to the state for a rearing pond. By 1909 the state legislature had authorized construction of three additional hatcheries: one near Springville, one at Fish Lake, and one at Panguitch Lake. The capacity of Utah's facilities for hatching eggs soon exceeded 12,000,000. At the same time large ponds were constructed near the Telluride Power Plant on the Provo River. These ponds were used to hold Bonneville cutthroat trout spawners from Utah Lake until eggs could be taken.

Powell's Slough, 4 miles north of the mouth of the Provo River in Utah Lake, was designated as a bass hatchery for the state and provided an ideal location and water supply for the hatching and rearing of large-mouth bass. Some 3,000,000 or more fish were hatched in each of several years prior to 1911.

In 1917 a federal hatchery was established at Springville, Utah. This hatchery was to provide a fair allocation of its fish to the state. The federal hatchery at Hagerman, Idaho had been providing fish to Nevada since at least as early as 1950 until recently. The Springville Hatchery in Utah played an important role in the rearing of the Lahontan cutthroat trout. In the early 1900s eggs taken from the Lahontan cutthroat spawning run in the Truckee River were shipped to the Springville Hatchery for hatching and rearing. The resulting fry were then shipped to various locations.

The Lahontan National Fish Hatchery at Gardnerville, Nevada was authorized by the United States Congress in August 1956 as part of the Washoe Project. Construction was completed in July 1966. Fish were first transferred to it from the Hagerman National Fish Hatchery, Idaho in October 1966. By fiscal year 1981 over 110,000 pounds of cutthroat and rainbow trout were being distributed by the Lahontan hatchery. The federally operated Lahontan National Fish Hatchery is now responsible for rearing and distributing Lahontan cutthroat trout into Pyramid and Walker lakes, Nevada. Restoration of the Pyramid Lake Lahontan cutthroat trout fishery is a prime objective of the hatchery (Duane Wainwright, personal communication, 1983).

Both states continued to evolve and develop their hatchery systems over the next fifty years. Problems associated with rearing large numbers of fish in restricted space included obtaining adequate feed. At one time or another feed included ground horse meat and canned carp and other nongame fish (in Utah). Eventually (in the early 1960s), both states shifted to dry pelleted trout feed. Disease problems were evidently minimal in many facilities in the early years due to the low numbers of fish being reared. As the demand for additional fish increased and facilities were utilized to capacity, diseases began to appear.

Fish were initially transplanted from rearing facilities to streams in railroad cars, with time and other costs generally being donated by the railroads. Buckboards or spring wagons carrying five-gallon milk cans full of fish and water and in some cases the use of pack animals allowed stocking of areas not accessible by railroad. Eventually, motorized tank trucks were devised, and later improvements in the size and capabilities of these vehicles permitted larger loads of fish to be carried greater distances. Air injection systems, circulation pumps, and ice helped extend the range of these vehicles.

Both states confronted philosophical problems about where to obtain eggs. Some eggs were obtained from wild stocks or from hatcheries outside of the Great Basin. Utah had maintained its own brood stock for many years. The cost of feeding brood stock in the years just after World War I became so prohibitive, however, that most of the brood fish were planted out or disposed of. Eggs then were obtained from hatcheries in other states. Both states continued to add hatcheries to better provide for distribution of fry and larger size fish in an equitable fashion.

Philosophies changed regarding the size of fish to stock. Small fish were easier to raise and cost less per fish to produce but had a lower survival rate. Larger fish were more costly to rear and fewer could be reared at a given facility, but they gave a higher return to anglers. Except in the early days when mature fish were received, both states almost exclusively stocked fry until experience showed that fry were lost at excessively high rates. Larger fish were then stocked, with a subsequent increase in return to the creel.

Diseases continued to be a problem for all hatcheries. Pollution and water shortages also caused difficulties at various facilities in both states. Production continued to increase, however, due to improved methodologies and increased numbers of hatcheries.

In 1981 the Nevada Department of Wildlife operated five fish-production facilities: the Verdi Hatchery at Verdi, the Washoe Rearing Station at Reno, the Gallagher Hatchery at Ruby Valley, the Spring Creek Rearing Station at Baker, and the Lake Mead Hatchery at Lake Mead. Production of the various facilities has been relatively consistent for several years. The combined production capability of the hatcheries in Nevada is now approximately 230,000 pounds per year. This total is made up of rainbow trout, brown trout, lake trout, cutthroat trout, and kokanee. In addition the department stocks selected warm-water species. These include walleye, channel catfish, white crappie, largemouth bass, yellow perch, black bullhead, and redear sunfish.

In 1962 Utah completed the Fisheries Experiment Station in Logan, adjacent to the older Production Hatchery. At this facility pathology, nutrition, and fish genetics are studied along with the potentials of new hatchery techniques and disease control methods. Work done at this facility contributed to the understanding of the problems of trout hepatoma, which was diagnosed as nutritional. Internal parasites, viral pancreatic necrosis, and bluesac disease are studied by personnel at this facility and nearby Utah State University.

In 1984 Utah was operating eleven state hatcheries: Beaver, Egan, Fountain Green, Glenwood, Kamas, Loa, Mantua, Midway, Panguitch, Springville, and White Rocks. Production at state hatcheries provides rainbow trout, cutthroat trout, brown trout, brook trout, lake trout, largemouth bass, walleye, striped bass, and salmon. Hatchery production is increasing as necessary (within budget constraints) to sustain the fishing demands of the public. Rainbow trout continues to be the species stocked most extensively. Rainbow trout generally comprises over 90 percent of the fish that are stocked into Utah waters by the state.

Philosophy and operating plans of both states have changed in response to new fish culture techniques and methodologies as well as the changing demands of the public. For example, to cope with disease problems affecting eggs, Utah developed an extensive brood stock of rainbow trout. Both states, however, still import some eggs each year.

During the 1970s the public became generally aware of the need to conserve resources as well as to eliminate pollution of air, water, and terrestrial resources. While much benefit was gained by this new involvement of the public, the hatcheries in both Utah and Nevada continued to experience restrictions due to inflation. In addition, hatcheries were called upon to produce ever-greater numbers of fish as more impounded waters, such as Flaming Gorge and Lake Powell became available for recreational fishing. The hatcheries support a fair portion of the recreational fishing in both states and are utilized as a management tool by planners to provide the fishing public with a quality resource.

While hatchery stocking programs assure fishing opportunities to large numbers of anglers, it must be remembered that many strains of hatchery rainbow trout (as well as some other species) are domesticated animals. As such they are rarely suitable as replacements for wild trout. A careful and well-planned balance must be struck between stocking and maintenance of wild populations so that both types of fish can be available to fishermen.

4

~~~~~~~~~~

The Endangered Species Act
and Desert Fishes of
the Great Basin

THE NATURE of the evolution of several fishes of the Great Basin has
resulted in their development in extremely limited and somewhat specialized habitats. In response to these specialized habitats the fish have
themselves become specialized. For example, Hubbs, Miller, and Hubbs
(1974) cite the development of the relict dace through evolution 1.5 to 2
million years ago. Much of the habitat of this species was unchanged
from the time of desiccation of Pleistocene Lake Lahontan some 10,000
years ago to when the white man in the Great Basin began modifying
the springs and other habitats of this particular fish. Many other species have been affected by the activity of man in the last 50 to 75 years.
The most striking example of this is probably the Devils Hole pupfish,
Devil's Hole, Nevada, which until recently existed in only one very
small area. The existence of this fish at one time was severely threatened when water withdrawals for irrigation caused a significant drop in
the water level of Devil's Hole, eliminating much of the spawning
habitat.

REASONS FOR PRESERVATION OF SPECIES

Fishes protected by the Endangered Species Act are distinct biological and ecological entities. In spite of warnings from many biolo-

gists, only a small minority of the general public realizes that human beings are extinguishing complex living assemblages as well as single species. A still smaller minority is doing anything about it (Fritz 1983). No one claims there would be an immediate or great economic disruption if one or more of the species were extirpated. Scientific losses can be more easily documented than economic losses, but there is a more basic threat: the disruption of the ecosystems on which human well-being depends. No matter how sophisticated modern technologies may seem, human livelihoods are ultimately grounded in biological processes, enmeshed in ecological webs so intricate that the consequences of destabilization such as habitat modification often cannot be foreseen. Crushed by the march of civilization, one species' extinction can take many others with it, and the ecological repercussions and rearrangements that follow may well endanger people. Without preserving wild habitats, we lose much of the value of saving endangered species. Plants or animals outside of their habitat are deprived of some of the challenges of natural selection. By preserving representative samples of our natural heritage we maintain the maximum diversity of evolutionary development and thereby assure a large and healthy pool of genetic resources for replenishing and expanding our foods, fibers, and medicines (Fritz 1983).

No one can claim that all existing species are ecologically essential to the viability of human culture, but scientists cannot say where the critical thresholds lie; that is, at what level of extermination the web of life will be seriously disrupted. Identifying and protecting those species whose ecological functions are especially important to human society are crucial tasks of citizens, scientists, and governments. In the long run, philosophical considerations may prove as potent as economic forces for species preservation. In short, we should keep our evolutionary options open (Eckholm 1981). The questions are often asked, "What good is this or that fish? Why worry about it?" Destruction of a species may be against the law, but falling back on the law is no answer. Presumably the rationale in back of the law has basis and we should address it.

HISTORY OF THE ENDANGERED SPECIES ACT

Early scientific and endangered species conservation literature (pre–1950) contains little or no information on threatened fishes or other aquatic species. Fisheries literature generally described the destruction resulting from pollution and disruption of spawning runs by dams blocking stream channels and the impacts of pollution on the sport and commercial fisheries of the United States. R. R. Miller's 1961 publication, *Man and the Changing Fish Fauna of the American Southwest*, and his 1964 publication, *Extinct, Rare and Endangered Freshwater Fishes*, were among the earliest and most comprehensive reports on the decline of western fishes.

The Endangered Species Act of 1973 is one of the strongest laws ever enacted by the United States Congress to protect threatened fish, wildlife, and plants. The 1973 act expanded coverage of two preceding laws: the Endangered Species Preservation Act of 1966 and the Endangered Species Conservation Act of 1969. These three statutes are the culmination of conservation efforts that began around the turn of the century. Early wildlife protection laws were aimed primarily at the problem of excessive killing and commercialization of terrestrial wildlife. The problem of habitat deterioration was realized at this time, but it was so overshadowed by excessive killing and selling of wildlife that it was rarely discussed (Williams 1981).

The 1966 and 1969 acts called for the establishment of a list of endangered species by the secretary of the interior and permitted the use of land and water conservation funds to acquire habitat for their protection. Funding was also provided and authorized for the management of listed endangered species. The 1973 act called for the establishment of two lists, one for foreign and one for native species. It prohibited importation of these species except under special permits and banned the purchase or sale of any animal illegally taken. It also provided for the acquisition of habitat. Both of the previous acts lacked provisions for habitat protection.

In passing the Endangered Species Act of 1973, Congress noted that human activities had already caused the extinction of several species of animals, and others were threatened with extinction. It was recognized that endangered species have educational, scientific, recreational, historical, and aesthetic values and should be preserved as part of the nation's natural heritage. The congressionally stated purpose of the Endangered Species Act is to preserve the ecosystems on which endangered and threatened species depend and to provide a program for their conservation. It also ensures that the United States lives up to the international treaties and conventions on conservation to which it is a party. It requires all federal departments to seek to conserve endangered and threatened species and to utilize their authority to further the provisions of the Endangered Species Act.

For the first time the 1973 act established two conservation status categories: endangered and threatened. An endangered species is defined as any species in danger of extinction throughout all or a significant portion of its range. A threatened species is one that is likely to become an endangered species throughout all or a significant portion of its range within the foreseeable future. A category of "special consideration" also exists that includes species or subspecies that are threatened by relatively minor disturbances of their habitat or that require additional information to determine their status. The 1973 act also provides protection for plants and all invertebrates, not just mollusks, as had originally been the case under the previous two acts. The 1978 amendments to the act redefined the term "species" to exclude populations of invertebrates and now reads, "Any subspecies of fish or wildlife or plants and any distinct population segment or any species of verte-brate, fish or wildlife which interbreeds when mature. . . ."

The determination of a species as endangered or threatened is presently based on one or more of the following factors: (1) the present or threatened destruction, modification, or curtailment of its habitat or range; (2) utilization for commercial, sporting, scientific, or educational purposes at levels that detrimentally affect it; (3) disease or predation; (4) absence of regulatory mechanisms adequate to prevent the decline of a species or degradation of its habitat; (5) other natural or man-made factors affecting its continuing existence. Mechanisms therefore exist to protect fish that are thought to be in danger of extinction (Williams 1981).

The 1978 and 1979 Endangered Species Act Amendments also define, for the first time, the critical habitat concept. Presently it is defined as "specific areas within the geographic area occupied by the species, at the time it is listed in accordance with the provisions of Section 4 of this Act, on which are found those physical or biological features (I) essential to the conservation of the species and (II) which may require special management considerations or protection; in specific areas outside the geographic area occupied by the species occupied at the time it is listed based upon a determination of the secretary of the interior that such areas are essential for the conservation of the species." Except in circumstances determined by the secretary of the interior, critical habitats shall not include the entire geographic area that can be occupied by the threatened or endangered species. The 1978 and 1979 amendments to this act made substantial changes. The 1978 amendments strengthened the consultation process with other federal agencies and expedited the consultation program by placing a ninety-day limit on it. Federal agencies are required to prepare a biological assessment for listed species that occur in the area in which a federal project is planned. The most drastic change in the Section 7 requirements is the addition of a two-tiered exemption process. This process is extremely complicated and provides for the establishment of a review board and cabinet-level committee authorized to exempt certain federal activities from compliance with some of the act's protective provisions. To date the exemption process has been used only twice, once involving the snail darter (Williams 1981).

LIMITING FACTORS

Two factors most severely decimate a population of native desert fishes in the Great Basin. The most direct and obvious decimating factor is destruction of habitat (including spawning areas) through modification. This may include pumping of water to such an extent that water levels are decreased in particular habitats or pumping of underground aquifers to such an extent that the continuous flow to these small habitats is interrupted or eliminated. Destruction or severe modification of habitat also results when small springs or streams are modified into reservoirs for irrigation or other purposes. These modifications often include the complete elimination of riparian and aquatic vegetation (to reduce transpiration losses) and occasionally excavation of the areas to deepen them or otherwise modify the bottom in size. The second most important decimating factor on populations of desert fishes in the Great Basin has been the stocking of exotic fishes into habitats previously inhabited by only one or occasionally two endemic species. Because these endemic fishes evolved without severe competition and with essentially no aquatic predators, they are ill equipped to sustain themselves when faced with either severe competition from exotics or pressures from highly predaceous fish, in particular members of the black bass group. Most of the exotics stocked in restricted habitats of the Great Basin are from the faunal-rich areas of the eastern United States, particularly the Mississippi River drainage and other warmwater habitats. Many of these species coevolved where competition, both inter- and intraspecific, has long been a factor in their existence. With few exceptions (such as the Lahontan cutthroat trout—tui chub predator-prey relationship in Pyramid Lake, Nevada), desert fishes of the Great Basin evolved in such a fashion that competition with other species was not an active force.

In addition to the predation aspects of introduced nonnative species are the problems of increased parasitism and hybridization. Hardy and Deacon (1986) point out that the introduction of "closely related species" has led to genetic extinction by mass hybridization. This is especially true among the salmonids, particularly the cutthroat trout. The establishment of mosquitofish and shortfin molly led to a significant increase in the incidence of parasitism in populations of the White River springfish and the Moapa River roundtail chub in the headwaters of the Moapa River, Nevada. Chemicals such as pesticides, rodenticides, and fertilizers that enter the environment are harmful to the delicate demands of some fish. Finally, over-collecting by scientists and aquarists can adversely affect these fish populations.

PRESERVATION OF SPECIES

Protection of the habitat required by the desert fish species in the Great Basin is essential if they are to survive. In many cases habitat has been severely reduced through the factors previously discussed. In order to ensure the continued existence of these species reserved areas may be required. These reserves must be structured so neither exotic species nor water reductions can affect them. This will require procuring control of sufficient area around the specific habitat and in some fashion preventing water withdrawals from aquifers or other sources that ultimately feed the habitat areas of concern. Elimination of the exotics from these areas may require some carefully planned and executed modification of the physical habitat so that the exotics are excluded or eliminated without the habitat required by the native species being destroyed.

5

$\approx\approx\approx$

The Evolution and
Classification of Fishes

EVOLUTION

SOMEWHERE IN THE then great oceans or areas of fresh water more than
500 million years ago, the first primitive fishlike animals made their
appearance on earth (Table 5.1). These first fishes predate early giant
insects, amphibians (including the original and now extinct giants),
reptiles (from the most primitive through dinosaurs and flying reptiles), specialized trees, shrubs, and grasses, and birds and mammals (including man). This discussion starts with the most primitive and ends
with the most recently evolved. Most of the early fishes are known
only as fossils.

Today we can fairly assume that almost every body of habitable
water has fish in it. Many waters have them in great abundance, so
much so that, like Sunday and apple pie, we take them for granted.
But it was not always this way; ancestors of today's fishes evolved
slowly and many dropped by the wayside, their remains lost in the deep
oceans. The original fishlike animals were probably not much to look
at by today's standards, but they were fish (fishlike, actually) and that
was a progressive change in evolution.

The early geological record has provided no evidence of the origin
of fishes, but shortly after the first fishlike fossils made their appearance, the jawless fishes Agnatha, the sharklike fishes Chondrichthyes,
and the bony fishes Osteichthyes were already differentiated, diversi-

Table 5.1. Range of Major Groups of Fishes through Time

Era	Period	Epoch	Dur[a]	BP[b]	Major Group
Cenozoic	Quaternary	Recent			
		Pleistocene	2	2	
	Tertiary	Pliocene	13	15	
		Miocene	15	30	
		Oligocene	10	40	
		Eocene	15	55	
		Palaeocene	10	65	
Mesozoic	Cretaceous		70	135	
	Jurassic		60	195	
	Triassic		130	225	
Palaeozoic	Permian		55	280	
	Carboniferous		70	350	
	Devonian		50	400	
	Silurian		50	450	
	Ordovician		50	500	
	Cambrian		100	600	

Major Group vertical ranges (left to right): Myxinoidea[c], Osteostraci, Anaspida, Petromyzonida, Heterostraci, Thelodonti, Acanthodii, Actinopterygii, Crossopterygii, Dipnoi, Placodermi, Elasmobranchii, Holocephali.

Source: Bond, *Biology of Fishes.*
[a]Dur: approximate millions of years duration.
[b]BP: approximate millions of years before present at beginning of epoch or period.
[c]Fossil examples and age unknown.

fied, and established (Greenwood 1975). The lack of jaws and paired fins and the presence of muscular gill pouches distinguish the agnathostomes from all that follow. These early jawless fish and the jawed fish, Gnathostomi, evolved from a common ancestry; the gnathostomes did not evolve from the present-day Agnatha (Greenwood 1975). (It is not the purpose of this book to discuss evolution of fishes in depth. Rather, we mention a few groups as examples of general interest. For anyone wishing to pursue the subject, an interesting and informative source of information is J. R. Norman's *A History of Fishes*, third edition by P. H. Greenwood.)

CLASSIFICATION

A fish is a cold-blooded animal that normally lives in water and has a backbone, cranium, gills that can extract oxygen from the water or in some cases from the air, and paired fins rather than five-digital limbs. There are probably eighteen to twenty thousand species of fish in the world today; however, scientists are not in agreement on the number. This means that a system is needed to identify, compartmentalize, and catalog fish into natural groups. The seven basic groups, starting with the largest and most inclusive, are kingdom, phylum, class, order, family, genus, and species (many authors use one or more subdivisions of class, order, and family). For example, the order Salmoniformes is classified as follows:

Kingdom   Animal
    Phylum   Chordate
      Class   Osteichthyes
        Order   Salmoniformes
          Family   Salmonidae
            Genus   *Salmo*
              Species   *clarki*
                Subspecies   *henshawi*

All fish and fishlike animals (the early jawless animals are not true fish) are in the animal kingdom and the phylum Chordate. Starting with kingdom, each descending division has more units than the preceding one; that is, there are more orders than classes, and so on down to species and subspecies.

We will discuss three groups ("classes" according to many authors) of living fishes: Agnatha, the jawless fishes; Chondrichthyes, the cartilaginous fishes; and Osteichthyes, the bony fishes.

The jawless fishes, represented today by the lampreys and the hagfishes, are the oldest known vertebrates. Lacking jaws, they take in food by a sucking action of the buccal cavity (Bond 1979). Vertebrae do not replace the notochord and the gill arches are considerably different from those of jawed fishes. Agnaths were apparently most abundant in the Silurian and the Lower Devonian periods, but their numbers decreased during the Middle and Upper Devonian. Only the lampreys and hagfishes have survived to modern times.

The cartilaginous fishes include sharks, skates, rays, mantas, and chimaeras (Robins et al. 1980). Gnathostomes include fishes known from the Upper Silurian more than 400 million years ago. These early jawed, cartilaginous skeletoned fishes have gill tissue and brachial arteries and nerves. Some of the extinct jawed fishes have a bonelike exo-skeleton. Present-day sharks have no operculum, no air bladder, and 5 to 7 gill openings on each side.

The bony fishes dominate most of the fresh waters of the world today, both in number of species and number of individuals. The lung-fishes and Crossopterygians are set apart taxonomically from other bony fishes. The other most ancient of the North American bony fishes fall into three orders: the sturgeons and paddlefishes (Acipenser-iformes), the gars (Semionotiformes), and the bowfin (Amiiformes).

We can loosely divide the remaining fishes into soft-rayed and spiny-rayed. Examples of the less specialized soft-rayed fishes are the trouts, herrings, and catfishes. The spiny-rayed representatives are perches, sunfishes, and basses.

Since the acceptance of evolution, modern systematics has endeav-ored to arrange fishes into natural groups, dictated by their hereditary history. Such a classification may be visualized as a dense bush with its roots deeply buried far back in geologic time, and in any succeeding period of history the branches have become more and more rami-fied (Greenwood 1975). Today's fishes are represented by the topmost branches, with the older branches and trunk representing older, largely fossil fishes. As expected, the older the fish, the less evidence there is of its body form and its relationship to other fishes. Almost all fossils are represented by only bony parts, leaving the systematists to make frequently subjective decisions regarding body form and functions.

The great Swedish naturalist, Linnaeus (1707–1778) was the first systematist to adopt binomial nomenclature (Greenwood 1975); that is, every animal has a genus and species scientific name (for example, *Salmo clarki*). A species is the basic unit of classification and a fish is given a scientific name that is recognized throughout the world. No two species may have an identical scientific name. Most fish also have binomial common names that may be more stable than their scientific names (Robins et al. 1980) but show considerable regional variation. Common names are easier to adapt to lay use and the need for each fish to have its own name is clear.

A genus shares some common specialized characters not found in other related groups. Genera are in turn grouped into families based on shared characteristics indicative of a common ancestry (Greenwood 1975). For example, the trouts, salmons, and whitefishes are put in one family based on common characteristics such as the presence of an adipose fin and the vestigial nature of the oviduct.

In most of the animal world the groups class, order, family, genus, and species are adequate divisions to describe all components. This is not true for fishes. Here the systematists must resort to further divisions of categories. The most commonly used device is prefixing sub or super; for example, subfamily, superorder. In *The Freshwater Fishes of Argentina* (Ringuelet, Aramburu, and de Aramburu 1967), for instance, the authors use relatively few families and large numbers of subfamilies to deal with the complexities encountered.

The Latin word "species" literally means a "particular kind." One of the basic criteria for a species is that it is reproductively isolated from other species. However, one of the fundamental characteristics of living organisms is that no two are ever exactly alike. This wide range of individual variation can at times pose a problem for systematists and laymen alike (Greenwood 1975). In certain cases species are divided into subspecies that may in turn be divided into races. The subspecies represents a population whose biological and morphological features are such as to indicate some degree of genetic isolation from related populations; that is, if physical barriers were removed, interbreeding would take place. A further taxonomic division is race, where each has its own morphological peculiarities, areas of distribution, and time and place of breeding (Greenwood 1975).

Generic names are generally descriptive of the main features of the group, they draw attention to morphologically distinguishing characteristics, or they may be a human name; for example, the genus of channel catfish is *Ictalurus*, a Greek word meaning "fish cat." The trivial (species) name may be descriptive or it may honor a person; for example, the species name of channel catfish is *punctatus*, meaning "spotted" in Latin, while the species name of the White River springfish is *baileyi*. The name of the author who first described a fish follows the scientific name. If the fish was later renamed, the original author's name is placed in parentheses.

Names of orders end in *iformes* (Siluriformes), names of families end in *idae* (Salmonidae). These names may be Anglicized by dropping the last two letters and adding *s* (salmonids).

FOSSIL GROUPS
Osteostraci

These fishes are small, few exceeding a foot in length. Their flattened head is covered with a bony shield, and the body has numerous bony plates. These were probably clumsy, sluggish creatures, living and foraging on the bottom. They disappeared in the Devonian more than 350 million years ago (Greenwood 1975).

Anaspida

This second group of fishlike animals is quite unlike the Osteo-straci in appearance. They have slender, torpedo-shaped bodies covered by small, regularly arranged bony plates; the head is armored with ir-regularly arranged plates. The body is rounded, the mouth terminal, the eyes lateral, and the nasal and pineal openings dorsal. The anaspids probably were good swimmers. They are known from about the same period as the Osteostraci.

Pteraspidomorphi

Chronologically, this is the oldest group. It first occurred in the Upper Cambrian over 500 million years ago and died out in the late Devonian. The pteraspids have the head and trunk enclosed in bony plates, while those on the posterior part of the body are smaller and have the general appearance of scales. The mouth is a transverse slit on the lower side of the head. There is no trace of true jaws (Greenwood 1975).

Placodermi

This group, appearing before the jawed cartilaginous fishes, has a stout exoskeleton of bony plates and is sharklike in appearance. The head portion is hinged to the boxlike armor of the thoracic region. The posterior is scaled or naked. The placoderms flourished for awhile and then disappeared (Greenwood 1975).

GREAT BASIN FOSSIL RECORDS

The paleontological record of Tertiary and Quaternary fishes in western North America is meager. Fossils representing nine families have been recorded from freshwater deposits of Miocene to Pleistocene epochs in western North America. They are minnows, suckers, bull-head catfishes, pirate perches, sunfishes, trouts, killifishes, sculpins, and sticklebacks (Miller 1958).

Cretaceous ichthyofaunas of western North America consisted only of archaic fishes. No recognized members of teleostean groups that now constitute most of the forms were present (Estes 1970). It was not until late Paleocene (approximately 55 million years ago) and dur-ing Eocene (37 to 53 million years ago) that freshwater faunas domi-nated by teleosts appeared in the fossil record (Patterson 1981). Eocene forms (Grande 1980; Grande, Eastman, and Cavender 1982; Wilson 1977) show little resemblance to those of Miocene (5 to 23 million years ago) to present (Miller 1958, 1965; Cavender 1968; Cavender, Lundberg, and Wilson 1970; Smith 1981). Miocene-Pliocene forms are usually judged specifically distinct from Recent faunal elements. Pleistocene taxa are not usually distinguishable at the species level from Recent taxa (Miller 1965; Smith 1981). Certain Great Basin Miocene fossils from the Humboldt Formation, Nevada indicate there were kinds of fish (a sucker, *Amyzon*, and a pirate perch, *Trichophanes*) quite unlike those that now inhabit the West (Miller 1958).

During or subsequent to the physiographic disruption of the West in the late Tertiary and Quaternary periods, the fish fauna differentiated within a group of isolated basins, each with a high incidence of endemism and generally lacking few strictly freshwater species in common (Hubbs and Miller 1948). Within the Great Basin, the Bonneville, Lahontan, and Death Valley drainages are centers of endemism (Miller 1958).

Modernization of the western ichthyofauna must have occurred in Oligocene since Miocene deposits yield diverse fossils, including mooneyes, trouts, smelts, mudminnows, pikes, minnows, suckers, bullhead catfishes, silversides, killifishes, sticklebacks, sunfishes, surfperches, and sculpins. Of these, all but the smelts, mudminnows, pikes, and bullhead catfishes remain abundant. Extirpation of nonteleosts and most of the last four families plus *Amyzon* must have been precipitated by the transition from Oligocene lowland rivers, which flowed over a broad erosional surface to diverse topography and disrupted drainages of the Miocene, perhaps aided by flows of molten rock (Minckley, Hendrickson, and Bond 1985). Evidence seems adequate to hypothesize a broadly distributed ancestral fauna consisting of the genera *Salmo* (or near relative), *Gila*, *Rhinichthys*, and *Catostomus* in streams flowing through low relief in the Great Basin region approximately 17 million years ago (Smith 1981).

The Bonneville basin, largest of the Great Basin drainages, has about 67 percent endemics and the Lahontan basin, second largest of the interior drainages, has 78 percent endemics. Five species of fish entered ancient Lake Bonneville from the Snake River: mountain whitefish, cutthroat trout, Utah sucker, longnose dace, and mottled sculpin (Miller 1958). The longnose dace probably gave rise to the Umpqua dace of the Umpqua River, Oregon (Bisson and Bond 1971) and its presence in the West may be ancient (Minckley, Hendrickson, and Bond 1985). Two primary genera, *Richardsonius* (minnow) and *Chasmistes* sucker), are present in both the Bonneville and Lahontan basins, as are four montane species: mountain whitefish, cutthroat trout, speckled dace, and Paiute sculpin. *Gila*, represented by the tui chub in the Lahontan basin and by the Utah chub in the Bonneville basin, is also common to these two drainages. These relationships indicate a former connection, perhaps of Pliocene or early Pleistocene, between these two drainages (Miller 1958). The highly saline, often warm, and alkaline waters of a large part of the much disrupted Death Valley drainage are particularly suited to the killifish family, of which all species and one of two genera are endemic (Miller 1948). This family's long existence in this drainage is supported not only by the high degree of endemism but also by the fossil record of *Cyprinodon* and *Fundulus* from Tertiary deposits in the valley. The endemic genus *Empetrichthys* was probably derived from *Fundulus*. The faunal relationship in this valley points to a former connection to the southeast in Pliocene time with what is now the Colorado River and to the north with the precursor of Lake Lahontan (Miller 1958).

Several authors have documented fossil and recent zoogeographic evidence linking aquatic faunal elements of the Snake River Plain southward to the Mojave Desert along the east side of the present Sierra Nevada. Fossil species noted in this evidence include *Chasmistes*, *Catostomus*, *Gila*, and *Archoplites* (Minckley, Hendrickson, and Bond 1985), all of which exist in the Great Basin today.

The earliest reliable dated remains of the sucker family in North America are from Miocene deposits in British Columbia, Nevada, and Colorado and are placed in the extinct genus *Amyzon*. The weight of present evidence indicates a cyprinid prototype as probably ancestral to suckers. A Pliocene minnow from the Esmeralda Formation of Nevada, *Leuciscus turneri* (Lucas 1900), is likely identical with modern *Gila*, which is widespread in the Great Basin today. A minnow from British Columbia, *Leuciscus rosei*, thought to be of Miocene Age, probably represents the living genus *Richardsonius*, which is also widespread in the Great Basin (Miller 1958).

Two early Pliocene fossils from beds within the Lahontan system of Nevada, a killifish (*Fundulus nevadensis*) and a stickleback (*Gasterosteus doryssus*), belong to genera of coastal and lowland distribution fishes living today in western North America only along the Pacific slope. Their entrance into Nevada, perhaps in late Miocene or early Pliocene times, may have been from the southwest by way of what is now the Death Valley region, since fossil killifishes of the same genus occur there (Miller 1945) and sticklebacks are found as far south today as northern Baja California.

Miocene and Pliocene sunfishes (centrarchidae) of extinct genera from Oregon, Nevada, and Utah demonstrate that this family, now largely restricted to eastern North America (an exception is the Sacramento perch), was once more widespread (Miller 1958).

Minckley, Hendrickson, and Bond (1985) and Smith (1978) provide additional information for fossil relationships to present-day fish. The modern Lahontan basin fauna includes a mixture of fishes of relatively recent derivation with older faunal elements. Fossil fishes related to those of the Pliocene Glenns Ferry Formation on the Snake River Plain, Idaho are present in fossil beds near Honey Lake, California and also resemble some species of the present Lahontan system (Taylor and Smith 1981). Included are *Rhabdofario*, which shows some characteristics of the Lahontan cutthroat trout of Pyramid Lake, Nevada; *Gila* sp., which is unlike the tui chub subspecies that now inhabits the region and resembles the fossil *Mylopharodon hagermanensis* and the hitch of the Sacramento River basin; Pliocene fish fossils from Mopung Hills, Nevada between Carson and Humboldt sinks, including kinds of fish referable to modern species; *Salmo* sp., which may be the same as the present-day Lahontan cutthroat trout; and *Salmo cyniclops* and *S. esmeralda*, fossil species probably from Miocene beds (La Rivers 1964, 1966), another trout from the Miocene Truckee Formation (Taylor and Smith 1981), and the species from the Mopung Hills site, all in Nevada and from Pliocene Lake Idaho, that appear of the lineage that gave rise to most western *Salmo* and attest to their remarkably long occupation of this region. Minnow family relationships are less clear. The Miocene *Gila esmeralda* (La Rivers 1966; Lugaski 1977) and Pliocene *Leuciscus* (equals *Gila turneri* [Lucas 1900; Miller 1958] and *Gila traini* [Lugaski 1979]), all from Nevada, have been somewhat arbitrarily considered as relatives of the present-day tui chub (Minckley, Hendrickson, and Bond 1984).

A fossil *Salmo* sp. from Pliocene Lake Idaho may be a relative of cutthroat trout, rainbow trout, or other *Salmo* species. The undescribed redband trout, which occurs in the Great Basin today, and both the Bear Lake whitefish and Bonneville whitefish can be traced to Pleistocene Lake Bonneville. An additional whitefish fossil *Prosopium prolixus* is from Pliocene Lake Idaho. The Tertiary of Death Valley produced *Cyprinodon breviradus*, which is related to the Owens pupfish, the Devils Hole pupfish, the Amargosa pupfish, and the Salt Creek pupfish. Five species of Late Cenozoic *Fundulus*, known from southern California and Nevada, are relatives of *Empetrichthys* and *Crenichthys*, both present in the Great Basin region (Smith 1978).

LIVING GROUPS
Agnatha

The Agnathas include both the living and the fossil fishlike, jaw-less vertebrates. These are the most primitive of living fishes and the oldest in point of fossil history and include the living lampreys and the hagfishes (no fossils of the latter have been found). Agnathostomes appear to have been most abundant in the Silurian and Lower Devonian but their numbers decreased through the Middle and Upper Devonian (Bond 1979).

Petromyzontiformes

The lampreys are characterized by the lack of paired fins, jaws, and scales; they are eellike with lateral eyes and a ventral mouth consisting of a disc set with horny teeth. The poorly developed skeleton is car-tilaginous. All lampreys have a long larval stage that may last up to five years. The nonparasitic lampreys confine their feeding to the larval stage; after metamorphosis they spend months in hiding while the gonads develop, then they spawn and die (Bond 1979). The adult stage of the parasitic lamprey lives by attaching itself to fish, rasping holes in the skin, and pumping out body fluids. After a period of growth the lamprey detaches itself from its victim, then returns to a freshwater stream to spawn and die.

Myxiniformes

This marine animal, with no larval stage, is found in temperate waters of the world. It lives on soft bottom and acts either as a scav-enger or an endoparasite on fish.

Gnathostomata

These earliest jawed fishes are known from the Upper Silurian more than 400 million years ago. They flourished in the Devonian and several species existed into and beyond the Carboniferous (Bond 1979).

Chondrichthyes

This group includes the modern sharks, skates and rays, mantas, and chimaeras along with their fossil relatives. These fishes have a car-tilaginous endoskeleton, often hardened by calcification, and placoid scales or no scales. There is no operculum. The 5 to 7 gill openings on each side are separate. Males are equipped with pelvic claspers for breeding. There is no gas bladder (Bond 1979). The Elasmobranchs have existed since the Upper Devonian. They are widely diverse in size, shape, food habits, and habitat. The smallest shark appears to be *Squaliolus laticaudus* from the Pacific near Japan. The largest is the whale shark, which may reach a length of 50 feet or more. The whale shark, even though it is the largest of the sharks, feeds only on small fish and invertebrates. The white shark, known for its voracious appetite, attacks large marine mammals and occasionally humans.

The skates and rays are characterized by a depressed body, with pelvic fins extending forward and fused to the head, so that the 5 pairs of gill openings are ventral. Some of these fish have stinging spines on the tail, some have a sawlike rostrum, some have electric organs, some are small, others may reach a length of over 20 feet. Most members of this large group are marine; however, a few live in fresh water.

Osteichthyes

The bony fishes form a large part of the living fish fauna of the world today. They are spread throughout all continents and oceans in every type of habitat. As the name indicates, the skeleton is typically bony, at least in part. These fish normally have an air bladder, ganoid or bony scales, and an operculum that covers the gills.

Dipnoi

There are six species of living lungfishes: one in Australia, one in South America, and four in Africa. Except for the Australian lungfish, the lungfishes have the unique ability to burrow into the mud and estivate when the water dries up. They remain in this state for months or even years until the water returns; they then become active.

Crossopterygii

The first modern specimen of a coelacanth, thought to be extinct 70 million years ago, was captured off the coast of South Africa in 1938. Some seventy specimens have been taken to date. This fish is of considerable interest to both systematists and paleontologists.

Actinoptergii

The spiny-rayed fishes form a large, diversified group that is abundant in both species and numbers. These are the fish most of us see when we study fish, go to the aquarium, or go fishing. The first group includes the sturgeons, the paddlefishes, the gars, and the bowfin.

Chondrostei

This somewhat artificial group contains the extinct palaeoniscoids and allies—sturgeons, paddlefishes, birchirs, and reedfish (Bond 1979).

Acipenseriformes

The sturgeons are an order of large, slow-growing, long-lived fishes that are famous for their roe, from which caviar is made. They are characterized by bony scutes on the back and sides. In North America the commercial interest in sturgeons is minor, but it is considerable in the U.S.S.R. and Iran. Sturgeons are found primarily in fresh water, but some species are marine and some are anadromous.

There are two living freshwater species of paddlefishes in the order Acipenseriformes: one in North America and one in China. These fishes are characterized by a long snout and sharklike body. They are naked except for scales on the upper caudal fin lobe, which is longer than the lower lobe. The paddlefish currently appears to be prospering in some of the impoundments on the Missouri River (Bond 1979).

Holostei

Two of the about five orders of this once widespread Jurassic period group remain today. There are seven species of gars and one bowfin. These fishes have an abbreviated heterocercal caudal and in living forms a spiral valve and cellular air bladder (Bond 1979).

Semionotiformes

The gars are elongate fishes with a body covered by armorlike ganoid scales. The long, tapered snout has two rows of sharp teeth. These are North and Central American freshwater fishes, except for the alligator gar that enters the Gulf of Mexico. Its large size and tenacity encourage a sport fishery in parts of its range, particularly in Arkansas. Landed specimens are generally released.

Amiiformes

There is only one species of living bowfin. This two- to three-foot-long fish lives in the temperate waters of North America. The stout body is nearly cylindrical. The tail fin is rounded and the body is covered with smooth-edged cycloid scales. The head is naked (Pflieger 1975).

Teleostei

The teleosts are characterized by cycloid or ctenoid scales, or some modification thereof, or they are secondarily naked (ancestors had scales at one time). The have a homocercal tail and no spiral valve. The first and less specialized group is the soft-rayed fishes, the second the spiny-rayed fishes. The soft-rayed fishes have an open pneumatic duct from the alimentary canal to the gas bladder (this is known as physostomous); this condition does not exist in spiny-rayed fishes, which are said to be physoclistous. These general rules have many exceptions (Bond 1979).

Salmoniformes

This order has marine, freshwater, and anadromous species. The Pacific and Atlantic salmons, the trouts, and the chars are of substantial value to both sport and commercial fisheries. The rainbow trout is the most widely cultured coldwater fish in America. The anadromous form, the steelhead, is one of the most widely sought sport fish in the western United States. There are six species of Pacific salmon (*Oncorhynchus* spp.): five in North America and one in Japan. These fish are anadromous, and they spawn once and die. The Atlantic salmon is also anadromous but is a repeat spawner, as is the steelhead. The chars (*Salvelinus* spp.) include lake trout, brook trout, Dolly Varden, and others. Some of the most bizarre deep sea fishes belong to this order.

The pikes also belong to this order; two of them, the muskellunge and the northern pike, are large, voracious predators that are highly prized as sport fish and within limits act as controls for nongame fish.

Cypriniformes

The fact that there are about three thousand species in this order points to its importance (Bond 1979). This number includes carps and minnows, suckers, characins, electric eels, and loaches. Many of these fish are very prominent in world food production, both wild and cultured.

The characins are abundant in Africa and South America where they are ecologically and economically important. The minnows are a dominant forage fish in many fresh waters of Europe, Asia, Africa, and North America. The carps, because of their rapid growth, large size, and ease of culture, produce large amounts of high protein food, especially in China.

The large-sized buffalofishes (*Ictiobus* spp.) and the medium-sized carpsuckers (*Carpiodes* spp.) are the two prime food producers in the North American sucker family. They are not often cultured. Several species of small suckers are food for predatory fish.

Siluriformes

Catfishes are worldwide in both fresh and salt water. North American freshwater catfishes (Ictaluridae) are naked. The family has three large species: the blue catfish, the flathead catfish, and the channel catfish. Channel catfish is the number one (greatest poundage) cultured fish in America. Those species collectively known as bullheads produce the most hours of sport fishing. South America has many diverse species of catfishes. The senior author once saw a Paraná River fisherman bring a catfish that was longer than he was into a restaurant. Many of the South American and marine catfishes are armored.

Gadiformes

The codfishes of this order support productive commercial marine fisheries for several nations.

Atheriniformes

This order includes the killifishes and livebearers, which have aroused considerable interest because of the endangered status of several species. Many are well known as ornamental fish. In the Great Basin species of this order are important due to their existence in unique habitats and the fact that they evolved in isolation. Several species in this order occupy extremely limited areas (sometimes a single spring source) in the Great Basin.

Perciformes

This largest of all orders of fishes typifies the spiny-rayed, advanced, bony fishes (Bond 1979). It includes temperate basses, sea basses, perches, sunfishes, mullets, barracudas, swordfishes, billfishes, and sculpins. The temperate basses include the freshwater white bass and the anadromous and the landlocked striped bass, both highly sought by American sportsmen.

The sunfishes include the largemouth and smallmouth basses (*Micropterus* spp.), two fish highly prized by sportsmen. However, the smaller and much more numerous sunfishes and the crappies provide more sport for larger numbers of people.

The perches reach their greatest development in North America. The pan-sized yellow perch is present in many waters. The walleye, a much larger member of the perch family than the yellow perch, is fished for sport and commercially. By far the largest number of species are the darters—small, highly colorful midwestern and eastern fishes.

Included in this order is the unusual family of climbing perches (*Anabas* spp.), which has the unfishlike trait of migrating over land when its habitat dries up.

The swordfishes and billfishes, two separate families, are known for their very large size, sporting qualities, and their habit of occasionally attacking small boats, much to the consternation and occasionally the harm of the occupants. These are the largest and perhaps the most prized of all sport fish.

Pleuronectiformes

The flatfishes get their name from their curious habit of swimming on their side instead of vertically. Early in the life of these fish, one eye migrates to the upper side of the body so that the lower side is sightless and colorless (Bond 1979). These mostly marine fishes are important in commercial fishing. The Atlantic halibut is the largest of all the flatfishes.

Tetraodontiformes

The headfishes deserve mention because of their unusual degree of specialization. The body of the headfishes is oval in shape, appearing to end just after the dorsal and anal fin. The largest of these, the ocean sunfish, basks at the surface. The senior author has watched these giants, some more than 5 feet long and 4 feet deep, only roll their eyes and make no attempt to dive when a ship passed within a few yards of them.

ETYMOLOGY, THE STUDY OF WORD ORIGINS

The meanings of both common and scientific names of fish are often confusing. Common names often vary from one geographic locale to another, but the American Fisheries Society (Robins et al. 1980) standardized them for fish in North America. With two exceptions (redfish and ocean perch for *Sebastes marinus*; cisco and lake herring for *Coregonus artedii*), fish in North America have only one accepted common name containing one or two (or rarely three) words. Scientific names are based on common characteristics for groups of fish (families and genera) and on generally descriptive terms for specific names. As with all other organisms, fish have binomial scientific names (genus and species). Occasionally it is necessary to use three names (or rarely four) to separate subspecies within a species or strains from one another. Scientific names, once origin, authorship, and taxonomic vagaries have been settled, tell something about the fish and the name generally describes either the fish or the reason for the specific name (for example, *cyanellus* equals green; *crysoleucas*, golden; *melas*, black; *nigromaculatus*, black-spotted; *williamsoni*, Williams). While

the names and their interpretations given below are not inclusive, they
represent the diverse, fascinating, and significant spectrum of scientific
names.

Several prominent ichthyologists contributed to the early documentation of the Great Basin fish fauna and added significantly to both
the early descriptions of new species and the now accepted nomenclature. Among these were John O. Snyder, Carl and Rosa Eigenmann,
Spencer Baird, Charles Girard, Carl L. Hubbs, David Starr Jordan, R. R.
Miller, and particularly Ira La Rivers in Nevada. The importance of
some of these individuals is reflected in the scientific names that follow. The parentheses around the author's name indicate authorship but
that the scientific name was later changed.

TROUTS

Oncorhynchus nerka (Walbaum)   Sockeye
  Oncorhynchus = hooked snout (from the appearance of fish when
  migrating to spawn).
  nerka : Russian name for the anadromous form of this species.

Prosopium williamsoni (Girard)   Mountain whitefish
  Prosopium = masked, from the large preorbitals.
  williamsoni : named for Lt. R. S. Williamson, who was in charge of
  one of the United States Pacific Railroad surveys.

Salmo clarki Richardson   Cutthroat trout
  Salmo from salio = to leap.
  clarki : named for William Clark of the Lewis and Clark expedi-
  tion of 1804–1806.

Salmo clarki henshawi Gill and Jordan   Lahontan cutthroat trout
  henshawi : H. W. Henshaw was a naturalist with the 1875–1877
  Wheeler Surveys west of the 100th meridian. David Starr Jordan and
  he reported on several Nevada species from the Wheeler Surveys and
  later Gill, an older associate of Jordan, named the distinctively different Lahontan cutthroat in his honor.
  Lahontan : Baron Louis Armand La Hontan (1666–1713) was an
  early French explorer in America. He did not enter the Great Basin
  but Hauge (La Rivers 1962) applied his name to the area of Pleistocene Lake Lahontan.

Salmo gairdneri Richardson   Rainbow trout
   gairdneri : Sir John Richardson, an English naturalist who originally
   described several Great Basin fishes, named this species. It was a
   trout from the Columbia River collected by Meredith Gairdner, a
   young doctor assigned to the Hudson Bay Company on the Columbia
   River. For his help in collecting this and other specimens, Richardson
   named the fish for Gairdner.

Salmo trutta Linnaeus   Brown trout
   trutta : Latin name for trout.

Salvelinus fontinalis (Mitchill)   Brook trout
   Salvelinus : an old name for char.
      fontinalis = living in springs.

Salvelinus namaycush (Walbaum)   Lake trout
   namaycush : an Indian name.

Thymallus arcticus (Pallas)   Arctic grayling
   Thymallus : based on the supposed odor of the flesh, like that of the
   herb, thyme.
      arcticus = of the Arctic.

PIKES

Esox lucius Linnaeus   Northern pike
   Esox : an old European name for pike.
      lucius : supposedly the Latin name for this species.

CARPS AND MINNOWS

Acrocheilus alutaceus Agassiz and Pickering   Chiselmouth
   Acrocheilus = sharp lip.
      alutaceus = leathery, referring to the tough appearance of the skin
      of this fish.

Carassius auratus (Linnaeus)   Goldfish
   Carrassius : Latinization of the vernacular name Karras or Karausche.
      auratus = gilded, referring to the coloration.

Cyprinus carpio Linnaeus   Common carp
   Cyprinus : ancient name for carp, probably derived from Cyprus,

abode of the goddess Venus, alluding to its fecundity.

    carpio : Latinization of the name carp.

Gila atraria (Girard)   Utah chub

    Gila : named for the Gila River.

      atraria = from *ater*, blackfish and *arius*, pertaining to; probably in reference to the coloration of this species in the waters of the type location.

Gila bicolor (Girard)   Tui chub

    Siphateles, now *Gila* = incomplete siphon.

      bicolor : probably in reference to the coloration of this species either normally (white ventrally and olive dorsally) or during spawning (when yellow or pink tints appear in the fins).

Notemigonus crysoleucas (Mitchill)   Golden shiner

    Notemigonus = back; half; angle, keellike back.

    crysoleucas = gold or white.

Richardsonius balteatus (Richardson)   Redside shiner

    Richardsonius : the genus was originally named by Girard for the prominent English zoologist Sir John Richardson, who described many species in the United States.

      balteatus = girdled, possibly referring to the brilliant red streaks that occur on males during breeding.

Richardsonius egregius (Girard)   Lahontan redside

    egregius = surprising, possibly alluding to the brilliant colors of this species that appear, predominantly in the males, during the breeding season.

SUCKERS

Catostomus ardens Jordan and Gilbert   Utah sucker

    Catostomus = inferior mouth.

      ardens = burning, probably referring to the bright red colors of the breeding males.

Catostomus tahoensis Gill and Jordan   Tahoe sucker

    tahoensis : named for the location of the type specimen, Lake Tahoe, California-Nevada.

Catostomus platyrhynchus (Cope)   Mountain sucker
   platyrhynchus = flat snout.

Chasmistes cujus Cope   Cui-ui
   Chasmistes = "one who yawns," possibly referring to the large terminal mouth of this sucker.
     cujus : assumed to be the Latinization of the Indian name rendered by Cope as "Couia."
      Cui-ui : pronounced "kwee-wee" commonly but the Paiute pronunciation is closer to "koo-ee-wee." Also spelled "Couia."

BULLHEAD CATFISHES

Ictalurus catus (Linnaeus)   White catfish
   Ictalurus = fish-cat.
    catus = cat.

Ictalurus melas (Rafinesque)   Black bullhead
   melas = black.

Ictalurus nebulosus (Lesueur)   Brown bullhead
   nebulosus = clouded, in reference to the mottled and gray coloring.

Ictalurus punctatus (Rafinesque)   Channel catfish
   punctatus = spotted, characteristic of individuals under 12 inches.

KILLIFISHES

Crenichthys baileyi (Gilbert)   White River springfish
   Crenichthys = spring fish (from their pothole spring habitat).
    baileyi : named in honor of the famous U.S. Bureau of Biological Survey field naturalist Vernon L. Bailey, who was one of the collectors of the type series.

Crenichthys nevadae Hubbs   Railroad Valley springfish
   nevadae : named for the collection location, the state of Nevada.

Cyprinodon diabolis Wales   Devils Hole pupfish
   Cyprinodon = carp tooth.
    diabolis : named for the type locality, Devil's Hole, Nevada.

Cyprinodon nevadensis Eigenmann/Eigenmann   Amargosa pupfish
   nevadensis : the type locality was in California. La Rivers (1962) indicates the describers must have desired to honor the region east of
   California.

Lucania parva (Baird)   Rainwater killifish
   Lucania : the meaning of this name is obscure, but was coined by
   Charles Girard.
      parva = literally, small.

LIVEBEARERS

Gambusia affinis (Baird and Girard)   Mosquitofish
   Gambusia : from *gambusino*, a Cuban word related to the fact that
   fishing for *gambusinos* is to fish for nothing.
      affinis = related (to *Gambusia holbrooki*).

TEMPERATE BASSES

Morone chrysops (Rafinesque)   White bass
   Morone : the origin of this word is obscured. Roccus, the other generic name that has been used for this fish, literally means rock.
      chrysops = golden eye, although in many fish the color is not
   conspicuous.

SUNFISHES

Archoplites interruptus (Girard)   Sacramento perch
   Archoplites : derived from the Greek words for anus and armature,
   referring to the conspicuous, spiny anal fin.
      interruptus : refers to the irregular bars on the sides.

Lepomis cyanellus Rafinesque   Green sunfish
   Lepomis = scaled cheek, referring to this characteristic, which was
   once thought to be a distinguishing trait.
      cyanellus = green, referring to the iridescent color of the fish.

Lepomis gibbosus (Linnaeus)   Pumpkinseed
   gibbosus = formed like the full moon or, literally, humped.
      pumpkinseed : referring to the overall body shape of this species.

Lepomis macrochirus Rafinesque   Bluegill
   macrochirus = literally, large hand, referring to the long pectoral
   fins.

Micropterus dolomieui Lacepède   Smallmouth bass
   Micropterus = short fin. The name comes from the original description for the genus by Lacepède, the single specimen of which was de-
formed and the last few rays were separated from the dorsal fin, giving the appearance of a separate fin.
      dolomieui : named for M. Dolomieu, a French mineralogist who
   was apparently a colleague of Lacepède.

Micropterus punctulatus (Rafinesque)   Spotted bass
   punctulatus = spotted.

Micropterus salmoides (Lacepède)   Largemouth bass
   salmoides = troutlike.

Pomoxis annularis Rafinesque   White crappie
   Pomoxis = cover-sharp, referring to the fact that the operculum ends
in a blunt point rather than a distinct flap.
      annularis = having rings, probably in reference to the color pat-
   tern of this species.
         crappie : is of unknown origin but is probably traceable to an In-
      dian word for these two species.

Pomoxis nigromaculatus (Lesueur)   Black crappie
   nigromaculatus = black-spotted.

PERCHES

Perca flavescens (Mitchill)   Yellow perch
   Perca : ancient Greek name for perch meaning dusky.
      flavescens = yellow.

Stizostedion vitreum vitreum (Mitchill)   Walleye
   Stizostedion = pungent throat.
      vitreum = glassy, alluding to the nature of the large, silvery eyes.

SCULPINS

Cottus bairdi Girard   Mottled sculpin
   Cottus : an old European name.
      bairdi : named for Fullerton Baird, first U.S. fish commissioner.

Cottus beldingi Eigenmann and Eigenmann   Paiute sculpin
   beldingi : named for the collector, L. Belding.

6

Unique Ways of Fish and Why We Study Them

FISH ARE UNIQUE and amazing creatures that represent many extremes. There are 18,000 to 20,000 species and many more if subspecies are counted. There are fish that walk, fly, or glide, live out of water for extended periods of time, hibernate in the mud when the water dries up, capture other fish with the aid of a lighted lure, and climb trees.

Fish mean many things to many people. The young fisherman's eyes light up when he thinks of the thrill of any catch no matter what the size or species and a chance to display it to peers and parents. The chef sees a fish as the main ingredient in a gourmet meal. The biologist sees it as a challenge and an object of scientific study. The adult sportsman dreams of catching a trophy fish to mount and hang on the living room wall. A commercial fisherman, perhaps the most pragmatic of participants, sees fish primarily as a livelihood. Millions of people each year are fascinated by aquarium fish, either at home or in public displays.

We think of fish as animals living in water and out of sight. But some fish drown if they are confined under water; they must breathe air to survive. Some fish spend much of their time out of water, returning to their native habitat only occasionally. Different species of fish have adapted to a wide range of temperatures, but few can tolerate quick changes. Some marine fishes live in near-freezing water. The Alaska blackfish reportedly has been found in a chunk of ice, but it survives because its flesh has a lower freezing point than fresh water. Some Antarctic fish rest on anchor ice at water temperatures of 28.4° to 30.2° F. In northern Utah there was a thriving population of mosquitofish in a 108° F spring, but when these fish were transferred directly to cold water or hotter water they died instantly. The lungfish of Africa, *Protopterus* spp., has a special way of dealing with the dewatering of its habitat: it simply burrows into the mud, forms a cocoon of spittle, and waits for rain. One family of deep sea fish is aptly known as the swallowers: they can swallow fish much larger than themselves.

The largest species of fish live in the great oceans, but others also live in unbelievably small areas. In a junk yard, in a hole 3 feet wide and 1.5 feet deep, there was a breeding population of mosquitofish. What was more surprising was that the hole was covered with a half-rotted wooden door. The Devils Hole pupfish lives in an area of about 24 square yards.

The world's largest fish, the whale shark, has a recorded length of 49 feet and a weight of 35,000 pounds, but Schultz and Stern (1948) state that specimens seen in the water have been estimated by experienced persons to be 70 feet long and weigh as much as 150,000 pounds. The largest sturgeon and the largest freshwater fish in the world is the beluga of the Caspian and Black seas. It is reported to reach a length of almost 30 feet and a weight of over 3,300 pounds, but Dr. Roald L. Potapov, U.S.S.R. Academy of Sciences, Leningrad states they have reached a weight of 5,500 pounds (personal communication, 1984). Large specimens may be 100 years old and carry over 7,000,000 eggs. In contrast, the pygmy goby that lives in the Philippines measures little more than one-third of an inch and weighs only a small fraction of one gram (Bond 1979).

Fish live in a wide range of altitudes both above and below sea level. Cutthroat trout in the Great Basin live well above timberline, while pupfishes in Death Valley live more than 300 feet below sea level. Some deep sea brotulids live in trenches almost 23,000 feet deep.

The life span of fish ranges from a few months to perhaps over 100 years. Some small warmwater fish may be born, grow to maturity, and die of old age all in about a year. Fish that grow slowly to a large size in cold climates may not mature until they are 10 to 15 years old and they live many years thereafter. In the Great Basin, brook trout in Bunny Lake, California have been reported to live to be 27 years old.

Fish are cold-blooded animals; their body temperature is controlled by their environment. However, not all fish are cold-blooded. The tunas and some of the sharks, for example, have a network of blood vessels in the skin that elevates their body temperature by as much as 18° F above the water in which they swim. The advantage is the reduced energy needed to flex the muscles that propel them and, therefore, they are able to attain greater speed (Carey 1973).

Rather than being the quiet creatures many people believe, fish are often quite noisy. They make a variety of noises, including grunts, growls, barks, chirps, hums, and other sounds less easily described. They apparently make sounds for about the same reasons other animals, including humans, do: to communicate, to frighten enemies, to express fear, and, it appears in some cases, just to entertain themselves. Boat fishermen on occasion may be amused by a school of croaking freshwater drum lurking in the boat's shade; channel catfish often express their displeasure when they are held out of water by making a grinding-croaking sound.

Another unique aspect of fish is the amount of time, effort, and money that people spend trying to catch them. In the United States people spend hundreds of millions of dollars each year on fishing and related efforts. Wildlife resource departments spend million of dollars each year stocking waters with fish acceptable to the public and ensuring that management practices and public policy support the continued availability of fishing waters. Sportsmen's organizations also spend countless hours and dollars lobbying in state and federal congresses and elsewhere to ensure continued quality fishing waters. No other group of animals is pursued by man for recreation or for sport as vigorously as are fish. The oldest sports in the world are fishing and hunting; the oldest tools of the trade are probably stone spears, fire-hardened wood spears, bone hooks, and traps and baskets woven from plant material. The inefficiency of these primitive tools undoubtedly caused the early food finders to look for a more efficient way to catch fish and to develop what we would now call research.

RESPIRATION

Respiration in fish is the process of extracting oxygen from the surrounding water and excreting carbon dioxide. This differs from humans only in that the fish have gills instead of lungs. No Great Basin fish has modified gills that function as lungs; that is, no Great Basin fish is capable of breathing for protracted periods out of water. Gills are a series of highly vascular filaments attached in double rows to 4 gill arches on either side. The surface that is exposed to oxygen-carrying water is increased many times by folds on the gill filaments (Greenwood 1975). The area of these folds is determined in part by the activity of the fish;

that is, it is much larger in a trout than a catfish. The blood in the gill folds extracts oxygen from water and excretes carbon dioxide. While there is less oxygen in a given volume of water than an equivalent amount of air, fish are able to extract up to 80 percent of the oxygen in water (Greenwood 1975). Trouts need a much higher concentration of oxygen in the water than do catfishes or tui chub to remain healthy.

MOVEMENT AND MIGRATION

One of the most fascinating things about fish is the many ways they travel exclusive of swimming. A number of species of Pacific flying fish become airborne by using their tail and caudal peduncle with a sculling motion until they clear the water, then they use the long pectoral fins, and to a lesser extent the pelvic fins, to help them glide for as far as one-fourth mile or sometimes much farther. When they begin to lose momentum and start touching the waves, they thrash their tail violently until they are again airborne. Generally they soar only 3 to 5 feet above the water, but sometimes they get much higher. When the senior author was cruising at 16 knots (18.4 miles per hour) in the Pacific, flying fish often glided alongside the ship, easily keeping abreast. Fish that are able to leave the water can better escape their enemies; they can also travel much faster.

People in Florida out for an evening stroll a few years back were amazed when they met catfish "walking" on dry land. These fish have been aptly named the walking catfish. Biologists were reportedly more than a little distressed when they tried to poison ponds containing these introduced fish; the catfish simply climbed out of the water and went to another pond. They are able to travel on land because of two adaptations: strong pectoral fins that function as front legs and modified treelike gills that can extract oxygen from the air. The walking catfish, brought into the United States from southern Asia, is now well established in parts of Florida. It has been stocked but presumably not established in the Great Basin.

American eels can at times effect a kind of portage around low dams when the ground is damp and the terrain is not too steep. They simply climb out of the water, go around the dam, slip back in the water, and proceed on upstream. Some of the lampreys have a more direct approach to dam navigation. They swim up the obstacle until they tire, then secure themselves to the face of the dam by means of their suckerlike mouth for a rest. The process is repeated until they clear the dam. Fish also travel by jumping, but whether this is to escape enemies or simply to travel faster is not always apparent. Possibly they are doing it for both reasons. Salmon jump to ascend waterfalls. Largemouth bass jump to capture food. Some appear to jump out of sheer playfulness and others from fright. In a two-acre pond on the Bear River Migratory Bird Refuge, hundreds of three- to four-inch common carp jumped repeatedly for thirty seconds after an air force jet broke the sound barrier over the pond. Many game fish such as rainbow trout and tarpon leap repeatedly when hooked and thrash their heads violently in an attempt to throw the hook.

In a cove on Spirit Lake, Iowa hundreds of common carp raced about just below the surface of the water and jumped repeatedly as a prelude to spawning. Schultz and Stern (1948) state that young needle-fish, about 1 foot long, playfully jump over such things as straws, feathers, floating paper, turtles, etc. They describe how Dr. Breeder found that throwing a splinter of wood or a straw into a school of needlefish invariably caused at least one of them to jump over it. The skipping gobies live among the mangrove roots along the shore of tropical seas or river mouths. According to Schultz and Stern (1948), although none ever wanders far from the water, some never go to sea. They simply rest on the roots of trees, occasionally leaving their perch to chase food or to take a quick dip. The lining of their mouth cavity is modified for air breathing so they can stay away from water even in hot sun.

There are numerous reports from many parts of the world of fish falling out of the sky during violent thunderstorms. There was a downpour of small fish in the midst of a storm in June 1924 in Long Reach, New Zealand. Within a few minutes after the storm struck the township, every hollow and rivulet was filled with thousands of one- to four-inch fish. These fish were a species unknown in the district; their nearest habitat was believed to be 500 miles away. In Cambridge, Maryland in 1829 a dry ditch filled with water during a thunderstorm; it was later discovered that it was also filled with hundreds of small sunfish (Dees 1967).

The migration of fish has been of interest to man from time immemorial. Fish migrate primarily for two reasons: to spawn or to feed. Chinook salmon travel from their birthplace in the small cold streams of northcentral Idaho down the Snake and Columbia rivers all the way to Alaska to feed and grow and then return to their home stream to spawn, feeding until they reach fresh water. American eels leave fresh water to migrate to the Sargasso Sea just southeast of the Bermuda Islands to spawn. Many freshwater and marine fish follow schools of small fish until they deplete the supply or have satisfied their hunger. Fish may migrate thousands of miles or only a few hundred yards.

LOCOMOTION

Great Basin fishes are not unique among fish in the way they move about, but they are nevertheless interesting. Basin fishes, and most others, swim by alternately contracting and relaxing the muscles on the sides of the body and by movement of the fins. A third method is by expelling jets of water from the gill openings as the fish breathes (Greenwood 1975). The first method is most important, but all three are related and used at one time or another or at the same time. A trout, for example, moves forward by contracting the muscles first on one side just back of the head, then by successive contractions and relaxations on both sides of the length of the body. This pulls the body into a series of alternating near S-shaped curves that propel the fish forward. The caudal fin also comes into play and water jets from the gill openings mostly when the fish first starts to move. There is relatively more thrust from the tail in a streamlined fish such as the trout, whereas there is relatively more thrust from the body in the deep-bodied bluegill.

The body of a fish (excluding bones, scales, skin, and internal organs) consists almost entirely of muscle for locomotion. Smaller muscle segments move fins, operate jaws and assist other bodily functions. Generally, Great Basin fishes have muscle tissue of two types. If the skin of a trout is removed, the sides of the fish can be seen to consist of broad bands of white (or pink) tissue with a thinner red band located in the center of the side. Both the "white muscle" and the significantly smaller "red muscle" are used for locomotion. Interestingly, it is the smaller red muscle that is used for routine locomotion and the white muscle tissue that is used for "burst" speeds in feeding, predator avoidance, or other activities requiring short bursts of high speed. Red muscle contains much fat and is well supplied with blood vessels. White muscle is low in fat and has a very limited blood supply. The relative amounts of each of these two muscle types is related to how the species lives and its energy requirements for survival (feeding, predator avoidance, etc.). Fish that cover long distances at leisurely speeds have greater amounts of red muscle while fish that must repeatedly or frequently produce burst speed have lesser amounts of red muscle. The paired fins, especially the pectorals, come into play in braking, turning, holding, or moving slowly forward or back. The median dorsal and anal fins serve primarily as a keel.

Locomotion in Great Basin fishes is used primarily for two broad categories of activity: routine movement and movement for survival. Routine swimming includes such activities as searching for food, diurnal migrations from one area to another, and parts of other migration events. Red muscle is used for these activities. Survival activities include capturing food (for those species that rely on speed to capture prey), predator avoidance, and some aspects of migration where speed or sustained swimming is required (such as negotiating swift waters). White muscle is utilized for these activities.

BODY SHAPE

The body shape of a fish gives some indication of where and how it lives. Torpedo-shaped streamlined trouts with pointed nose and fins are equipped to navigate and survive in swift streams. The more platelike sunfishes are at home in lakes, ponds, and streams where slower flowing waters exist. Sculpin have flattened heads that are consistent with their bottom-dwelling character and their habit of burrowing or settling down among rocks in the substrate. On mud of silt bottoms, sculpins may burrow into the mud and become almost invisible, their body coloration generally matching the surrounding substrate.

Although the eyes of most fish are built upon the same basis as those of other vertebrates, several species have unusual modifications that enable them to live in a wide range of habitats (Bond 1979). The four-eyed fishes of the West Indies have eyes that are modified to see both above and below the surface of the water; the upper half of each eye is adapted to aerial vision and the lower half to water, a sort of bifocal lens. The fish must submerge its eyes frequently to prevent drying. This adaptation presumably enables it to better forage for food and escape enemies. The northern cavefish of Mammoth Cave, Kentucky has adapted to total darkness by losing its sight (it has eye buds beneath the skin) and by losing its color. Some deep sea fish have telescopic eyes attached at the end of a stalk. Members of the trout family, particularly those anadromous forms, have highly developed sense organs for navigation orientation. Smolts migrate downstream tail first. Most species of fish use the lateral line (a series of pressure-sensitive receptors in the body midline) to sense motion in the surrounding waters, thereby sensing prey or predators.

SCALATION

Great Basin fishes have either cycloid scales (cui-ui) or ctenoid scales (sunfishes) or they are naked (catfishes). Generally, the scales are regularly and evenly spaced over the body and overlap like the shingles on a roof. Once an individual fish is completely scaled its number of scales does not increase as it grows older, but they do increase in size. The number of scales in the lateral series may vary between individuals of a species. As a fish grows it lays down growth rings (circuli) on the scales or other bony parts. When these rings are interrupted, as in winter, the mark is known as an annulus, or year mark. These can be used to age many species of fish. Cycloid scales are roughly oval in shape, like a fingernail, and the part that is exposed is smooth. Ctenoid scales tend to be more rectangular in shape and the exposed portion generally has a series of fine comblike spines. Scales provide protection against abrasion of the skin and against external parasites. Catfishes, which have no scales but an extremely tough skin, may be aged by counting the year marks on the opercle or other bony parts of the body. It is interesting to note that some scaled fish, such as cui-ui and common carp, can be more accurately aged from opercles than scales.

FEEDING

In streams fish often feed in or just below fast water riffles; in lakes they catch prey by sudden bursts of speed. Most suckers (the cui-ui of Pyramid Lake and the June sucker of Utah Lake are exceptions) have a ventral mouth that enables them to feed comfortably on or near the bottom. They are not as streamlined or as swift as the trout; they feed by just moving slowly but steadily along and their food is not composed of items that can avoid them by speed. The largely omnivorous catfishes of the Great Basin have large heads with a wide mouth and a moderately tapering body. They are at home in lakes or in moderate to slow streams, where, aided by their fleshy sensory barbels, they feed near the bottom. Smell is also used to locate decaying material that is edible. The channel catfish readily comes to the surface to feed on terrestrial insects and fleshy plant seeds. Native fishes that inhabit some of the small, remote springs with little or no current in the Great Basin are typically chubby-bodied with short, rounded, paired fins. They are neither agile nor fast and they are almost invariably omnivorous.

Most fish feed by outswimming or by ambushing their food, but some have more novel methods. The archer fish of the South Pacific hunts its food by cruising along just below the water surface; when it spots an insect, the quarry is shot down with a drop of water. This is accomplished by a special mechanism. Lengthwise along the roof of the mouth is a groove with a funnellike opening at the rear. When the fish presses its tongue against the roof of the mouth, a tube is formed with the tongue acting as a valve to build water pressure. Accuracy of up to 6 feet is possible because of the efficiency of the water pellet—firing mechanism and the keen aerial vision of the fish (Schultz and Stern 1948).

Equally specialized and efficient in collecting food is the angler fish. It has a rod and bait consisting of wormlike tentacles that it dangles just above its upper jaw. When a fish moves in to get an easy breakfast, it is gobbled up so quickly that only a slow-motion camera can detect it. This placid, neutral-colored, ocean-dwelling fish lies on the bottom and waits for its prey. Occasionally it changes diet by swimming near the surface and feeding on unwary birds that are diving for food. Some other deep sea fish use a lighted lure to attract victims.

The fish with the most sure-fire method of getting food is the electric eel of the Amazon River. This fish, which may reach a length of 8 feet, is capable of producing up to 600 volts and 1,000 watts of electricity. The resultant shock can be very painful or even fatal to man or beast. The electric eel also uses its unusual powers to ward off enemies. Interestingly, it will drown if it cannot reach the surface to gulp air. Other fish with electric powers include certain catfishes and rays in both fresh and salt water.

The majority of fish in the Great Basin have less spectacular feeding methods. Members of the sucker family, equipped with inferior mouths on the bottom of the head, actually "vacuum" food particles (and quantities of the substrate) from the bottom. Piscivorous or predatory fish such as the larger members of the trout family feed by capturing smaller fish. Large adult Lahontan cutthroat in Pyramid Lake, Nevada feed almost exclusively on tui chubs, which they capture by a burst of speed and then ingest the prey, generally head first.

Most fish are neutral in their behavior toward humans, but a small percent are truly dangerous. In the fish world, shark is a word that gets quick attention. Deserved or not, and in many cases it is not, the shark is stuck with a black hat. Of course some do deserve the fear associated with them. Where it occurs, the great white shark should be given a wide berth at all times; it can be truly dangerous. Two or three species of piranhas are the most feared fish in South America. A school of palometa (piranha), for example, has been known to leave only the skeleton of a full-grown cow in just a few minutes. We (the senior author and others) swam with no fear in the great Paraná River where there are millions of piranhas, but as the water level dropped in the smaller bodies of water and food for fish became scarce, we, as prudent people, no longer swam with the piranhas.

When humans turn the tables and bite the fish, they may also be in danger; that is, some fish have toxic flesh. In the tropical oceans some species of fish should never be eaten, others at only certain times of the year. The malady that results is known as ciguatera, a general term covering poisoning by fish flesh. Large-sized barracuda are more likely to be toxic than small ones. The toxin is passed up their food chain from algae. Ciguatera is always painful and sometimes fatal. The effects of eating the purgative fish need no explanation. Freshwater fish flesh is relatively free of toxins; the eggs of gar are an exception. A sick humorist in northwest Iowa, many years back, persuaded his neighbor that his hens would lay better if he fed them shortnose gar eggs.

Several marine fish, such as some of the rays, have poisonous spines. The freshwater madtoms have mildly poisonous pectoral fins. We learned the hard way how not to collect them; don't grab a handful of aquatic vegetation that is hiding one of these little three-inch fish.

REPRODUCTION

If fish behavior is sometimes unusual, certain breeding habits border on the bizarre. Some tropical fish often change sex. A pair may mate, change sex, and then mate again. The pair may alternate this way as many as five times in a single mating.

Sex changes occur in either direction; however, the change from female to male is more common. Many of the coral reef fishes change sex in this way, including the large sea basses, groupers, parrot fishes, and wrasses. Scientists at one time had trouble explaining why there were no young male wrasses on reefs. It appeared as though the large, brightly colored males had sprung full-formed on the reefs without ever having been juveniles or small adults. In a sense they had, because individuals there spend their youth as females and then change to males when they become older and larger. As it turns out, sex change is the normal occurrence in the lives of a large number of coral reef fishes. It apparently has evolved over a long period of time and includes many species of fish (Warner 1982).

Why should an individual fish change sex? What possible evolutionary advantage might there be? One example is when large males monopolize mating by guarding a group of females on a scarce breeding site. Here small males have little or no chance to breed. By changing sex there is less chance of a scarcity of eggs than when only one of the two fish in the mating act is able to produce eggs. Males on some coral reefs mate in harems; a single male controls a group of females. As Warner (1982) says, "Among tropical fish, when the going gets tough, the tough change sex."

Fish normally reproduce either by the female laying eggs in the water that are then fertilized by the male or by giving birth to the young. The number of eggs produced per female ranges from a few to many million. One 7-inch female cutthroat in upper Logan River had 8 mature eggs. One fish spawns in such a peculiar manner that it deserves attention. The California grunion spawns on certain beaches along the California coast from Point Conception south. What makes the grunion different is that these 5- to 7-inch fish spawn not in the water but on the beach. Approximately fifteen minutes after high tide, the grunion begin riding waves up on the beach, where the female buries herself tail first up to her pectoral fins in the sand. One or more males burrow down beside her, fertilize the eggs, then they all ride the next wave out. Two weeks later, at the next series of high tides, when the eggs are wet by the salt water and agitated by the tide, they quickly hatch and the young fish head out to sea.

What might be deemed a single-parent arrangement is found among some seahorses. Perhaps the most intriguing characteristic of seahorses, whose life span is brief, is their unparalleled manner of reproduction. As the season for reproduction approaches, the bodies of the males and females change. The female cloaca distends and becomes an ovipositor and the walls of the male brood pouch thicken and become highly vascular. Courtship is an elaborate ceremony in which the male and the female give out intense mating signals while swimming around and around each other. The female produces as many as 600 eggs, which she deposits, a few at a time, into the brood pouch of the passive male. As they are deposited they are fertilized. She repeats this several times until all her eggs are gone. Then with her trim figure restored, she swims away, carefree, and leaves the hatching and rearing of the family to the male (Dees 1969).

Great Basin fishes reproduce in a variety of ways, ranging from involved courtships to seemingly indiscriminate broadcasting of eggs and sperm. Members of the trout family prepare extensive redds into which eggs and sperm are deposited and covered. Eggs and developing embryos are protected from predators and to some extent from environmental conditions by the gravel covering of the redd. Members of the bullhead catfish family construct nests in secret and guard eggs and young tenaciously for varying periods of time. The livebearers produce young alive, eliminating the period of time when the defenseless embryos are subject to predation.

Carp and many other members of the minnow family produce large numbers of eggs but prepare no nest and provide no parental care for either embryos or young. Generally speaking, the numbers of young or eggs produced is inversely proportional to the amount of protection provided by the adults. Species that produce few offspring per generation provide more parental care (in the form of nests or protection of eggs and young) than do species that produce large numbers of eggs or young per generation.

Some species of killifishes or livebearers may produce multiple generations (particularly in warm springs where temperature is stable) in a year. Members of the trout family produce only one generation per year and some species such as kokanee die after spawning. Their decaying carcasses provide nutrients for subsequent production of food, which can be utilized by the next generation.

WHY WE STUDY FISH

Why do people study fish? For enjoyment, curiosity (both scientific and casual), and often just for entertainment. Nutritionists and laymen are interested in the food value of fish and epicurian oddities in certain marine fish, which are often unsafe to eat. The hagfish, with its four hearts, is of interest to the medical profession for insight into heart disease research. Medical researchers are also interested in the array of contractile structures in the vascular system of some species.

Almost everyone is intrigued with dangerous fishes. Sharks, barracudas, piranhas, electric fishes, stinging fishes, fishes with toxic flesh—all have a special fascination (preferably at a safe distance).

Culture of fish for food is seated in antiquity and today is one of the fastest-growing aspects of American agriculture. The aquarium trade sells hundreds of millions of pet fish each year, many from the far reaches of the world, to people who expect no more from their wards than long hours of entertainment and relaxation. Sport fishing, one of the largest participation sports in America, is enjoyed by millions of people of all ages, from the robust to the somewhat less than healthy. The sport in turn furnishes employment for several thousand biologists and administrators and associated staff at state and federal levels. Universities and private organizations also carry on both basic and applied research to protect and perpetuate sport fisheries. Suppliers of everything from palatial fishing boats to cane poles profit by and participate in the sport. Commercial fishing provides a livelihood for thousands and food for millions each year. It is a necessary industry for many nations such as Japan, with its limited land-based resources.

The management of sport and commercial fisheries requires an in-depth understanding of population dynamics, behavior, growth rate, and longevity. Public attitudes, which sometimes determine how many fish to harvest, are sometimes influenced by rather bizarre preconceptions. Fish are studied as bioassay organisms; that is, the fish is the biological entity exposed to various levels of toxicants to determine ultimately what the possibly dangerous compounds do to the fish and can potentially do to humans. Several species of fish are sensitive indicators of pollution in aquatic ecosystems.

The systematists study fish, living and fossil, to understand better the relationship of fish to each other. Ichthyologists are concerned with pure science—knowledge for its own sake—but beyond that most of them are interested and involved in the practical aspects of fishery science. It is understood that today's basic research may have a very practical application tomorrow.

As a resource, fish provide a renewable source of protein. In the temperate portions of the world greater production of food per acre can sometimes be derived from fish than from beef cattle. This protein is readily available and easily harvested. Additionally, fish farming generally requires less energy input than cattle ranching and is less subject to adverse impacts from climate and harsh weather conditions.

Ocean ranching, to supplement natural runs of anadromous fish and reap the benefits of the ocean's productivity, has increased vastly in the 1980s, particularly in Alaska, Oregon, Washington State, Norway and the U.S.S.R. In "salmon ranching" large tonnages of fish protein can theoretically be harvested with minimum effort, because the fish return to the ponds from which they were released after being reared for one or more years in the ocean, where they can feed for free. Many fishery biologists are concerned about the impact of large numbers of these semidomestic fish on wild populations.

As fellow inhabitants of the earth, fish offer a widely diverse group of organisms for study. Fish occupy ecological niches that range from high mountain lakes to deep ocean trenches, from water that is near freezing to ponds over 100° F, from large lakes, rivers, and streams to puddles and small farm ponds, from lakes and estuaries that are extremely salty to icy mountain streams that are essentially distilled water, from acid to alkaline pH conditions, and from well-lighted to totally dark water of caves. Fish have adapted to these wide-ranging conditions over thousands of years, gradually spreading throughout the world to occupy all bodies of water that will support them. For these reasons we can learn from fish as representatives of a successful organism type and profit by the experience that they have lived through.

7

Key to Native and Introduced Fishes of the Great Basin by Gerald R. Smith

The following numbered statements describe fishes or groups of fishes. By treating the *a* and *b* statements as choices, one of which leads to another choice or to the name of a fish, one can follow the numbers to an identification of a fish in the hand. Begin with couplet 1 in the family key. Compare the statements and the accompanying pictures to the fish. If the fish has an adipose fin, go to the indicated numbered step (couplet 2), and so on. Asterisks indicate figured characters.

First learn the names of some of the main structures of fishes in the first figure. The later figures, accompanying each key, are numbered to correspond to the couplets in order to assist in making the key choices. Sometimes it is easier to make a guess at the identification by comparing the fish to the figures, then working through the key, backward and forward.

Fish identification is based heavily on shapes, the nature of the fins, scale size, gill rakers, teeth and other structures around the mouth, and the lateral line.

Fins. It is important to determine whether fins have spines or only soft rays: spines are segmented, unbranched, and (except in sculpins) hard and sharp; soft rays are segmented and usually branched. The origin of a fin is the anteriormost point on its base.

Counting fin rays. In catfishes each ray, even the smallest, is counted separately. In other fishes, the one or two short rays at the beginning of the fin are not counted at all and the first full-length ray is counted as number one; the last ray is usually branched to the base and counted only once.

Scale size. Scale size is described in terms of the number along the body, usually in or near the lateral line. Sometimes the number of scale rows between the head and the beginning of the dorsal fin is counted— the "number of predorsal scales."

The lateral line consists of a row of scales bearing tubes containing nerves. It is easy to count these scales, starting with the first one behind the upper shoulder and ending with the one over the crease where the caudal fin bends at its base. If the lateral line is interrupted or incomplete, that fact is usually important to the identification.

Gill rakers. These are the food-straining structures on the front of the gill arches. They are easiest to count after the first (front) gill arch is carefully dissected out. (Replace it for future reference after counting.)

Teeth. In the mouth, teeth can usually be examined directly with a hand lens or microscope. Pharyngeal teeth must be dissected from the back of the throat behind the last normal gill arches: cut the muscles at the bottom center and at the top sides of the pharyngeal arches and pull them out with forceps; replace after cleaning them off and studying them.

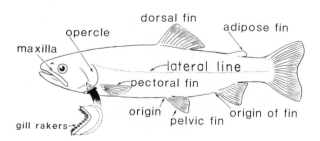

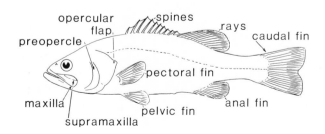

Barbels. These are flaps of skin with taste buds. In minnows they may be small and partly hidden in the groove at the end of the upper lip.

A fish is most valuable if you know what it is, and accurate identification often requires dissection. But if you think you have a rare or protected species, get professional advice before you kill it.

Several species of fishes that have been stocked but are not established in the Great Basin do not appear in the key.

KEY TO NATIVE AND INTRODUCED FAMILIES

1.a. Adipose fin present on back between dorsal and caudal fins* trout and catfish 2
1.b. Adipose fin absent* 3

2.a. No spines in dorsal or pectoral fins*—trouts, salmon, whitefish, Salmonidae
2.b. Dorsal and pectoral fins each with one strong spine*—catfish, Ictaluridae and Loricariidae

3.a. No teeth in mouth, head without scales (suckers and minnows) 4
3.b. Mouth with teeth on jaws, head with scales 5

4.a. Mouth with fleshy lips* nearly meeting at midline, ventral, except in some lake suckers; caudal fin with 18 principal rays—suckers, Catostomidae
4.b. Mouth without fleshy lips* (except, in some dace, at corners of mouth), usually terminal; 19 principal caudal rays—minnows, Cyprinidae

5.a. Dorsal fin small, without spines;* pelvic fins midway back on body, well behind pectoral fins* (but absent in some topminnows and forward in male live-bearers) 6
5.b. Dorsal fin large and with two parts, the first with 3 or more spines;* pelvic fins positioned under pectoral fins* 8

6.a. Mouth much larger than eye diameter*—northern pike, *Esox lucius*, Esocidae
6.b. Mouth not much larger than eye diameter* (killifish and live-bearers) . .7

7.a. Dorsal fin usually with 6 rays;* anal fin modified into a sperm transfer organ in males;* origin of dorsal fin over or behind vertical from the origin of the anal fin*—live-bearers, Poeciliidae
7.b. Dorsal fin usually with 8 or 9 rays;* anal fin not modified;* origin of dorsal fin over or ahead of vertical from the origin of anal fin*—killifish, pupfish, and springfish, Cyprinodontidae

8.a. Three separated dorsal spines; sides with large vertical plates; caudal peduncle slender, with lateral keels—threespine stickleback, *Gasterosteus aculeatus*, Gasterosteidae*

8.b. Six or more dorsal spines; sides with scales or minute prickles, but not plates; caudal peduncle much deeper than eye diameter, without keels 9

9.a. Scales absent; head wider than high; eyes dorsal; pelvic fin with one soft spine and 3 or 4 rays—sculpins, Cottidae
9.b. Scales present; head as high or higher than wide; eyes lateral; pelvic fin with one hard spine and 5 branched rays 10

10.a. One pair of nostrils;* lateral line discontinuous below soft dorsal fin;* 16 principal caudal rays—Cichlidae
10.b. Two pair of nostrils;* lateral line continuous under soft dorsal fin;* 17 principal caudal rays 11

11.a. Preopercle strongly serrated;* dorsal fins not connected;* supramaxilla absent; pseudobranch present (perch, walleye, and white bass) 12
11.b. Preopercle weakly serrated or nearly smooth;* dorsal fins connected,* even if only slightly; supramaxilla present; pseudobranch weak or absent— bass and sunfish, Centrarchidae

12.a. Anal spines 2;* dorsal spines 12 or 14 *—walleye and perch, Percidae
12.b. Anal spines 3;* dorsal spines 10 *—white bass, *Morone chrysops*, Percichthyidae

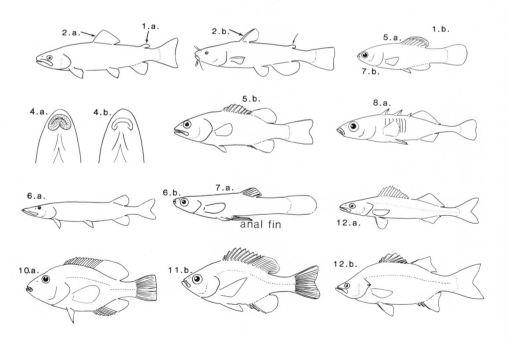

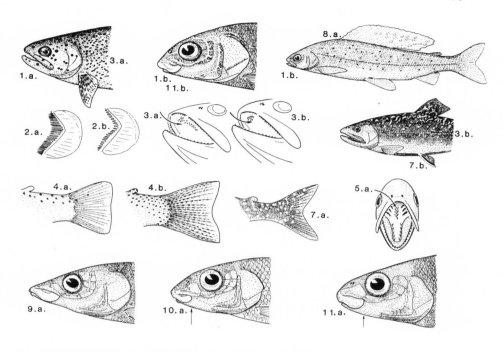

KEY TO NATIVE AND INTRODUCED TROUTS (SALMONIDAE)

1.a. Scales small,* more than 100 in lateral line; mouth large* with large teeth (trout, salmon, and chars) 2
1.b. Scales larger,* fewer than 100 in lateral line; mouth small* with small or minute teeth (whitefish and grayling) 8

2.a. More than 30 gill rakers on first gill arch;* gill rakers long and slender;* body silvery with few distinct spots; anal rays usually 13 to 14—sockeye or kokanee salmon, *Oncorhynchus nerka*
2.b. Fewer than 26 gill rakers on first arch;* gill rakers short;* color pattern usually including distinct spots; anal rays fewer than 13 (trout and chars) . . . 3

3.a. Black spots present on head and body;* lower fins usually lack white leading edges,* though they may have white tips; vomer with a long double row of teeth* (trouts) 4
3.b. Red, cream, or whitish spots or wavy markings on darker background of body;* lower fins usually with snow white leading edges;* vomer with a cluster of several teeth only at its head* (chars) 7

4.a. Tail fin without numerous distinct black spots;* body often pale brown, sides with round, red spots in white or bluish rings; caudal fin not forked;* young with orange adipose fin lacking black margin or spots*—brown trout, *Salmo trutta*

4.b. Caudal fin with rows of numerous, distinct black spots;* no round red spots on sides; caudal fin often moderately forked; adipose fin of young spotted or edged with black* (native trouts of western United States) 5

5.a. Red or orange cutthroat marks in grooves between each lower jaw and throat; small teeth present on back of tongue between first gill arches;* dorsal, anal, and pelvic fins not tipped with white—cutthroat trout, *Salmo clarki* 12
5.b. Cutthroat marks usually absent (except in hybrids and redband trout, a rainbow trout relative in the Harney basin); no small teeth on back of tongue near first gill arches (all trout have large teeth on front of tongue); dorsal, anal, and pelvic fins often tipped with white. 6

6.a. Black spots large, regular in size and shape, and restricted posteriorly; scales small, usually 150 to 180 in lateral line; parr marks usually present in adults as well as young—golden trout, *Salmo aguabonita*
6.b. Black spots small, irregular in size and shape, covering much of back and sides; scales larger, usually 120 to 150 in lateral line; parr marks present in young, not adults—rainbow trout, *Salmo gairdneri*

7.a. Caudal fin deeply forked;* no black slash marks on lower fins; body pale with whitish bean-shaped spots* and no bright orange or red; parr marks in young narrow and irregular—lake trout, *Salvelinus namaycush*
7.b. Caudal fin no more than slightly forked; black slash bordering snow white edges of lower fins;* back with wavy pattern of dark and light* extending onto dorsal and caudal fins; sides with red or pink spots in bluish circles; young with 8 to 10 regularly spaced parr marks—brook trout, *Salvelinus fontinalis*

8.a. Dorsal fin large, saillike in adults* with more than 17 rays; color blue, green, and purple—arctic grayling, *Thymallus arcticus*
8.b. Dorsal fin small with 11 to 13 rays; color silvery with blue-green back (whitefishes). 9

9.a. Snout long and sharp;* gill rakers 37 to 45; maxilla long and slender*— Bonneville cisco, *Prosopium gemmiferum*, Bear Lake
9.b. Snout not long and sharp; gill rakers 18 to 26; maxilla shorter and deeper 10

10.a. Maxilla short, not reaching to end of lacrymal* (the lacrymal is the bone in front of the eye and above the maxilla); scales large, 67 to 78 in lateral line— Bear Lake whitefish, *Prosopium abyssicola*, Bear Lake
10.b. Maxilla reaching to end of lacrymal;* scales smaller, 75 to 94 in lateral line. 11

11.a. Anal rays 9 to 11; dorsal rays 10 to 12; length of upper jaw usually less than 1/2 length of dorsal fin base—Bonneville whitefish, *Prosopium spilonotus*,* Bear Lake
11.b. Anal rays 11 to 13; dorsal rays 12 to 13; length of upper jaw shorter, less than 1/2 length of dorsal fin base—mountain whitefish, *Prosopium williamsoni*,* mountain streams and lakes of Great Basin

12. A large number of more or less differentiated cutthroat trouts inhabit the Great Basin in addition to those introduced. They have large, evenly distributed spots (with a few exceptions) and fall into two general groups. Each has been transplanted elsewhere in the basin. The first of these groups lives in the Lahontan basin and is characterized by possession of 21 to 28 gill rakers and 40 to 75 pyloric caeca. It includes *Salmo clarki henshawi* (Pyramid Lake and elsewhere) and its generally spotless (except posteriorly) close relative, *S. c. seleniris* (Silver King Creek, California). The second group has 16 to 21 gill rakers. It includes *S. c. utah* of the Bonneville drainage and the similar (introduced) Yellowstone cutthroats from the upper Snake and Yellowstone drainages.

KEY TO SUCKERS (CATOSTOMIDAE)

1.a. Lower lips separated by a gap in the midline, with papillae weak or absent;* mouth subterminal; gill rakers 37 to 47 in outer row of first arch; each raker branched like broccoli*—*Chasmistes* 2
1.b. Lower lips in contact or joined at the midline and covered with papillae;* mouth ventral; gill rakers fewer than 37 (except in some mountain suckers; see below); each raker only slightly branched*—*Catostomus*.................. 3

2.a. Scales around caudal peduncle 22 to 26; scales in lateral line 59 to 68—Cui-ui, *Chasmistes cujus*, Pyramid Lake
2.b. Scales around caudal peduncle 19 to 20; scales in lateral line 55 to 62—June sucker, *Chasmistes liorus*, Utah Lake

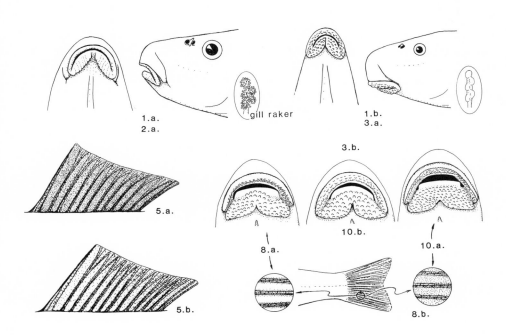

gill raker

1.a.
2.a.

1.b.
3.a.

3.b.

5.a.

5.b.

8.a.

10.b.

10.a.

8.b.

3.a. Jaws with weak, rounded scraping edges projecting beyond lips; * lower lips cleft to base, no notches at outer corners of lips; * head large, fontanelle wide— valley suckers, subgenus *Catostomus*.................................... 4
3.b. Jaws, especially lower, with squared scraping edges projecting well beyond lips; * notches at outer corners of upper and lower lips; * lower lips not cleft to base; * head small; fontanelle narrow or closed (bridgelip sucker, *Catostomus columbianus* in the Harney basin has these characteristics, but the first two are weakly developed)—mountain suckers, subgenus *Pantosteus* 8

4.a. Dorsal rays usually 12 or more; lateral line scales fewer than 70 (except in largescale sucker, *Catostomus macrocheilus* of the Harney basin)......... 5
4.b. Dorsal rays usually 9 to 11; lateral line scales usually more than 70..... 6

5.a. Predorsal scales 28 to 32; gill rakers 28 to 31; dorsal fin usually with 12 rays, membranes densely pigmented, dark*—Utah sucker, *Catostomus ardens*, Bonneville basin
5.b. Predorsal scales 36 to 52; gill rakers 23 to 29; dorsal fin usually with 13 rays, membranes lightly speckled*—largescale sucker, *Catostomus macrocheilus*, Harney basin and Snake River drainage

6.a. Lateral line scales usually more than 80 (77 to 93)—Tahoe sucker, *Catostomus tahoensis*, Lahontan and some adjacent drainages
6.b. Lateral line scales usually fewer than 79 (68 to 85) 7

7.a. Belly dusky with melanophores in breeding males—Owens sucker, *Catostomus fumeiventris*, Owens Valley
7.b. Belly white or yellow, without melanophores—Warner sucker, *Catostomus warnerensis*, Warner Valley

8.a. Anterior papillae of lower lip grouped in a half-rosette pattern with blank spaces on either side; * caudal fin membranes spotless between rays *—mountain sucker, *Catostomus platyrhynchus*, Bonneville, Lahontan, and Snake River basins
8.b. Anterior papillae of lower lip evenly spaced, * not grouped into a half-rosette pattern; caudal fin membranes densely pigmented* 9

9.a. Predorsal scales 21 to 32—desert sucker, *Catostomus clarki*, White River drainage
9.b. Predorsal scales 43 to 62 10

10.a. Lateral line scales 90 to 107; lower jaw with broad square-edged cartilage; * lips deeply notched at outer corners *—bluehead sucker, *Catostomus discobolus*, northern Bonneville basin
10.b. Lateral line scales usually fewer than 90; lower jaw cartilage rounded; * lips not deeply notched at outer corners *—bridgelip sucker, *Catostomus columbianus*, Harney basin

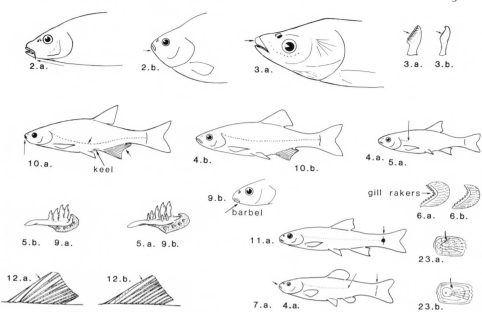

KEY TO THE NATIVE AND INTRODUCED CARPS AND MINNOWS (CYPRINIDAE)

1.a. Dorsal fin with more than 12 rays 2
1.b. Dorsal fin with fewer than 12 rays 3

2.a. Upper jaw with 2 barbels on each side;* lateral line with more than 32 scales or with some scales greatly enlarged; gill rakers 21 to 27—common carp, *Cyprinus carpio*
2.b. Upper jaw with no barbels;* lateral line with fewer than 32 scales; scales of similar size; gill rakers 37 to 43—goldfish, *Carassius auratus*

3.a. Position of anal fin well back, distance from anal fin origin to caudal base is 1/3 distance from anal fin origin to snout tip; head wide and flat, eyes low on side of head; upper lip thickened anteriorly;* pharyngeal teeth strongly serrated*—grass carp, *Ctenopharyngodon idella*
3.b. Position of anal fin farther forward, distance from anal fin origin to caudal base goes 2 to 2-1/2 times in distance from anal origin to snout tip; head rounded in cross section, eyes high on side of head; upper lip not thickened anteriorly; pharyngeal teeth not serrated* 4

4.a. Number of pored lateral line scales reduced, lateral line not reaching to end of caudal peduncle* 5
4.b. Lateral line complete, pored scales extending to end of caudal peduncle*
.... 11

5.a. Fewer than 40 lateral scale rows; lateral line absent or with 1 or 2 pored scales; * pharyngeal teeth 2, 5–4, 2—least chub, *Iotichthys phlegethontis*, Bonneville basin
5.b. More than 40 lateral scale rows; pharyngeal teeth usually 4-4 6

6.a. Gill rakers 13 to 22 * 7
6.b. Gill rakers 7 to 12 * 9

7.a. Mouth small and oblique; anterior predorsal scales smaller and more crowded than other scales; end of caudal peduncle with a faint, slightly oblique band of pigment—fathead minnow, *Pimephales promelas*
7.b. Mouth larger and less oblique; predorsal scales evenly spaced; no oblique band of pigment at end of caudal peduncle—certain isolated populations of the *Gila bicolor* complex. 8

8.a. Dorsal and anal fin rays typically 8; scales with radii in posterior fields only—tui chub, *Gila bicolor* (most will key though 4.b.)
8.b. Dorsal and anal fin rays typically 7; scales with radii in all fields 30

9.a. No barbel at lateral corner of mouth; no frenum bridging snout and upper lip; pharyngeal teeth usually 4-4; * dorsal fin rays usually 8—relict dace, *Relictus solitarius*, Ruby, Butte, Goshute, and Steptoe valleys, Nevada (desert dace, *Eremichthys acros*, which may key out here, has scraping sheaths on the jaws; see 16.b.)
9.b. Maxillary barbel at corner of mouth; * frenum between snout and upper lip; pharyngeal teeth usually in two rows, 2, 4-4, 2 * or 1, 4-4, 1; dorsal fin rays 7—speckled dace, (*Rhinichthys osculus* will key here only rarely; most have complete lateral lines)

10.a. Belly between pelvic fins and anal opening keeled; * mouth very small, oblique; * lateral line complete and strongly decurved; anal fin rays 11 or 12—golden shiner, *Notemigonus crysoleucas* *
10.b. Belly not keeled behind pelvic fins; mouth larger and less oblique; lateral line usually only slightly decurved; anal fin rays fewer (except in redside shiner, *Richardsonius balteatus* which have 10 to 13) 11

11.a. Combination of the following: fewer than 50 scales in lateral line; large, distinct black spot on caudal peduncle at base of caudal fin; snout blunt; body silvery in life—spottail shiner, *Notropis hudsonius* *
11.b. Lacking at least one of the above combinations of characters. Usually more than 50 scales in lateral line; caudal spot absent, indistinct, dusky, or not ahead of base of caudal fin; snout not blunt (except in *Acrocheilus* and some *Rhinichthys osculus*), sides not uniformly silvery. 12

12.a. Dorsal fin with an anterior spine; * pelvic fins spiny (spinedace) 13
12.b. Dorsal * and pelvic fins of flexible rays only 15

13.a. Mouth slightly oblique; almost no pigment on shoulder girdle ahead of scapular bar of pigment; dorsal spine strong; dorsal fin high, depressed length extending less than 2.1 times in predorsal length—Pahranagat spinedace, *Lepidomeda altivelis*,* Pahranagat Valley, Nevada

13.b. Mouth less oblique; pigment on shoulder girdle extending ahead of scapular pigment bar and under opercular flap; dorsal spine weaker; dorsal fin lower, length included more than 2.2 times in predorsal length 14

14.a. Melanophores extending across opercle and subopercle and to angle of preopercle; shoulder girdle with much pigment directly in front of pectoral fin base—White River spinedace, *Lepidomeda albivallis*,* White River Valley, Nevada

14.b. Melanophores confined to upper half of opercle and preopercle; no pigment on shoulder girdle directly ahead of pectoral fin base—Big Spring spinedace, *Lepidomeda mollispinis pratensis*,* Big Spring, Meadow Valley Wash, Nevada

15.a. Jaw edges with hard, biting sheaths 16
15.b. Jaw edges without hard, biting sheaths 17

16.a. Lower jaw with a hard, square biting surface;* usually 10 dorsal fin rays; usually 9 anal fin rays; adult size large—chiselmouth, *Acrocheilus alutaceus*, Harney basin

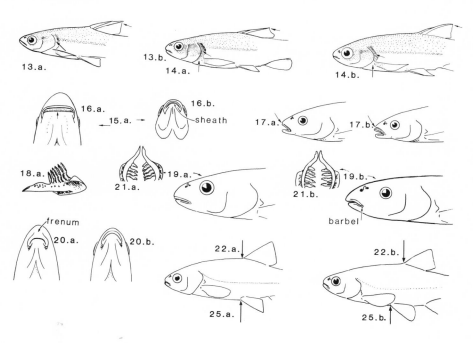

16.b. Upper and lower jaws with easily removed, rounded biting edges;* usually 8 dorsal fin rays; usually 8 anal fin rays; adult size small; lateral line sometimes interrupted or incomplete—desert dace, *Eremichthys acros*, Soldier Meadows, Nevada

17.a. Premaxillae not protractile,* a bridge of skin (frenum) between lip and snout prevents extension (the bridge of skin may be hidden in shallow groove between snout and lip) 18
17.b. Premaxillae protractile,* a deep fold of skin above the upper lip allows extension 21

18.a. Scales small, more than 90 in lateral line; pharyngeal teeth usually 6-6,* Sacramento blackfish, *Orthodon microlepidotus*
18.b. Scales larger, 47 to 89 in lateral line 19

19.a. Pharyngeal teeth usually 4 to 5;* no maxillary barbel*—moapa dace, *Moapa coriacea*, Warm Springs, Clark County, Nevada
19.b. Pharyngeal teeth usually 2, 4-4, 2 or 1, 4-4, 1;* maxillary barbel usually present*—dace, *Rhinichthys* 20

20.a. Snout projecting well ahead of mouth and connected to upper lip by a broad bridge of skin*—longnose dace, *Rhinichthys cataractae*
20.b. Snout projecting slightly ahead of mouth;* frenum usually hidden— speckled dace, *Rhinichthys osculus*

21.a. Pharyngeal teeth in one row, usually 5-4 or 5-5. 22
21.b. Pharyngeal teeth in 2 rows, usually 2, 5-4, 2 or 2, 4-4, 2. 24

22.a. Origin of dorsal fin directly over origin of pelvic fins;* 26 to 33 predorsal scale rows; teeth 5-4 or 5-5; lateral line sometimes incomplete 23
22.b. Origin of dorsal fin well behind vertical from pelvic fins;* 32 to 38 predorsal scale rows; teeth 5-4—California roach, *Hesperoleucus symmetricus*

23.a. Dorsal and anal fins usually with 7 rays; radii in all fields of scales; lateral scales in 50 to 74 rows, embedded (see also 30)—Alvord chub, *Gila alvordensis*, Alvord basin
23.b. Dorsal and anal fins usually with 8 or 9 rays; radii only in posterior field of scales; lateral line scales usually 45 to 63—tui chub, *Gila bicolor*

24.a. Scales large, fewer than 66 in lateral line 25
24.b. Scales smaller, more than 66 in lateral line 28

25.a. Dorsal fin origin directly over pelvic origin* (chubs, *Gila*) 26
25.b. Dorsal fin origin behind vertical from pelvic origin* (redsides, *Richardsonius*). 27

26.a. Usually 9 dorsal and 8 anal fin rays; gill rakers 8 to 16—Utah chub, *Gila atraria*, Bonneville basin, introduced elsewhere

26.b. Usually 8 dorsal and 7 anal fin rays; gill rakers 7 to 10—arroyo chub, *Gila orcutti*, Mojave basin

27.a. Anal fin rays 10 to 13, usually 11 to 12—redside shiner, *Richardsonius balteatus*, Bonneville, Snake, and Harney basins
27.b. Anal fin rays 8 to 10, usually 8 to 9—Lahontan redside, *Richardsonius egregius*, Lahontan basin

28.a. Lateral line scales 89 to 94; dorsal and anal fin rays usually 9—Pahranagat roundtail chub, *Gila robusta jordani*, White River, Nevada
28.b. Lateral line scales fewer than 85; dorsal and anal fin rays usually 8 ... 29

29.a. Scales small and embedded, giving the impression of leathery skin, 75 to 85 in lateral line; snout short; mouth not large, not extending to below front of eye—leatherside chub, *Gila copei*, Bonneville basin
29.b. Scales larger and distinct, 67 to 75 in lateral line; snout long; mouth large, extending to below front of eye—northern squawfish, *Ptychocheilus oregonensis*, Harney basin

30.a. Pored lateral line scales usually reaching at least to caudal peduncle; gill rakers 18 to 22; pectoral rays usually 14; head length 25 to 29 percent of standard length; head profile convex above—Alvord chub, *Gila alvordensis*
30.b. Pored lateral line scales not reaching caudal peduncle; gill rakers 13 to 20, pectoral rays usually 13; head length 28 to 36 percent of standard length; head profile slightly concave above—Borax Lake chub, *Gila boraxobius*

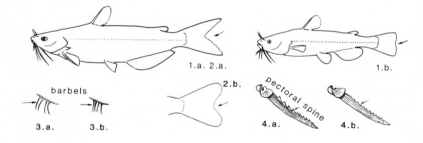

KEY TO SUCCESSFULLY INTRODUCED CATFISHES (ICTALURIDAE AND LORICARIIDAE)

1.a. Caudal fin forked;* body usually pale or silvery on sides (or blue-black in breeding adults), some with black spots 2
1.b. Caudal fin more or less squared or rounded behind;* color darker yellow, brown, or black, not distinctly spotted 3

2.a. Caudal fin deeply, sharply forked;* black spots present except in very large adults; anal fin rays 24 to 30 (count all rays in catfish)—channel catfish, *Ictalurus punctatus*

2.b. Caudal fin rounded, moderately forked; * no distinct spots; anal rays 19 to 23—white catfish, *Ictalurus catus*

3.a. Barbels on chin unpigmented, whitish; * anal fin rays more than 23—yellow bullhead, *Ictalurus natalis*
3.b. Barbels on chin pigmented, dark; * anal fin with 16 to 24 rays 4

4.a. Posterior serrations of pectoral spine in the form of regularly spaced sharp barbs; * anal fin rays 21 to 24; gill rakers 14 or fewer; belly usually whitish—brown bullhead, *Ictalurus nebulosus*
4.b. Posterior serrations of pectoral spine in the form of irregularly spaced jagged edges; * anal fin rays 17 to 21; gill rakers 15 to 21; belly usually yellowish; light-colored vertical bar at base of caudal fin—black bullhead, *Ictalurus melas*

Aquarium catfishes of the family Loricariidae may be recognized by their flattened shape and numerous rows of bony plates. The suckermouth catfish, *Hypostomus plecostomus*, has been introduced and is established in Indian Springs, Clark County, Nevada.

KEY TO NATIVE AND INTRODUCED KILLIFISHES (CYPRINODONTIDAE)

1.a. Origin of dorsal fin vertically above the origin of anal fin; * no pelvic fins; * jaw teeth conical or bicuspid, never tricuspid (springfish, poolfish) 2
1.b. Origin of dorsal fin well ahead of vertical from origin of anal fin; * pelvic fins present * or absent; teeth conical or tricuspid 5

2.a. Jaw teeth conical; * pharyngeal teeth somewhat molariform; * intestine in an *S* curve (poolfish, *Empetrichthys*) 3
2.b. Jaw teeth bicuspid; * pharyngeal teeth not molariform; * intestine coiled (springfish, *Crenichthys*) 4

3.a. Body deep; 20 to 30 scales in lateral series; usually 14 anal fin rays—Ash Meadows killifish, *Empetrichthys merriami*, Ash Meadows, Nye County, Nevada (probably extinct)
3.b. Body slender; usually 31 to 32 scales in lateral series; anal fin rays usually 12 to 13—Pahrump killifish, *Empetrichthys latos latos*, * Pahrump Valley, Nye County, Nevada (extinct in native range, under cultivation elsewhere)

4.a. Side usually with 2 dark stripes or 2 rows of dark blotches—White River springfish, *Crenichthys baileyi*, * White River drainage, Nevada
4.b. Side with one row of dark blotches—Railroad Valley springfish, *Crenichthys nevadae*, * Railroad Valley, Nevada

5.a. Teeth tricuspid * (pupfish) 6
5.b. Teeth conical * 9

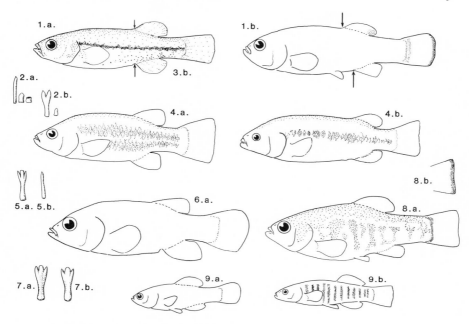

6.a. No pelvic fins; vertical bars indistinct in adults; dwarfed, adults usually shorter than 20 mm standard length; caudal fin margin convex—Devils Hole pupfish, *Cyprinodon diabolis*,* Ash Meadows, Nevada
6.b. Pelvic fins usually present on at least one side; vertical bars evident on adult females; not so dwarfed; caudal fin margin usually nearly straight.....7

7.a. Scales small and crowded, usually 28 to 29 in lateral series and 33 or more around body; outer face of teeth with prominent median ridge*—Salt Creek pupfish, *Cyprinodon salinus*, Death Valley, California
7.b. Scales large and regular, usually 25 to 27 in lateral series and fewer than 32 around body; outer face of teeth without median ridge* 8

8.a. Caudal fin without a terminal black band;* breeding males blue with yellowish margins on dorsal and anal fins and yellowish or pale margin on caudal; pelvic fin rays 7—Owens pupfish, *Cyprinodon radiosus*, Owens Valley, California
8.b. Caudal fin of males usually with a terminal black band;* breeding males blue without yellowish markings on fins; pelvic fin rays usually 6—Amargosa pupfish, *Cyprinodon nevadensis*, Amargosa Valley, California and Ash Meadows, Nevada

9.a. Scales large, fewer than 30 in lateral series; dorsal and anal fin rays fewer than 13; plainly colored—rainwater killifish, *Lucania parva**
9.b. Scales small, more than 50 in lateral series; dorsal and anal fin rays more than 13; color pattern of vertical bars—plains killifish, *Fundulus zebrinus*

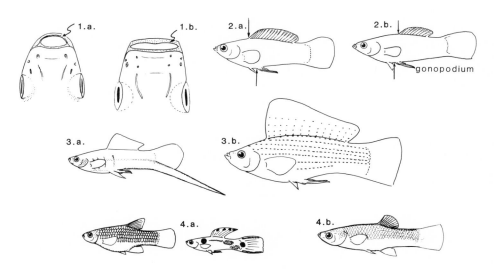

KEY TO SUCCESSFULLY INTRODUCED LIVEBEARERS
(POECILIIDAE)

1.a. Border of upper jaw a narrow, convex arch* viewed from above; origin of dorsal fin well behind vertical line from origin of anal fin; 30 to 32 lateral scales; gonopodium usually longer than 1/3 standard length; caudal fin with a vertical row of small spots, no large spots except from parasite infections—mosquitofish, *Gambusia affinis*

1.b. Border of upper jaw broad, slightly concave, or nearly straight* viewed from above; origin of dorsal fin approximately over or ahead of origin of anal fin (except in male guppies, which have large black and colored spots); 25 to 30 lateral line scales; gonopodium usually shorter than 1/3 standard length; caudal fin with large or diffuse spots or no spots 2

2.a. Origin of dorsal fin ahead of vertical from origin of anal fin;* dorsal fin rays 12 or more 3

2.b. Origin of dorsal fin over or behind vertical from origin of anal fin;* dorsal fin rays 12 or fewer...4

3.a. Sides usually with several longitudinal stripes; males with swordlike extension of lower caudal fin rays;* dorsal fin of males not high and saillike* (colors green, red, or black)—green swordtail, *Xiphophorus helleri*

3.b. Sides usually with 5 to 6 rows of (red, blue, and green) spots;* males with large, saillike dorsal fin;* no swordlike extension of caudal fin* (color green, brown, or black)—sailfin molly, *Poecilia latipinna*

4.a. Dorsal fin rays 7 to 8; males dwarfed and variably colorful, with large red, blue, green, and black spots;* females larger, but rarely over 50 mm; female color pattern reticulate*—guppy, *Poecilia reticulata*

4.b. Dorsal fin rays 8 to 11; males with small blue or green spots; both sexes larger; female color pattern spotted or criss-crossed, * not reticulate—shortfin molly, *Poecilia mexicana*

KEY TO SUCCESSFULLY INTRODUCED SUNFISHES (CENTRARCHIDAE)

1.a. Anal spines 3 * 2
1.b. Anal spines 5 to 8 * 8

2.a. Body slender, about 1/3 as deep as long; * scales small, more than 58 in lateral line (bass) 3
2.b. Body deep, rounded in side view, more than 1/3 as deep as long; * scales large, fewer than 52 in lateral line (sunfishes) 5

3.a. Upper jaw large, extending past vertical from back of eye * (except in young, which have bicolored caudal fin); spiny and soft dorsal fins narrowly connected at their bases; * 9 to 12 rows of scales on cheeks—largemouth bass, *Micropterus salmoides*
3.b. Upper jaw smaller, usually extending to vertical from pupil of eye * (young with tricolored caudal fin); spiny and soft dorsal fins with broader connection at their bases; more than 12 rows of scales on cheek. 4

4.a. Sides plain olive green or with faint vertical bars; * scales small, usually 68 to 76 in lateral line; usually 13 to 15 soft dorsal fin rays; young without black spot at base of caudal fin *—smallmouth bass, *Micropterus dolomieui*
4.b. Side with irregular, dark horizontal stripe; * scales larger, usually 59 to 65 in lateral line; usually 12 soft dorsal fin rays; young with black spot at base of caudal fin *—spotted bass, *Micropterus punctulatus*

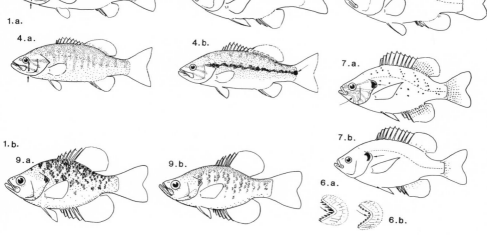

5.a. Mouth large, upper jaw as long as or longer than longest dorsal spine; * pectoral fin short and rounded; * not reaching front of eye when bent forward across eye—green sunfish, *Lepomis cyanellus*
5.b. Mouth small, upper jaw much shorter than longest dorsal spine; pectoral fin long and pointed, reaching beyond eye if bent forward across eye. 6

6.a. Opercular flap black to margin, * without white border or reddish spot; last rays of soft dorsal fin with black blotch near middle; * gill rakers on first arch long and slender*—bluegill, *Lepomis macrochirus*
6.b. Opercular flap with white border and reddish spot or margin; no large black blotch in back of dorsal fin; gill rakers short and thick* 7

7.a. Cheek with wavy, iridescent blue or green lines; * soft dorsal fin with distinct spots; * opercular margin stiff to edge (except for skin); body contour more rounded—pumpkinseed, *Lepomis gibbosus*
7.b. Cheek without wavy blue-green lines; * soft dorsal fin without distinct spots; * opercular margin thin and somewhat flexible; body contour more rhomboidal—redear sunfish, *Lepomis microlophus*

8.a. Dorsal spines 6 to 8 (crappies) 9
8.b. Dorsal spines 11 to 12—Sacramento perch, *Archoplites interruptus*

9.a. Dorsal fin spines usually 7 or 8; length of dorsal fin base greater than distance from dorsal fin origin to eye; pattern on sides consisting of irregular dark blotches—black crappie, *Pomoxis nigromaculatus**
9.b. Dorsal fin spines usually 6; length of dorsal fin base less than distance from dorsal fin origin to eye; pattern on sides consisting of vertical bars—white crappie, *Pomoxis annularis**

KEY TO SUCCESSFULLY INTRODUCED PERCHES (PERCIDAE)

1.a. Anal fin soft rays 6 to 8; no canine teeth; body not long and slender—yellow perch, *Perca flavescens*
1.b. Anal fin soft rays 12 to 13; large canine teeth in jaws; body long and slender (Fig. 2:12a)—walleye, *Stizostedion vitreum vitreum*

KEY TO SCULPINS (COTTIDAE)

1.a. Preopercle with a single spine at the posterior edge; * palatine teeth weak or absent; lateral line usually complete*—Paiute sculpin, *Cottus beldingi*
1.b. Preopercle with one spine on posterior edge and 2 or 3 spines along ventral edge; * palatine with well-developed tooth patch; lateral line incomplete* . . . 2

2.a. Last spine on ventral limb of preopercle directed postero-ventrally; prickles widely distributed on back and sides; body slender (Bonneville Lake sculpins) 3
2.b. Last spine on ventral limb of preopercle directed antero-ventrally; * prickles limited to anterior sides or absent; body robust—mottled sculpin, *Cottus bairdi*

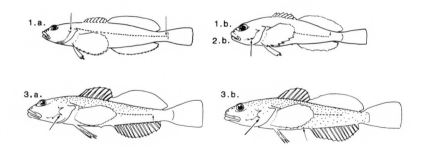

3.a. No prickles on breast and belly—Bear Lake sculpin, *Cottus extensus**
3.b. Prickles present on breast and belly—Utah Lake sculpin, *Cottus echinatus** (extinct)

KEY TO SUCCESSFULLY INTRODUCED CICHLIDS (CICHLIDAE)

1.a. Anal fin spines 8 to 9 (Fig. 2:10a); branched anal fin rays 6—convict cichlid, *Cichlasoma nigrofasciatum*
1.b. Anal fin spines 3; branched anal fin rays 7 to 10—redbelly tilapia, *Tilapia zilli*

8

Salmoniformes

TROUTS (Salmonidae)

THE SALMONIDS constitute economically the most important family of coldwater fishes in North America. Most valuable as sport fish, they are also harvested in large numbers commercially and are reared extensively in hatcheries and other aquaculture operations (fish farming) and as fish that have been allowed to run to the sea and then return to their original rearing areas (ocean ranching). This family includes the trouts, salmons, chars, whitefishes, and grayling. Most species inhabit fresh water. However, the Pacific salmon (*Oncorhynchus* spp.) are anadromous; that is, they spawn in fresh water but migrate to sea to attain most of their growth. Most species of trout have anadromous populations. Many trout populations exhibit anadromous tendencies, sometimes seasonally, when they are in streams flowing into salt water. This tendency is probably a reflection of "crossed-over" anadromous genes somewhere in their past. The arctic char, Dolly Varden, brook trout, brown trout, and Atlantic salmon all have searun races, as do the rainbow (steelhead) and the cutthroat. The Pacific salmons may also be landlocked; most or all species have the ability to reproduce without being able to run to sea.

Sizes of fish in this family vary widely: the chinook salmon occasionally reaches weights of over 100 pounds, while the Bonneville cisco rarely attains weights in excess of 2.5 ounces. As artificial propaga-

tion has increased, disease has become an important negative factor
in rearing and to some extent in wild populations. Temperature preferences range from those of the arctic grayling, which chooses water in
the low 40s (F), to some trout that tolerate temperatures of almost
80° F. Reproductive strategies range from the Pacific salmon, which
spawns once and dies, to other family members that are generally repeat spawners.

The salmonids are characterized by the presence of an adipose fin
and a small fleshy appendage (auxiliary process) at the base of the pelvic fins. The lateral line is well developed. The scales are cycloid and
generally small (Simpson and Wallace 1978). The group is widespread
and numerous in northern regions that were under glaciers less than
15,000 years ago.

Jordan and Evermann (1904), in a more poetic fashion, provide the
following information on the genus *Salmo*.

> There is no other group of fishes which offers so many diffi-
> culties to the ichthyologist, with regard to the distinction of the
> species, as well as to certain points in their life history, as this
> genus. The colouration is, first of all, subject to great variation,
> and consequently this character but rarely assists in distinguish-
> ing a species, there being not one which would show in all stages
> the same kind of colouration. The water has a marked influence
> on colours: trout with intense ocellated spots are generally found
> in clear, rapid rivers and in Alpine pools; in the large lakes, with
> pebbly bottom, the fish are bright silvery, and the ocellated spots
> are mixed with or replaced by x-shaped black spots; in dark lakes,
> or lakes with peaty bottom, they often assume an almost uniform
> blackish colouration.

The current American Fisheries Society list of fishes (Robins et al.
1980) lists thirty-nine species and seven genera of trout in the United
States and Canada. Twelve species, including three subspecies with five
genera, occur in the Great Basin. Of the twelve species, three are endemic to Bear Lake, Utah-Idaho, three more are native (occurring in
Great Basin and other western waters), and six are introduced.

Members of the trout family occur in a wide range of habitats,
stream and lake types, and elevations in the Great Basin. They occur in
high mountain lakes, in small streams, and in large rivers. Where water
temperatures are cool enough, they may occur throughout a drainage
system from headwaters to valley locations. They inhabit streams of
high to low gradient and occur over a wide range of environmental
quality waters.

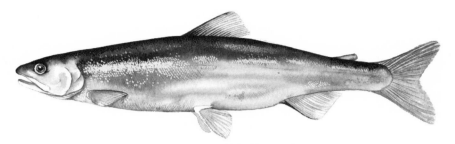

Sockeye salmon (Kokanee)
Oncorhynchus nerka (Walbaum)

Importance

The kokanee is a landlocked sockeye salmon. Its importance varies from that of a valuable sport and forage fish to having slight or negative value. Two benefits of the kokanee stem from the fact that it may be noncompetitive with other game fish for food and it can function as forage for other sport fish. It is considered an excellent table fish and is reasonably sporting, considering its small size (Sigler and Miller 1963).

Historically, the kokanee fishery of Pend Oreille Lake in northern Idaho was unique among kokanee fisheries in the United States. The lake supported a fishery with high catch rates for both sport and commercial fishing. During the 1950s and 1960s, a hand-line fishery that supported average catch rates of 3 fish per hour and as high as 10 to 20 fish per hour existed. In the late 1960s, a decline in the catch rate was obvious.

Range

The original populations of kokanee probably developed from sockeye runs along the west coast of the United States and Canada that were trapped or planted where they could not return to sea. The kokanee was first stocked in various waters in the Bonneville basin in 1922 and in Lake Tahoe, California-Nevada in 1950 (La Rivers 1962). Limited stocking continues in the Great Basin and elsewhere in the United States. The kokanee also occurs in the coastal range lakes of British Columbia and Washington and is present in Lake Tahoe, California-Nevada and in Porcupine and East Canyon reservoirs, Utah in the Great Basin.

Description

The kokanee has a dark-blue back and silvery sides. The anal rays generally number 14 to 16 and not fewer than 13. This characteristic helps separate the kokanee from rainbow, cutthroat, and brown trout, which have fewer than 13 anal rays. The tail is deeply forked, which readily distinguishes it from rainbow, cutthroat, and brown trout. Another separating characteristic is the number of branchiostegals. There are 13 to 19 for kokanee and 10 to 12 for trout. As the spawning season approaches, both male and female kokanee turn a deep red and the lower jaw of the male develops a characteristic hook common to the Pacific salmon.

Size and Longevity

The kokanee population of Pend Oreille Lake, Idaho commonly reached sizes of 14 to 16 inches in the 1930s but had declined to 9- to 10-inch fish at maturity by 1942. Most mature populations average 10 to 12 inches in length. Record fish may weigh more than 6 pounds, but the range in most areas is 1 to 2 pounds. Kokanee may live as long as 7 years but more often live only 3 to 5 years. They die after spawning. Janssen (1983) reported no fish over 34 months old in Porcupine Reservoir, Utah.

Limiting Factors

Obstructions blocking spawning runs is the most severe limiting factor. Since kokanee are pelagic zooplankton grazers that prefer well-oxygenated water and 50° to 60° F temperatures, any deviation from that will have an adverse effect on their growth and development. Occasionally, kokanee mortality will occur when the hypolimnion becomes depleted of oxygen (Moyle 1976). Depletion of their food (large zooplankton) has caused stunting in some populations such as Lake Tahoe. Competition with *Mysis* in Lake Tahoe is a possible cause of decreased growth (Cooper and Goldman 1980).

Food and Feeding

Kokanee eat primarily zooplankton. Feeding is generally heaviest from sundown to dark. They often travel in large schools and sometimes near the surface but in the vicinity of deep water. The kokanee does not feed after it begins its spawning run, although it will strike a lure (Sigler and Miller 1963). Emerging insects, especially midges, are fed on occasionally, and newly emerged fry in streams may subsist on aquatic insects for a short time. The food of kokanee changes little as the fish grow larger.

Breeding Habits

As spawning time approaches, generally in their third or fourth year (although they may be as young as 2 and as old as 7) the kokanee stop feeding and seek one of the lake's tributary streams in which to spawn. Spawning is from late August to January. In Idaho there are two recognized stocks: one spawns from August to October, the other from late October to January (Bruce Rieman, personal communication, 1984). Females sometimes die before releasing all of their eggs. Cordone et al. (1971) note particularly low spawning success in Lake Tahoe, where only 11 percent in 1967 and 28 percent in 1968 of the dead females examined were spawned out and 30 percent and 46 percent, respectively, had died without spawning.

Like other salmon, kokanee generally home to the stream in which they were hatched or planted as fry. However, Simpson and Wallace (1978) found there were notable exceptions to this. They found that, for some unexplained reason, the majority of a population will desert their area and spawn elsewhere and then, just as suddenly, the population or a part of it will return to the original spawning site. Kokanee generally spawn in gravel bars of streams, but they will spawn along lakeshores when only unsuitable or insufficient stream spawning areas are available. The female builds the redd and defends the area from other females, while the male defends the area from other males. Generally, each female contains from 200 to 1,800 eggs. After spawning, the female may occasionally defend the area, although she will die shortly thereafter. Required spawning temperatures range from 43° to 55° F. When the kokanee spawns along the lakeshore the depth is generally less than 30 feet. Stream spawning sites occur in much shallower water.

Habitat

Kokanee thrive best in high, cold, large mountain lakes. They inhabit the surface waters as long as the temperature remains between 50° and 60° F. Then, as the surface water warms, they move down and away from the warmer water, very often into the thermocline.

Preservation of Species

Because kokanee are planted at a small size and grow on natural food, the cost for sustaining a fishery, even where natural reproduction does not occur, is smaller than for planting catchable trout (Wydoski and Whitney 1979). Kokanee are generally stocked to produce forage for trout and for a sport fishery. According to Moyle (1976), kokanee has largely failed as a forage fish for trout in Lake Tahoe, although it is eaten in small numbers by lake trout. Moyle believes in small lakes it may actually depress trout growth and population size by competing with trout for zooplankton. Although angling for kokanee has become a popular sport in recent years, the kokanee is generally underexploited because it takes a rather specialized technique to catch it during much of the season. Low fishing mortality and a small plankton population may lead to stunted kokanee populations. As previously noted, the kokanee in Pend Oreille Lake, Idaho decreased substantially in size only a few years after they entered the lake. Unless there is an adequate zooplankton population and an adequate fishing pressure, it may be unwise to stock kokanee in some deep, cold lakes.

The presence of direct competitors such as *Mysis* for large zooplankton may alter the growth rate of kokanee, reducing the number of large fish (Cooper and Goldman 1980). Detailed study of both the kokanee population and the prey base is needed before *Mysis* is stocked in any water body where a kokanee fishery is maintained. In Pend Oreille Lake, *Mysis* may have contributed to the reduced size of kokanee by altering the species composition of the zooplankton population, making a large part of the food supply unavailable to small kokanee when they first enter the lake.

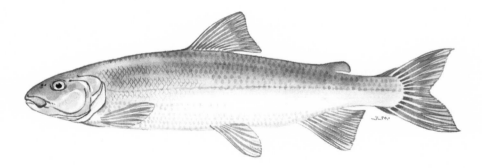

Bear Lake whitefish
Prosopium abyssicola (Snyder)

Importance

The Bear Lake whitefish is endemic to Bear Lake; that is, it is found nowhere else in the world. It probably provides limited forage for large trout, but it is rarely taken by hook and line. Although its economic value is minimal, its value as a unique ecological entity is much greater.

Range

Bear Lake, Utah-Idaho.

Description

The Bear Lake whitefish is not easily distinguished from another Bear Lake inhabitant, the Bonneville whitefish. The Bear Lake whitefish has larger scales than the Bonneville whitefish and has a "Roman nose." The Bonneville whitefish has spots until it is about 10 inches long; the Bear Lake whitefish has none. It has an average of 11 dorsal rays and 10 anal rays. Scales in the lateral series usually number 69 to 74 and scales around the body 39 to 43. As the name implies, it is whitish in color.

Size and Longevity

The Bear Lake whitefish seldom exceeds 9 inches in length. The largest individual taken during a five-year study on Bear Lake was just short of 11 inches. This individual was judged to be 11 years old. Whitefish caught between 1952 and 1954 measured the following year-end size in inches for fish age 1 to 8: 1.3, 3.0, 4.4, 5.2, 5.9, 6.5, 7.0, and 7.5 (Sigler 1958a).

Limiting Factors

Predation and senility appear to be the two main enemies of the Bear Lake whitefish. No other mortality factors are apparent.

Food and Feeding

The Bear Lake whitefish feeds heavily on tiny invertebrates: ostracods, copepods, insects, and aquatic oligochaetes. This habit of feeding suggests complete dependence on the soft marl bottom that is primarily in deep water.

Breeding Habits

The Bear Lake whitefish spawns in water 50 to 100 feet deep from late December to early February. However, ripe females have been taken as late as March, when water temperatures are 36° to 39° F.

Habitat

Basically the Bear Lake whitefish is a deep-water fish that lives near the bottom in cold oligotrophic Bear Lake. It rarely frequents shore areas in either summer or winter.

Preservation of Species

Maintenance of an acceptable water quality appears to be the only need of the Bear Lake whitefish.

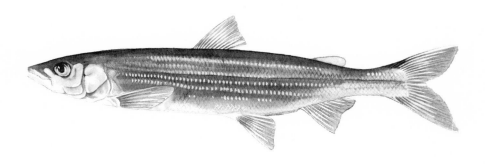

Bonneville cisco
***Prosopium gemmiferum* (Snyder)**

Importance

The Bonneville cisco is endemic to Bear Lake and therefore has a unique importance in natural history. Bear Lake, Utah-Idaho is the only lake in North America (Great Lakes as a unit excluded) with 4 endemic fishes: Bonneville cisco, Bonneville whitefish, Bear Lake whitefish, and Bear Lake sculpin. All 4 originated between 10,000 and 35,000 years ago.

Although the Bonneville cisco is vulnerable to fishing for only about 16 days each year, it provides thousands of recreational fishing days and food for fishermen. It supplied a limited commercial fishery for local fishermen before that activity was barred in 1911. As the most numerous fish in Bear Lake, it is an important forage fish for cutthroat trout and lake trout (Sigler 1962).

Range

The Bonneville cisco was originally present only in Bear Lake, Utah-Idaho. It has been stocked in Lake Tahoe, Nevada-California, Twin Lakes, Colorado, high mountain lakes in South Dakota, and Flaming Gorge Reservoir, Utah-Wyoming. There has been no survival in Lake Tahoe and none has been documented in other areas. Fossils of the Bonneville cisco were discovered in the Stansbury level of prehistoric Lake Bonneville, which was of much greater area than present-day Bear Lake or other Lake Bonneville remnants.

Description

The Bonneville cisco has a long, sharply pointed snout, with a projecting lower jaw and a thin body. Its overall appearance is that of a herring, pale moss green above, with silver sides that have a pearly iridescence. It is a brassy color during the breeding season. The eye is large, the maxillary is entirely in front of the eye, it has no teeth, and the gill rakers are longest near the center of the arch.

Size and Longevity

The Bonneville cisco rarely attains a length of much over 8.5 inches and a weight of 2.5 ounces. It rarely lives longer than 7 years, although a few have been aged at 10 and 11 years. Male and female Bonneville cisco grow at about the same rate in both length and weight. Typically the Bonneville cisco yearly length in inches for fish age 1 to 8 is: 2.9, 4.6, 5.8, 6.4, 6.9, 7.2, 7.6, and 8.1 (Sigler and Workman 1978).

Limiting Factors

Predation and fishing are the primary decimators of the Bonneville cisco. Disease and parasites appear to be minor mortality factors. Occasionally a fish is infested with stomach nematodes.

Food and Feeding

The principal diet of the Bonneville cisco is zooplankton. The copepod *Epischura* is the predominant item of food and is of considerable importance throughout the year. In winter, when *Epischura* numbers may be low, the Bonneville cisco feeds heavily on cladocerans, principally *Bosmina*. It also feeds on chironomid larvae, primarily in winter and early spring. The Bonneville cisco feeds year-round.

Breeding habits

Each year hundreds of thousands of Bonneville cisco move inshore to spawn in waters ranging in depth from a few inches to 40 feet. They predictably start on January 15, plus or minus 5 days, and continue for 12 days plus or minus 4 days (Sigler and Workman 1978). Males move inshore ahead of females and remain there throughout most of the spawning season. Females move inshore only when they are ripe and move back out to deep water after they have spawned. Large schools of mature Bonneville cisco move inshore, then swim parallel to shore at varying distances from it, depending upon the turbulence of the water, the presence of fishermen, and whether or not there is ice cover. During spawning a female is typically attended by 3 to 5 males. When the group stops to spawn, they are particularly vulnerable to dip-net fishermen. The Bonneville cisco spawns at temperatures from 33° to 42° F. The nuptial attire consists of tubercles that project above the scales as much as a millimeter and bright colors, primarily yellow. Although the tubercles are confined primarily to the male, an occasional female may have fewer and smaller ones. The Bonneville cisco matures at 3 years of age and produces from 2,000 to 3,600 eggs (Sigler and Workman 1978).

Habitat

The Bonneville cisco appears to prefer temperatures of 58° F or less. It is widely scattered throughout Bear Lake when the temperatures are colder than this, but as the water warms in the spring and early summer it descends into the deeper, colder water. After Bear Lake is stratified, the greatest concentration of Bonneville cisco is in the thermocline. Although the cisco may leave this area and move into the warm surface waters to feed, it is generally at depths of 50 to 100 feet during the summer months. The greatest movement of Bonneville cisco occurs near twilight when it moves inshore, then swims parallel to shore. Movement is generally between early twilight and dark.

Preservation of Species

Bonneville cisco, taken almost entirely with dip nets while on the spawning ground, are vulnerable for only 12 to 16 days a year. The catch rate by dip netting is 4 to 5 males for each female. This presents an interesting management possibility. If fishing pressure is depressing the numbers markedly, the summer (mixed) population will show a predominance of females, which should indicate overfishing. However, the sex ratio and depression of the population present an enigma. The fishing success over the past few years has shown a marked decline, yet the sex ratio in the lake remains at 1:1. Other management requirements include maintenance of the present quality of Bear Lake water, including oxygen saturation down through the thermocline and the exclusion of pollutants.

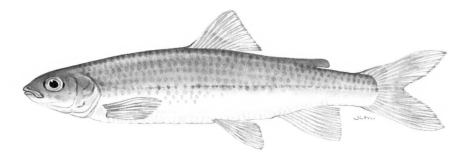

Bonneville whitefish
Prosopium spilonotus (Snyder)

Importance

The Bonneville whitefish is taken by hook and line in limited numbers from Bear Lake, Utah-Idaho. It has not found favor with large numbers of sportsmen. Its additional value is that it provides forage for large trout. Perhaps its most unique value from a natural history standpoint is that it is endemic to Bear Lake.

Range

Bear Lake, Utah-Idaho.

Description

The Bonneville whitefish is whitish in color and has spots until it is about 10 inches long. The dorsal rays number 10 to 12 and the anal rays 9 to 11. Scales along the lateral series total 74 to 94; gill rakers total 19 to 26. The mouth is small and slightly inferior. The caudal fin is deeply forked.

Size and Longevity

In a 1951 to 1954 study, the yearly length in inches of Bonneville whitefish age 1 to 8 was 3.2, 5.7, 7.5, 9.2, 10.7, 12.7, 14.6, and 16.4. Fishermen occasionally report catching 18- to 22-inch Bonneville whitefish. The average life span is 6 to 8 years (McConnell, Clark, and Sigler 1957). The hook and line record is 3 pounds, 6 ounces, but most fish caught weigh less than 2 pounds.

Limiting Factors

A small number of Bonneville whitefish are caught by hook and line each year and an unknown number fall prey to other fish. The balance of this relatively abundant fish dies from disease (a minor factor) or advanced age.

Food and Feeding

Chironomid larvae and pupae constitute the bulk of the diet of the Bonneville whitefish. Miscellaneous aquatic and terrestrial insects make up the balance of the diet, although it probably takes an occasional fish. The food habits of the Bonneville whitefish indicate that it is not only wide ranging but frequently moves into shallow water, particularly during the winter months.

Breeding Habits

The Bonneville whitefish in Bear Lake spawns from mid-February to early March. The temperature preference is about 45° F. When a female stops to spawn, 5 or 6 males attend her. After the spawning act, which lasts from 5 to 15 seconds, the fish resume travel with the school.

Spawning takes place over rocky, shallow areas or sandy points. The fish matures in its third or fourth year. One 9-inch female contained 1,200 eggs (Sigler 1958a).

Habitat

Bonneville whitefish are frequently taken by experimental gill nets in 40 to 100 feet of water. Adult fish apparently frequent the shallow water more often than the young ones. The Bonneville whitefish is more inclined to inhabit shallow water, summer and winter, than either the Bonneville cisco or the Bear Lake whitefish.

Preservation of Species

Since the Bonneville whitefish is taken only occasionally by hook and line, it appears fishing pressure can have slight effect on the total population. As with other Bear Lake coldwater fish, the primary requisite for their continued welfare is maintenance of an optimum water quality.

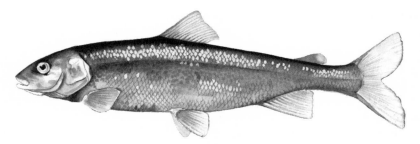

Mountain whitefish
Prosopium williamsoni (Girard)

Importance

The mountain whitefish is viewed by fishermen with mixed emotions. Some believe it is a good food and sport fish, others feel it is definitely a second-class citizen. As a result of this attitude and the mountain whitefish's rather high reproductive potential, it is more abundant in many waters than many fishermen and fishery managers prefer. Angling for whitefish is more popular in winter, when they feed more actively than do trout. At this time many fishermen catch them to be smoked and more recently to be canned. They are also very good fresh.

Range

The mountain whitefish is widely distributed over the western United States, both east and west of the Continental Divide. It is present in southwestern Canada, particularly Alberta and British Columbia. In the Great Basin it is present in many cold waters such as in the Truckee River, Nevada and the Bear River drainage, Utah. It occurs in other drainages such as the Sevier. Most populations are semi-isolated.

Description

The back and fins of the mountain whitefish are light brown and the sides and belly are silver to white. The depth is approximately 0.2 of the length. The snout and lower jaw are short and blunt, and there is a flap between the nostrils. The dorsal fin has 10 to 12 rays, the anal fin 9 to 11. The cycloid scales in the lateral series number 75 to 94, although 80 to 90 is the usual range. The young have several parr marks on each side.

Size and Longevity

The average age reached by mountain whitefish is 7 or 8, although a few fish may live 10 or more years. The yearly average length in inches for whitefish age 1 to 9 in Logan River, Utah is 4.6, 8.1, 10.2, 11.6, 12.8, 14.1, 15.4, 16.4, and 17.4 (Sigler 1951). In studies in Canada, California, and the Rocky Mountain area, mountain whitefish did not grow as long or as fast as those from the Logan River, but some of them lived longer. Logan River anglers report mountain whitefish weighing up to 4 pounds, but most of those examined during a 1950 study weighed under 2 pounds with a few slightly over 3 pounds. The hook and line record fish weighed 5 pounds.

Limiting Factors

Limited sport and even commercial fishing apparently do not seriously reduce established mountain whitefish populations. However, where it is eagerly sought after by anglers, fishing pressure may affect the population. Small mountain whitefish are preyed upon by trout, but even when they are with a heavy population of trout the trout apparently do not make inroads into the whitefish population.

Food and Feeding

The mountain whitefish feeds generally at twilight or at night and often on the bottom, but occasionally schools surface to feed. Food of the mountain whitefish in the Logan River, Utah in order of importance by volume is caddisfly larvae, truefly larvae, and mayfly and stonefly nymphs. Feeding habits are similar in Walker River, Nevada (Ellison 1980). They also feed on terrestrial insects that are unfortunate enough to fall into the water. The mountain whitefish has an interesting trait of feeding more actively in the cold winter months than it does in some of the warmer summer months. In the Columbia River it feeds at times on hatchery salmon fry as the latter drift out of the tributaries and on salmon eggs when available (Sigler and Miller 1963). Simpson and Wallace (1978) report that whitefish in Idaho commonly feed on whitefish eggs during spawning season.

Breeding Habits

Late in the fall, generally mid to late November or early December depending on latitude and temperature, whitefish in streams move from pool areas to riffles to spawn. Mountain whitefish living in lakes move up the nearest stream. They generally move only a short distance and spawn 6,900 to 9,400 eggs per pound of female. The eggs hatch in about 5 months at temperatures above 35° F. Spawning activity lasts approximately 2 weeks. Whitefish do not build redds. In northern Idaho they spawn during late October and early November when water temperatures range between 40° and 45° F. Although the mountain whitefish prefers the riffle areas of streams for spawning, it has been known to spawn in the shallow water along the gravel shores of lakes. Spawning takes place where there is adequate current to remove silt from the eggs. The eggs, when discharged, are adhesive and stick to the stream bottom substrate. Maturity is reached at age 3 to 4 years.

Habitat

The mountain whitefish apparently prefers streams rather than lakes. It does, however, occur in some mountain lakes such as Lake Tahoe. In the Logan River, Utah the whitefish prospers in waters with a mean temperature of 48° to 51° F, a near saturation of oxygen, and a pH of 8.1 to 8.4. It lives anywhere in the Logan River where pools are at least 16 feet wide and 3 to 4 feet deep at the season of least flow. It does not live in the river above elevations of 6,250 feet.

Preservation of Species

The mountain whitefish appears to be prospering throughout its range with the present level of protection it enjoys. Even an experimental commercial fishery, designed to improve trout fishing in eastern Idaho several years ago, appeared not to notably decimate the whitefish population. In fact, fishery managers were so discouraged by the results that they discontinued the project.

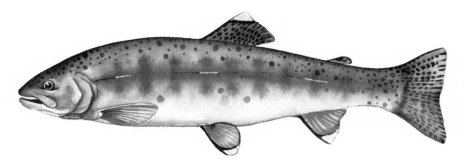

Golden trout
***Salmo aguabonita* Jordan**

Importance

The golden trout is of minor importance in the Great Basin. In California it is the official state fish, and in Wyoming it is an important sport fish. It attracts fishermen primarily because of its relative scarcity and its brilliant colors. It is said to have fighting ability equal to the rainbow trout but is easier to catch.

Range

The golden trout is native to the upper Kern River basin, Tulare and Kern counties, California. Today it is present in over 300 high mountain lakes and streams in California. There is a lesser number in Wyoming and a limited number in the Humboldt River drainage of the Great Basin.

Description

Golden trout is spectacularly bright in color. Belly and cheeks are both bright red to orange, but the lower sides are bright gold. A central lateral band is red-orange and the back is deep olive green. About 10 parr marks are usually present, even in adults. It is distinguished from the cutthroat by the absence of the cutthroat mark and the lack of basibranchial teeth. The dorsal, anal, and pelvic fins have distinct white tips offset by a black bar (Moyle 1976). Scales in the lateral series number from 175 to 210; scales above the lateral line, 34 to 45; pelvic rays, 8 to 10; gill rakers, 17 to 21; pyloric caeca, 25 to 40 (Schreck and Behnke 1971). Jordan and Evermann (1904) report it as the most beautiful of all the many beautiful western trout.

Size and Longevity

The golden trout is a slow-growing, relatively short-lived fish. An average yearly length in inches for fish age 1 to 5 may be as follows: 1.5, 5.5, 8.4, 9.9, and 10.4 (Carlander 1969). Although a 10- to 12-inch golden trout is average, fish up to 24 inches are taken occasionally. The hook and line record golden trout weighed 11 pounds.

Limiting Factors

Golden trout interbreeds readily with rainbow trout and loses its identity. It also hybridizes with cutthroat trout. Three-way hybrids (rainbow, cutthroat, golden) are commonly found in the upper Wind River drainage, Wyoming (Robert Behnke, personal communication, 1983). Lake populations that are introduced tend somewhat to migrate into streams where they are less able to compete. Golden trout is one of the easiest of all trouts to catch; perhaps its best defense is the remote areas it inhabits.

Food and Feeding

The golden trout is primarily insectivorous, preferring caddisfly larvae, midges, and other available insects. In lakes it feeds on zooplankton, particularly copepods and cladocerans.

Breeding Habits

Spawning may occur any time from late May to August, depending on the altitude, when water temperatures reach 45° to 50° F. According to Moyle (1976), golden trout requires gravel riffles for successful spawning. Although spawning has apparently been observed in lakes, it rarely if ever is successful. Golden trout does, however, spawn successfully in inlet or outlet streams of lakes. The fish mature in their third or fourth year and females produce 300 to 2,300 eggs, depending on fish size.

Habitat

The golden trout does best in swift, high-altitude streams and in lakes at altitudes ranging from 6,000 to 11,500 feet. It is a true wilderness animal.

Preservation of Species

The golden trout needs protection from other fish, especially the salmonids, and from heavy angling pressure. Its range may be extended by stocking it in fishless, remote lakes and streams.

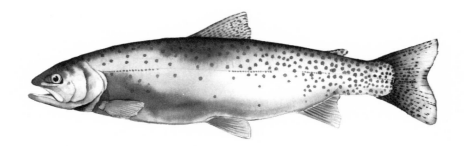

Cutthroat trout
***Salmo clarki* Richardson**

Lahontan cutthroat trout *S. c. henshawi* Gill and Jordan
Paiute cutthroat trout *S. c. seleniris* Snyder
Bonneville cutthroat trout *S. c. utah* Suckley

Importance

The cutthroat trout is one of the most popular sport fish in western America. It is avidly pursued, not only by elite fishermen but by the rank and file as well. In the view of many its sporting and table qualities exceed that of all other trout. It is, however, not nearly as abundant over much of its range as the rainbow trout.

The Lahontan cutthroat trout in Pyramid Lake is of substantial economic and social importance to the Pyramid Lake Paiute Indian tribe and to numerous sport fishermen from near and far. Its adaptation to the highly saline waters of Pyramid Lake also makes it unique. It has been estimated that the historic annual production of Lahontan cutthroat trout in the Pyramid Lake–Truckee River ecosystem was at least 1,000,000 pounds (Behnke 1974). At one time the Pyramid Lake cutthroat trout was the mainstay in the diet of the Pyramid Lake Paiutes and many other Indian tribes. It was also shipped to mining camps and other markets as far away as San Francisco (Sigler et al. 1983). It is listed by the U.S. Fish and Wildlife Service as threatened.

Ancient Lake Lahontan in what is now western Nevada reached its maximum size about 75,000 years B.P. There were many fluctuations in water levels over the next 65,000 years, but the great lake finally desiccated into nine smaller lakes, one of which was Pyramid Lake, about 8,000 B.P. (Benson 1978). A large, fast-growing predatory trout, the Lahontan cutthroat, emerged as the dominant fish in the Truckee River–Pyramid Lake ecosystem. Over the years the load, including salts, of TDS in waters of terminal Pyramid Lake increased. The Lahontan cutthroat trout adjusted as TDS increased until in 1976 the level was 5,228 ppm. The tui chub also adapted to Pyramid Lake and a predator-prey relationship of immense benefit to the Lahontan cutthroat evolved. The Lahontan is also important over other parts of its range.

At the same time the Lahontan cutthroat was adjusting to Pyramid Lake, a stream form of cutthroat trout was adapting in the Humboldt River drainage. Behnke (1981) believes this fish is a different subspecies from the Lahontan cutthroat. He calls this undescribed subspecies the Humboldt cutthroat trout and believes it is taxonomically and ecologically different. Thomas Trelease (personal communication, June 19, 1983) disagrees. Trelease reasons that many waters in the Humboldt drainage system and other waters of central Nevada were planted in the early days with Pyramid Lake stock. Later these same waters were stocked with Summit Lake and Heenan Lake strains of Lahontan and Yellowstone Lake cutthroat. He believes these waters now contain a mixture of the above strains and subspecies that cannot be positively differentiated. Trelease further states that dams constructed on small streams where fish over one-half pound were unheard-of until the reservoir formed behind them later had fish as large as 5 pounds.

Behnke (1981) also reports an unnamed stream form of cutthroat trout in Willow and Whitehorse creeks of the Alvord basin and the Paiute trout of Silver King Creek (a tributary of the Carson River drainage in California) that represents an isolated population of cutthroat trout with few or no spots on the body. The Paiute cutthroat trout is listed by the U.S. Fish and Wildlife Service as threatened.

Historic Lake Bonneville established three distinct levels over much of what is now western Utah. The cutthroat trout native to the Bonneville basin probably gained entrance into the basin when the Bear River changed its course from the Snake River to the Bonneville basin about 30,000 years ago (Broecker and Kaufman 1965). After the Bear River became tributary to Lake Bonneville, the lake reached its maximum size some 16,000 to 18,000 years B.P. (Broecker and Kaufman 1965). The Bonneville cutthroat trout evolved into three groups that can be recognized morphologically and ecologically (Behnke 1981). The Bonneville cutthroat, native to the Bear River division of the basin, is adapted to a harsh, highly fluctuating stream environment, which parallels the evolution of the cutthroat in the Lahontan basin. In the Thomas Fork and Smith Fork drainages near Cokeville, Wyoming, the Bonneville cutthroat is dominant in turbid streams that carry heavy sediment loads. According to Behnke (1981), the environment appears to be marginal for trout, but the cutthroat dominates over brown trout. Another group of Bonneville cutthroat is native to the Snake Valley region of western Utah. At the maximum elevation of Lake Bonneville Snake Valley was an arm of the lake, but after a slight decline in lake level it became isolated from the rest of the basin. The Snake Valley group of Bonneville cutthroat lives in small, clear, isolated streams. It is not competitive with introduced salmonids. The third group constitutes the balance of the Bonneville cutthroat in the Bonneville basin. The Bonneville cutthroat trout is listed by the U.S. Fish and Wildlife Service as threatened.

Range

The cutthroat trout has the widest distribution of any species of trout in western North America. Its range along the Pacific coast is from southeastern Alaska to the Eel River in northern California. It is native to all major river drainages in western North America as far east as central Colorado. In the northern part of its range it is present on both sides of the Continental Divide. It occurs in fresh, brackish, and salt water. While its original populations have been reduced by a number of factors, they have been concurrently increased to some extent by extensive planting.

The cutthroat is the only trout native to the Great Basin except the rainbow in Eagle Lake, California (see also redband under rainbow trout). The cutthroat trout is present in many high, coldwater streams and lakes of the Great Basin. The range of the Lahontan cutthroat trout is the Truckee, Carson, and Walker rivers, Donner Creek, and Pyramid, Walker, Donner, Independence, and Summit lakes, Nevada (Coffin 1981). The Paiute cutthroat trout is from Silver King Creek, a tributary of the Carson River in California. The Bonneville cutthroat trout is present in Snake Valley, western Utah and in Pine Creek, Nevada. A small population exists in Willow Creek, Jordan River drainage, Utah. The largest populations are in Lake Alice, a tributary to Smith Fork, and in Thomas Fork and Smith Fork, Bear River drainage, Wyoming (Behnke 1979, 1981).

Lahontan cutthroat trout.

Description

The back and sides of the cutthroat are frequently a steel gray covered with spots. These spots are larger, more regular in size and shape, and more restricted than those on brown or rainbow trout. A slash mark, usually red or orange in adults but sometimes lacking in young, runs along both sides of the lower jaw. The body is elongate and typically troutlike, rounded and slightly compressed; scales are cycloid and small to medium in size, 125 to 190 in the lateral series (Behnke 1981). The head is conical, moderate to short, eyes moderate, and snout rounded. The mouth is terminal and rather large. There are small sharp teeth on the jaw, vomer, tongue, and median basibranchial plate between the lower end of the gill arches. The gill rakers total 16 to 28, less on the upper than the lower limb (Behnke 1981). The dorsal fin has 8 to 11 rays, the anal fin has 10 or 11, the caudal is slightly forked. The color and spotting is highly variable, often differing between watersheds, subspecies, and local populations. The young have 9 or 10 oval parr marks along the lateral line (Simpson and Wallace 1978).

The Lahontan trout is characterized by its large size, spots evenly distributed and extending from the head onto the caudal fin, and by having a higher number of pyloric caeca than other subspecies of cutthroat. The Paiute trout, close to the Lahontan taxonomically, has few or no spots on the body. The Bonneville cutthroat trout has large, evenly distributed spots on the side but seldom on the ventral region.

Size and Longevity

The growth of cutthroat trout depends primarily on two factors: water temperature, and abundance and kind of available food. The slowest growth is in cold, high lakes or streams with a short growing season where food is generally limited to invertebrates. The anadromous cutthroat trout grows fast in saltwater during the summer, but returns to fresh water during the winter months. Cutthroat trout in high coldwater areas usually attain a length of 14 to 16 inches and a weight of 1 pound or more in 4 to 5 years. The average life span of the cutthroat trout is about 7 to 8 years, with few living more than 10. Bulkley (1961) reports the yearly length in inches for cutthroat age 1 to 7 in Yellowstone Lake, Wyoming as 1.8, 5.1, 8.9, 12.3, 15.5, 17.5, and 19.1. In a three-year study on Pyramid Lake, Nevada (Sigler et al. 1983), 562 Lahontan cutthroat trout ranged in size from 7.5 inches and 2.9 ounces to 31 inches and 13.5 pounds. A total of 676 fish age 1 to 7 reached the following yearly total length in inches: 9.1, 12.3, 15.2, 18.2, 20.6, 23.7, and 25.5. The hook and line record cutthroat trout was a Lahontan that weighed 41 pounds and was caught in Pyramid Lake, Nevada in 1925. The largest recorded Lahontan cutthroat trout caught in Pyramid Lake in 1976 weighed 28 pounds.

Limiting Factors

Since cutthroat trout are taken quite readily on a large variety of lures, hook and line fishing is the predominant mortality factor. The cutthroat trout often does not have the ability to compete favorably with introduced fish such as rainbow trout, brown trout, or brook trout in a degraded habitat. Once widespread populations of cutthroats in streams and lakes of the Lahontan basin have now been largely replaced by other trout species. In many streams they have hybridized with rainbow trout, which has become the dominant species. Possibly, pure rainbow trout are more aggressive than either cutthroat or the hybrids and displace them from feeding territories (Moyle 1976). Displacement not only makes the cutthroat trout more vulnerable to predation and fishing, but it also decreases its growth rate and reproductive potential. According to Moyle, competition and predation from introduced lake trout were presumably important factors in the complete elimination of cutthroat trout from Lake Tahoe.

In the early 1930s the level of Pyramid Lake dropped so much that a delta was formed at the mouth of the Truckee River. This obstacle, which persisted for more than 10 years, prevented spawning runs of Lahontan cutthroat upriver and the original population of Lahontans in Pyramid Lake was essentially gone by 1940. A few may have persisted until 1943.

Nevertheless, in prime cutthroat trout habitats, genetically pure cutthroat compete very well. For example, when rainbow trout were introduced into Yellowstone Lake, Yellowstone National Park, Wyoming, the rainbow trout did not prosper. In Bear Lake, Utah-Idaho, the cutthroat trout fare better than the rainbow trout. In Thomas Fork and Smith Fork drainages, Wyoming, Bonneville cutthroat are dominant (Behnke 1981).

Disease sometimes devastates cutthroat populations, and this is something that has happened more often since the advent of fish hatcheries. Females may spawn only once or twice in a lifetime, and post-spawning mortality is often high. The most serious environmental hazard facing stream-dwelling cutthroat trout is the loss of habitat due to reduced flows, degradation of water quality, or change in stream configuration. In some streams, the major factor adversely affecting salmonid densities may be inadequate overwintering habitat. Boulders, log jams, and debris are all important (Hickman and Raleigh 1982).

Food and Feeding

Wydoski and Whitney (1979) found that inland subspecies of cutthroat trout feed primarily on aquatic insects, although the larger fish may feed entirely on fish. They report that in the Oregon coastal subspecies there is a preference for insects, along with frogs, earthworms, and juvenile salmon. Other foods include crayfish, terrestrial arthropods, salamanders, and sculpins.

Scott and Crossman (1973) report coastal cutthroat food consists mainly of insects, both aquatic and terrestrial. Other food includes various plankton, crustaceans, crayfish, salmon eggs, and dead salmon.

Midges and other truefly larvae, mayflies, and beetles also enter the diet. Older fish in rivers and lakes feed almost exclusively on fish. Young cutthroat start feeding in 14 to 23 days after hatching.

Small cutthroat trout in Pyramid Lake, Nevada feed largely on insects and zooplankton. They start feeding on fish when they are 12 to 13 inches long and eat a higher percent of fish as they grow older. The diet of fish that are 20 to 30 inches long is about 94 percent fish (Sigler et al. 1983) and almost entirely tui chubs.

Moyle (1976) states that stream-dwelling cutthroat trout defend feeding territories and feed mostly on drift; their food is often a mixture of terrestrial and aquatic insects. In some of the high Uinta Mountain lakes, where the growing season is less than 6 weeks and lake productivity is very low, cutthroat apparently subsist primarily on terrestrial insects, including large swarms of migrants.

Breeding habits

In the spring, after the ice has disappeared, cutthroat trout spawn in the clear, cold, shallow riffles of streams. Typically, when the temperature is greater than 40° F (daily maximum), some males move into spawning areas. First spawning is when daily maximum is 42° to 45° F, peaking at 44° to 48° F. The upper safe range for gravid females and egg incubation is considered to be 57° F. Coastal cutthroat spawn in the winter months, usually January or February. Both lake-dwelling and coastal cutthroat migrate up streams to spawn. Cutthroat trout do not spawn in lakes. According to Moyle (1976), the distances migrated are generally short, but there are migrations of over 60 miles. There is good evidence that some Lahontan cutthroat trout, before the construction of Derby Dam in 1905, migrated from Pyramid Lake up the Truckee River into Lake Tahoe to spawn in tributaries, a distance of more than 120 stream miles (Sigler et al. 1983).

The female fans out a redd in a gravel bed with her tail and deposits her eggs. The eggs are then fertilized, and the female moves immediately upstream to cover the eggs and spawn again; she moves downstream after covering the eggs when spawning is complete. A typical redd is 2 feet long by 1.5 feet wide in 7 to 10 inches of water. The eggs may be covered with 5 to 7 inches of coarse gravel (Wydoski and Whitney 1979).

The cutthroat trout generally mature in their second to fourth year. In Pyramid Lake many males mature at age 2 and females at age 3 or occasionally 4. One lot of hatchery-held Lahontan cutthroat trout males matured at age 1. Fecundity of Pyramid Lake cutthroat ranges from 1,241 to 7,963 eggs, with a mean of 3,815 (Sigler et al. 1983). According to Moyle (1976), the stimulus for upstream migration in coastal cutthroat is not clear, but lake-dwelling Lahontan cutthroat appear to respond to increasing day length and increasing stream temperatures.

Around the turn of the century the Pyramid Lake Lahontan cutthroat trout had two distinct spawning runs, one beginning in December and lasting until March, the other starting in March and lasting into May or June. In general the winter spawning run was composed of larger fish than the spring run. There has been minimal or no reproduction in the Truckee River for many years although the Marble Bluff Fishway became functional in 1976. In 1981 there was a substantial run of spawning fish, starting in January, into a small artificial stream running into the lake just south of Sutcliffe, Nevada. In 1982 the run again started in January and numbered more than 9,000 mature fish. An estimated 2.2 million eggs were taken in 1982 and 3 to 5 million in 1983 (Alan Ruger, personal communication, 1983). The run in 1983 was substantially higher than in 1982.

The oldest male in the Pyramid Lake study (Sigler et al. 1983) was 7 years; the oldest female was 6 years. This does not mean there are no fish older than this in the lake. There is evidence that the Pyramid Lake female Lahontans are alternate year spawners. This means many of them will spawn no more than twice. Considering the relatively high post-spawning mortality, many probably spawn only once.

Habitat

The cutthroat trout is present in streams ranging from sea level to altitudes of over 10,000 feet. The coastal cutthroat, an anadromous fish, spends its summers in saltwater and winters in fresh water. The cutthroat is established in a wide variety of cold waters, ranging from large alkaline lakes such as Pyramid Lake, Nevada to small mountain lakes and from major rivers to small tributaries (Moyle 1976; Sigler et al. 1983).

In large bodies of water the cutthroat trout prefers areas around rocks, sandy or rubble shores, and deep waters. In mountain streams the fish choose habitat around rocky areas, riffles, deep pools, and near or under overhanging logs, shrubs, or banks. Fry do best in stream areas with 40 to 60 percent pool areas. The cutthroat trout does well in high altitude lakes of clear, cold water that are low in fertility.

Some thriving populations of cutthroat in the Uinta Mountains live in waters with a pH of 7.0, TDS of 40 ppm, and a very sparse benthic fauna. Some of these small lakes are fed by glaciers.

Preservation of Species

The maintenance or upgrading of cutthroat trout habitat is the most urgent need today. Cover is recognized as one essential aspect of good cutthroat trout habitat. In streams, brush and undercut banks are used, as is depth (Hickman and Raleigh 1982). Competition from other trout species should be reduced and possibly removed. No other trout should be stocked with cutthroat trout unless it can be demonstrated that they do not compete or interbreed with them. Different subspecies, races, or strains of cutthroat should not be indiscriminately mixed in hatcheries. Genetic strains should be stocked where they have evolved and adapted over a long period of time or, better, where they can encourage or support weak populations.

Angling restrictions should be compatible with numbers of fish available and fishing pressure. Where the number of spawning fish each year is limited, restrictions on the number of mature fish that can be taken should be high. The number of smaller fish taken may then be more liberal.

Recent research (Busack and Gall 1981) indicates that introgressive hybridization (assimilation of genes from one species into another) can occur and is a cause of decline in many native western trout populations.

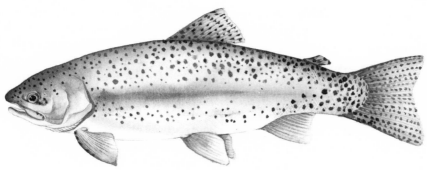

Rainbow trout
Salmo gairdneri (Richardson)

Importance

On the basis of its contribution to the fishery, the rainbow is the most important trout in North America as well as one of the most important game fish in the Great Basin. This species is continuously stocked in substantial numbers in almost all habitable trout waters in the United States. It fights well, leaps repeatedly when hooked, and, whether smoked, eaten fresh, or canned, is highly palatable. Therefore the total catch (and catch rate) is very high.

The main reason the rainbow is stocked so widely is that it is the easiest and most economical of all trout to raise. Admittedly, some strains are domesticated, but in the eyes of hatcherymen and fishermen alike this is not important. Commercial trout farmers raise and sell more rainbow trout than any other coldwater fish in North America. The Thousand Springs area of south-central Idaho alone produces millions of pounds of rainbow trout each year for commercial markets.

The steelhead, a sea-run form of rainbow, adds an especially important dimension to the fishery in the Pacific Northwest. It grows faster and is larger than most inland rainbow. It is eagerly sought by fishermen, and a catch of one fish per day satisfies many anglers. Another form of rainbow trout, the Kamloops, grows to a large size in big lakes that contain an abundance of forage fish. The Eagle Lake, California rainbow trout is the only native rainbow trout in the Great Basin (Peter Moyle, personal communication, 1983), with the possible exception of the unnamed redband trout (*Salmo* sp.) of the Oregon Desert basins (Behnke 1981).

Range

The original range of the rainbow trout (including all forms) is the

Pacific coast of North America, mainly west of the Rocky Mountains in the north and the Sierra Nevada in the south. It extends from Rio del Presidio, Durango, Mexico to the Kuskokwim River, Alaska. In addition to being introduced widely throughout the United States, this species has also been introduced into New Zealand, Australia, Tasmania, South America, Africa, Japan, southern Asia, Europe, and Hawaii (Lee et al. 1980). In Canada it occurs in British Columbia and from the Avalon Peninsula of Newfoundland across the southern portions of the provinces from Nova Scotia to Ontario, north through central Manitoba and central Saskatchewan, to northern Alberta and the Yukon Territory (Scott and Crossman 1973).

The steelhead, the anadromous form of this species, originally was native to the Snake River, Idaho and its tributaries as far upstream as Shoshone Falls. Dams have now reduced this range in the Snake River to below Hell's Canyon and to the drainages of the Salmon and Clearwater rivers, Idaho. The Kamloops was introduced from British Columbia into Pend Oreille Lake, Idaho (Simpson and Wallace 1978).

Fish hatcheries operated by state fish and game departments stock rainbow heavily in almost every habitable drainage in the Great Basin. The Great Basin, however, does not have large populations of lake-dwelling rainbow. Bear Lake has a moderate to small population. There are rainbow trout in the Truckee River and in Lake Tahoe, but none in Pyramid Lake. The Great Basin has no steelhead and few or no Kamloops. The Eagle Lake trout, which inhabits a pluvial Lake Lahontan basin where cutthroat would be expected, may have replaced the cutthroat many years ago, or may be the result of an early introduction (Busack et al. 1980).

Behnke (1981) points out that several desiccated basins north of Lahontan and west of Alvord basins in Oregon have the interior form of rainbow trout (equals redband trout) as their native trout. The redband trout is the interior form of rainbow trout that is not presently recognized taxonomically but considered a part of *Salmo gairdneri*.

Description

The body is elongate, moderately compressed, and rather deep; the cycloid scales number 120 to 160 in the lateral series. The head is short, the snout rounded, eyes moderate, and the mouth terminal. There are small sharp teeth on the jaws and tongue, but they are poorly developed on the vomer and are absent from the basibranchial plate between the lower ends of the gill arches. The dorsal fin rays and anal fin rays both number 11; the caudal fin is slightly forked (Robert Behnke, personal communication, 1983; Simpson and Wallace 1978).

Color in the rainbow trout is variable and depends on habitat, size, and sexual condition. Stream residents and spawners have darker and more intense colors than do lake residents, which tend to be silvery. Bear Lake rainbow tend to be quite silvery and some of them almost entirely lose their spots.

The adult is normally bluish to olive green on the back; the sides are lighter and silvery with a reddish horizontal band; the belly may either be white or silvery. There are generally irregular black spots on the back, sides, and head. The dorsal, adipose, and caudal fins are also spotted. Although there are no nuptial tubercles during the breeding season, minor changes in shape of the head and mouth occur among males during spawning.

The young trout is blue to green on the dorsal surface, silver to white on the sides, and white below. There are generally 5 to 10 irregular marks on the back between the head and the dorsal fin. There are also 5 to 10 oval parr marks spaced on the sides and straddling the lateral line. Steelhead and Kamloops are generally more silvery than other forms of rainbow. Some stocked rainbow trout in the Great Basin have a trace of a cutthroat slash along the crease of the lower jaw. This mark presumably indicates some cutthroat ancestry.

Size and Longevity

Adult nonmigratory rainbow trout, excluding Kamloops, average 2 to 4 pounds in size and are considered large at 6 to 8 pounds. Simpson and Wallace (1978) report a 37-pound Kamloops taken from Pend Oreille Lake in 1947. They also report that Idaho steelhead range from 4 to 20 pounds. Steelhead weighing 28 pounds have been taken from the Columbia River (Don Chapman, personal communication, 1983). The all-tackle hook and line record (probably a steelhead), weighing 42 pounds, 2 ounces, was from Belle Island, Alaska (Kutz 1982). It is interesting to note that the Kamloops, when introduced from Pend Oreille Lake into other areas in Idaho, shows no better growth than other forms of rainbow trout (Simpson and Wallace 1978). This response is at times true of other strains of rainbow trout when introduced outside their natural habitat. This may in some cases be due to differences in forage availability (that is, prey species of fish).

Rainbow trout markedly larger than 2 to 4 pounds in size are often piscivorous. For example, the steelhead trout on the west coast, the Kamloops in Pend Oreille Lake, and the rainbow trout in Fish Lake and Bear Lake, Utah are piscivorous and subsequently reach large size.

However, there are some notable exceptions to this rule. Kamloops introduced into some fishless lakes that contained vast numbers of *Gammarus* and other large crustaceans grew to 14 pounds in as few as 3 years. According to Scott and Crossman (1973), growth rate in these lakes often decreases gradually as the trout population increases and food decreases. However, they state that other lakes are able to maintain populations of fish to 4 or 5 pounds on invertebrates alone. Johannes and Larkin (1961) report on the long-documented history of a single population of Kamloops trout in Paul Lake, British Columbia. The invertebrate population was adequate to produce large trout before the introduction of the redside shiner. The shiner competed with the trout for food to the detriment of the Kamloops fishery, which subsequently produced larger but fewer Kamloops. By feeding on the shiners, the trout got bigger after the shiner was introduced—a tradeoff of a few large trout for a good population of moderate-sized trout.

As soon as the fry absorbs its yolk sack it emerges from the gravel. At this time it is from 0.37 to 0.62 inch long. By the end of the first summer it may be 4 inches long and weigh 0.4 ounce.

Rainbow trout from high mountain lakes live only 4 to 5 years. Simpson and Wallace (1978) believe the life span of rainbow trout is fairly short, few living beyond 5 years of age. Moyle (1976) states the oldest known rainbow, age 11 years, was from Eagle Lake, California, an alkaline former arm of ancient Lake Lahontan. He further states that steelhead occasionally reach 9 years of age, but the maximum age for most rainbow is 7 years. In a Logan River, Utah study only about 3 percent of the rainbow stocked lived through the first winter. It is believed that fish stocked in lakes have a somewhat higher overwintering survival rate. However, the mortality rate for rainbow trout stocked in Bear Lake when they were less than 8 to 9 inches long was extremely high the first 18 months (McConnell, Clark, and Sigler 1957). Scott and Crossman (1973) state that the life expectancy may be as low as 3 or 4 years in stream and lake populations, but for steelhead and Great Lakes populations it would appear to be 6 to 8 years.

Limiting Factors

Since the rainbow trout is easily caught and avidly sought by fishermen, fishing is by far the number one mortality factor. Most domestic strains of rainbow trout are also relatively short-lived in the wild. The eggs and young of rainbow trout that spawn in the spring in high-flow turbulent streams face the twin hazards of scouring or siltation with resulting oxygen depletion of the redd. Both the numbers and health of emerging fry are affected. Under these flow regimes the fry may also be pushed downstream into undesirable habitat. According to Wydoski and Whitney (1979), although 95 percent of the rainbow trout eggs are fertilized, only 65 to 85 percent survive the embryonic stage. Chapman (personal communication, 1983) believes the average embryonic stage survival may be as low as 30 percent.

Temperatures of 60° F are ideal for rapid growth of rainbow trout (Leitritz and Lewis 1980). Female rainbow are most productive when they are in water where temperatures do not exceed 56° F (preferably 54° F) for six months before spawning. Temperatures of 42° F or lower also adversely affect egg development in females (Leitritz and Lewis 1980). Water temperatures in the high 70s, except under otherwise ideal conditions, may cause stress, which predisposes disease or, in some cases, death for fish of all ages. According to Leitritz and Lewis (1980), yearlings and adults can withstand temperatures up to 78° F for short periods of time. Black (1953) states that the upper lethal temperature for fingerling Kamloops was 75.2° F when they had been acclimated at 51.8° F. Scott and Crossman (1973) believe rainbow trout are most successful in habitats with temperatures of 70° F or slightly lower, but can survive if there is cooler, well-oxygenated water into which they can retreat as the surface waters warm over 70° F.

Moyle (1976) states rainbow trout will survive temperatures to 82° F if they have been acclimated to the upper temperature and the water is saturated with oxygen. The rigors of spawning induce stress that not infrequently results in up to 100 percent post-spawning mortality (Simpson and Wallace 1978; Wydoski and Whitney 1979). This applies to long-distance migrating fish. Idaho steelhead populations that migrate in excess of 700 miles to spawn and through several dams probably have few repeat spawners. On shorter coastal rivers, repeat spawners may constitute 5 to 20 percent of steelhead runs, and in some years repeat spawners may equal up to 38 percent of the run in the Gualala River, California (Robert Behnke, personal communication, 1983).

Moyle (1976) believes that the mortality is highest when stocked rainbow are planted in relatively small numbers in a stream that already contains a wild trout population. The planted fish are evidently unable to break into the established dominance hierarchies of the wild trout. Diseases carried by the planted fish may also decimate them without seriously affecting the wild stocks. When the stocked trout are put there in large numbers, the effect of sheer numbers may disrupt the established hierarchies of the wild fish, making the wild fish population more vulnerable to angling and dislocation. This factor, Moyle believes, does not operate in lake stocking.

Rainbow trout are subject to predation by other trout, diving birds, and a variety of mammals. Logan River, Utah periodically produces prize-winning (14 to 23 pounds) brown trout. The associates of these large, fast-growing brown trout are a few mottled sculpin, a moderate number of mountain whitefish, and very large numbers of rainbow trout. It seems highly probable that the brown trout would not grow to the size they do if there were no stocked rainbow trout on which to feed.

Changes in water quality, particularly pH, may adversely affect rainbow trout populations. Rainbow do well in waters of pH from 7 to 8 but can survive in waters ranging from 5.8 to 9.6 pH. The Eagle Lake, California population has adapted to the highly alkaline water there, which has a pH of from 8.4 to 9.6.

Food and Feeding

Young rainbow trout feed on small benthic invertebrates, primarily insects and crustaceans. Rainbow trout more than any other trout tend to feed on algae and, to a lesser extent, on vascular plants. This may in part be incidental and the nourishment may be slight. The rainbow continues the primarily invertebrate diet until it reaches a size of 1 to 2 pounds; there is then a tendency to turn to a fish diet when it is available. Although rainbow trout are primarily drift feeders, they tend to rise to the surface and feed on surface insects. This is a fact fly fishermen know quite well.

In the summer months, stream-dwelling rainbow tend to feed heavily on the abundant drift organisms, but they still feed actively on bottom invertebrates. The rate of feeding and available food are considerably reduced in winter, primarily due to an almost complete lack of drift organisms and, perhaps more important, to the fact that trout metabolism is reduced by the cold water.

Moyle (1976) believes rainbow trout in lakes have a greater proclivity for feeding on fish than do stream-dwelling rainbow, although he states that fish do not normally become an important element in the diet until trout are 12 to 14 inches long. In some high-altitude, low-productivity mountain lakes, rainbow may be forced to feed heavily on terrestrial insects. Many of the rainbow trout stocked in Bear Lake in years past did not reach a large size. After a stocking of Kamloops, however, many rainbow weighing 8 to 9 pounds were caught. One rationale is that these trout learned to feed on the abundant forage fish while the previously stocked rainbow did not. Rainbow trout in Fish Lake, Utah, after reaching a size of about 1.5 pounds, feed almost exclusively on Utah chub and grow rapidly thereafter (Sigler 1953).

In general, rainbow trout feed on various invertebrates, including zooplankton and crustaceans such as *Gammarus*; at older ages it may continue to feed on these organisms rather than shifting to fish.

Breeding Habits

Nonmigratory rainbow trout normally spawn in the spring; however, hatchery strains have been developed that spawn every month of the year. In Washington State there is a winter and a summer spawning run of steelhead, although some rainbow probably migrate upstream in every month of the year (Wydoski and Whitney 1979). Both winter and summer steelhead spawn in spring.

The rainbow trout is a stream spawner and, unlike the chars, is generally unable to spawn in lakes. There are, however, instances where rainbow populations have successfully spawned in lakes, generally on gravel bars formed near the outflow. Some of these populations are rainbow-cutthroat hybrids. To spawn, rainbow trout seek out gravel bars in streams in the early spring when water temperatures reach 50° F or more. The female digs a redd in the gravel by turning on her side and beating her tail up and down. In this way she cleans the gravel and excavates a pit that is longer and deeper than her body. Nest building takes place day and night. When ready to spawn, the female rests near the bottom at the center of the redd, and the dominant male moves into position parallel to her. Both bodies are pressed together and the eggs and milt are released over a few seconds. The male courts the digging female and aggressively tries to drive other males away from a redd, although in the spawning process there is generally more than one male spawning with each female. As soon as the female has spawned, she immediately moves upstream to the edge of the nest and begins displacing gravel to cover the eggs. Scott and Crossman (1973) state females may dig and spawn in several redds with one or more males. Chapman doubts this; he believes the defense of the redd is a key adaptive mechanism and multiple redds are maladaptive (Don Chapman, personal communication, 1983).

Eggs usually hatch in 4 to 7 weeks and alevins take an additional 3 to 7 days to absorb the yolk before becoming free-swimming. At a water temperature of 50° F, eggs hatch in about 31 days (Leitritz and Lewis 1980).

The average age at first spawning is 2 to 3 years; some hatchery rainbow spawn at age 1 and some wild fish do not first spawn until they are age 5. A high percentage of some strains of hatchery rainbow do not spawn in the wild. Many others are caught and some do not adapt to the environment. Rainbow and cutthroat that spawn in the same area often hybridize.

According to Scott and Crossman (1973), individual rainbow have been known to spawn in as many as 5 successive years. They note that the survival rate for repeat spawners is often very low, probably less than 10 percent. Simpson and Wallace (1978) believe mortality is close to 100 percent for spawning steelhead in Idaho.

Habitat

The rainbow trout has adapted to a wide range of aquatic habitats. It prospers in large deep lakes and in small farm ponds. It lives in some of the largest rivers of North America and in small creeks with a flow of only a few cubic feet per second. Some strains of rainbow trout in lakes tend to stay close to shore, rarely moving into deep water except to avoid high temperatures. Other strains are far-ranging and pelagic. In Bear Lake, Utah-Idaho in the 1950s, most stocked rainbow were littoral zone fish, but another group, presumable Kamloops, was rarely taken inshore.

Optimum temperatures are 54° to 56° F for reproduction and 60° F or somewhat above for growth. At low temperatures the rainbow can withstand low oxygen concentrations if it is inactive, but at high temperatures it requires near-saturation levels. It survives in lakes ranging in pH from 5.8 to 9.6 and the Eagle Lake, California population has adapted to pH levels from 8.4 to 9.6. Best growth is achieved in alkaline water of pH 7 to 8.

Stream-dwelling rainbow trout tend to be highly aggressive, setting up feeding territories and defending them against intruders. This territoriality is not evident in lakes. In lakes, rainbow trout tend to form schools and move about in a more or less systematic fashion in search of food and optimum temperature habitats. Generally, their area of school movement is not large. The area inhabited by stream-dwelling rainbow may be only a few hundred yards or, in some cases, it may be confined to one or two pools and the riffles just above them. Steelhead, in contrast to resident rainbow trout, are highly migratory. Some stocks of "resident" rainbow trout that are descendants of anadromous stock may migrate intermediate distances.

Preservation of Species

The preservation of the major forms of rainbow trout can best be discussed separately. The maintenance of native runs of the anadromous steelhead trout is dependent on such environmental factors as dams, flows, water quality, and quality spawning substrate. Kamloops trout generally prosper in large lakes with an abundance of forage fish. They need tributary streams with adequate physical and chemical characteristics for spawning. The remaining forms of rainbow can be lumped into two groups: the nonanadromous trout that reproduce in the wild, and the many strains that are produced and stocked by hatcheries. The Eagle Lake trout is unique and has a restricted habitat. Measures to preserve this species for further study should be implemented.

All forms of rainbow need an acceptable habitat, legal protection from excessive exploitation, and at times supplemental stocking. Some strains of hatchery-reared rainbow are stocked to be caught in a relatively short time. Overwinter mortality of these fish in streams is generally high and somewhat less in lakes. In this "put and take" type of management, it is not preservation but rather the opposite that is in order.

Brown trout
***Salmo trutta* Linnaeus**

Importance

Once an adequate breeding population has been established, brown trout provides some of the finest wild trout fishing in North America. At a time when hatchery costs are increasing and more fishing hours are being spent, a trout that can reproduce in the wild and hold its own against both the hazards of its environment and heavy fishing pressure is unique. The brown trout is more difficult to catch than most trout; a bonus for the exceptional fisherman and a frustration for those with less experience. It is more aggressive than most trout and readily feeds on other fish. Fishermen sometimes catch a high percentage of other trout in a stream but few or no brown trout, thereby reaching the conclusion that there are no fish left. At one time the brown trout was considered by both biologists and fishermen as a mixed blessing. This attitude is changing. Biologists are more appreciative of self-sustaining populations and fishermen are learning to catch them.

Range

The brown trout is native to Europe and western Asia. It is partially anadromous there and is therefore also present in the British Isles and Iceland (Moyle 1976). The brown trout was first introduced into North America in 1883. In the Great Basin it was first introduced in the Truckee River in 1895 (La Rivers 1962). The brown trout was introduced into Utah Lake prior to 1900 and stocked regularly by 1910 (Heckmann, Thompson, and White 1981). It was spread throughout the Great Basin shortly thereafter and is now present in most trout waters throughout the United States and Canada. It has been stocked in South America, Africa, India, Australia, and New Zealand.

Description

The brown trout has a back of olive to greenish-brown. Lower portions of the body are often yellow, fading beneath to gray or white. Yellow coloring is more likely to be found in mature fish, especially in males during the breeding season. Rather large dark spots appear upon the back and sides but are not developed on the caudal fin. Reddish spots that have pale borders are profuse over the upper part of the body. Frequently, the front edge of the pelvic fins and the anal fin has a yellow margin. In young brown trout the adipose is orange, without dark spots or margins. The tail fin is truncate, not forked. Scales number 115 to 120 in the lateral series (Sigler and Miller 1963). Basibranchial teeth are absent. The dorsal fin has 9 to 12 major rays; the anal fin, 10 to 12; the pelvic fins, 9 to 12 each (almost always 9); and the pectoral fins, 12 to 14 each. There are 14 to 21 gill rakers on each arch and 9 to 11 branchiostegal rays.

Size and Longevity

Brown trout usually average 4 to 7 pounds by their sixth year. Fish weighing 8 to 12 pounds are not uncommon. In a Utah stream study, the yearly length in inches of brown trout age 1 to 6 was 3.5, 6.0, 10.0, 14.0, 16.0, and 18.0. Brown trout are fast-growing, moderately long-lived (10 years or older) fish. Scott and Crossman (1973) give the often-quoted but unrecognized world's hook and line record as 39 pounds, 4 ounces, caught in Scotland in 1866. The Great Basin has produced some very large brown trout. In 1937, a 37-pound, 12-ounce brown trout was taken from the lower impoundment of the Logan River, Utah; it is, however, not a hook and line record since it was hooked, lost, and later retrieved by a couple of youngsters. In one week on the Logan River, one fisherman caught a 14-pound, 4-ounce and a 14-pound, 14-ounce brown trout from the same general area. Other large fish captured in the Logan River include an 18-pound and a 23-pound fish.

Limiting Factors

The brown trout is limited by low water temperatures; it is rare in the cold high reaches of mountain streams. It is also restricted from waters that warm to the high 70s. Optimum temperatures are 45° to 68° F. Neither does it prosper in very small bodies of water. Brown trout stocked in small natural ponds in northern Utah (0.5 to 2 acres) grew slowly and remained in poor condition, even though there was an abundance of fish and other food. It is believed that the little fish in the pond were so well protected by an abundance of cover that the brown trout were not able to feed on them, although there were undoubtedly other factors that were not recognized. The brown trout is, to some extent, preyed upon by fish-eating birds, mammals, and fish. However, the main causes of mortality are fishing and habitat destruction, especially stream channelization.

Food and Feeding

In both lakes and streams small brown trout feed heavily on zoo-plankton and bottom-dwelling insects. A typical stream feeding pattern for brown trout as it grows older is from drift organisms and zoo-plankton, to aquatic and terrestrial insects, to small fish and finally to large fish. Brown trout less than 2 pounds live largely on such insects as mayflies, caddisflies, stoneflies, and midge larvae and pupae. Other invertebrate foods include aquatic earthworms, freshwater clams, and crayfish. At an earlier age than most trout it feeds largely on fish. Brown trout, except the young, feed more actively at twilight than during midday. Scott and Crossman (1973) report that brown trout eat a variety of organisms, including aquatic and terrestrial insects, crayfish, mollusks, salamanders, frogs, rodents, and fish.

Logan River, Utah has produced a number of large brown trout. In the areas where the large fish were caught, the food consists of a few mottled sculpin, a moderate number of mountain whitefish, and often a large number of stocked rainbow trout. It is likely that the stocked fish have been an important factor in producing the trophy fishery by providing food for the brown trout.

Breeding Habits

The brown trout spawns in the fall from late October to December, initiating spawning on a decreasing temperature scale between 50° and 45° F. Mature brown trout move out of deep pools or lakes upstream to the nearest acceptable riffle area where the female selects the redd site and starts a depression by turning on her side and digging with her tail. This initial activity attracts a male, who defends the female and redd from other males. The male does not help with the construction of the redd, although he may continuously court the female as she works. After the redd is complete, the female sinks to the bottom of the depression, the male swims alongside, the eggs and sperm are released, and fertilization occurs. Following this the female moves upstream and covers the eggs by digging a new redd. This procedure may be repeated several times. A female lays from 200 to more than 6,000 eggs, which hatch in 41 days at a constant water temperature of 50° F (Leitritz and Lewis 1980). The average age of maturity is 2 to 3 years, with males often maturing earlier than females. Brown trout are reared in hatcheries, but most hatcherymen consider them more difficult to raise than rainbow trout.

Habitat

Adult brown trout inhabit glide or rubble areas or the bottom of deep pools in streams; the young may be in shallow pools, close to shore in shallow water, or in riffles. At twilight adults often move to the surface or into riffle areas to feed. It is more of a big-water fish than most trout. It inhabits large lakes and streams, and in medium-size streams it frequents the deepest pools. It does not seek small streams. Anadromous brown trout may at times be in saltwater except during the breeding season. In Logan River, Utah it does not generally move upstream above an altitude of 5,250 feet, although browns inadvertently stocked at 6,975 feet appeared to prosper.

Preservation of Species

Once a brood stock has been established in an acceptable habitat, the brown trout is able to produce a sustained and substantial population. Although it is somewhat difficult to catch, it can be overfished by above-average fishermen. It is questionable whether or not brown trout should be stocked over existing or proposed rainbow or cutthroat trout populations due to competition between the species. Unfortunately, in many cases this is an after-the-fact decision. In northern Utah it did not prosper in small spring-fed ponds. In Flaming Gorge Lake, Utah-Wyoming on the Green River, it is producing a trophy fishery.

Brown trout suffer from habitat degradation such as stream channelization and dredging. On one occasion an extensive riffle area in the Logan River, Utah was dredged just after large numbers of brown trout had spawned there. Another time farther downstream the river was straightened and deepened by removing bank cover and bottom substrate and depositing it on the banks. In both cases, required habitat was destroyed, resulting in reduced brown trout numbers in those areas.

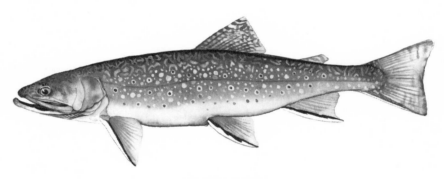

Brook trout
***Salvelinus fontinalis* (Mitchill)**

Importance

The ability of the brook trout to reproduce and sustain a fishable population in high, cold lakes and streams makes it a valuable component in the trout fishery. It is a popular game fish over much of its range. Small individuals are readily caught on both live baits and artificial lures; large ones are exceptionally wary. Many populations of brook trout are self-sustaining. Today only limited numbers are raised in hatcheries, although the species is easy to raise. At the turn of the century it was the most frequently stocked trout. Although it is one of the few trout that will perpetuate itself in lakes without tributaries, it also tends to overpopulate these lakes. This results in large numbers of small trout that are of little or no interest to most fishermen.

Range

The brook trout is endemic to northeastern North America, from the north Atlantic seaboard south to Cape Cod, in the Appalachian Mountains southward to Georgia, west of the upper Mississippi and Great Lakes region to Minnesota, and north to Hudson Bay (Lee et al. 1980). The brook trout has been stocked in many other parts of North America. In the Great Basin it was stocked extensively in the latter part of the nineteenth century (Heckmann, Thompson, and White 1981; La Rivers 1962). It has been stocked in South America, the Falkland Islands, New Zealand, Asia, and Europe (Scott and Crossman 1973).

Description

The brook trout has a streamlined, somewhat compressed body that is about 5 times as long as it is deep. The fins are soft-rayed with the dorsal fin having 10 rays and the anal fin 9. The caudal fin is square or only slightly forked. The head is large but not long; the mouth is terminal and reaches behind the eye. There are well-developed teeth on the maxillary, premaxillary, and the head of the vomerine bone inside the mouth.

The color of the brook trout ranges from olive to blue-gray on the back to white on the belly. Red spots, with or without bluish rings around them, are evident on the sides, although they are not numerous. Wavy marks on the back are characteristic and are probably its most distinguishing feature. This, along with the white and then black stripe along the fore edge of each of the lower fins, helps separate this trout from any other (Sigler and Miller 1963). The caudal fin has variable black lines, sometimes two or three, parallel to the trailing edge of the fin. All colors intensify at spawning time; the lower flanks and belly of males becoming orange-red with black pigment on either side of the belly. Sea-run brook trout become silvery with purple iridescence; only red spots are visible on the sides.

Size and Longevity

Brook trout are neither fast-growing nor long-lived fish. Two ecologically distinct forms have been identified by some researchers. A small form that lives 3 to 4 years and reaches 8 to 10 inches is found in small, cold streams and lake habitats, and a larger form that lives 8 to 10 years and reaches weights of 9 to 13 pounds inhabits large lakes, streams, and estuaries (Raleigh 1982). Approximate yearly length in inches for fish age 1 to 6 in stream populations is 2.4, 5.0, 7.1, 9.2, 10.8, and 12.9 (La Rivers 1962). Even more than in most fish, growth is highly variable. When food is abundant and temperature moderate, growth may be quite rapid. In cold, infertile, overpopulated waters the brook trout may reach no greater size than 6 to 8 inches. Most brook trout do not live beyond 5 to 7 years. Reimers (1979) documented brook trout ages to 24 years in Bunny Lake, California. Most other published data record ages to a maximum of 7 years for this species. It is interesting to note that fish in Bunny Lake reach a length of only 9.5 to 11 inches. Scott and Crossman (1973) state that a number of brook trout weighing 5 to 6 pounds are caught each year. They point out that in the 1968–70 Ontario Federation of Anglers' and Hunters' Big Fish Contest there are many brook trout in the 6-pound class. The world record brook trout weighed 14 pounds, 8 ounces. The largest brook trout caught in the Great Basin weighed 5 pounds, 10 ounces.

Limiting Factors

The brook trout generally does not live as many years as most trout and has an above-average vulnerability to fishing. Overpopulation results in intensive competition for food and at times cannibalism of eggs and young. Brook trout living in beaver dam ponds may at times be displaced through the destruction or abandonment of the dam. In beaver ponds and streams they are vulnerable to mink and other fish-eating mammals. In some areas the most serious predators of brook trout are fish-eating birds such as kingfishers and mergansers. In some high mountain lakes, brook trout may live only three years because they spawn in the fall and then cannot survive the winter.

Seegrist and Gard (1972) published information on brook and rainbow trout populations affected by winter and spring floods in Sagehen Creek, California. Fall-spawned brook trout redds were decimated by winter floods while spring-spawned rainbow were not (in a particular year). The reverse was also true. Floods dramatically altered species composition and these changes persisted for several years.

Food and Feeding

The brook trout is a voracious feeder. It eats insects throughout its life. A 1-inch fish may subsist mainly on small invertebrates, 2-inch fish prefer midges, and when they grow to 4 inches there is an increased consumption of mayfly nymphs and caddisfly larvae. After 4 inches the dominant aquatic insects eaten are midge larvae, mayfly nymphs, caddisfly larvae, pupae, and adults, and stonefly nymphs. Terrestrial insects, worms, mollusks, crustaceans, and fish are also taken (Sigler and Miller 1963). According to Scott and Crossman (1973) brook trout also occasionally take frogs, salamanders, snakes, and small mammals such as field mice and shrews.

Breeding Habits

The spawning season occurs as early as late summer in the northern part of its range and as late as early winter in the southern portion. The brook trout initiates spawning activities when water temperatures drop to the low 50s or less. Brook trout reach sexual maturity in 2 or 3 years, although some males may mature after only 1 year. Spawning takes place over gravel beds in the shallows of headwaters of streams, but it can also be successful in gravelly shallows of lakes if there is a spring upwelling and a moderate current. They may spawn successfully in spring-fed ponds.

The female chooses a spawning site and digs the redd by turning on her side and moving gravel by rapid movements of her tail. Usually this behavior does not begin unless there are males in the vicinity. Several males may be attracted to one digging female. One male quickly becomes dominant and defends the redd site against all other males. According to Moyle (1976), redds often are located in territories already defended by males. In this case the female chases away other females, although on occasion the male may help. As the female digs, the male constantly courts her by swimming alongside and nudging and quivering. When the redd is complete, the female swims slowly to the bottom of the redd where she is joined by the male, then eggs and sperm are released simultaneously. The female almost immediately begins to sweep gravel over the eggs with her tail. This new digging activity not only covers the newly spawned eggs but serves to start a new redd. Only 15 to 60 eggs are laid at one time and since brook trout females contain anywhere from 50 to 2,700 eggs, each female has to repeatedly dig new redds. In California, the average fecundity is between 200 and 600 eggs.

Since the eggs of fall- and winter-spawning fish have to overwinter at low temperatures, developing time is usually much longer than it is for spring or summer spawners. Development takes only 35 days at 55° F, but it takes 68 days at 45° F (Leitritz and Lewis 1980).

Habitat

The brook trout reaches its greatest abundance in cool, clear headwater ponds and spring-fed streams or lakes. It tends to seek water temperatures of 55° to 60° F; waters much warmer than this may cause dislocation and discomfort or occasionally mortality. Only the golden trout and the arctic grayling consistently seek lower water temperatures than the brook trout. In streams, brook trout, like several other trout, defend their territories against all comers, including other brook trout. In lakes they are apparently less inclined to form large schools than many other fish, although they may school when alarmed or in an area of exceptionally desirable habitat such as near a spring. Large brook trout are almost invariably loners in either streams or lakes.

Preservation of Species

Fishing regulations can generally be quite liberal. Although small brook trout are easy to catch, stunted and underexploited populations are the rule. The larger fish are quite wary and difficult to overfish. Brook trout prosper in the cold, well-oxygenated, clear waters of the high country. Where overpopulated, they are their own worst enemy. Limited stocking or the encouraging of self-sustaining populations and liberal regulations for small-sized (5- to 6-inch) populations may be the answer. Without heavy fishing pressure, management is difficult.

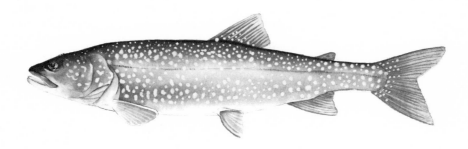

Lake trout
***Salvelinus namaycush* (Walbaum)**

Importance

The lake trout is highly prized as a sport fish, primarily because of its large size and trophy value. The process of hooking a lake trout may be long and tedious, but once hooked it shows relatively little spirit. It is important commercially, mainly in the Great Lakes and parts of Canada. It is prized both fresh and smoked. Some excessively fat ones (particularly a subspecies in the Great Lakes) must be smoked to be edible. There are, at times, conflicts between sporting and commercial interests. The lake trout was fished commercially around the turn of the century in the Great Basin (Utah Lake), but the venture was short-lived because the lake trout did not prosper. The lake trout is popular with trophy fishermen in the Great Basin in such waters as Bear Lake, Utah-Idaho and Lake Tahoe, Nevada-California. The Colorado Division of Wildlife and some other states cross the lake trout with brook trout in hatcheries. Male brook trout and female lake trout produce a fertile hybrid known as the splake, which inhabits an ecological area somewhere between that of the two parents and is valued by fishermen.

Range

The native range of the lake trout extends on the north from Alaska to Labrador and on the south from the Fraser and Columbia rivers to the northern New England states. Included are the Great Lakes states of New York, Pennsylvania, Michigan, Wisconsin, and Minnesota. In Canada, it occurs in southwestern Nova Scotia, New Brunswick, and northern Quebec. It is present throughout Ontario, but not generally through the Hudson and James Bay lowlands. Lake trout is present through northern Manitoba and Saskatchewan and in the southwestern portion of Alberta and northern British Columbia, and it is widely distributed in the Yukon and Northwest Territories and many Arctic islands (Scott and Crossman 1973). Even within the lake trout's general range, the distribution pattern exhibits peculiar clustering in certain regions and complete absence from others that appear to be equally suitable. In the Great Basin it is present in Bear Lake, Utah-Idaho and Mary's and other lakes at the head of Big Cottonwood Canyon, Utah; in Nevada-California it is present in the Tahoe basin in Tahoe, Donner, Fallen Leaf, and Stony Ridge lakes. All these are introduced populations (Sigler and Miller 1963; Moyle 1976).

Description

Not as highly colored as other trout, the lake trout has a background color of gray overlaid with light spots that vary in intensity with age and environment. This background color covers the back, sides, and fins and serves to highlight the lighter gray spots and vermiculations. Generally no white edging appears on the lower fins, but an occasional narrow band is present (Sigler and Miller 1963). The background color varies greatly and trout in large lakes are sometimes so silvery that the spots are difficult to see. Spotting is usually more intense on small fish. Red spots are absent on lake trout but orange or orange-red coloration may be evident on pectoral, pelvic, and especially anal fins and sometimes caudal fins. Young lake trout have distinctive parr marks, about 7 to 12 in number (Scott and Crossman 1973).

Vomerine teeth, as in brook trout, are confined to the head of that troughlike bone. The caudal fin is deeply forked and the pyloric caeca are numerous (95 to 170). The oblique rows of scales just above the lateral line number 175 to 228 and are deeply imbedded (Sigler and Miller 1963). The head is stout, broad dorsally, its length about 21 to 28 percent of the total length; the eye is relatively small in adults, 12 to 20 percent of head length; the snout is long, its length greater than eye diameter. The mouth is large and terminal. The teeth are developed on the upper and lower jaws. Gill rakers range from 16 to 26 and branchiostegal rays total 10 to 14.

Size and Longevity

The lake trout is a slow-growing, long-lived fish. The record all-tackle hook and line fish weighed 65 pounds (Kutz 1982). The largest lake trout recorded for the Great Basin weighed 37 pounds, 6 ounces. The largest known lake trout in North America was caught in a gill net in Lake Athabasca, Saskatchewan. It weighed 102 pounds and was 49.5 inches long. According to Scott and Crossman (1973), it was a relatively young fish, 20 to 25 years old. They attribute the rapid growth to the fact that it had never become sexually mature. The yearly length in inches for Montana lake trout age 1 to 6 is 3.0, 6.0, 9.0, 14.0, 20.0, 26.0, and 30.0 for a 9-year-old fish (Brown 1971). In Lake Tahoe the yearly fork length in inches for fish age 1 to 10 is 4.7, 7.0, 9.8, 12.6, 15.0, 16.9, 18.9, 20.8, 22.0, and 24.4 (Moyle 1976). Moyle points out that Lake Tahoe trout are long-lived, up to 17 years, but that elsewhere ages of 41 years have been reported. Most lake trout growth takes place from June to September, although growth continues slowly in winter.

Limiting Factors

Other fish, both game and nongame, prey on small lake trout. In addition, many fish feed on their eggs. In Bear Lake, Utah-Idaho there are relatively few good spawning areas. This has the net effect of low or zero reproduction some years. Lake trout cannot tolerate temperatures of over 70° F; their preference is closer to 55° F. Their salinity tolerance is also low for a salmonid: 11,000 to 13,000 ppm. The famous commercial lake trout fisheries of the Great Lakes have been decimated by the sea lamprey and by pollution, particularly DDT. Some Adirondack population declines have been associated with high DDT and other pesticide levels.

Food and Feeding

Young lake trout feed on small insects, crustaceans, and other zoo-

plankton. Lake trout over 2 pounds in many instances feed almost entirely on fish. Fish eaten in Bear Lake, Utah-Idaho are almost entirely
sculpins, whitefishes, and Utah suckers; in Fish Lake it is predominantly Utah chub.

In Lake Tahoe, lake trout less that 5 inches feed on zooplankton
and midge larvae and pupae. As they grow in size they graduate to
Paiute sculpins, a relatively small fish. The diet of larger fish consists of
fish and, to a lesser extent, crayfish. The fish taken are Tahoe suckers,
tui chubs, and mountain whitefish; interestingly enough, very few
kokanee are eaten by the lake trout (Moyle 1976). Recent studies by the
Nevada Department of Wildlife and others indicate adult lake trout
feeding heavily on *Mysis*.

Breeding Habits

Lake trout spawn in the fall on a dropping temperature (50° F ± 5°).
The time may range from mid October to early December. Lake-
spawning lake trout move inshore and initiate spawning just at dusk
and may continue until midnight. They prefer silt-free, rocky, boulder-
strewn areas that may range in depth from a few feet to 200 feet. No
redd is prepared and no territory is established. The fertilized eggs
settle into crevices and between rocks. Neither the eggs nor the young
are guarded. the 4- to 5-week incubation period may last from mid February to the end of March. River-spawning lake trout may spawn as
early as mid September over gravel and boulders. The eggs may hatch as
early as late November. The eggs, measuring 0.20 to 0.24 inches in diameter, are produced at the rate of about 750 per pound of female
(Becker 1983; Sigler and Miller 1963).

Habitat

Except in the northern part of its range, lake trout generally lives
only in deep, cold, stratified lakes. Much of the time it lives in the hypolimnion near the bottom. In such lakes the fertility is low, resulting
in a relatively sparse growth of aquatic plants and small animals. An
adequate amount of oxygen in the hypolimnion and thermocline is
necessary. In Great Basin lakes it is usually in water 100 feet or deeper
and in Lake Tahoe it has been reported at depths of 1,400 feet. In the
spring and fall it moves into shallow water to feed or spawn. Lake trout
in Canada occurs only in relatively deep lakes throughout the southern
part of its range, but in the northern half, especially in the Territories,
it also occurs in shallow lakes and rivers. It is present in the upper
Green River, Wyoming as well as in the reservoirs. It often occurs in

surface waters immediately after ice breakup. As the surface water warms with the advance of spring, lake trout retire to the cooler waters, eventually to the hypolimnion (Scott and Crossman 1973).

Preservation of Species

Maintenance of an optimum habitat and stocking (in some areas) are the prime requisites of sustained lake trout populations. Where there is both summer and winter fishing pressure, monitoring numbers of large fish caught may be required and fishing restricted. Management practices have long included the use of hatcheries for artificial propagation. Young fish are often reared to fingerling or even yearling stage before they are released. *Mysis* in Lake Tahoe may have adversely affected the numbers of large lake trout caught. The lake trout are feeding on *Mysis* rather than fish, potentially decreasing growth rates.

Arctic grayling
***Thymallus arcticus* (Pallas)**

Importance

Arctic grayling is sought by anglers who prize it highly for its gameness when hooked, its rare beauty, and its table qualities. It is also valued for its prestige; many people have never seen a grayling. The grayling is one of the important sport fishes of Alaska and northern Canada. It also makes a significant contribution to subsistence fishing in some remote areas (Morrow 1980). This species is not highly important in the Great Basin because of its limited range and scarcity.

Range

The native range of this species is eastern Siberia, across North America to Hudson Bay, and south to Michigan, Montana, and British Columbia. Originally there were 2 isolated populations in the United States. One, the Michigan grayling, has been extinct for more than 25 years. The other, sometimes known as the Montana grayling, has had its range greatly reduced from the original, which included the Missouri River and its tributaries above Great Falls, Montana. It occurs in the Great Basin in Lobdell Lake, California and its outlet, Desert Creek, in the western Lahontan basin (Reiber 1983).

Description

The relatively slender grayling is gray to olive green on the back, silvery to light purple on the sides, and bluish-white on the belly. The most distinguishing characteristic is a long, high, brilliantly colored, principally purple dorsal fin. The upper margin of the dorsal is green with pink or red spots and has gray and rose-colored bands. The pectoral fins are blue and shot through with pink colors at the tip. A black slash runs along the chin in the same manner as the red slash of a cutthroat trout. The grayling has an adipose fin, a dorsal fin with 18 to 25 rays, and pelvic fins with 5 or more rays. The large-pored cycloid scales number between 77 and 103 in the lateral series. The head is average size for salmonids, the mouth small with sparse teeth on the jaws, prevomer, and palatines. The caudal fin is forked.

Size and Longevity

The grayling is slow-growing and moderate-lived. The yearly length in inches for grayling age 1 to 6 in Yellowstone Lake, Wyoming is 3.5, 8.0, 11.0, 13.0, 14.5, and 15.5 (Varley and Schullery 1983). Most grayling live less than 6 years, but a few live as long as 10 (Brown 1971). The average size is about 1 pound, although fish in many populations do not reach this size. The all-tackle hook and line record weighed 5 pounds, 15 ounces. The Lobdell Lake, California population, sampled in 1980, contained young-of-year fish 3.4 inches long, 1-year-old fish 12 inches long, and 3-year-old fish 14.6 inches long (Reiber 1983).

Limiting Factors

The grayling is so easy to catch that it may be overfished. It suffers quickly from habitat degradation. The stream form is listed as threatened (Williams 1981). It is not considered an able competitor with most trout. There was a marked decline in the grayling population in Upper Granite Lake, Washington after cutthroat trout were planted there. The amount of adequate spawning space limits population size since the aggressive territoriality of the male grayling limits the number of spawners at any one time (Eschmeyer and Scott 1983). It is easy prey for birds since it does not always seek cover.

Food and Feeding

Virtually the entire diet of the grayling is composed of insects—larvae, pupae, and adults—that are taken from the drift. The majority of these aquatic forms have been moved from the bottom by one means or another and thus become part of the drift. The grayling is primarily a surface and mid-depth feeder; it does not feed on the bottom except in the fall when drift is reduced. It occasionally eats fish (Morrow 1980). The fry begin searching for food about a week after hatching. The yolk sac of grayling disappears much more rapidly than that of trout, which explains why it begins feeding earlier in life than do trout. Brown (1971) states that aquatic insects and crustaceans form the bulk of the diet and that grayling are extremely voracious, feeding without caution.

Breeding Habits

Grayling spawn early in the spring immediately after ice breakup. In Alaska they begin to congregate at the mouths of clearwater tributaries and start upstream in channels cut though the ice by surface run-off. As soon as the stream opens, the fish move upstream to the spawning grounds, a migration that may be 100 miles long. When spawning, wild adults tend to ignore danger. Spawning in Alaska takes place from mid May to June (Morrow 1980). Grayling usually reach sexual maturity in 2 years. A 1-pound female produces about 7,000 eggs, while a 2-pound one may have as many as 12,000 (Brown 1971). The grayling shows no particular preference for substrate when spawning, although sandy gravel with overhead cover seems to be used most often, perhaps because it is most abundant. A male establishes a territory that he defends against other males by erecting his dorsal fin, opening his mouth, and assuming a rigid posture. Persistent intruders may be rushed and driven off. Rarely, females may be attacked. The male follows the female, courting her with displays of his dorsal fin. He then drifts beside her and pulls his dorsal fin over her back. Both fish arch and vibrate. The female releases eggs and the male releases milt. No redd is constructed (Morrow 1980). The orange-colored eggs are about 0.1 inch before water hardening. The young have been described as "two eyeballs on a thread."

The adhesive eggs stick to particles of sand or gravel. In 52° F water the eggs hatch in 17 days (Varley and Schullery 1983). At Grebe Lake in Yellowstone National Park the grayling generally begin spawning the day after the ice goes off, migrating only a short distance upstream before spawning. The grayling run in many areas is of shorter duration than it is for trout, being completed in not more than a week and at times in no more than 2 or 3 days. In Yellowstone National Park, grayling fry begin their migration from the stream to the lake between 7:00 and 10:00 P.M. (Varley and Schullery 1983). In Lobdell Lake, California grayling have been observed spawning in the lake inlet stream (Reiber 1983).

Habitat

Grayling prefers clear, very cold streams with stretches of bottom that have abundant plant life. It has succeeded as a lake fish in several instances, but apparently is more at home in streams. An analysis of lakes that have successful populations reveals an abundance of aquatic vegetation over as much as 50 percent of the bottom. In streams it chooses deep pools where it forms large schools. Unlike the trout, the grayling remains in the open, often in the middle of the stream in plain sight even when approached. Temperatures from 38° to 52° F are best suited to grayling. In the fall there may be a downstream migration when the fish leave the small tributaries and move to overwinter in lakes or deep pools in the stream. Grayling tend to establish territories although this tendency is not evident when they form schools.

Preservation of Species

The grayling is a desirable game fish even though relatively few people have ever seen it in the wild. Since it can easily be captured it requires an unusual amount of protection where fishing pressure is heavy. Grayling are more difficult than rainbow trout to raise in hatcheries, and relatively few attempts have been made to carry them to maturity. Nevertheless, propagation is necessary if the range of the grayling is to be expanded or in some cases maintained. On the other hand, in hatcheries grayling are more docile during spawning than trout, they are less afraid of people, and the eggs can be taken from the females without difficulty. Stocking should be in waters where there is a minimum or no competition from trout. In the wild additional stream cover may provide visual isolation for territorial males and therefore increase total spawning. Stream improvement structures may also increase spawning success.

PIKES (ESOCIDAE)

This Holarctic family contains one genus, *Esox*, with five species in North America and one in the U.S.S.R. Members of the family are easily recognized by the ducklike bill and long teeth. They have a short and far back dorsal fin and forked tail (Smith 1979). Teeth on the jaws are large and prominent. There are large patches of cardiform teeth on the vomer, palatines, and tongue. The pectoral fins are low and the pelvic fins abdominal. The native range of the pikes is over much of the northern hemisphere. Only one species occurs in the Great Basin.

Northern pike
***Esox lucius* Linnaeus**

Importance

Sportsmen eagerly seek northern pike because of its large size and fighting antics when hooked. Since it is highly piscivorous in nature, the pike is a valuable management tool in waters inhabited largely by nongame fish. Stories of its eating inordinate numbers of young waterfowl should be viewed with skepticism. It is an important commodity where commercial fishing is legal. The northern pike is not an important game fish in the Great Basin because of its limited range and relatively sparse populations.

Range

This species has circumpolar distribution in the northern hemisphere. Its native range in North America is from Alaska south to Missouri and Nebraska, east of the Rocky Mountains, and west of the Appalachians. It is native in Lake Champlain and the Hudson River and south but east of the mountains to the Connecticut River, and in New Hampshire and central Massachusetts. Its original range includes the

United Kingdom and Ireland, all of Europe south to northern Italy around the Dead and Caspian seas, northeast into Siberia in lakes Balkhash and Baikal, and east to the Chukchi Peninsula. It has not been planted as extensively in the United States as many other game fish (Scott and Crossman 1973). In the Great Basin it is present in Redmond Lake and Yuba Reservoir, Utah and Bassett and Comins lakes and Dakes and J. D. reservoirs, Nevada.

Description

The northern pike is distinctive because of a pattern of light-colored marks on a green or brown background. It also differs from other species of the genus in having fully scaled cheeks, although only the upper half of the opercle is scaled. The teardroplike mark below the eye is usually weak. The young have discrete black over brown spots on the dorsal, anal, and caudal fins and lack dark-color markings on the back and sides (Smith 1979). The background color of the flanks is light. In pike over 15 inches long, there are markings of 7 to 9 irregular, longitudinal rows of yellow to whitish bead-shaped spots, some as long as the eye diameter. The body has the appearance of being flecked with gold, which is caused by tiny gold spots on the tip of the exposed edge of most body scales. Juveniles have a pattern of long, wavy, white to yellow vertical bars extending up almost to the lateral line. These bars break into the rows of spots in the adults. Because of this distinctive juvenile coloration, they are sometimes confused with other species. The sides of the head are vermiculated with bright golden marks (Scott and Crossman 1973).

Size and Longevity

The northern pike is a fast-growing, long-lived fish. In the southern part of the range it may live 10 to 12 or more years, whereas the somewhat slower-growing Arctic populations may reach ages as high as 24 to 26 years. The growth in length of young fish is very rapid. They are about 0.33 inch long when hatched and may be as long as 6 to 12 inches at the end of the first year. In a Missouri River backwater area with a large number of gizzard shad, young pike reached 20 inches the first summer, indicating the growth potential when abundant food is available. The average yearly length in inches of northern pike age 1 to 6 years in Montana is 10.0, 15.0, 18.0, 21.0, 24.0, and 30.0 and, for 10-year-olds, 40 inches. Growth in length is rapid during the first 3 years but slows after sexual maturity, when weight increases more rapidly. In one study in Lake Athabasca, Canada, one group of fish grew to a length of 45.9 inches in 24 years. Northern pike of the Great Basin generally do not reach a weight of over 20 pounds, the record being 27 pounds. The angling record for pike in North America is 46 pounds, 2 ounces, while the world record is 62.5 pounds (Scott and Crossman 1973; Kutz 1982).

Limiting Factors

Since northern pike spawn in very shallow weedy areas, there is always the chance that the young, and occasionally the adults, will be trapped by falling water levels. In Spirit Lake, Iowa there is no evidence that dropping water levels initiated a migration of young into deeper, safer waters, potentially leaving the young prey to fish, aquatic insects, birds, and even mammals. Eggs are also preyed upon. Spawning northern pike lose their wariness and are susceptible to predation by humans, bears, eagles, and ospreys. In Spirit Lake, Iowa one year they stacked up two to three deep when a headgate that had been inadvertently closed blocked their spawning run. The fish were so abundant and so unwary in this area that at one point a Labrador retriever was picking up fish and bringing them ashore. In other seasons the adults are secretive and belligerent; they have only humans to fear. They are, however, vulnerable to overfishing since they strike lures readily and often inhabit inshore areas.

Food and Feeding

As soon as young northern pike have absorbed the yolk sac, they start feeding heavily on large zooplankton and immature insects. After a few days, small fish enter the pike's diet and by the time young are two inches long they may eat primarily fish. Northern pike are visual predators and are primarily active during daylight (Inskip 1982). Adult pike feed largely on fish, although they are omnivorous carnivores that eat virtually any living vertebrate they can catch and swallow. Adults at times feed heavily on frogs and crayfish and they are not reluctant to take such unwary animals as mice, muskrats, and ducklings (Scott and Crossman 1973). Young pike do not prosper in hatcheries unless given an opportunity at a very early age to feed on fish.

Breeding Habits

Almost immediately after the ice goes out in the spring, mature northern pike move into shallow weedy areas and commence spawning, generally when temperatures range from 40° to 52° F. In general, pike spawn in heavily vegetated flood plains of rivers, marshes, and bays. One female, along with a generally smaller male, swims through the vegetation in water, often only 4 or 5 inches deep, and distributes eggs, more or less randomly, near the surface. The spawning act is usually followed by a thrust of the tail that both moves the female out and scatters the settling eggs. The pike builds no nest; the eggs are adhesive and attach to vegetation or debris. The northern pike is highly prolific. One estimate of fecundity is as high as 395,000 eggs; the estimated number of eggs per pound of female is 9,000. While the number of eggs is high, so is the mortality. Scott and Crossman (1973) quote a 99.8 percent mortality from egg to young at the time they are leaving the spawning grounds. Eggs hatch in from 4 to 14 days depending upon water temperature.

The spawning act is repeated many times during a 2- to 5-day period. After spawning is complete, adults move out of the area immediately. The young begin feeding early and leave the area in 4 to 6 weeks. In southern Canada and northern United States, females mature at age 3 to 4 and males at 2 to 3 years of age, whereas in the northern part of its range the female may not mature until it is 6 years of age and the male 5 (Scott and Crossman 1973).

Habitat

Northern pike habitat ranges from the large, relatively cold, deep lakes to small, warm farm ponds. In rivers they prefer slow, meandering, heavily vegetated habitat to the fast, shallow areas. In lakes, unless the water is too warm, they are generally present inshore, where there is an abundance of vegetation that provides both cover and food. They are more active in summer than winter, although they are active enough in winter to provide a sport fishery in many areas. They occur in lakes with total alkalinities as high as 1,000 ppm and pH as high as 9.5. Although the northern pike is a freshwater fish, it at times moves into brackish (estuarine) waters.

Preservation of Species

Two important components of preservation are stable water levels in spawning areas until adults and young have emigrated and catch regulations. Stocking is often in order for areas fished heavily, both in summer and winter. It should not be overlooked that at times the northern pike is both a competitor with and a predator on more desirable game fish. In the Great Basin this species may require supplemental stocking to support sport fisheries. More important may be the need for habitat preservation and an adequate prey base.

9

Cypriniformes

CARPS AND MINNOWS (CYPRINIDAE)

THIS LARGE and widely distributed family inhabits fresh waters of four continents: North America, Europe, Asia, and Africa. Worldwide there are over 1,500 species; in North America they occur mostly east of the Continental Divide. They occupy almost every conceivable niche and range in size from less than an ounce to nearly 300 pounds; however, most species are small. They are important as food, both wild and cultivated, forage, and pets and in research.

This family is characterized by cycloid scales and abdominal pelvic fins. The fins have soft rays without true spines. In a few species the first ray of the dorsal and sometimes the anal fin is hardened into a spinelike structure resembling a true spine. All members of this family have toothless jaws, but strong pharyngeal teeth break up and help swallow food. There is no adipose fin. A unique structure called the Weberian apparatus, a series of small bones that connects the gas bladder to the inner ear, probably gives them an acute sense of hearing (Simpson and Wallace 1978). The current American Fisheries Society list of fishes (Robins et al. 1980) lists 221 species and 43 genera of cyprinids in the United States and Canada. Sixteen native species in 8 genera and 10 introduced species in 10 genera occur in the Great Basin.

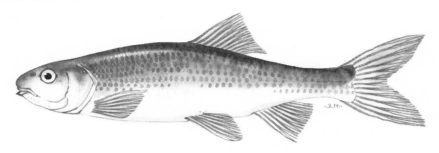

Chiselmouth
Acrocheilus alutaceus Agassiz and Pickering

Importance

The chiselmouth is distinguished taxonomically by being the only living species in this genus and is therefore of great interest to naturalist historians. It was probably used as food by Indians at one time. The chiselmouth is important in the food web because it provides a link between the primary plant producers and piscivorous fish (La Rivers 1962; Wydoski and Whitney 1979).

Range

The chiselmouth is a strictly western fish, occurring in the Columbia River system of Washington and Oregon, the Fraser River system of British Columbia, and the Harney-Malheur system of the Great Basin (Scott and Crossman 1973; La Rivers 1962).

Description

The overall coloration of this species is rather drab with dark brown above and lighter sides. The sides may have many small black dots that are lighter on the lower sides. Young fish may have a vague dark spot at the base of the caudal fin. There is an orange coloration in the axils of the pectoral and pelvic fins.

The body is elongate and only slightly compressed. The caudal peduncle is slender, appearing pinched posteriorly. The head is blunt and approximately as long as the body depth. The snout is bluntly rounded and the lower jaw has a distinguishing hard, sharp plate, giving rise to both the common and generic names. It has 1 dorsal fin with 10 rays that starts behind the origin of the pelvic fins. The caudal fin is distinctly forked; the anal fin has 9 or 10 rays. The pelvic fins are well developed and narrow with 9 or 10 rays; the pectoral fins have 15 to 18 rays. The scales are small and cycloid, numbering from 85 to 93 in the lateral series. The lateral line is complete (La Rivers 1962; Scott and Crossman 1973; Wydoski and Whitney 1979).

Size and Longevity

The chiselmouth may reach a size of 12 inches and live 6 years. Newly hatched larvae are about 0.3 inch long and difficult to distinguish from other cyprinids until they reach a length of 0.6 inch, when the chisellike mouth becomes evident. Other age and growth data are sketchy and difficult to obtain because of the unreadability of the otoliths (Moodie 1966).

Limiting Factors

The chiselmouth is preyed upon by piscivorous fish and is affected by parasitism. Hybridization occurs with the northern squawfish.

Food and Feeding

The chiselmouth eats mostly vegetation (predominantly algae) and associated animals, as is suggested by the long, convoluted intestine and the cartilaginous sheathing of the mouth. Young fish feed upon surface-occurring insects. Feeding behavior is unique and very specialized, consisting of scraping the chisellike lower jaw along rocks or other substrate in quick, short, darting movements of about 1 inch. Filamentous algae are ingested but probably not digested to any significant degree. The primary food is diatoms (Wydoski and Whitney 1979; Scott and Crossman 1973; La Rivers 1962).

Breeding Habits

Males probably attain sexual maturity at age 2 or 3 and females at age 3 or 4. Spawning occurs in late June and early July in streams at temperatures of 62° F. Females produce about 6,200 eggs. Spawning has not been directly observed but eggs have been collected on open bottoms and among boulders (Scott and Crossman 1973; Wydoski and Whitney 1979).

Habitat

The chiselmouth apparently prefers warm areas of streams in moderately fast to very fast water. It also lives in lakes but migrates into streams to spawn. Almost nothing is known about its behavior, although it occurs in abundance in many rivers within its range (Scott and Crossman 1973; Wydoski and Whitney 1979).

Preservation of Species

This fish is abundant and relatively unimportant economically, so probably all that is required for the preservation of this species is that established populations be protected from habitat destruction or introduction of competing species.

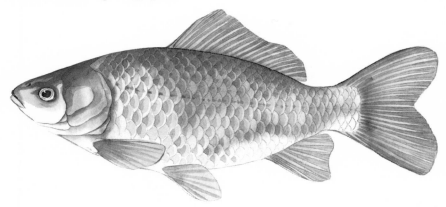

Goldfish
***Carassius auratus* (Linnaeus)**

Importance

The goldfish is highly valued as an aquarium fish and in research. In the wild it falls somewhere between an annoyance and a nuisance. It seldom furnishes fishing and at times is a competitor of more desirable fish, especially native killifishes. The goldfish has been cultivated for centuries and there is extensive literature covering every phase of its life history.

Range

Goldfish, a native of China, has been introduced in all inhabited parts of the world as an ornamental aquarium fish (Brown 1971). It is not known when goldfish was introduced in America, but there was a goldfish farm in Maryland in 1889. It has been accidentally and intentionally stocked by well-meaning citizens in much of North America. There are a number of small populations scattered throughout the Great Basin.

Description

The goldfish has a moderately compressed, robust body covered

with large scales. The color is variable in the wild, and at times it re-
verts to a drab gray, much like the common carp. The head is short and
mouth oblique, and jaw teeth are absent. The dorsal fin, with an anterior serrated spine, has 18 to 20 rays. There are no chin barbels as in the
common carp.

Size and Longevity

Goldfish do not reach a large size in the wild; 6 to 8 inches is the
average maximum size in many areas, with a few reaching twice or
more that length. Longevity is 5 to 8 years, much less than in aquarium-
reared fish.

Limiting Factors

Competition and predation are probably the worst enemies of wild
goldfish. It lives and reproduces in badly polluted waters in some areas.

Food and Feeding

Food is largely algae and aquatic invertebrates.

Breeding Habits

Goldfish mate at 1 to 3 years of age in the wild. The spawning season lasts for several weeks, starting in early summer, when temperatures
range from 63° to 68° F. The adhesive eggs stick to plants, debris, and
other bottom substrate. Unlike the common carp, it does not thrash
about in shallow water when spawning. The choice spawning areas are
warm, shallow, weedy waters. In some areas goldfish hybridize with
common carp.

Habitat

The habitat of goldfish ranges from small, sluggish, warm streams
and ponds to the backwaters of large rivers and lakes. It is abundant in
the Illinois River, Illinois in the Chicago area, where few other fish have
survived the stream degradation. To a moderate extent it lives where it
has been put. In the Great Basin, populations have been established
where it was intentionally or accidentally stocked.

Preservation of Species

It is considered an undesirable species in the wild and is offered no
specific protection.

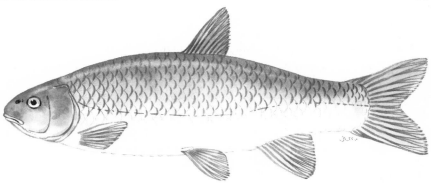

Grass carp
Ctenopharyngodon idella (Valenciennes)

Importance

The grass carp was imported into this country as a biological control for aquatic vegetation, largely in reservoirs. In some countries it is reared as a food fish. Its flesh is reported to be on a par with that of the common carp. There is strong concern in the United States that where the grass carp has become established in natural waters it may be a liability. It can in time become a competitor of native species and in some cases it may destroy habitat of both fish and waterfowl (Pflieger 1975). The jury is still out on the ecological effects of the grass carp. In the meantime its range should not be deliberately extended.

Range

The grass carp is a native of eastern Asia. It was brought to this country in 1963 and introduced into the open waters of Arkansas. It has been reported in waters of both the Missouri and the Mississippi rivers. In the Great Basin it is present in a few ponds near Las Vegas, probably from aquarium releases or unauthorized stocking by people who believed it would control aquatic vegetation. It may also have been introduced in western Utah.

Description

The grass carp is a thick-bodied, silvery fish with a short, pointed dorsal fin and a broad, blunt head. It is generally pale gray in color. Scales on the back and sides have prominent dark edges, which give the fish a crosshatched effect. The dorsal fin, located just above the pelvic fins, has 8 rays.

Size and Longevity

The grass carp grows rapidly under favorable conditions. A specimen caught in the Missouri River had grown from a length of 4.8 inches to 25.8 inches in 1 year. Twenty specimens caught by commercial fishermen in 1974 ranged in length from 24 to 34 inches and in weight from 6 to 14.7 pounds. Most were in their third summer (Pflieger 1975). Pflieger reports that in its native range the grass carp may reach a length of 4 feet and a weight of 100 pounds.

Limiting Factors

Little is known of the grass carp in this country. Probably the grass carp is susceptible to the same factors that adversely affect the common carp.

Food and Feeding

Young grass carp to 8 inches in length feed mainly on small crustaceans and other invertebrates. Fish larger than this prefer aquatic vegetation. However, the grass carp reportedly eats a wide variety of plant and animal material (Pflieger 1975). Feeding is evidently selective, however, and the overall result may be just a change in plant community composition.

Breeding Habits

Smith (1979) states that the grass carp in China spawns from April until mid August, producing hundreds of thousands of eggs that float until hatched. In large streams during periods of high flow, eggs and young may be carried a considerable distance, thus expanding the fish's range.

Habitat

The grass carp is typically a fish of large, slow, warm rivers, but it can be propagated in ponds.

Preservation of Species

Grass carp is possibly a negative ecological force in western North America and the Great Basin. It is similar in palatability to common carp and therefore is not a favored food fish. More important, many aspects of its ecology in Great Basin waters and elsewhere are poorly understood. Its use as an aquatic weed control mechanism may change to an uncontrolled experiment with potentially disastrous results.

Restraint in utilizing grass carp should be maintained until responsible agencies can investigate and document long-term ecological effects. Only time and study will tell how the grass carp should be handled or utilized in North America.

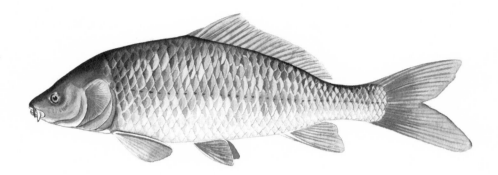

Common carp
Cyprinus carpio **Linnaeus**

Importance

The common carp is viewed with mixed emotions in North America. In the last twenty or more years of the nineteenth century, it was praised lavishly as a delicacy and was stocked extensively by state and federal fish commissioners and private landowners. Shortly thereafter, attitudes toward the carp changed abruptly. Three factors work against the acceptance of carp in the United States and Canada. The culinary qualities of wild North American carp do not match those described for Asian and European carp. This may be due in part to the muddy flavor it often picks up in many habitats in early to late spring and that it keeps until winter. This unpalatable taste is caused by a soil-inhabiting bacteria ingested by carp via aquatic invertebrates. Not all carp have a muddy taste; it depends on the habitat (many other species of fish suffer from the same problem). Strike two against the carp is that it competes intensely for food with native fish. Strike three is the tendency for large schools of carp to be destructive of habitat for fish and waterfowl in some areas.

The common carp is important in North American warm waters, but in many areas from a negative standpoint. There are exceptions; in quite a number of places in North America it is sought after as a sport and food fish. Its great abundance makes it a good potential source of high-protein food. Over the years carp has been used as food for poultry, fur bearers, and trout as well as human consumption. A commercial fishery in northwest Iowa ships carp, live, dressed, or smoked, to many metropolitan areas of the United States. Carp, when hooked, put up a substantial and satisfying fight. Young carp furnish a limited amount of forage, but their agility and rapid growth reduce the amount of predation on them. Use of the young as forage by other species is further reduced by the young's tendency to hide in aquatic vegetation until they reach 3 to 9 inches. Their strong spines also render them unsuitable for many predators.

Range

The carp is native to Asia, where it is extensively cultivated for human consumption. It was brought into Germany and other European countries from the Orient many centuries ago. From about 1876 to 1910 it was stocked in the United States initially from Europe (Hessel 1878) and later from both European and local stock. It was introduced in the Great Basin in large numbers from approximately 1878 to 1905. Today it ranges over most of the warm waters of the contiguous forty-eight states, including Great Basin waters, and also lives in some cold waters such as Bear Lake, Utah-Idaho.

Description

The carp is a deep-bodied fish with a triangular head. The adult is usually olive green to gold on the back, becoming yellow on the belly. The lower half of the caudal fin and the anal fin may have a reddish hue with stronger coloration in large adults. The young, after reaching a size of 4 to 5 inches, have essentially the same body form as the adult, but the colors are less intense. The mouth has a pair of barbels on each side, one barbel shorter than the other. The rather long dorsal fin has 17 to 21 rays and a stout serrated spine (much like a saw blade turned upside down) on the leading edge of the fin. The anal fin also has a spine. The deep body is laterally compressed, and the scales are large, numbering 35 to 38 in the lateral series. The carp may be fully and uniformly scaled, partially and irregularly scaled, or nearly naked. Local names such as mirror and leather carp apply to the latter category. Carp that are irregularly scaled may have several sizes of scales, ranging from quite small to very large. It is interesting to note that these scales are not reliable for determining age.

Size and Longevity

Carp is a relatively long-lived, fast-growing fish. It reportedly may reach an age of 20 years or more, although this is undoubtedly the exception. The world's largest carp, weighing 82 pounds, 8 ounces, was taken from near Pretoria, South Africa. The North American record carp, weighing 59.5 pounds, was taken in Iowa in 1955. The Great Basin record is 35 pounds, taken from an experimental duck pond on the Bear River Migratory Bird Refuge, Utah. The length at the end of each year in inches of carp age 1 to 8 from the Ogden Bay Bird Refuge near Ogden, Utah is 6.8, 13.9, 20.4, 25.0, 27.2, 28.2, 28.5, and 28.4. There was a measurable increase in rate of growth of carp in the Ogden Bay Bird Refuge immediately after a heavy reduction in numbers. Carp in nearby Bear River Migratory Bird Refuge, at the mouth of the Bear River near Brigham City, grow at a slightly slower rate. No fish older than 8 years was taken from Odgen Bay; none older than 7 years from Bear River Refuge. In cold, inhospitable Bear Lake, the carp grow to a length of 26.7 inches, but it takes them 13 years (Sigler 1958b).

Limiting Factors

The carp is fed upon by fish, birds, and occasionally mammals. In the Bear River Migratory Bird Refuge, the white pelican feeds extensively on primarily young or yearling carp. Rapid drop in water levels just after spawning is destructive to carp eggs and young. In the Bear River Migratory Bird Refuge during the hottest part of the summer, young carp sometimes inadvertently move into the very shallow, hot water and die before they can escape. Carp is sometimes killed by pollution or siltation, but its tolerance is much higher than that of native cyprinids. When it is spawning, the adult carp loses much of its natural wariness and therefore becomes quite vulnerable. A rare disaster killed large numbers of carp in the Ogden Bay Bird Refuge when high winds and high water caused the saline waters of Great Salt Lake to sweep over an Ogden Bay dike into the area inhabited by carp.

Food and Feeding

The carp feeds primarily on aquatic invertebrates, mostly insects. Algae is fed upon if the more desirable invertebrates are lacking, but nutrient value may be low. Insects, primarily midge larvae and pupae, make up as much as 87 percent of the diet in the Bear River Migratory Bird Refuge population. In Bear Lake, where aquatic invertebrates are much less abundant, the carp feeds more on algae. Carp in the Bear River Migratory Bird Refuge were observed sucking midge larvae from vascular plants, starting at the bottom and ending at the surface with a loud slurp. On a few occasions, large adults fed on young carp; possibly those that had been killed or immobilized by hot water (Sigler 1958b).

Characteristically, the carp is an omnivorous and opportunistic feeder. One school of carp was observed feeding on maggots as they emerged from an animal carcass partly submerged in a riverbed. In other areas it has been reported feeding on various kinds of seeds, wild rice, aquatic plants, and algae as well as terrestrial insects floating on the surface.

Breeding Habits

The carp is a spring spawner, in water ranging in temperature from 58° to 67° F with an optimum of 62° F. Spawning carp move into warm, shallow, often weedy areas and commence spawning either by day or night, but the preference is apparently twilight. Spawning often takes place in water so shallow that the backs of the carp are exposed. There is much disturbance created by spawning carp; they race about, break water, and splash loudly. On one occasion in Spirit Lake, Iowa spawning carp were moving such large boulders that the noise could be heard for half a mile. The carp builds no nest and does not care for its young. The slightly adhesive eggs stick to debris or plants or occasionally sink to the bottom substrate. The spawning period may last from early May to late August. The female lays from 500 to 600 eggs at a time; one large female was estimated to have more than 100,000 eggs. Carp first spawn at age 2 to 4. In some areas carp hybridize with goldfish.

Habitat

The carp is adapted to a wide range of habitats, from large, deep, and sometimes cold lakes, rivers, and reservoirs to small, warm farm ponds. Many waterfowl refuges of the Great Basin are judged to be ideal carp habitat where there is an abundance of food, the water warms rapidly in spring in the shallow areas, and there are deep canals to retreat to in winter or when the shallow water becomes too warm. The carp is exceptionally wary; at the slightest sign of danger it rapidly retreats to safety. In a flooded cornfield along the Illinois River, Illinois, carp cruised leisurely down the rows of corn until there was a 2- to 3-inch drop in water level, then they went scurrying through a break in the dike and back into the river. Unmolested populations of carp in small artesian-fed ponds in northern Utah have standing populations of from 1,000 to 2,000 pounds per surface acre. One January morning in 1942, thousands of pounds of carp were located by commercial fishermen in a small cove in West Okoboji Lake, Iowa, resting under the ice in a semi-dormant condition. After a number of these fish had been taken with gill nets, the others became very active and escaped. Carp generally do not form well-defined schools. However, in the Bear River Migratory Bird Refuge, they form schools of several thousands, both when they are spawning and feeding.

Preservation of Species

Preservation of common carp is rarely a problem. Efforts to eliminate or markedly reduce populations have had only limited success. Probably the only way to reduce carp numbers to acceptable levels is to substantially increase utilization. This is currently not economically feasible over much of the carp's habitat, but can be promoted by resource agencies where possibilities exist.

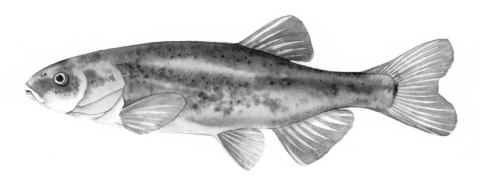

Desert dace
***Eremichthys acros* Hubbs and Miller**

Importance

The desert dace is an interesting natural history entity and a unique native desert fish. It should be protected and preserved. It is listed by the U.S. Fish and Wildlife Service as threatened.

Range

The desert dace is restricted and native to the warm springs and creeks of Soldier Meadows in western Humboldt County, northwest Nevada.

Description

This small fish is olive green on the back and silvery below and has pronounced yellow reflections along the sides. The sides are weakly and vaguely mottled, with a blackish spotting and a dorso-lateral deep green streak. Both the dorsal and the anal fin usually have 8 rays. It has 5 to 9 gill rakers, 36 to 38 vertebrae, and a blackish peritoneum (La Rivers 1962).

Size and Longevity

This little fish apparently does not reach a size of over 2.5 inches. It probably lives 2 to 3 years.

Limiting Factors

Degradation of habitat and introduction of exotics have threatened the desert dace. Wherever possible this process should be reversed. It is not a strong competitor and it is adapted to a highly specialized habitat (see chapter 4).

Food and Feeding

The desert dace feeds on available aquatic invertebrates, primarily insects. It also feeds on algae. In an aquarium, it fed on other fish (La Rivers 1962).

Breeding Habits

It probably breeds throughout the early and midsummer months, producing limited numbers of untended adhesive eggs.

Habitat

The desert dace lives in warm springs and creeks of Soldier Meadows, Nevada, a high mountain basin at an elevation slightly under 5,000 feet. It can tolerate temperatures from 67° to 100° F (Nyquist 1963).

Preservation of Species

This species' limited habitat necessitates that it be protected from physical alteration and/or changes in water levels and chemistry. Additionally, no other fish species should be stocked in this restricted habitat. Measures to ensure the continued existence of this species may, of necessity, include the establishment of reserves or refuges specifically for this species.

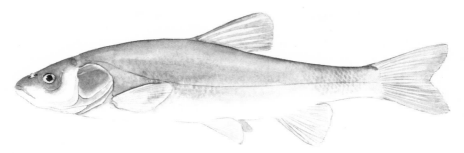

Alvord chub
Gila alvordensis Hubbs and Miller

Importance

The Alvord chub is endemic to the Alvord basin, Oregon-Nevada. Its importance is related to its severely restricted distribution and its occurrence as a rare natural history entity. It is listed by the U.S. Fish and Wildlife Service as of special concern.

Range

This species' distribution is restricted to a relatively small area of southeastern Oregon and northwest Nevada. It occurs in selected springs, marshes, and tributary streams in the Sheldon National Wildlife Refuge, Nevada and in one location outside of the refuge (Williams, Williams, and Bond 1980). Williams and Bond (1983) collected Alvord chub from 16 locations.

Description

The Alvord chub is generally gray to whitish overall with a darker back. A faint, indistinct band that may be interrupted occurs on the sides from the head to the caudal peduncle. The single dorsal fin has 7 rays, the caudal 19 rays, and the anal 8 rays. The male has longer fins than the female (Williams, Williams, and Bond 1980). Specimens from canyon areas are darker than those on the valley floor (Williams and Bond 1983).

Size and Longevity

Williams and Bond (1983) report adult males about 2 inches in length and females about 2.5 inches in one habitat, while in other habitats fish as large as 4.8 inches were present. It probably lives 4 to 5 years.

Limiting Factors

The habitat of the Alvord basin is fragile and water is scarce. This means the welfare of the Alvord chub can easily be threatened by even limited human activities. It also appears the Alvord chub can be eliminated by the introduction of exotic fishes. Since the Alvord chub has evolved without companion species of fish (with one exception), it is not an able competitor.

Food and Feeding

The Alvord chub is an opportunistic feeder. Specimens collected from Thousand Creek, Nevada in 1978 had eaten 10 food items. Midge larvae, cladocerans, copepods, and ostracods are of greatest importance. Midges account for 26 percent of the volume of food. Terrestrial insects were not eaten. Food is variable with season, possibly reflecting seasonal changes in abundance (Williams and Williams 1980).

Breeding Habits

Williams and Bond (1983) collected Alvord chubs in spawning condition in mid June. Young of the year present in June indicate a spawning season from at least April until July.

Habitat

In a series of collections in the Sheldon National Wildlife Refuge, the Alvord chub was not taken with other fish. Later it was collected in Trout Creek with rainbow trout (Williams and Bond 1983). It inhabits springs and ponds in an extremely limited area in and around the refuge. Temperatures in the habitats range from 58° to 80° F. Water depth in these areas ranges from 3 inches to over 3 feet, the bottom varies from silt to gravel, and there is 0 to 90 percent cover. The habitat in which it occurs indicates requirements are not stringent. Cool- and warmwater springs as well as creeks, reservoirs, and lakes have populations. High temperatures evidently inhibit this species. None was found above an 88° F boundary area in one location (Williams, Williams, and Bond 1980).

Preservation of Species

The Alvord chub is present in at least sixteen locations in the Alvord basin. This habitat should be protected from degradation, especially the lowering of water levels. No introductions of any species of fish should be made in the Alvord basin where there are Alvord chubs.

Utah chub
Gila atraria (Girard)

Importance

Because of its great abundance, wide distribution, moderate size (occasionally 16 inches), and generalized feeding habits, this species may become a serious competitor of game fish, especially trout in a delicate or disrupted habitat. It is significant that those waters in which the species has become a nuisance are either not within its native range or, if so, have been much modified by man. The Utah chub has become so abundant in some areas that special eradication programs have been initiated to eliminate it. The result of these efforts has been to dramatically reduce the population, but the chub has rebounded quite readily. "Spot poisoning" programs have met with minimal success. There is presently no economically feasible way of eradicating Utah chub once it is established and well distributed.

The Utah chub is easily taken on hook and line and has proved to be a nuisance to fishermen, who find difficulty in avoiding it while fishing for trout. On a positive note, it provides important forage for game fish in some waters. While its abundance and relative ease of capture would make it attractive as a source of protein for human consumption, the presence of intramuscular bones and the fairly small average size for a sport fish detract from its usefulness as a human food under present economic conditions.

Range

The native range of the Utah chub lies largely within the drainage basin of ancient Lake Bonneville in Utah, Idaho, Wyoming, and Nevada of the Great Basin. It is also native to the Snake River drainage above Shoshone Falls and the lower Wood River system, Idaho. In Henry's Fork of the Snake River, its range is restricted to the area below Mesa Falls.

The Utah chub's range has been extended, via the bait bucket of well-meaning fishermen, into a number of lakes, including Fish Lake, Utah, reservoirs and streams in the Colorado River system, and in Hebgen Lake and the Madison River, Montana. It is in Panguitch Lake in the Sevier River basin, Utah. It has also been introduced in northeastern Nevada.

Description

The Utah chub is highly variable in coloration, changing with age and habitat. The back and upper parts vary from metallic or olive green, sometimes distinctly blue on the back, to dark olive brown or almost blackish; the sides are silvery or brassy to golden. The male, especially in breeding season, is distinctly more golden than the female. Often there is a narrow golden stripe along the upper side that is brighter in the male than the female. The fins may be dull olive, yellow, or golden. The dorsal fin sometimes has a blue sheen. In the breeding male there is often a trace of yellowish or orange in the axil of the pectoral fins, about the mouth, and along the preopercle. The belly is whitish or silvery in most, blackish in some.

The body is rather robust. The origin of the dorsal fin lies directly over the origin of the pelvic fins. There are typically 9 rays in the dorsal fin. The scales number about 45 to 65 in the lateral series, while the gill rakers vary from 8 to 16, being most numerous in those populations that naturally inhabit lakes.

Size and Longevity

An 11-year-old Utah chub in Bear Lake attained a length of 22 inches and a weight of 3 pounds. This is atypical; it generally does not reach a size of more than 16 inches and 2 pounds. Elsewhere it grows to 10 to 12 inches, but more commonly 5 to 8 inches. Utah chub commonly attains an age of 5 to 8 years and exceptional individuals may live to be 11 years old (Carbine 1936; Neuhold 1957). The length in inches of Utah chub age 1 to 7 in Hebgen Lake, Montana is 1.6, 3.5, 6.1, 8.2, 9.7, 10.9, and 12.4 (Graham 1961). Utah chub in Panguitch Lake, Utah have a yearly average length in inches of 1.3, 2.3, 3.6, 4.9, 5.7, 6.3, and 6.8 (Neuhold 1957). Growth is generally rapid for the first 3 or 4 years but tapers off markedly thereafter.

Limiting Factors

The Utah chub is preyed upon by fish and to a lesser extent by birds and mammals. When fluctuating water levels occur during the spawning season, eggs and young may be stranded. The chub has few serious enemies and is well able to sustain itself even under adverse conditions.

Food and Feeding

The Utah chub is an omnivorous feeder, readily eating plants, aquatic and terrestrial insects (including mosquito larvae), snails, crustaceans, and occasionally small fish and fish eggs. As it increases in size it is able to feed on a larger variety of foods. The bulk of its diet then consists of plants and invertebrates. It has been observed eating green algae in desert springs and feeding upon its own eggs. In Fish Lake, Utah, where it has become established, it regularly eats about the same food as do the small trout (Sigler 1953).

Breeding Habits

Spawning takes place during late spring and summer, with the peak between June 5 and 15 in Scofield Reservoir, Utah and between late June and early July in Hebgen Lake, Montana. Spawning was first noted in Scofield Reservoir on May 15, and the last mature fish was taken August 15 (Olson 1959). At Utah Lake, Utah mature fish were taken in April (Carbine 1936). The water temperature during spawning varies from 52° to 62° F in Scofield Reservoir and from 54° to 68° F in Hebgen Lake (Olson 1959; Graham 1961).

Spawning takes place in water generally less than 2 feet deep. A female is escorted by 2 to 6 males; the yellowish eggs are deposited at random. When held in the laboratory at a constant temperature of 64.8° F, the eggs hatched within 9 days; at 67.3° F they hatched within 6 days.

Spawning migrations have been noted in lake populations. In late spring fish move from deep to shallow water. In 22 females ranging in total length from 5.2 to 15.2 inches, the number of eggs varied from 10,470 to 38,123, the average being 25,282. These fish were from 2 to 7 years old (Olson 1959). Seven females, ranging in length from 8.8 to 13.8 inches, averaged 40,750 eggs in Hebgen Lake (Graham 1961). Male chub in Scofield Reservoir mature at age 2 and females at age 3; in Hebgen Lake males mature at age 3 and females at age 4 or older.

Habitat

Utah chub is present in a wide variety of waters and thrives over a broad range of temperatures. It predominates at elevations between 5,000 and 9,000 feet (Neuhold 1957). It seems to be equally at home in cool waters (60° to 68° F) or warm waters (81° to 88° F). It is present in irrigation ditches, ponds, sloughs, creeks, large rivers, large lakes, and reservoirs. It is typically associated with dense vegetation. It prospers in streams with currents from slow to swift near bottoms that range from clay, mud, or sand to gravel, peat, rubble, and marl. It seems to frequent depths between 1.5 to 4 feet, but in Bear Lake it was captured at 75 feet (McConnell, Clark, and Sigler 1957). It is present in springs and in spring-fed ditches on the desert floor that are often alkaline or salty. It thrives under a wide range of chemical and physical conditions and readily adapts to conditions not encountered in its natural range.

Preservation of Species

The Utah chub is obviously a fish that needs little or no protection, at least from the standpoint of fishermen and fishery biologists. Attempts to eradicate it have proven both futile and costly. Utah chub has been used extensively as a bait minnow, resulting in its unwanted spread to waters that it previously did not occupy. To prevent the spread of this and other unwanted species, many western states have outlawed the use of live fish species as bait. Further distribution of this species to new waters should be discouraged.

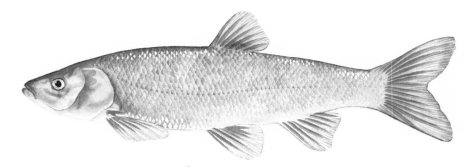

Tui chub
***Gila bicolor* (Girard)**

Importance

The tui chub is quite important as forage over most of its range; only rarely is it a serious predator of game fish. Marrin and Erman (1982) document no feeding competition between tui chub and introduced trouts in Stampede Reservoir, California. Lahontan cutthroat trout in Pyramid Lake, Nevada feed on tui chub after the trout reach a size of 12 inches and more heavily as they become larger. The tui chub reproduces rapidly and, because of its slow growth and relatively small size, is vulnerable throughout its life. Coevolution of the tui chub and Lahontan cutthroat trout has resulted in a somewhat unique predator-prey system in Pyramid Lake. The historically large size of Lahontan cutthroat trout in Pyramid Lake was due to the abundant tui chub prey base, resulting in more efficient energy transfer and subsequently larger cutthroat. In Pyramid Lake the tui chub also provides a vital food base for nesting birds on Anahoe Island. It is easy to catch on hook and line.

Range

The tui chub is native and widely distributed in the Lahontan and Central systems and in the Owens and Mojave rivers of the Great Basin. It is in the upper Pit River and Goose Lake of the Sacramento–San Joaquin system, California and in the Klamath system. It is widespread in the Columbia River drainage of Washington and Oregon, into which it may have been introduced, and in the interior basin of Oregon. It is present in drainages on both sides of the Sierra Nevada. It is abundant in Pyramid, Tahoe, Eagle, and Walker lakes and in the Humboldt River system reservoirs, Nevada.

Description

The tui chub is highly successful over a wide variety of habitats and it responds to these variations by changes in color, shape, size, and at times morphology. Its adaptability is accomplished at the subspecies level. Almost every isolated or partially isolated drainage system in California, Nevada, and Oregon supports at least one distinctive subspecies or form. According to Moyle (1976), one of California's early ichthyologists, J. O. Snyder, was so impressed by the differences in populations of tui chub that he described many of them as separate species. Today most of Snyder's species have been reduced to subspecies. The tui chub's adaptability and Snyder's nomenclature have understandably created considerable confusion and some disagreement among taxonomists as to what should be recognized as species or subspecies. For example, there are forms with numerous fine gill rakers inhabiting open waters, and other forms of coarse gill-rakered fish live inshore in lakes or streams. In some cases there are intergrades between these two. In Pyramid Lake there are both forms, but they do not appear to hybridize, at least not extensively.

The color is deep olive above, lighter on the sides, and white below. The upper parts and sides have a very pronounced brassy reflection. Some of the scales are darker than others and some are pinkish. The fins are olive and may be strongly tinted with red, and the belly may be suffused with yellow. Others are more green than olive and some have a dark lateral color extending almost to the ventral surface. The colors are more pronounced in lake dwellers. Young have a narrow dark stripe along the lateral line. The head is pointed, the mouth is rather oblique, the eye is large, and the lateral line is curved down slightly. The peritoneum is dusky, the intestine is short—about equal to the body length. The scale count in the lateral series ranges from 44 to 60 (La Rivers 1962; Moyle 1976).

Size and Longevity

The tui chub is neither fast-growing nor long-lived. It occasionally reaches a size of more than 16 inches, but the average length in many areas is 9 to 11 inches. In a 3-year study, the total length at the end of each year in inches of Pyramid Lake tui chub age 1 to 7 was 5.4, 7.5, 9.4, 11.3, 13.6, 15.8, and 16.4. Females in Pyramid Lake grow faster than males and live 7 years. The oldest males were 4 years old (Sigler and Kennedy 1978).

Limiting Factors

The tui chub is preyed upon heavily throughout its life by fish (particularly cutthroat trout), several species of birds, and occasionally mammals. In some areas water diversions seriously damage its habitat. A dominant subspecies of tui chub may extirpate another subspecies.

Food and Feeding

This species eats invertebrates, vascular plants, algae, and occasionally fish. A fish less than 4 inches long eats very little plant material, but as it increases in size it feeds more frequently on algae. In Pyramid Lake the bottom-dwelling (coarse-rakered) form eats more plants and algae than the open water (fine-rakered) form. The bottom-dwelling form feeds only inshore, but the open water form feeds both inshore and offshore. The fine-rakered form feeds more on plankton than the coarse-rakered does. Tui chub of all sizes feed most heavily on zooplankton in winter and spring. Large tui chub feed to some extent on fish. In a 1976 Pyramid Lake study involving 551 tui chub, food ranked by volume is as follows: algae, zooplankton, ostracods, midge larvae and pupae, vascular plants, fish, terrestrial insects, and amphipods (Sigler and Kennedy 1978).

In Lake Tahoe the inshore form eats 89 percent invertebrates, 5 percent fish and fish eggs, 3 percent plankton, and 3 percent plants.

Bottom food consists mainly of snails, small clams, caddisfly larvae, midge larvae, and crayfish. The open water form feeds almost exclusively (92 percent) on plankton, mostly crustaceans (Miller 1951). The young feed on crustaceans and rotifers, gradually shifting to larger organisms as they increase in size (Moyle 1976).

In Pyramid Lake, the tui chub moves to the surface to feed between 8:00 P.M. and 4:00 A.M., following the zooplankton that migrate upward at night. In summer it may feed in water more than 200 feet deep and in dissolved oxygen concentrations of less than 2 ppm.

Breeding Habits

Tui chub may spawn from as early as late April to as late as early August. In Pyramid Lake, spawning temperatures range from 62° to 72° F. The peak of spawning is reached in June when the water temperature is in the low to mid 60s. The female matures at age 2 or 3 at a length of 8 to 10 inches. Occasionally a male will mature at age 1, but most mature at age 2 when they are 8 inches long. The number of eggs produced by tui chub in Pyramid Lake varies from 6,100 to 68,900, with an average of 23,300. Males move inshore ahead of the females, generally in the vicinity of heavy beds of vegetation in quite shallow water. The female, attended by several males, deposits adhesive eggs over a wide area. There is no care of eggs or young. The young remain close to shore in the vicinity of heavy vegetation for most of the summer.

In Lake Tahoe, Nevada-California some tui chubs spawn in or near the mouth of streams. Spawning ends in the latter part of July.

Habitat

Tui chub adapts to a wide range of habitats from small streams to large lakes. It occurs as a distinctive form (subspecies in many cases) in most isolated or partially isolated drainage systems in California, Nevada, and Oregon (Moyle 1976). Tui chub are also very successful in reservoirs and are the most abundant fish in many Lahontan drainage reservoirs such as Stampede and Boca on the Little Truckee River (Marrin and Erman 1982). It prospers in cold Lake Tahoe and small streams that sometimes reach temperatures in the high 70s. In summer near midday in Pyramid Lake, it forms large doughnut-shaped schools near the surface but only over deep water. Some of these schools are more than 100 yards across. Schools in shallow water move randomly or parallel to shore. In large lakes it is dispersed in at least limited numbers throughout the lake during all seasons. However, it is most abundant in shallow waters from late spring until early winter. There is a tendency to disperse into deep water in late fall, but many remain in relatively shallow water or near the surface in deep water. The young form schools and swim parallel to shore in quite shallow water or congregate in heavy vegetation.

Preservation of Species

The tui chub, with its high reproductive rate and great adaptability to habitat, needs no protection at the species level other than from degradation of habitat caused by water diversions or pollution. Several named and potential subspecies do need protection. The number of subspecies of *Gila bicolor* is not firmly established at present. At least 16 subspecies potentially exist and further study might increase or decrease that number. The important consideration is that the tui chub, being somewhat unique in its ability to adapt to a wide range of habitat and climatic conditions, should be preserved at the subspecies level as a representative of biological diversity (see chapter 4).

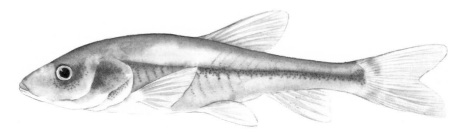

Borax Lake chub
Gila boraxobius Williams and Bond

Importance

The Borax Lake chub is important as a natural history entity. Because it occurs in a very restricted habitat, it has developed over time in a unique fashion suitable for survival in that habitat. Species of this type are important for biological study because of their ability to survive in adverse environments (poor water quality, periods of low water, high temperatures). They may in time become important for culture or insect control in addition to providing insights into adaptability. The Borax Lake chub is listed by the U.S. Fish and Wildlife Service as endangered (Williams 1981).

Range

This Great Basin species is restricted to Borax Lake, Oregon outflows in the immediate vicinity of the lake and two small adjacent
pools (Williams and Bond 1980).

Description

The Borax Lake chub is moderately dark olive green on the dorsal
surface of the head and body with a dark line extending along the
length of the dorsal midline. Lateral surfaces are mostly silvery with
numerous small melanophores. The sides display a purple iridescence.
The belly is silver. The fins are colorless except for many melanophores
along the rays of the dorsal and caudal fins and the first four rays of the
pectoral fins.

It has 7 dorsal and anal fin rays and 13 pectoral fin rays. The anterior margin of the rather small dorsal fin and of the anal fin is slightly
rounded and the posterior margin is slightly convex. The posterior tips
of the slightly forked caudal fin are rounded. All fins are proportion-
ately larger in males than females. The head is longer, wider, and deeper
than that of the Alvord chub and the eye is larger. In profile, the dorsal
surface of the head is concave. The lateral line is reduced. The jaw is
long and the mouth oblique. The caudal peduncle is noticeably slender.
It has fine, deeply embedded scales (Williams and Bond 1980).

Size and Longevity

The Borax Lake chub, typically about 2 inches in length, is a dwarf
species of *Gila*. Occasionally females reach 3.5 inches. Williams and
Bond (1983) report that Borax Lake chubs probably live only 1 year,
with a small number (mostly females) surviving 2 or 3 years.

Limiting Factors

The Borax Lake chub is restricted to the thermal waters of Borax
Lake, Oregon and its outflows (Williams and Bond 1983). Borax Lake is
relatively shallow and ranges in temperature from 63° to 95° F. It is supplied with water (95° to 104° F) from thermal springs. This naturally
restricted but stable habitat has been threatened by geothermal energy
development and alteration of the north and east shoreline in 1979. As
a result, Lower Borax Lake and the marsh and pools to the south and
west dried up, eliminating the chub in those areas (see chapter 4).

Food and Feeding

Williams and Williams (1980) found 24 different foods eaten by

Borax Lake chub. Many items fluctuate seasonally in occurrence, but some insects, especially midge larvae, diatoms, and microcrustaceans, are important throughout the year. During the spring, algae, midge larvae, copepods, adult dipterans, and ostracods are the predominant food items. Algae, mostly diatoms, account for 70 to 80 percent of the food volume of some individuals, suggesting that not all diatoms are the result of secondary ingestion with microcrustaceans but are a preferred food. During autumn, terrestrial insects, midge larvae, and diatoms are the principal food, but in winter it relies more heavily on autochthonous food items such as ostracods, copepods, midges, and cladocerans. Terrestrial insects are of importance in spring, summer, and autumn but seldom occur in the winter diet.

The Borax Lake chub feeds primarily by rooting around in bottom material and picking up food. However, if benthic food is scarce or other foods are more abundant, it will readily feed on materials drifting in the water column or occurring on the surface. There is some difference in feeding habits and prey selection between adults and juveniles. It feeds throughout the day and activity peaks shortly after sunset. Minimal activity occurs after sunrise (Williams and Williams 1980). It is basically an exploitive omnivore (Williams and Bond 1983).

Breeding Habits

Most spawning for the Borax Lake chub probably occurs in early spring. Williams (1980) reports females with mature or nearly mature ova in September, December, and January, indicating that some spawning activity may occur at any time of the year. Due to the relatively constant temperatures in the Borax Lake environment, it is likely that spawning activity is initiated in relation to photoperiod rather than prevailing water temperatures. The number of ova produced per female may range from 75 to 6,924.

Habitat

Borax Lake, Oregon outflows in the immediate vicinity and two small, adjacent pools are the habitat for this species. No other fish inhabit these waters. Borax Lake is a relatively shallow, small, clear, natural lake. The water of the lake is slightly alkaline (pH near 7.3). Sodium is the major cation and bicarbonate, sulfate, and chloride (in decreasing abundance) are the major anions. Specific conductance is 2,410 (Williams and Bond 1980; Mariner et al. 1974). Borax Lake receives water from several thermal springs at 95° to 104° F, and lake temperatures vary from 62.6° to 95° F. The chub avoids water temperatures above

93.2° F (Williams and Williams 1980; Williams and Bond 1983).

Preservation of Species

Geothermal energy development and shoreline alteration have dramatically changed the habitat of this species in Borax Lake and resulted in a partial loss of habitat and reduced population numbers. As a result of emergency listing and subsequent final rule making under the Endangered Species Act, geothermal exploration is prohibited within a one-mile buffer zone around the lake. It is imperative that there be no further degradation of habitat if the species is to survive (see chapter 4).

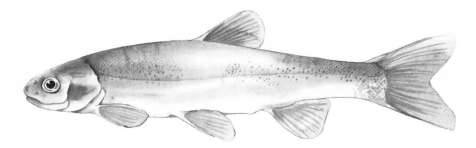

Leatherside chub
***Gila copei* (Jordan and Gilbert)**

Importance

The leatherside chub is an excellent bait minnow. It has been used for this purpose in the lower Colorado River and elsewhere. It is also utilized as forage by game fish.

Range

In the Great Basin in Utah, this species is native only to the eastern and southern parts of Bonneville basin in the rivers draining into Great Salt Lake (Bear, Logan, and Weber), into Utah Lake (Provo River), and into the Sevier River system (Beaver and Sevier rivers and their tributaries). It occurs locally in the upper part of the Snake River, Wyoming and in Little Wood River, Idaho. It was not taken in the Snake River until 1934 and may have been introduced. It has been introduced into the Colorado River system, notably Strawberry Reservoir and Price River, Utah.

Description

The trim, gradually tapering, silvery body has very small scales, about 75 to 85 in the lateral series, and rounded dorsal and anal fins. Both dorsal and anal fins typically have 8 rays, which readily distinguishes the leatherside chub from most other minnows. The pharyngeal teeth are in 2 rows and typically number 2, 4-4, 2. In Great Basin populations the dorsal fin originates behind the insertion of the pelvic fins. The skin has a leathery texture, from which the fish derives its name.

Males have orange to red on the axils of the paired fins, on the base of the anal fin, and on the lower lobe of the caudal fin. There is a golden-red speck at the upper end of the gill opening and also between the eye and the upper jaw. The body is bluish above and silvery below in both sexes (Sigler and Miller 1963).

Size and Longevity

The average length reached is from 3 to 5 inches, with a maximum length of about 6 inches. It probably lives no more than 5 years.

Limiting Factors

Fish, other predators, and habitat degradation are probably the only enemies of the leatherside chub. Where this practice is legal, it may be heavily seined for bait.

Food and Feeding

Food habits of this species have not been studied, but based on the ecology of the water it inhabits, it probably feeds on small drift organisms, algae, and aquatic insects.

Breeding Habits

This species probably spawns from June to August in waters ranging in temperature from 60° to 68° F. It probably does not build a nest or protect its eggs or young.

Habitat

The leatherside chub typically seeks cool to cold creeks and rivers. Adults live in either pools or riffles; young seek brush areas or quiet pockets near shore. The water may be clear to slightly turbid or occasionally muddy. The bottom in areas typically inhabited includes gravel, sometimes exclusively, but there may also be sand, rubble, stones, boulders, or silt. It is an inhabitant of rivers as well as creeks, in water temperatures ranging from 50° to 74° F, usually 60° to 68° F. The current is typically moderate, varying from slight to swift. The vegetation may be dense but is more frequently sparse, sometimes absent, and may consist primarily of algae and pondweeds. It generally frequents waters 2 to 3 feet deep or less (Sigler and Miller 1963).

Preservation of Species

At one time, the seining and selling of leatherside chub for bait was a drain on the population. Since the use of live minnows as bait has been outlawed over much of its range, the only enemies it has are predatory animals. Rapid fluctuations in water levels should, if possible, be avoided.

Arroyo chub
Gila orcutti **(Eigenmann and Eigenmann)**

Importance

The arroyo chub is a native western minnow, although not native to the Great Basin. As a member of the unique fauna of the western United States, it deserves special consideration.

Range

The arroyo chub is native to the streams of the Los Angeles plain, the upper Santa Clara River system, and the San Luis Rey and Santa Margarita river systems of San Diego County, California. It has been introduced into the Santa Inez system in California and the Mojave River system of the Great Basin (Lee et al. 1980).

Description

Coloration is olive green on the back and white on the belly with a dull gray lateral band on the sides. The arroyo chub has 8 dorsal rays and 7 anal fin rays. The lateral line series contains 48 to 62 scales. The lateral line reaches the caudal peduncle but is not decurved. This small, chunky minnow has a small mouth and large eyes (Hubbs and Miller 1942).

Size and Longevity

Age and growth data are not available for this species. Moyle (1976) reports the usual size is less than 5 inches but it may occasionally be nearly 12.

Limiting Factors

The arroyo chub is subject to predation and the effects of expanding human populations. It has been reduced in many of its native streams but is still common. Hybridization with both the Mojave tui chub and the California roach takes place (Hubbs and Miller 1942).

Food and Feeding

Arroyo chub feeds heavily on algae, crustaceans, and other aquatic invertebrates, including snails. Because of availability, diet in spring is more varied than in winter (Moyle 1976).

Breeding Habits

Breeding takes place in pools in April and May (Lee et al. 1980).

Habitat

Prior to the white man's settlement of the native range of the arroyo chub, it inhabited muddy, torrential streams in the winter and clear, intermittent brooks in the summer. It prefers the slower-moving segments of streams with bottoms of sand or mud. The arroyo chub had adapted to warm, fluctuating streams of the Los Angeles plain prior to the white man's disruption of these ecosystems (Greenfield and Deckert 1973).

Preservation of Species

Populations of arroyo chub have been affected by human population growth within its native range. Moyle (1976) states serious consideration should be given to managing stream sections specifically for the chub and other native fishes in the areas in which it occurs, including the elimination of predatory species such as green sunfish and largemouth bass. Conversely, introductions of this species into waters with wild populations of Mojave tui chub have led to the Mojave tui chub's extirpation from its native Mojave River. Further introduction of arroyo chub in the Great Basin should be discouraged.

Pahranagat roundtail chub
Gila robusta jordani Tanner

Importance

The Pahranagat roundtail chub is listed by the U.S. Fish and Wildlife Service as endangered. Its importance is due to its uniqueness and its existence as a natural history entity that has evolved over thousands of years in a specialized habitat. This subspecies is the most endangered fish in the Great Basin. Fewer than forty adults exist in the only known population.

Range

The range of the Pahranagat roundtail chub is extremely restricted. It occurs in a very small area in the outflow of Ash Springs, eastern Nevada. It was first found in Hiko Springs, Nevada, on Mrs. Wipple's ranch in May 1949 (Hardy 1980; La Rivers 1962).

Description

The Pahranagat roundtail chub is olive green on the head and back with silvery sides in winter. It is more active and streamlined than its associates. It has a moderately forked caudal fin with slightly rounded edges. There is a complete lateral line. A single dorsal fin has approximately 9 rays; the anal fin also has 9 rays. Dark blotches appear on the sides, mostly above the lateral line. The type specimen description is as follows: ". . . body somewhat elongate, more robust than *Gila elegans*, back only slightly elevated and head depressed; proximal portions of the fins are whitish and may turn orange in preservative. The scales number 89 to 94 in the lateral series, 26 to 27 above and 13 to 14 scales below the lateral line. The young have a silvery color when preserved in alcohol" (Tanner 1950).

Size and Longevity

The type specimen of Tanner was 6.25 inches long (Tanner 1950). It probably lives 3 to 5 years.

Limiting Factors

The head pool of Ash Springs is substantially higher than the bed of the White River, preventing contamination of Ash Springs' fish by individuals from Crystal Springs or the river in floods (Williams and Wilde 1981).

The introduction of exotic species, particularly the Oriental snail, are implicated in the decline of this native fish, as are predation, parasitism, and competition for food and space (Hardy 1982). Locally it is sometimes called trout and will take a baited hook, but it is scarce and Tanner (1950) presumed it would become extinct (see chapter 4).

Food and Feeding

Under controlled conditions aquatic insect larvae were exposed to adult chubs, but none were ingested (Hardy 1982). Only on one occasion was an invertebrate taken and that was an adult aquatic dipteran. In general, both adult and larval insects, whether aquatic or terrestrial, were ignored. Algae, on the other hand, were taken readily on all occasions, with *Spirogyra* preferred over other species. Data for other subspecies of *Gila robusta* indicate filamentous algae comprise as much as 90 percent of the diet. La Rivers (1962) indicates it may also feed on associated springfishes.

Breeding Habits

Adult chubs move upstream to spawn in February and March, and this may coincide with the time of year when ambient water temperatures in the system of Ash Springs are their lowest. Spawning behavior is similar to other *Gila* species.

Habitat

Hardy (1982) found adult Pahranagat roundtail chub in only a single microhabitat in his Ash Springs, Nevada study area. This microhabitat consists of a large pool with overhead cover adjacent to a deeply undercut bank. Maximum depth is about 8 feet and the average a little over 4 feet. The pool area is 16 feet long by 10 feet wide, with a firm sand bottom. Maximum velocity is 0.6 foot per second. Young chubs utilize runs with an average depth of less than 2 feet, but are common in water to depths of 7.5 feet. Substrates where juvenile chubs are present vary from soft detrital mud to firm sand. Most often overhanging banks and submerged vegetation are utilized as cover. Young avoid the more open areas of the stream. Smaller fish, about 0.8 inch long, school with speckled dace in the deeper portions of the stream. No young chubs are in the shallow, quiet water where other fish reached their maximum densities. Hardy's (1982) work indicates this subspecies prefers deep, slow runs and pools. Temperature may be an important limiting factor for the Pahranagat roundtail chub within the Ash Springs system. This subspecies, and closely related forms, has been collected at temperatures ranging from 59° to 86° F, but it is most often collected at temperatures below 77° F. Additional specimens obtained from Crystal Springs in April 1950 indicate this fish is very active and hard to catch.

Preservation of Species

This subspecies has evolved in a relatively stable environment (in terms of temperature and water level) with little direct or indirect competition. Modification of the habitat and introduction of non-native fish (or other organisms) threaten its continued existence through predation, parasitism, and competition for food and space. Preservation will require the reversal of these trends and future assurance of a stable habitat with no competitors, predators, disease, or parasites (see chapter 4).

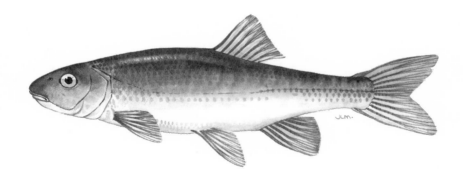

California roach
Hesperoleucus symmetricus **(Baird and Girard)**

Importance

The California roach is a native western species, abundant in intermittent streams of central California. It probably provides some forage for piscivorous species.

Range

California roach is found throughout the Sacramento–San Joaquin drainage system, including the Pit River and Goose Lake (Moyle 1976; Coombs, Bond, and Drohan 1979). Populations in the Cuyama River, San Luis Obispo and Santa Barbara counties, California may be the result of a bait-bucket introduction or earlier natural "stream capture" (Moyle 1976). Coombs, Bond, and Drohan (1979) report it in the Warner Valley, Oregon in the Great Basin. It is not considered native to the Great Basin.

Description

The California roach's body color is two-tone: the upper half is usually dark, dusky gray to steel blue, while the lower half is dull but silvery. Red-orange blotches appear on the chin, operculum, and at the bases of the paired and anal fins during the breeding season. The California roach is a small, chunky-bodied fish. A relatively large head and large eyes contrast with a small mouth, which is slanted downward. The single dorsal fin is short with 7 to 10 rays; the anal fin has 6 to 9 rays. Scales are small, numbering 47 to 63 in the lateral series (Moyle 1976).

Size and Longevity

California roach grow rapidly in summer when food is abundant. Growth is highly variable between California populations, presumably in response to food availability. Yearly size in inches was 1.7, 2.8, and 3.5 for specimens from California populations. The oldest specimen collected was 5 years (Fry 1936).

Limiting Factors

The roach is preyed upon by piscivorous fish, particularly green sunfish, and it hybridizes with hitch and arroyo chub. Roach has been adversely impacted by barriers to migration and the introduction of green sunfish over portions of its range.

Food and Feeding

California roach is primarily a bottom feeder, picking up detritus and debris along with food items. It also takes aquatic insects, crustaceans, and terrestrial insects at the surface. Filamentous algae are the main food but aquatic insects and crustaceans make up 25 to 30 percent of total food volume. Crustaceans are important food items for small roach (Fite 1973).

Breeding Habits

March through June is the principal spawning period but it has been observed spawning in late July in the Russian River, California. Fish move from pools into shallow, flowing water where small rocks cover the bottom. The roach spawns in schools. Each female lays a few eggs at a time and between 250 and 900 eggs are laid by an average female. Eggs are laid in crevices between rocks and then fertilized. The adhesive eggs stick to rocks as they are deposited. Eggs hatch in 2 to 3 days. Fry remain in the crevices until they grow large enough to swim actively (Barnes 1957).

Habitat

California roach survives in certain California waters because it can tolerate conditions that other native species cannot. Intermittent streams that are tributary to larger streams are typical habitat. Populations are found in warm, alkaline streams and in coastal streams. Large numbers occur in pools left when foothill streams dry in the summer. These pools may have temperatures to 95° F and low dissolved oxygen levels. Streams heavily polluted by sewage may also support large populations (Murphy 1948b).

Preservation of Species

Preservation of habitat and access to spawning areas are required to sustain this species. Introduction of green sunfish or other predatory species in waters where roach exist adversely affects them.

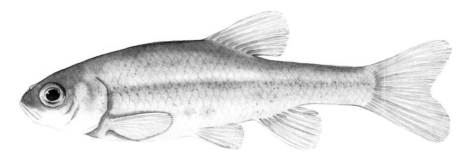

Least chub
Iotichthys phlegethontis (Cope)

Importance

The least chub is of value as a natural predator of mosquito larvae and if abundant it might provide forage for other fish. However, its short life span and low annual reproductive rate indicate its value as forage is minimal. Perhaps most important of all, it should be preserved because it is an interesting element of the native fauna. It is listed as threatened by the U.S. Fish and Wildlife Service.

Range

The original range of the least chub was in the Bonneville basin, in streams near Salt Lake City, Utah, and in freshwater ponds and swamps around Great Salt Lake. It was also present in Utah Lake, Beaver River, Paraowan Creek, Clear Creek, and Provo River. The first specimens to be taken from Millard County, western Utah were from springs in Snake Valley by C. L., L. C., and E. L. Hubbs in 1942. It was first collected in Leland Harris Spring, Juab County, Utah by R. R. Miller in 1970. Its present range may now be limited to Snake Valley, western Utah (Sigler and Workman 1975). Recent stockings have not been evaluated.

Description

The extremely small size, very oblique mouth, large scales (34 to 38 along the side), and absence of a lateral line (rarely with 1 or 2 pored scales) readily distinguish the least chub. The males are olive green above and steel blue on the sides, with a golden stripe behind the upper end of the gill opening. In the brightest males, the lower sides are golden, becoming reddish dark-gold, in a band running from the bright red pectoral fin axis to above the front of the anal fin. The fins are lemon amber and sometimes the paired fins are bright golden-amber. In some males the entire sides are suffused with brassy yellow. The females and young are pale olive above and silvery on the sides and have watery-white fins. The eyes of females are silvery, with only a little gold rather than definitely golden as in the males. The pharyngeal teeth are in 2 rows, 2, 5-4, 2. The dorsal fin lies behind the insertion of the pelvic fins. The dorsal fin rays number 8, or rarely 9, and the anal rays number 8 (Sigler and Miller 1963).

Size and Longevity

The least chub is short-lived and slow-growing. In 3 separate studies totaling 112 fish from the Leland Harris Spring area, Juab County, Utah, the total length in inches for fish age 1 to 4 at the end of each year was 0.7, 1.3, 2.0, and 3.0. Only 2 fish reached a length of 3 inches and 4 years of age. In another study totaling 207 fish from the same area, the total length in inches at the end of each year was 1.0, 1.4, and 1.6. Only 6 percent (12) of these fish reached age 3. A least chub 1.3 inches long weighs 0.02 ounce (Sigler and Workman 1975; Workman, Sigler, and Workman 1976; Crawford 1979).

Limiting Factors

The most serious hazard the least chub faces today is predation by introduced species such as game fishes, Utah chub, and bullfrog. Trampling and organic pollution by livestock in the vicinity of Leland Harris Spring is a problem to fish in this area. Various fish-eating ducks and gulls also prey on the least chub during part of the year. Additional adverse effects occur from hybridization with Utah chub and speckled dace. These species have similar food habits that potentially could adversely affect least chub survival. In the spring area the least chub is apparently able to avoid or survive the hazards of cold weather. Habitat degradation and predation by exotic fish probably caused the elimination of the least chub over much of its range.

Food and Feeding

The most common food of the least chub is algae, diatomaceous material, and midge adults, larvae, and pupae. It also eats copepods, ostracods, and whatever other invertebrates are available. One was observed swimming up to a clump of algae, grabbing a mouthful, and thrashing about until the algae were freed.

Breeding Habits

The least chub spawns in the spring when water temperatures

reach 60° F. Both males and females mature at age 1 when they are slightly over 1 inch long. Spawning occurs in vegetation, primarily algae, from April to July. The number of eggs produced ranges from less than 300 to over 2,700. Mature eggs range in diameter from 0.03 to 0.05 inch. The eggs are adhesive and heavier than water; they sink until they strike some object to which they attach. The eggs hatch in a little over two days at 72° F. The female spawns intermittently throughout the late spring and early summer (Crawford 1979).

The newly hatched least chub lives on its yolk sac for 3 to 4 days. After that it begins to feed. The initiation of least chub spawning is a function of both temperature and sunlight. Least chub held in an aquarium at a constant photoperiod and temperature did not show a tendency to spawn until they were exposed to sunlight (Crawford 1979).

Habitat

The least chub originally was an inhabitant of slow rivers, clear creeks, springs, ponds, and swamps that at times were quite alkaline. The Leland Harris Spring area, where the chub is present today, is moderately heavily vegetated with algae, chara, duck weed, and watercress with bulrushes, cattails, and sedges at the margin. Other plants include rabbitfoot grass, water parsnip, muskgrass, wire rush, and motherwort. The pH of the water in Leland Harris Spring in 1975 was 8.0, oxygen 4.5 ppm, total hardness 120 ppm, calcium hardness 63 ppm, and alkalinity 150 ppm. The bottom material in least chub habitat may consist of hard to very soft clay, mud, soft mud, or peat. Water temperatures range from 55° to 75° F (some shallow areas in winter are below freezing). The Leland Harris Spring area varies in depth from a few inches to 10 or more feet. Some of the area is covered by a floating bog with openings only 3 to 4 feet across. The hazard of walking over this area is demonstrated by the number of cattle skeletons scattered around two particularly attractive but lethal waterholes.

Preservation of Species

The primary need of the least chub today is protection from predators. It is not possible to protect it from birds, mammals, or amphibians, but there are areas where all introduced fish could be removed. Probably the most serious type of habitat degradation would be a lowering of the water table. Hybridization with Utah chub and speckled dace is also occurring. Similar food habits of all three species and hybridization have adverse effects on least chub populations.

The Bureau of Land Management controls most of the property surrounding least chub habitat in western Utah (that is, Leland Harris Spring). These areas are managed for the least chub under its designated "sensitive species" status. No physical modification or other potentially adverse actions can occur without agency review.

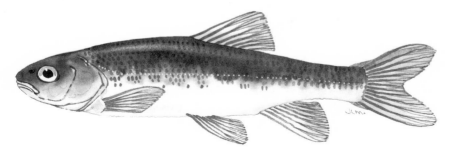

White River spinedace
***Lepidomeda albivallis* Miller and Hubbs**

Importance

The White River spinedace was once used to some extent as a bait fish, but this was discouraged by R. R. Miller in 1952 because of its restricted range and interest to science as a natural history entity (La Rivers 1962). It is listed as threatened by the U.S. Fish and Wildlife Service.

Range

It occurs in the upper pluvial White River of southeastern Nevada (Miller and Hubbs 1960; La Rivers 1962). It has been extirpated in Preston Big Spring near the headwaters of the White River, Nevada (Deacon and Williams 1984).

Description

The body is bright brassy green to olive above, brassy over bright silvery on the sides, and silvery-white on the belly. There may be sooty splashes on the sides. The dorsal and caudal fins are pale olive brown to pinkish-brown, with the rays often deep olive and the clear interradial membranes faintly rosy. The pectorals are yellowish with orange-red axils and the anal and pelvic fin membranes are bright red-orange but otherwise white. Some coppery-red to red color occurs on the side of the face at the upper end of the gill opening on the preorbital just behind the mouth and along the upper arm of the opercle. The lateral line is more strongly gilt than adjacent parts of the body. The single dorsal fin has 7 rays, the anal fin 8 rays. The pelvic fins usually have 7 rays. Lateral series scales number 79 to 92 (La Rivers 1962).

Size and Longevity

Largest size appears to be about 4 inches. Specific growth data is not known. It probably lives 3 to 5 years.

Limiting Factors

The White River spinedace is now confined to one area of cool springs (65° to 71° F) in the upper White River drainage. Disruption of this area could result in extirpation of this species (see chapter 4).

Food and Feeding

It is probably an opportunistic omnivore. Specific feeding habits and preference data have not been published. Constantz (1981) believes all spring-feeding species are omnivorous and that specialized feeders cannot persist in desert springs.

Breeding Habits

Like most cyprinids, it probably broadcasts large numbers of eggs that are fertilized and mature in the substrate or on vegetation with no parental care provided.

Habitat

It occurs in one cool (65° to 71° F) spring area and its overflow in the upper portions of the pluvial White River, Nevada. The bottom of the area is mostly gravel and sand with some mud. Swift to moderate currents prevail in much of the habitat. Watercress, a fine-leafed *Potamogeton*, and rushes are common plants (La Rivers 1962).

Preservation of Species

Any disturbance of the White River spinedace's habitat or an introduction of exotic fish will endanger it (see chapter 4).

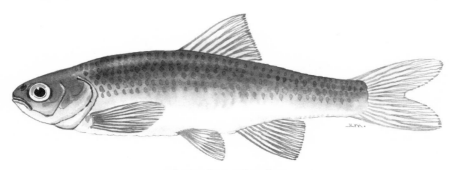

Big Spring spinedace
Lepidomeda mollispinis pratensis Miller and Hubbs

Importance

The Big Spring spinedace was first used as a bait fish in the early 1900s. It was once an intermediate link in the food web. It is now important from an ecological standpoint and is listed by the U.S. Fish and Wildlife Service as endangered.

Range

This subspecies was once present in Big Spring and the spring-fed marsh northeast of Panaca, Lincoln County, Nevada. La Rivers (1962) reported it as extinct following a collection in 1959. Deacon and Williams (1984) report it in Meadow Valley Wash in the course of the pluvial Carpenter River.

Description

The body is bright silvery. The axils of the paired fins may be lemon to orange as is the basal part of the anal fin and the upper edge of the shoulder girdle above the mouth. The single dorsal fin has 8 rays, the anal fin 9, and the pelvic fins 7. Scales in the lateral series number 82 to 90 (La Rivers 1962; Miller and Hubbs 1960).

Size and Longevity

Its largest size appears to be about 3.5 inches (La Rivers 1962). No age and growth data are available for this subspecies.

Limiting Factors

The population of Big Spring spinedace is currently limited by acceptable habitat. The hazards of water development and introduction of exotics pose serious problems for the continued existence of this subspecies (see chapter 4).

Food and Feeding

No data are available on feeding habits or preference. Big Spring spinedace probably feeds on algae, aquatic insects, and other invertebrates; that is, it is an opportunistic omnivore.

Habitat

The natural channel of Meadow Valley Wash near Ash Springs is generally 1 to 3 feet wide and as deep as 2 feet. It contains watercress, *Potamogeton*, and rushes. The bottom is firm to soft clay with some gravel. Current is slight and water temperature is 84° F in July (La Rivers 1962). Original habitat has been severely modified by man's development.

Preservation of Species

This subspecies has been severely impacted by both water course alterations and by the introduction of exotic species, particularly common carp and mosquitofish. This subspecies is now restricted to a single habitat area and could easily be extirpated. Measures to insure its protection and possible reestablishment in previous habitat should be investigated.

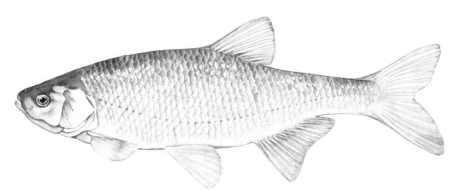

Golden shiner
Notemigonus crysoleucas (Mitchill)

Importance

The golden shiner is a valued forage fish over most of its native range; it has been introduced extensively elsewhere as a forage and bait fish. It lends itself well to pond culture and is probably the most widely cultivated bait minnow in the United States. One reason for this is its rapid growth; it achieves a moderately large size quickly. Bait dealers can, by selecting the proper gear, market the desired size of fish. The golden shiner is a good indicator of pollution or habitat modification when it markedly outnumbers other species at a site (Smith 1979). It is occasionally used as an ornamental fish.

Range

The original range of this species is eastern North America, from the Maritime Provinces south to Florida, west to the Dakotas and Texas, and north to Quebec. It is absent from Newfoundland and provinces west of Saskatchewan. Golden shiner has been introduced in Utah Lake, Utah in the Great Basin and in Amargosa River, Nye County, Nevada. It has been reported in the Malheur Lake basin, Oregon.

Description

The golden shiner has a green to olive back with a faint dusky stripe along the midline. The sides are golden or silver, the belly silvery or white. The fins are without markings. Young, from clear waters, may have a definite dusky stripe along midside. This deep-bodied, slab-sided minnow has a sickle-shaped outer margin on the anal fin and a strong downward curve in the lateral line. It has a fleshy, scaleless keel along the midline of the belly from the anus forward to the base of the pelvic fins. The mouth is slightly upturned and small; the eye does not reach the jaw. There are no barbels. Dorsal rays number 8, anal fin rays 11 to 15. The lateral series has 45 to 54 scales (Pflieger 1975).

Size and Longevity

This species is one of the larger of the small cyprinids. Becker (1983) notes Wisconsin golden shiners age 1 to 7 have yearly lengths in inches of 1.1, 2.3, 3.3, 5.0, 6.1, 6.8, and 7.3. Females grow more rapidly and attain a larger size than males. Golden shiners as large as 8 to 10 inches are occasionally taken on hook and line. Moyle (1976) states that in some California ponds golden shiners reach a length of 3 inches in 1 year and 5.5 inches in 2 years. At higher elevations they are less than 2 inches long at the end of the first year. Carlander (1969) states that the maximum age is 9 years.

Limiting Factors

The golden shiner is preyed upon heavily by game fish. According to Smith (1979), its decline in western and northern Illinois is probably due to the draining of marshes and swales. It has also been affected by the draining of flood plain lakes and swamps along rivers. It has great ecological tolerance and can persist in badly polluted and highly turbid streams and swamps where water temperatures are high.

Food and Feeding

Zooplankton, particularly cladocerans like *Daphnia*, seem to be the most important food for golden shiners of all sizes. In Clear Lake, California, 95 percent of the golden shiner diet is zooplankton. Next in importance are small flying insects taken at the surface. It occasionally takes small fish, mollusks, and aquatic insect larvae. When animal food is in short supply it may feed on filamentous algae. According to Becker (1983), it is a sight-feeder.

Breeding Habits

The golden shiner may spawn as early as March or as late as August. The beginning and cessation of spawning are determined by temperature. Spawning generally occurs early in the morning. It matures at age 1 or 2 and probably spawns each year thereafter. In California it begins spawning at 68° F, although it has spawned at temperatures as low as 59° F (Moyle 1976). In Missouri ponds, it spawns from late April to early June, beginning when water temperatures rise to 70° F and ceasing when temperatures exceed 80° F. Spawning may be resumed in mid or late summer if water temperature is sufficiently reduced by cold rain (Pflieger 1975). This is in agreement with Wisconsin studies (Becker 1983). It does not prepare a nest or guard its eggs or young. The adhesive eggs are scattered over filamentous algae or higher plants. At times it spawns over the nests of largemouth bass or green sunfish. Eggs hatch in about 4 days and the young form schools just below the surface near shore.

Habitat

Golden shiner prefers quiet waters and rarely occurs in streams with a detectable current. The largest populations are in sloughs, ponds, lakes, impoundments, quiet pools of low gradient streams, and ditches. It thrives best in clear waters with dense mats of vegetation, but will tolerate high turbidity and pollution and oxygen as low as 1.4 ppm (Becker 1983).

Preservation of Species

Cultivation as a bait fish alone assures the preservation of this species. It is also widely distributed in the wild. In some instances the golden shiner is a problem species in mountain lakes where it has been introduced by fishermen and competes with trout. Eradication programs are common in California (Peter Moyle, personal communication, 1983).

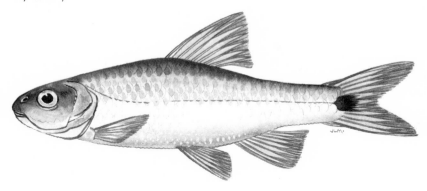

Spottail shiner
Notropis hudsonius **(Clinton)**

Importance

The spottail shiner is an important bait fish over much of its native range. It is the preferred bait fish for walleyes in Iowa. It is also an important link in the food web for larger fish.

Range

One of the most wide-ranging North American fishes, the spottail shiner occurs from Georgia north through Canada and from the upper Mississippi River basin to northwest Canada (Lee et al. 1980). In the Great Basin it has been stocked into Willard Bay Reservoir, Utah as a forage species.

Description

The overall coloration is silvery with yellowish or golden overtones. The back is pale green to olive and the sides silvery. The belly is silvery-white. The fins are mainly clear except for the black spot at the base of the caudal fin. This is most conspicuous in small fish and fades in larger specimens (Scott and Crossman 1973).

The body is stout and laterally compressed. The head is bluntly triangular and the eye relatively large. The snout is rounded and distinctly overhangs the mouth, which is subterminal. The single dorsal fin has its origin over the origin of the pelvic fins and has 8 rays. The caudal fin is distinctly forked. The anal fin has 8 or rarely 9 rays. Pharyngeal teeth are variable, but generally are 2, 4-4, 2. The pelvic fins are small with 7 or rarely 8 rays and the pectoral fins are of moderate size with 12 to 17 rays. The scales are cycloid, numbering 36 to 41 in the lateral series. The lateral line is complete (Becker 1983; Smith 1979).

Size and Longevity

Spottails over 5 inches in length are unusual, except in Lake Erie populations. It is a relatively fast-growing but short-lived species. Females are generally larger than males. Total length of Wisconsin spottail shiners age 1 to 5 in inches is 2.5, 3.8, 4.3, 4.7, and 4.9 (Becker 1983; Trautman 1981).

Limiting Factors

Spottail shiners may be parasitized by a variety of organisms, including trematodes, cestodes, nematodes, and protozoans. It is preyed upon by piscivorous fish, including larger spottail shiners.

Food and Feeding

This species feeds on many organisms, including masses of filamentous algae, aquatic insect larvae (especially chironomids and mayflies), crustaceans, aquatic insects, and its own eggs (Smith 1979). It tends to shift from small invertebrates to large insects as it increases in size (Becker 1983).

Breeding Habits

The spottail shiner spawns at age 1 in spring and early summer throughout its range but the timing varies highly with latitude and seasonal weather. It spawns over gravelly riffles in 3 to 15 feet of water. Spottail shiner may spawn near the mouths of tributary streams or along the sandy shoals of lake shores. Ripe females contain 100 to 4,600 yellowish eggs, the number varying with adult size. Spawning occurs in closely packed groups, with no evidence of nesting (Becker 1983; Smith 1979).

Habitat

The spottail shiner is a large lake and river fish, but it also occurs in smaller lakes and streams. Large schools occur near the shoreline with sparse to moderate vegetation in Lake Michigan. It is generally in moderately shallow water or shoal areas, but has been reported at depths of 150 feet (Becker 1983; Smith 1979).

Preservation of Species

Its abundance and wide distribution within its native range indicate that no special preservation requirements are necessary, although its numbers have been depleted by seining in some areas. In the Great Basin it has been stocked as a forage species in a 10,000-acre reservoir. The spottail's future here depends on its ability to reproduce and avoid excessive predation.

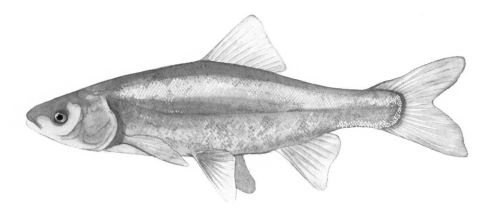

Sacramento blackfish
Orthodon microlepidotus (Ayres)

Importance

Fifty to one hundred thousand pounds of Sacramento blackfish, most of which are sold in the Oriental fish markets in San Francisco, are taken annually from Clear Lake and other California waters. It is not generally useful as a forage fish because of its rapid growth, but does contribute to the forage base for some piscivorous species. Because of its herbivorous nature, it is an important entity in the food web, converting plant production to a form usable by piscivorous fish (Moyle 1976). It has considerable potential for commercial aquaculture.

Range

The Sacramento blackfish is native to the main Sacramento–San Joaquin drainage system, Clear Lake, California and the Pajaro and Salinas rivers, California. It has been introduced into reservoirs on the Carmel River, California. In the Great Basin it has been introduced in Lahontan Reservoir on the Carson River, western Nevada, where it is abundant (Nevada Wildlife Department 1982). It was also introduced near Reno, Nevada but did not survive (La Rivers 1962).

Description

The Sacramento blackfish is generally silvery-gray but larger fish may become darker, especially on the back. It has a dull, olivaceous sheen. It can be easily recognized by the large number of tiny scales (numbering up to 110) in the lateral series. The lateral line is curved gently downward. The Sacramento blackfish has a cone-shaped head with a flat, sloping forehead, round elongate body, a small eye, and a wide, slightly upturned mouth. The single dorsal fin has 9 to 11 rays. The anal fin has 8 to 9 rays and is smaller than the dorsal fin. The pectoral fins are rounded and slightly exceed the pelvic fins in height. The caudal fin is large and deeply forked (La Rivers 1962).

Size and Longevity

The Sacramento blackfish is a rapid-growing but relatively short-lived fish. It lives about 5 years. In Clear Lake, California it reaches 4 inches and 1 ounce the first year, 10 inches the second year, and 13 inches the third year. During the third year, growth differences between male and female become evident, the female being larger by about 1 inch. The longest fish recorded in Clear Lake was almost 20 inches and the heaviest was 3.3 pounds (Murphy 1950).

Limiting Factors

The Sacramento blackfish is fed on by piscivorous species in some habitats. It is somewhat less abundant now than previously in California, but is prospering in Lahontan Reservoir, Nevada. It has hybridized with the tui chub (La Rivers 1962). There is a heavy post-spawning mortality.

Food and Feeding

Its food habits are unusual for a North American cyprinid. It is primarily a filter feeder on planktonic algae and zooplankton, including rotifers, cladocerans, copepods, and suspended detritus. It is not selective in its feeding, but eats plankton in roughly the proportion of occurrence. The presence of sand and other bottom materials in the food indicates bottom feeding. Young are evidently more selective feeders than adults, feeding more on the bottom and on invertebrates (Murphy 1950).

Breeding Habits

Sexual maturity occurs at age 2 or 3. The Sacramento blackfish spawns generally in lakes from April to July at temperatures between 54° and 75° F. Spawning takes place in warm, shallow areas with heavy growths of aquatic plants. Males follow females closely, fertilizing the adhesive eggs as the females lay them. A 17-inch female may produce 350,000 eggs. Spawning is evidently physiologically difficult for this species, as evidenced by spawning checks on the scales and because most fish die after their second spawning (Murphy 1950).

Habitat

This species is most abundant in warm, shallow waters where current is slow or absent. It tolerates moderately high levels of turbidity and total dissolved solids. Young occur in schools close to shore and adults school in open water away from shore.

Preservation of Species

The Sacramento blackfish's tolerance of changing environmental conditions, its ability to withstand high turbidity and total dissolved solids, as well as its general abundance throughout its range preclude the necessity for any special preservation considerations other than commercial overfishing.

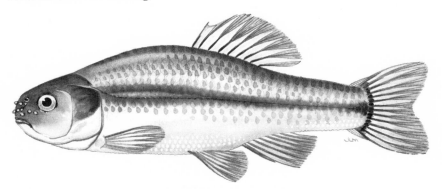

Fathead minnow
***Pimephales promelas* Rafinesque**

Importance

The fathead minnow is important mainly as a forage fish. In its native range it is propagated in hatchery ponds as bait and as food for smallmouth bass and other game fish. Adults are placed in ponds in the spring so that their young hatch throughout the summer and provide feed for young game fish. It provides an important link in the food web, converting algae, organic detritus, and planktonic organisms to food for other fishes. It is used extensively as a bait fish where this practice is legal (Sigler and Miller 1963).

Range

This species occurs naturally through most of central North America, from Louisiana and Chihuahua, Mexico north to Great Slave Lake, Canada and from New Brunswick to Alberta, Canada on the west (Scott and Crossman 1973). In the Great Basin it was stocked in Utah Lake, Utah in 1969 where it is considered rare (Heckmann, Thompson, and White 1981). It is established in the western states of Arizona, California, and New Mexico.

Description

The fathead minnow is generally dark overall, olive green or brown above and white below. The sides have brassy or silvery reflections. The young and nonbreeding adults are lighter in color and exhibit a distinct lateral band that extends from the head to the caudal peduncle. Breeding males are very dark, including the fins. Nuptial tubercles on breeding males are light in color and the spongy pad on the back is slate blue or gray (Sigler and Miller 1963).

The body is short, thick-set, and laterally compressed, often with a pronounced belly. The head is rather sharply triangular. The mouth is small and nearly terminal, the snout protruding slightly beyond the upper lip. The single dorsal fin has 8 rays and begins over the pelvic fin origin. The caudal fin is shallowly forked; the anal fin has 7 rays. The pelvics are small, with 8 rays originating below the dorsal origin and extending to the anal fin origin in the male but not in the female. The pectoral fins are short with usually 15 or 16 rays. The cycloid scales, numbering 41 to 54 in the lateral series, are crowded before the dorsal fin and are conspicuously smaller than elsewhere on the body. The lateral line is complete except for 3 or 4 pored scales. The lining of the body cavity is dusky or black (Scott and Crossman 1973; Sigler and Miller 1963).

Size and Longevity

In warm waters with abundant food supplies, growth is rapid. Adult sizes of 2 to 2.8 inches are reported for Canadian populations. A maximum size of 3.5 inches is reported for Utah populations. It is a short-lived species, rarely reaching more than 2 years of age. In all populations, the male grows faster than the female and achieves a larger size (Scott and Crossman 1973; Sigler and Miller 1963). This is typical of species in which the male guards the eggs and sometimes the young.

Limiting Factors

Fathead minnow is parasitized by protozoans, trematodes, cestodes, nematodes, and crustaceans and is preyed upon by various piscivorous fish and birds.

Food and Feeding

The principal food of the fathead minnow is probably algae. Other food includes organic detritus, bottom material, aquatic insect larvae, and zooplankton. The long intestine is indicative of a vegetative diet.

Breeding Habits

Spawning begins in May as water temperatures near 64° F and continues until August. The male selects a spawning site on the underside of a log or branch, large rock, board, or occasionally a lily pad in water depths of 2 to 3 feet. A female is sought and herded into position below the nest site, the male positioning himself on the left side of the female. After much circling, the female is nudged and lifted by the male's back until she lies on her side immediately below the selected substrate. The adhesive eggs are deposited, fertilized, and the female is driven off. The male aggressively guards the nest, driving off all small fish in the area. A male may seek out a number of females, the nest eventually containing eggs from several. The female also spawns with more than 1 male and produces up to 12,000 eggs. The male not only guards the nest but provides some care for the eggs during incubation. Eggs hatch in 4 to 6 days in temperatures of 77° F. Females may reach sexual maturity the following spring when they are 1 year old (Scott and Crossman 1973; Sigler and Miller 1963).

Habitat

The preferred habitats are varied, including sluggish brooks, lakes, bogs, ponds, and streams that may be clear or silty, cool or warm. In Iowa it is most abundant in ponds and lakes but avoids running water (Harlan and Speaker 1956).

Preservation of Species

Generally, its abundance and high productivity preclude the necessity for special preservation considerations. However, heavy predation on a limited population may endanger it.

Northern squawfish
Ptychocheilus oregonensis (Richardson)

Importance

Although edible, the flesh of squawfish is bony, reducing its quality in the eyes of many. Potentially, it is a fair game fish. Its predatory habits are important management considerations because it preys upon game species and may seriously impact hatchery-released salmon (Wydoski and Whitney 1979). Brown and Moyle (1981) believe that predation on salmonids by northern squawfish is not significant except in localized situations.

Range

This species occurs on the Pacific slope of western North America, in the Malheur Lake system of Oregon, the Columbia River system, and north in the Pacific slope drainages to the Nass River, British Columbia (Lee et al. 1980). It occurs in the Harney system of the Great Basin.

Description

The northern squawfish is dark green or green-brown above with lighter sides and a silvery or white belly. The male is colorful during spawning when the lower fins become yellow or yellow-orange. The body is elongate, somewhat laterally compressed and not deep. The head is moderately long and the snout is long. The mouth is large and terminal, extending to below the anterior margin of the eye. The single dorsal fin has 9 or sometimes 10 rays with its origin over or slightly behind the origin of the pelvic fins. The caudal is distinctly forked and has pointed lobes. The anal fin has 8 or seldom 9 rays. The pelvic fins are small, with 9 rays. The pectorals are short, with 15 or 16 rays. Small cycloid scales number 67 to 75 in the lateral series. The lateral line is complete (Scott and Crossman 1973).

Size and Longevity

The northern squawfish is a relatively slow-growing, long-lived species. A Canadian population had the following lengths in inches for fish age 1 through 11: 1.9, 3.9, 5.8, 7.8, 8.9, 10.8, 11.9, 13.6, 14.4, 15.2, and 16.2 (Clemens 1939). A maximum weight of 29 pounds has been reported. It may live 15 to 20 years.

Limiting Factors

This species is parasitized by trematodes, cestodes, nematodes, acanthocephalans, leeches, crustaceans, and mollusks. Its large size precludes most predation except at younger ages.

Food and Feeding

Young squawfish, 1 to 4 inches long, feed on insects but shift to fish at larger sizes. Very large squawfish feed on fish almost exclusively but may also eat crayfish. Male squawfish have been observed feeding on squawfish eggs (Patten and Rodman 1969).

Breeding Habits

Squawfish spawn from late May to July over gravelly shallows, generally along a lakeshore or in lakes near tributary streams. Sexual maturity occurs at about 6 years. It tends to gather in large numbers but builds no nest. A female may be accompanied by several males. The small, adhesive eggs are broadcast and fertilized and then sink to the bottom. The eggs may be greenish to pale orange. Females carry as many as 6,700 to 83,000 eggs but do not deposit them all at once. The eggs hatch in about 1 week at 65° F (Wydoski and Whitney 1979).

Habitat

The squawfish is typically a large river species, preferring the still waters of large pools and reservoirs. Young inhabit inshore waters in summer months, moving to deeper waters in fall. Older, larger fish tend to remain offshore. Temperature preferences appear to be 68° to 73° F. Tagging studies indicate it does not move great distances (Wydoski and Whitney 1979).

Preservation of Species

The large size and abundance probably preclude the necessity of special consideration. Where it is considered a management problem, squawfish numbers may be locally reduced through control methods (MacPhee and Ruelle 1969).

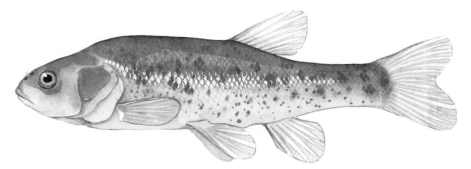

Relict dace
***Relictus solitarius* Hubbs and Miller**

Importance

The relict dace has been used for human food (like sardines) and as live bait for game fish, feed for various other animals, and mosquito control (Hubbs, Miller, and Hubbs 1974). Under natural conditions the relict dace is poorly suited as forage for game fish. It does not compete well with exotic species and, where they are stocked, a relict dace population will often be greatly reduced. Other uses of this species such as for aquarium fish and experimental animals have been attempted with somewhat limited success. Significance and value are difficult to define but are related to the fact that it is a unique species, contributing to both the diversity of life and the opportunity to study a life form that has been in existence in excess of one million years. It is the only surviving fish species from a large area of Pleistocene Lake Lahontan, remaining when this lake desiccated over the last ten thousand years.

The relict dace is currently listed as "of special concern" by the Endangered Species Committee of the American Fisheries Society. It has, however, recently been taken off the state of Nevada's protected list (Deacon et al. 1979; Vigg 1982).

Range

Hubbs, Miller, and Hubbs (1974) indicate that *Relictus* takes its place along with *Moapa* and *Eremichthys* among the distinctive endemic relict fishes that occupy limited areas of spring water within the Great Basin. It is somewhat less restricted in its distribution than the other two genera, being native throughout many of the basin bottom springs of Ruby and Butte valleys, Nevada and the pluvial drainages of lakes Franklin and Gale in the Goshute and Steptoe valleys, Nevada.

Description

Coloration in the relict dace is extremely variable. The general background color is dusky, with olive to brassy colors on the dorsal surface, the ventral surface being lighter and covered with interspersed melanophores. It is strongly speckled with brown or occasionally moss green. There are bright blue reflections apparent, sometimes with a tinge of violet. A narrow stripe of pearly or golden yellow occurs on the dorsal and ventral surfaces. The midsides are often silvery with reflections of brassy or violet color. The lower fins are often yellowish or lemon-colored and occasionally bright golden. Occasionally a completely golden fish is observed. The male has longer and wider fins with thicker rays than the female. Breeding males exhibit more extensive adult coloration at a smaller size than do females. The male develops a characteristic pattern of nuptial tubercles on his head and fins but not on the body.

The mouth is oblique and terminal and completely lacking in horny cutting edges. The lateral line originates above the opercle and rarely extends beyond the insertion of the dorsal fin. It is commonly disrupted. The 50 to 70 scales in the lateral series are rather small and are markedly irregular. The fins are small and strongly rounded; the pelvics are especially and uniquely paddlelike. The dorsal and pelvic fins are both placed far back on the body (Hubbs, Miller, and Hubbs 1974; Vigg 1982).

Hubbs, Miller, and Hubbs (1974) note that this dace provides an excellent example of modification that is, in part, a degeneration characterizing fishes, particularly cyprinids and cyprinodontids, that are confined to isolated springs in the Great Basin and elsewhere. These modifications include a body form adapted to mid-water swimming in quiet water, with more or less symmetrical curved dorsal or ventral contours of body and head. It is generally rather chubby, with a deep caudal peduncle and a terminal and rather large mouth suited for engulfing organisms living at various depths. The small, weak, rounded fins are adequate only for limited locomotion in quiet water. The barbels are reduced or obsolete. The lateral line and other sense organs are not critically needed in the absence of enemies. Scales tend to lose their orderly arrangement and color and may develop radii on all fields.

Size and Longevity

Size varies tremendously in different populations of relict dace. Vigg (1982) indicates that extremely variable environmental conditions may affect growth and size of fish in localized populations. Because of the constant temperature of many of the habitats for relict dace, normal aging techniques using scales may not be valid. Determination of age is therefore difficult. Relict dace probably reach an age of at least 5 years and possibly 7 or 8. The largest relict dace sampled by Vigg was 4.25 inches and weighed less than 0.5 ounce. In the warm environments typical of some populations, where relict dace is less influenced by cold winter air temperatures, it probably grows at almost a constant rate for most of the year.

Limiting Factors

Seasonal and artificial desiccation of habitats and other adverse environmental conditions, cannibalism, and predation by birds, mammals, insects, and parasites all affect relict dace. Introduction of diseases, competitors, and exotic predatory fish is detrimental.

Food and Feeding

Like many cyprinid species, relict dace is an opportunistic feeder, eating whatever is available and digestible. In a sample of 5 springs in 3 different valleys, Vigg (1982) found amphipods and gastropods were the most prevalent food items, constituting over 80 percent of the diet. Relict dace also eats insects, ostrocods, and leeches. In a laboratory environment it readily feeds on commercial dry feed and cultured *Daphnia* (Vigg 1982).

Breeding Habits

Little data exist on the reproductive biology of relict dace and spawning behavior is basically unknown. Hubbs, Miller, and Hubbs (1974) speculate that relict dace spawns on vegetation, since the mud-soft substrate in its habitat is typically anaerobic. Hubbs, Miller, and Hubbs conclude that (1) both sexes spawn first as yearlings, (2) the smallest yearlings reproduce in their second year of life, (3) many females reproduce when 2 or more years old, and (4) few males breed at an age older than 1 or 2. It is a very prolific fish and has a long breeding season, extending at least from late June to late September (Hubbs, Miller, and Hubbs 1974). Observation of some Nevada habitats indicates young are present at all times of the year, which supports the hypothesis that relict dace spawns over an extended period.

Habitat

Relict dace is found only in a relatively few, small thermal springs, creeks, and marsh areas in Nevada. Heavy growths of filamentous algae, rushes, and mosses are characteristic of these habitats. Watercress may be the most prevalent plant in undisturbed relict dace habitat (Vigg 1982). Dense aquatic vegetation is an important consideration for relict dace. It is extremely secretive (Hubbs, Miller, and Hubbs 1974) and is especially retiring during cold months. It is a mid-water swimmer and is seldom observed on the surface or the bottom. This may be in response to potential predators such as birds. When alarmed, it will dive into the soft mud substrate or submerged vegetation. When held in laboratory tanks, it spends most of its time hiding. Many of the habitats in which relict dace is present are supplied by thermal springs, providing a relatively constant year-round temperature. However, dace also exist in nonthermal springs and creeks as well as ponds and intermittent lakes and marshes. Vigg reports the maximum water temperature in relict dace habitat is 74° F.

Preservation of Species

Preservation of habitat without modification or alteration and maintenance of minimum water levels are necessary for this species' preservation. Special reserves may be required to ensure its continued existence. Also essential is the elimination of stocking of other fishes in reservoirs created for relict dace habitat. It can neither compete with nor adequately protect itself from large fish.

Longnose dace
***Rhinichthys cataractae* (Valenciennes)**

Importance

The longnose dace is important as a bait fish. Because of its wide distribution, it also has utility as forage for trout and other game fish. It occurs in both streams and lakes and grows to a fairly large size.

Range

This species is widely distributed in North America, from the Atlantic coast to Washington on the Pacific coast. In eastern North America it occurs along the mountains south to Virginia, west to the Mississippi River drainage, and as far south as Iowa. It is present from Labrador south along the Rocky Mountains into New Mexico, Texas, and northern Mexico (Lee et al. 1980). It occurs in the Great Basin in the northeastern part of the Bonneville system in a wide range of habitats (Sigler and Miller 1963), but has not been reported elsewhere in the Great Basin except in southeastern Oregon (Lee et al. 1980).

Description

The color of the back varies from olive green to brown, shading to cream or silvery-white on the belly. In lakes the back may be grayish. There may be a faint mottling, formed by scattered, darkened scales, in the middle of the sides. The lateral line is dark from the gill cover to the base of the caudal fin in many fish, but this line may occur only on the posterior portion or be totally absent. The young have a distinct lateral stripe. Breeding males may display orange-red coloration at the edge of the mouth that spreads lightly onto the cheeks. A trace of orange-red color may occur in the posterior axis of the pectoral fins, pelvic fins, and occasionally along the anterior base of the anal fin. Females are generally much more dully colored than males (Scott and Crossman 1973; Sigler and Miller 1963).

The slender body, long conical head and snout, inferior mouth, and small maxillary barbels readily distinguish this species, with the exception of the speckled dace, from other Great Basin minnows (Sigler and Miller 1963). It is nearly round in cross sections with a broad, triangular head. The head length is approximately 20 percent of the total length. It has a single dorsal fin with 8 rays. The caudal fin is shallowly forked with rounded lobes. The pelvic fins, with 8 rays, are small, with the origin forward of the dorsal fin origin. The short pectoral fins have 13 rays and are rounded and paddlelike. The small cycloid scales number 61 to 72 in the lateral series. The lateral line is complete and straight or nearly so (Scott and Crossman 1973; Sigler and Miller 1963).

Size and Longevity

The longnose dace is a relatively slow-growing, short-lived fish, reaching a total length of 5 inches and attaining 5 years of age (Wydoski and Whitney 1979). Minnesota populations are reported as reaching yearly total lengths in inches of 1.9, 2.4, 2.9, 3.3, and 3.9 for fish age 1 to 5. In Utah it generally does not exceed 4.5 inches in length and most individuals are between 2.5 and 3.5 inches long (Sigler and Miller 1963). Growth rate between the sexes is equal but older and larger fish are generally females (Wydoski and Whitney 1979).

Limiting Factors

This species is preyed on by trout and other game fish. Longnose dace is infested to some extent with trematodes, nematodes, and other parasites.

Food and Feeding

This species is a benthic feeder as an adult. Young feed on drift in the mid-water column. Its food may consist of as much as 98 percent aquatic insect larvae and small amounts of algae. Like many species, its food selection is based upon abundance and availability. Some populations feed on fish eggs (Sigler and Miller 1963; Wydoski and Whitney 1979).

Breeding Habits

Spawning occurs in riffles over a gravelly bottom, beginning in late spring or early summer at a temperature of 53° F. No nest is built but a territory is established and defended by one parent who also guards the eggs. Females lay 200 to 1,200 transparent, adhesive eggs that hatch in 7 to 10 days at 60° F. The yolk sac is absorbed in about 7 days and the young rise to the surface when the posterior lobe of the swim bladder is inflated. The young live in the mid-water column, unlike adults, which exhibit a bottom-dwelling pattern, and they inhabit quiet waters near shore. The pelagic stage of the young lasts about 4 months before they assume the bottom existence of adults (Scott and Crossman 1973; Sigler and Miller 1963).

Habitat

The adult longnose dace is a bottom-dweller. Its body form is adapted to swift waters and at times it may inhabit turbulent streams. In lakes it occurs near inshore waters over boulder or gravel bottoms, moving into deeper waters during the heat of summer to maintain its preferred temperature of 53° to 70° F (Sigler and Miller 1963; Trautman 1981).

Preservation of Species

Due to its wide range and abundance, general habitat protection and maintenance of acceptable water quality are all this species requires.

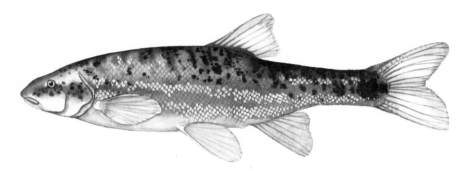

Speckled dace
***Rhinichthys osculus* (Girard)**

Importance

Throughout its range in North America the speckled dace, principally due to its abundance, has value as a bait and forage fish, a value reduced only slightly by its small size. The speckled dace occurs over wide and diverse habitats in the western United States. Its adaptability is reflected at the subspecies level in the many distinct forms it takes in response to variable habitats. This adaptability is rooted in evolutionary trends within the species and gives importance to both the species as a whole and the numerous subspecies as mechanisms for evolutionary studies.

Range

The speckled dace occurs in western North America in Pacific watersheds from the Columbia River to the Colorado River drainage. It is in interior drainages of California, but only rarely in coastal streams, and is the only fish species native to all of the major western drainage systems (Lee et al. 1980). Previously the species was divided into 12 separate species (Jordan and Evermann 1896) and the present status of both described and undescribed subspecies is largely unresolved. Deacon and Williams (1984) list 5 undescribed and 10 described subspecies for Nevada. Isolated populations exist in the Death Valley system and others exist elsewhere in California and in Utah (Moyle 1976). It is present throughout the Great Basin.

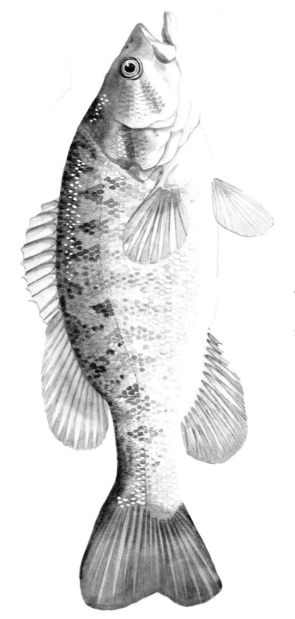

Smallmouth Bass

Largemouth Bass

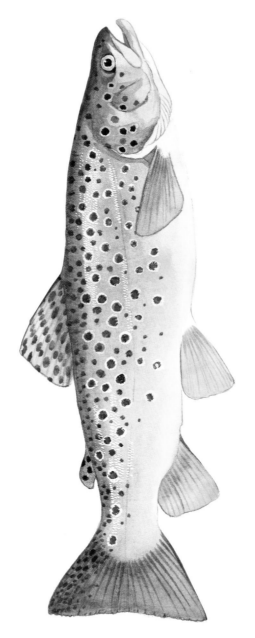

Brown Trout

Cutthroat Trout

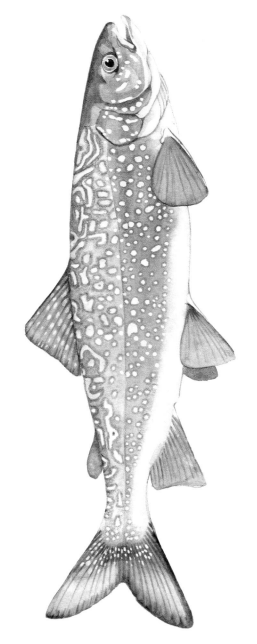

Lake Trout

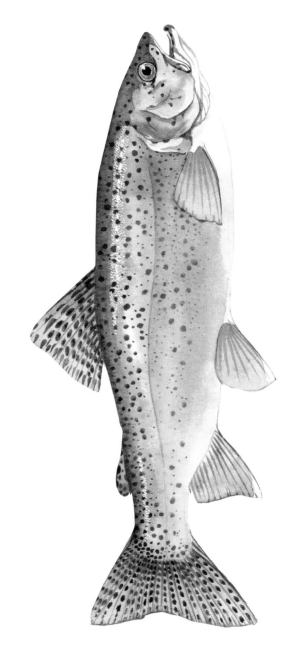

Rainbow Trout

Brook Trout

Golden Trout

Mountain Whitefish

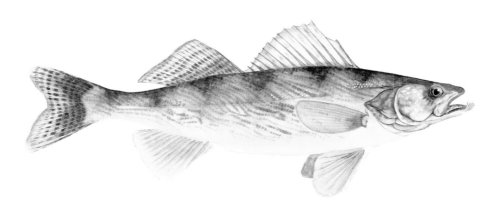

Walleye

Bonneville Cisco

Description

Overall coloration is gray or gray-brown with scattered and vague darker flecks, usually above the midline of the sides. The lower sides and belly are yellowish or creamy-white. It has a faint lateral band of darker color that begins weakly under the dorsal fin and extends onto the caudal peduncle, terminating with a diffuse spot on the caudal fin base; the spot and band are both more conspicuous on young fish. In spawning males, an orange-red color appears around the mouth, the upper part of the gill opening, the base of the anal fin, and the lower caudal lobe (Scott and Crossman 1973; Sigler and Miller 1963).

The body is elongate but somewhat laterally compressed. The mouth is subterminal, the snout pointed, and the head triangular. Speckled dace has one dorsal fin with 8 or 9 rays. The caudal fin is forked with rounded lobes. The anal fin has 6 or 7 rays and the origin is under the posterior base of the dorsal fin. The pelvic fins are relatively small and rounded with 8 or 9 rays. The pectorals are small and rounded with 13 or 14 rays. The cycloid scales number 47 to 89 in the lateral series. The lateral line is complete or terminates before the base of the caudal fin (Moyle 1976; Sigler and Miller 1963).

Size and Longevity

Speckled dace has a short life span, few living beyond 3 years. It is small, reaching only a length of 3 to 4 inches. In the Trinity River, California lengths in inches were 0.6 to 1.6 for young and 2.0 to 2.5 for fish age 2 and 3. Females are generally larger than males (Moyle 1976; Wydoski and Whitney 1979).

Limiting Factors

Speckled dace is prey for game fish and is parasitized by a variety of organisms. Its abundance and wide distribution ensure its survival at the species level.

Food and Feeding

The bottom-dwelling speckled dace feeds primarily on benthic organisms, predictably because of its subterminal mouth. Young feed primarily on mid-water plankton and adults on bottom-dwelling aquatic insects, freshwater shrimp, plant material, and zooplankton. Algae may constitute 21 percent of the food by volume (Wydoski and Whitney 1979). Some populations may occasionally feed on eggs and larvae of suckers and minnows.

Breeding Habits

The speckled dace usually matures during its second summer. It may spawn throughout the summer months but peak activity occurs in June and July at temperatures near 65° F. Males congregate in a small spawning area from which they remove the detrital material, clearing a small patch of bare rocks and gravel. The male develops nuptial tubercles on the rays and the axils of the paired fins. The base of the anal fin and the lower caudal lobe may become deep orange to scarlet, as may the area around the mouth and the upper part of the gill opening.

The female is surrounded by a group of males when she enters the area. Eggs are deposited underneath a rock or close to the bottom and fertilized. The adhesive eggs stick to the bottom substrate and hatch in 6 days at approximately 65° F. Larval fish remain in the gravel for an additional 7 to 8 days. When fry emerge from the gravel, they tend to congregate in the warm shallows of streams near large rocks. They generally move into quiet, swampy coves in lakes (Sigler and Miller 1963).

Habitat

This ubiquitous species lives in a wide variety of habitats, from swift, cold riffles of mountain streams to the quiet waters of isolated cool or warm springs, but it is uncommon in water over 3 feet deep. It may be the only species present in intermittent streams and outflows of desert springs. It is rarely found singly, yet avoids forming large schools except during spawning. It is most active at night, spending the day among rocks in shallow water or in slightly deeper areas. In streams, it may be active all year (Moyle 1976; Sigler and Miller 1963).

Preservation of Species

Maintenance of acceptable water quality and spawning and nursery areas is required at the subspecies level. Each subspecies is very tolerant of the environmental variation of its particular habitat and efforts should be made to preserve these unique and unusual habitats along with the fish they support.

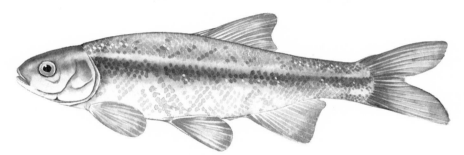

Redside shiner
Richardsonius balteatus (Richardson)

Importance

The redside shiner is important as a forage fish for several species of game fish. Its usefulness as forage lies in its small size and slow growth rate, which render it useful as prey for its entire life. Some game fish, such as rainbow trout, have sufficiently different daily movement patterns and do not greatly overlap the redside shiner's patterns, thus reducing its availability to those populations (Wydoski and Whitney 1979). In some habitats it eats the same foods as small game fish, detracting from its value as a forage fish. It is extremely common in Utah. It is used as a bait fish in some states. It may be a predator of young trout and other game fish (Sigler and Miller 1963; Wydoski and Whitney 1979).

Range

The native distribution of the redside shiner is mostly west of the Rocky Mountains in North America, south through Washington, Oregon, and the Columbia drainage. In the Great Basin it occurs in northern Harney basin, Oregon and Nevada and throughout the Bonneville basin (Lee et al. 1980).

Description

The coloration in this species is vivid. Adults have a prominent orange to red or pink stripe on each side that lies just below a dark band running from behind the head to the base of the caudal fin. The red stripe, running from the shoulder girdle to above the anal fin, is especially bright in breeding males and tends to be broadened and intensified fore and aft. The stripe is present in females in a more somber shade, especially during the breeding season. During part of the year the red stripe is absent. The side above the dark band may be bright golden. The upper parts are bluish to metallic green and the sides are silvery. Below the red stripe the sides may be pale golden. The axils of the pectoral fins may be golden to red (Sigler and Miller 1963).

The length of the head goes 4 to 4.5 times into total body length. The mouth is terminal and somewhat oblique. The lateral line is weakly decurved with 50 to 60 moderate-sized cycloid scales in the lateral series. The large anal fin is sickle-shaped with 10 to 13 rays. The dorsal fin, originating behind the insertion of the pelvic fins, has 8 to 10 rays. The caudal fin is definitely forked (Sigler and Miller 1963; La Rivers 1962).

Size and Longevity

The maximum length reached by redside shiners is about 7 inches, but most are less than 5 inches. It is a relatively short-lived species, with a maximum life span of 5 years. The size at the end of each year in inches for fish age 1 to 4 in Montana is 0.8, 1.7, 2.7, and 4.0 (Brown 1971).

Limiting Factors

The redside shiner is preyed upon by a variety of game fish. It is cannibalistic of its own eggs and may be its own worst predator (La Rivers 1962).

Food and Feeding

This species is largely omnivorous. Adults feed primarily on aquatic and terrestrial insects and snails as well as zooplankton when it is in a pelagic area. It may feed upon fish eggs and fry, including its own. Fry feed on zooplankton and algae (Wydoski and Whitney 1979).

Breeding Habits

Spawning usually takes place in the second year of life in shallow streams in groups of 2 to 15 fish during April to June. The female deposits only a few eggs at one time that sink and readily adhere to rocks or detritus as they are broadcast. Egg production varies from 829 to 3,602 for females 3.3 to 4.1 inches in length. Those eggs left exposed are generally eaten. Spawning activities may be initiated in water as cool as 50° F over fine gravel, rocky riffles, or in upwelling springs. It may also spawn over submerged plants along lakeshores. The eggs hatch in 3 to 7 days at 70° to 73° F (Sigler and Miller 1963; Wydoski and Whitney 1979).

Habitat

The redside shiner is present in a wide variety of habitats. It occurs in ponds, lakes, streams, and irrigation ditches. It is present most often where summer temperatures range from 44° to 75° F. It moves in schools and tends to stay in vegetated areas in shallow water. In many lakes it exhibits daily and seasonal movement patterns. During the day it remains in shallow water but moves into deeper water after dark. In streams it may occur in both turbid and clear water in either swift or slow currents and over varied bottom types. In spring it moves inshore and remains there until July when it migrates to deep water, moving to still deeper areas when surface waters warm. It returns to shallow water in September and October when near-shore water temperatures decrease (Wydoski and Whitney 1979; Sigler and Miller 1963).

Preservation of Species

Due to its ubiquitousness and abundance, preservation of this species requires only maintenance of acceptable water quality and habitat.

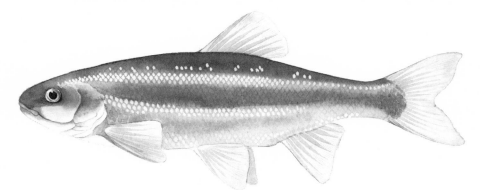

Lahontan redside
***Richardsonius egregius* (Girard)**

Importance

The Lahontan redside is an important species from an ecological aspect because it is endemic to a relatively small area. It is important as forage for various game fish and has been used as a bait fish. The Lahontan redside is abundant in most of its native range but is gone from many of the upstream areas in Nevada where it previously occurred (La Rivers 1962). It has been observed preying on eggs and fry of cui-ui in the lower Truckee River.

Range

This species is native to the extensive Lahontan drainage system of Nevada and California. It occurs in the Walker, Truckee, Susan, Quinn, Reese, and Humboldt rivers. It is rare in Walker and Pyramid lakes and is present in greater numbers in Lake Tahoe. It has been introduced into portions of Nye County, Nevada but the status there is unknown (La Rivers 1962).

Description

Snyder (1918) notes, "This beautiful little fish is almost universally distributed throughout the brooks, rivers and lakes of the region." It has large eyes but is best identified by its spectacular breeding colors, which are a scarlet stripe on the sides, a shiny olivaceous back, and a silvery belly. In nonbreeding fish the red color is greatly reduced, but the stripe is still visible as a dark lateral band (La Rivers 1962).

It is a rather small, slender minnow, in which the body depth goes about 4.5 times into the standard length. The mouth is slightly oblique and the maxillary barely reaches the front edge of the eye. The single dorsal fin has 7 to 8 rays and the anal fin 8 to 10 rays. The lateral line is generally complete and originates at the upper edge of the operculum. There are 52 to 63 scales in the lateral series.

Size and Longevity

The Lahontan redside does not generally live longer than 4 years and is relatively slow-growing. The yearly average lengths of Lake Tahoe redsides in inches is 1.3, 2.0, and 3.0 for fish age 1 to 3. The largest specimen collected was 5.5 inches, but it rarely reaches lengths over 4 inches (Evans 1969; La Rivers 1962).

Limiting Factors

This species is preyed upon by fish and hybridizes with tui chubs and speckled dace in Lake Tahoe (Hopkirk and Behnke 1966). It may have been adversely affected by alterations in habitat over portions of its range.

Food and Feeding

The Lahontan redside is an opportunistic feeder on invertebrates. A Lake Tahoe study reports food is 38 percent by volume surface insects, 28 percent bottom-living insect larvae, and 25 percent planktonic crustaceans. Moyle (personal communication, 1983) has documented redsides feeding on aquatic and terrestrial drift in a Truckee River basin stream. Eight percent of the food by volume consists of Tahoe sucker eggs when these fish are spawning. Redsides feed at any time of day or night. Flying insects appear to be favored in the evening and at night, while bottom and planktonic forms are favored during the day (Miller 1951).

Breeding Habits

The Lahontan redside generally matures in its second or third year. Spawning occurs from late May to August but peaks in June when water temperatures are between 55.5° and 57° F. In Lake Tahoe, Stampede Reservoir (Little Truckee River), Nevada and Sagehen Creek, California, spawning populations migrate upstream into tributaries to sand and gravel bottoms at the downstream end of pools. In shallow lake waters it spawns near shore over bottoms of gravel or small rocks. Females average 1,125 eggs, most of which are contained in the right ovary. Groups of 20 to 100 fish swim about in a tight school close to the bottom, and females and males release the eggs and sperm as a small cluster of fish presses against the bottom. The eggs sink into crevices between the rocks and adhere to the undersurfaces (Miller 1951; Evans 1969). After hatching, the young leave the spawning grounds and inhabit shallow areas of quiet water with a protective cover of floating debris. They frequently form schools with other minnows.

Habitat

Snyder (1918) reports that the Lahontan redside is widely distributed throughout the brooks, rivers, and lakes of the region. It is found in the lower courses of the rivers in deep, quiet water at the heads of pools but avoids high gradient areas. In lakes it congregates in large schools, generally in sheltered areas about logs, rocks, etc. In Lake Tahoe it is a littoral zone fish, but has been collected at depths to 100 feet. Typically, large schools swim close to the surface over rocky bottoms. When fall water temperatures drop to less than 50° F, it leaves the shallow water areas and inhabits rocky bottom areas in water 10 to 60 feet deep (Evans 1969; Miller 1951).

Preservation of Species

Its abundance and wide distribution within its native range ensure its existence if water quality and habitat are maintained.

SUCKERS (CATOSTOMIDAE)

The suckers make up a characteristic element of the North America fish fauna and include approximately 100 species distributed from the Arctic to the tropics (Simpson and Wallace 1978). One species, *Myxocyprinus asiaticus*, is known from China where it represents the only survivor of an early stage in the evolution of this family. The blue sucker of the Mississippi River drainage is also considered a "primitive" species (Peter Moyle, personal communication, 1983). Only one other species, *Catostomus catostomus*, occurs in the Old World (Siberia) (Sigler and Miller 1963). It probably invaded there from North America during the Pleistocene two million years ago.

The suckers have soft fin rays, cycloid scales, and toothless jaws. There are 10 or more pharyngeal teeth in one row on the two pharyngeal arches. The mouth is typically fit for sucking, as the name implies, and is in a more or less ventral position. It is protrusible with papillose lips. However, the shortnose sucker, June sucker, and cui-ui (*Chasmistes* spp.) have terminal and rather oblique mouths, with thin lips and almost no papillae. Suckers are very closely related to minnows and the young may be misidentified quite easily. Most suckers run upstream in the spring to spawn, but they also spawn along lakeshores. These fish characteristically use the mouth as a suction device, picking up detritus, plants, and animals, especially aquatic insects. Some species are of substantial commercial value, especially in the midwest and eastern United States. The Utah sucker was, at one time, the most important commercial fish in Utah, primarily because of its great abundance and ease of capture. The June sucker of Utah Lake may also have made a substantial contribution to the early commercial fishery. Young suckers provide forage for predatory fish and birds and several species are used for bait.

Fifty-nine species of suckers in eleven genera are listed in the American Fisheries Society's *List of Common and Scientific Names of Fishes from the United States and Canada* (Robins et al. 1980). Eleven species in two genera occur in the Great Basin, all are native, and three have official status under the Endangered Species Act.

Utah sucker
Catostomus ardens Jordan and Gilbert

Importance

The Utah sucker at one time was of considerable value as a food fish, particularly to early-day Utah Mormon pioneers. In years when crop production suffered and food was in short supply, the Mormons readily turned to Utah Lake, Utah and to a lesser extent to Bear Lake, Utah-Idaho for suckers. The Utah sucker was used fresh, smoked, and brined. It is used today as a human food, but to a far lesser extent. It is also important as a forage fish over much of its range and is a potential bait fish. A 1957 study shows that it accounts for the greatest total weight of any fish in Bear Lake; numerically it ranks third (McConnell, Clark, and Sigler 1957).

During the 1830s to 1850s, trappers' diaries tell of hundreds of Indians during Indian-trapper early summer rendezvous dropping whatever they were doing and catching thousands of fish on the east side of Bear Lake. This could only have been during spawning when it would have been easy to catch Utah suckers.

Range

Utah sucker is native to the drainage of old Lake Bonneville. It is also present in the Snake River drainage above Shoshone Falls in Idaho and in Wyoming. It has become established in several areas, including parts of the Colorado River drainage, presumably via the bait bucket.

Description

The color of the Utah sucker is bronze or gray above, whitish below, with dark fins. Breeding males usually have a bright rosy lateral stripe. It has relatively large cycloid scales, about 60 to 70 in the lateral series, and 11 to 13 dorsal fin rays. The body is long and slightly compressed; the back is broad and somewhat elevated. The head is short, conical, and broad. The eye is small and the mouth is inferior, with relatively weak lips that are without a lateral notch. The caudal fin is short, broad, and weakly forked.

Size and Longevity

The Utah sucker is relatively fast-growing and lives 10 to 12 years. In a sample of 144 Utah suckers taken by nets from Bear Lake, the median size was 10.5 inches. The yearly size in inches of Utah suckers age 1 to 10 in Bear Lake is 1.5, 5.1, 8.4, 10.3, 13.1, 14.6, 16.5, 17.6, 19.9, and 22.0.

In Blackfoot Reservoir, Idaho, specimens weighing over 8 pounds have been taken by commercial seiners. In other areas it attains a length of 25.5 inches and a weight of more than 5 pounds. The average weight of spawning adults in Bear Lake ranges between 2 and 3 pounds.

Limiting Factors

Of the 200 Utah suckers examined from Bear Lake, Utah-Idaho in 1955, almost all were parasitized by *Liguala intestinalis*, a body cavity tapeworm. The larva is a plerocercoid, but is free in the body cavity. No other Bear Lake fishes examined were so highly parasitized. Although there appears to be no loss of condition in these parasitized suckers, the tapeworms must have some detrimental effect. Fish as small as 7 or 8 inches often contained 3 or 4 feet of tapeworm (McConnell, Clark, and Sigler 1957). In 1983 we examined 100 Utah suckers from Bear Lake. None was parasitized. Young Utah suckers are preyed upon by other fish, birds, occasionally mammals, and by humans for food. There is frequently a high post-spawning mortality of stream-spawning and possibly lake-spawning suckers.

Food and Feeding

In areas where there is not a large selection of food, the young and adults feed on the same items. Utah sucker feeds freely on both plants and animals. Adults take most of their food from the bottom in deep lakes, feeding throughout the year and at all depths in Bear Lake. Some young remain near shore in shallow water or in the tributary streams where they were spawned. It is not uncommon to observe them grazing on the filamentous algae and other algae on fixed objects.

Breeding Habits

The Utah sucker is a spring spawner, moving out of lakes or large rivers into streams when water temperatures reach about 60° F. A female is usually attended by 2 or more males. When the female is ready to spawn, 2 males approach her, one on either side, and as all 3 fish quiver rapidly the eggs and milt are spread. The gravel and sand are then stirred by violent tail movement of the males. Maturity is at 2 or 3 years of age.

In Bear Lake and quite probably many other lakes, there is a discrete lake-spawning population of Utah suckers. These fish congregate offshore and move inshore either day or night but more often just at dusk, where spawning activities become frenzied with much splashing and disturbance. The average date that spawning starts in Bear Lake is June 12. In mid June 1976, at 2:30 A.M., we observed one continuous school on the east side of Bear Lake that was in excess of 3 miles long and about 6 feet wide, extending from water 6 inches deep out to water 18 to 24 inches deep. These fish were almost without fear, showing little or no concern when a person walked near them or shone a light directly on them. On June 13, 1983, around midday we observed spawning schools of 400 to 500, but they were wary. It is believed the undertow, prevalent along that area of the lake, acts to aerate the eggs until they hatch.

Two groups of Utah suckers appear in St. Charles Creek, Idaho (a tributary of Bear Lake) in early to mid June. One consists of smaller, darker, immature fish and the other large, bleached-out, and sometimes battered spawning adults.

Habitat

The Utah sucker is an adaptable species. It prospers in a wide range of habitats from large, deep, cold lakes to relatively small, warm streams (above 80° F). It may be in streams where the current is rapid or where it is slight. The water may be turbid to clear, the bottom varying from mud and clay to sand and gravel. It prospers in Bear Lake in deep water, feeding on the bottom when temperatures are 42° to 46° F. Adults often feed in water more than 100 feet deep. The young are more likely to be in a tributary stream or near shore. Often adults are present in all areas of a lake.

Preservation of Species

The Utah sucker is so well adapted that it apparently needs no protection from the usual and accustomed manner of taking fish or from predators.

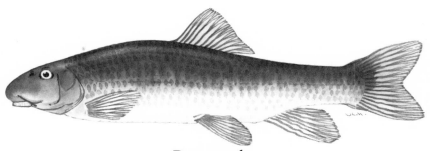

Desert sucker
Catostomus clarki **Baird and Girard**

Importance

The desert sucker is preyed upon by other fish and used to some extent as bait; its main value is that it is an interesting desert fish. In the Gila River basin, Arizona, it provides considerable sport for bow and arrow enthusiasts.

Range

This species is present in the lower Colorado River basin downstream from Grand Canyon, in south central and southern Arizona, and in western New Mexico. In the Great Basin it is present in the pluvial White River near Preston and Lund, White Pine County and Meadow Valley Wash, Lincoln County, Nevada (Deacon and Williams 1984).

Description

The desert sucker is silvery tan to darkish green above, silvery to yellowish below; the caudal pigment is dispersed over fin rays and membranes. Scales in the lateral series vary widely, ranging from 61 to 104, usually 75 to 90 in the White River drainage. The dorsal rays number 8 to 12, usually 10 to 11, pelvic rays 8 to 12, usually 9 or 10. The caudal peduncle is 6.9 to 11.2 percent of the standard length. There is a distinct notch at each corner of the mouth. The edge of the jaw inside the lower lip has a hard cartilaginous sheath. The upper lip is recurved and there is a small flap of skin at the base of each pelvic fin (Minckley 1973).

Size and Longevity

Adults reach a maximum size of 13 inches and probably live 8 to 10 years.

Limiting Factors

This species is preyed upon by other fish, occasionally is used as bait, and in general suffers the hazards that many small suckers do. It may hybridize with other suckers.

Food and Feeding

The desert sucker is an herbivore, feeding on encrusted diatoms and additional algae scraped from stones and other surfaces by its cartilage-sheathed jaws. It has been observed to pull itself along with the expanded suctionlike mouth and scrape not only the top of the stones but also the sides, at times feeding belly up on various items (Minckley 1973).

Breeding Habits

In Arizona the desert sucker spawns at age 3 in late winter to early spring on riffles in a manner similar to other suckers. The young tend to congregate in tremendous numbers along the bank in quiet waters, then progressively move into the mainstream as they increase in size (Minckley 1973).

Habitat

The desert sucker tends to live more in rapid waters than in pools, or at least it moves to swift areas to feed and spawn, then lives in pools during the day. Waters are frequently muddy or turbid but it also occurs in good trout waters. Water temperatures are variable with season but may fluctuate from 45° to 85° F during June to September. Adults may live in water as deep as 6 to 8 feet but are frequently found in depths of 3 to 4 feet. Young and juveniles occur in water only 6 to 18 inches deep.

Preservation of Species

Since enemies of the desert sucker are few and hazards are at a minimum it probably needs no special protection at the species level. This may not be true of the subspecies. The above life history is largely from Minckley (1973).

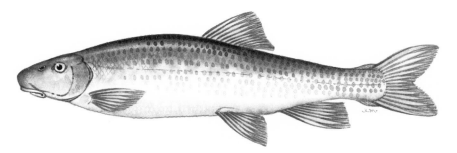

Bridgelip sucker
Catostomus columbianus (Eigenmann and Eigenmann)

Importance

The impact of the bridgelip sucker on the environment is probably near neutral. It furnishes a limited amount of forage for game fish, but it may, at times, also compete with their young for food.

Range

This species is restricted to the fresh waters of northwest North America. It is in the Columbia River drainage from British Columbia south to southern Oregon, below the Great Falls of the Snake River, from Idaho west to eastern Oregon and Washington, and north in the Fraser River to central British Columbia. It is present in the Harney drainage of the northwest section of the Great Basin (Scott and Crossman 1973; Lee et al. 1980).

Description

The back and top of the head of this species is brown to olive; the upper sides are somewhat mottled and paler brown; the lower sides and head, below the eye and ventral surface, are white to pale yellow. The lateral line is prominent near the head and paler than the background. Breeding males have a prominent orange lateral band. The young often have three dark lateral blotches.

This rather small fish is torpedo-shaped with a cylindrical body, not laterally compressed, with the greatest body depth ahead of the origin of the dorsal fin. The head is moderately long, about 20 percent of the total length. The eye is high on the head at mid length and is moderately large. The mouth is ventral, little overhung by the snout, and capable of being extended forward. It is characterized by an incomplete cleft lower lip and very slight notches in the corners of the mouth. The gill rakers are short and fleshy. The branchiostegal rays number 3; the cycloid scales, crowded anteriorly, usually number less than 90 in the lateral series. The lateral line is complete, but often with breaks and branches. The peritoneum is black and the intestine long. There is no pyloric caecae. The swim bladder has 2 chambers (Scott and Crossman 1973; Wydoski and Whitney 1979).

Size and Longevity

This relatively small sucker apparently seldom reaches a length over 15 inches. The young are about 3 inches at the end of the first year. It probably lives 6 to 8 years.

Limiting Factors

Adverse factors such as predation and habitat destruction through channelization or dredging probably affect the bridgelip sucker. It hybridizes with the largescale sucker and is parasitized by trematodes, cestodes, and other organisms. Mammals and some birds prey on it.

Food and Feeding

The cartilaginous edges of the jaws and the black peritoneum of the species suggest its food is obtained by scraping algae from rocks. This food would include invertebrates taken incidentally while feeding on or near the bottom (Carl, Clemens, and Lindsey 1967).

Breeding Habits

The bridgelip sucker probably spawns in the spring when water temperatures reach the mid 50s. The rather large eggs are 0.11 inch in diameter. Sexual maturity is reached when the fish is about 5 inches long. This probably represents age 2 or occasionally age 3 (Scott and Crossman 1973).

Habitat

The habitat of this species is usually the cold waters of small, fast-flowing streams with gravelly, rock bottoms. It may also inhabit rivers where the current is moderate and the substrate is composed of sand and silt. It is seldom found in lakes (Simpson and Wallace 1978).

Preservation of Species

Apparently little or no protection is needed to preserve this small sucker, although its biology is incompletely understood.

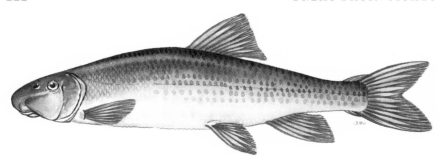

Bluehead sucker
Catostomus discobolus Cope

Importance

This species is a good bait and forage fish. In the upper tributaries of the Green and Bear rivers it provides an important link in the food chain of carnivorous game fish, especially trout, and its feeding habits offer little competition with them. When both game fish and suckers are in the same area, the suckers may take the predator pressure off the game fish by being more readily taken. Suckers of this type are particularly valuable in converting algae into fish food (Sigler and Miller 1963).

Range

The bluehead sucker is widely distributed in the Colorado River drainage from Bill Williams River in western Arizona, where it is scarce, northward into Colorado and Wyoming, where it is abundant. It is present in the Snake River above the Great Falls. In Utah it is common in the Green River and in the Bear River of the Great Basin (Sigler and Miller 1963).

Description

This species is distinguished by a blue head, bluish-gray to olivaceous back and upper sides, and whitish belly. The breeding male has yellow or orange lower fins and a more or less interrupted red or rosy band along the lateral line. There are considerable brassy reflections on the sides and some green reflections along the opercle region.

The bluehead sucker, like *Gila robusta*, varies in body form according to the size and swiftness of the waters it inhabits. The caudal peduncle may be pencil-shaped, though compressed, or it may be relatively deep. The dorsal fin may be enlarged with 11 or 12 rays, expansive and strongly falcate, or it may be smaller with 9 or 10 rays, less expanded and with only a slight concave margin. The scales are moderate to small, ranging from 90 to 107 in the lateral series. The head is short and broad with a heavy snout that overhangs the large mouth. The upper lip is large and forms a fleshy hood over the mouth opening. The lower lip is shallowly notched at the midline. Both jaws have well-developed cartilaginous scraping edges, hence one common name, chiselmouth sucker (Sigler and Miller 1963).

Size and Longevity

Although this species occasionally reaches a length of 16 or more inches, most adults are between 6 and 10 inches long. It probably lives 6 to 8 years, or occasionally longer.

Limiting Factors

Predation by trout and other game fish is the primary decimator of the bluehead sucker. It also hybridizes with other species of the genus *Catostomus*.

Food and Feeding

The cartilaginous scraping edges of the jaws enable this species to feed effectively on algae-covered rocks and other fixed objects. Aquatic insects living in algal communities are eaten incidentally. The bluehead sucker also feeds in riffles where there is a strong current or in deep rocky pools. It may be seen on its sides, or even upside down, feeding along the bases of boulders. The type of food taken does not vary much throughout its life.

Breeding Habits

Spawning has not been described but probably occurs in the spring and early summer at lower elevations and mid to late summer in colder waters. Specimens less than 1 inch long were netted in a cut-off channel of the Gunnison River, Colorado on October 20, and young as small as 0.33 inch were collected in southeastern Utah on June 17. It probably spawns at a length of about 5 inches and 2 years of age.

Habitat

The bluehead sucker usually occurs in the main current of streams. It mainly inhabits very large streams, but may also occur in small creeks. Although it is usually found in cooler waters, it can tolerate temperatures as warm as 82° F. It may greatly outnumber other larger species of *Catostomus* with which it is a common associate. Reportedly a nervous, cautious fish, it flees at the sight of a shadow or the sound of a crunch of gravel (Sigler and Miller 1963; Baxter and Simon 1970).

Preservation of Species

The bluehead sucker requires little specific protection in its present habitat.

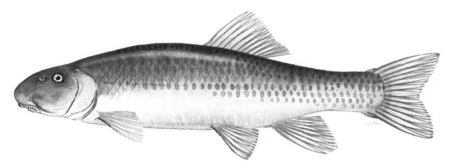

Owens sucker
Catostomus fumeiventris **Miller**

Importance

The Owens sucker is probably not important from an economic standpoint. Ecologically it is important because it seems to be the one species native to the Owens River that has thrived despite the disruption of the system by the activities of the city of Los Angeles (Moyle 1976).

Range

This species is native to the Owens River and tributaries in Death Valley, but has been introduced into June Lake in the Mono Lake basin and into the Santa Clara River basin (the latter by escape from the Los Angeles aqueduct) (Miller 1973).

Description

The dusky, smoky-colored belly of this fish, from which its scientific name is derived, is especially noticeable in spawning males, which, however, do not develop the lateral red stripe characteristic of Tahoe suckers. For the balance of the year, male and female are slate-colored, occasionally becoming dusky and usually having dark bellies. It is similar to the Tahoe sucker except it has coarser scales. The lateral series is 68 to 85, usually fewer than 79. It has more pectoral rays (16 to

19) and is duller in color than the Tahoe sucker, especially during the breeding season (Miller 1973).

Size and Longevity

The maximum size and longevity of the Owens sucker is unknown, but it is presumably similar to the Tahoe sucker: 12 to 18 inches and 5 to 8 years.

Limiting Factors

Although this species appears to have thrived despite the disruption of the Owens River system, habitat destruction is potentially the most serious hazard it faces. It hybridizes with the Santa Ana sucker in the Santa Clara basin of California (Hubbs and Miller 1942).

Food and Feeding

The dietary habits of the Owens sucker are presumably similar to those of the Tahoe sucker, its diet consisting primarily of invertebrates, algae, and vascular plants.

Breeding Habits

The Owens sucker apparently spawns from late May through early July, at least in the tributary streams of the Owens River and Lake Crowley, Mono County, California. The larval suckers are abundant in weedy edges of backwaters of streams (Miller 1973).

Habitat

The habitat of this species is similar to that of the Tahoe sucker; that is, it occupies both lakes and streams.

Preservation of Species

As a precautionary measure, the Owens sucker has been introduced into a native fish sanctuary in Owens Valley, California. The status of this introduced population is uncertain.

Largescale sucker
Catostomus macrocheilus Girard

Importance

The largescale sucker plays a part in the food chain by converting plant material to animal protein, which in turn is consumed by carnivorous fish. This species was much used as a food staple in the early American Indian economy. Although it has been accused of feeding on trout and salmon eggs, it is doubtful that it eats many other than those that would not have survived (La Rivers 1962).

Range

The native range of this species is in the streams tributary to the Pacific Ocean between the Skeena River in British Columbia and the Sixes River in Oregon. In Montana it is common throughout the Clark Fork and Kootenai river drainages in both streams and lakes (Brown 1971). It is present in the Harney drainage in the northwest Great Basin (Smith 1978).

Description

The adult largescale sucker is dark and noticeably counter-shaded. The back and upper sides to just below the lateral line and the head to just below the eye are blue-gray to olive. The lower sides and the lower part of the head and ventral surface are cream to white. A dark band runs below the lateral line to the base of the caudal fin. The fins are immaculate to dusky, with a dark leading edge or a white edge with dark behind it. The young, up to 6 inches, have 3 or 4 diffused dark spots on the sides. Counter-shading and the lateral band are darker and more pronounced on breeding males. Above the lateral line in breeding individuals of both sexes there is an iridescent olive green to ochre band and a narrow, yellowish stripe between the lateral band and the white of the ventral surface. The large cycloid scales, 62 to 69 in the lateral series, are somewhat crowded anteriorly, but increase in size from head to tail. The peritoneum is dark; the intestine long and coiled. The stomach is little differentiated. There is no pyloric caeca. The body tapers rapidly behind the dorsal fin. The head is moderately long, 20 to 23 percent of the total length, and is deep and wide, with the eyes high, a little ahead of the center of the head (Carl, Clemens, and Lindsey 1967).

Size and Longevity

The approximate total length of largescale suckers at the end of each year for fish age 1 to 5 in Montana in inches is 2.0, 3.5, 5.5, 7.5, and 10.0 (17.0 at age 8). It lives 11 or more years. The largest one known in Montana was 22.5 inches and weighed 4.3 pounds (Brown 1971). Clemens (1939) reports fork length in inches at the end of each year for Okanagon Lake, British Columbia as 1.8, 3.0, 4.9, 6.7, 7.5, 9.0, 11.2, 12.0, 13.4, 14.0, and 14.8 for fish age 1 to 11.

Limiting Factors

The young of this species are eaten by a number of predators such as squawfish and mergansers. Adults in shallow water are doubtless eaten by bears, other mammals, ospreys, and eagles. Largescale sucker occurs in areas where it is relatively free of predation by larger fish (Scott and Crossman 1973). The upper lethal temperature has been calculated at 85° F for fish acclimated at 66° F (Black 1953).

Food and Feeding

Largescale sucker fry eat small zooplankton when they are near the surface or in mid-water. After the fish becomes larger and is a bottom dweller, it changes its diet to aquatic insect larvae, diatoms, and other plant material. Large fish feed on such bottom organisms as crustaceans, aquatic insect larvae, earthworms, and snails (Wydoski and Whitney 1979).

Breeding Habits

Although most largescale suckers do not spawn until their fourth or fifth year, some males become sexually mature in 3 years. Females produce 20,000 or more eggs. Spawning occurs when mature fish move upstream during April or May at temperatures of 46° to 48° F. The eggs are deposited in gravel riffles where the current is strong. No nest is prepared and eggs are abandoned after they are laid and fertilized. The adhesive eggs stick to bottom substrate, which prevents them from being carried away by the current. Hatching time is about 2 weeks, then fry move away from the current into backwater areas or downstream to lakes. Spawning is generally in water averaging about 8 inches deep, along the edges of downstream ends of pools, in streams having a bottom of fine gravel and sand or occasionally boulders. The largescale sucker also spawns along lakeshores. Although it generally spawns at night, it has been observed spawning in the daytime in large streams (Brown 1971; Wydoski and Whitney 1979).

Habitat

The largescale sucker lives in lakes and large rivers. Fry remain in the gravel or near the surface, close to where they were spawned, for the first few weeks until the elongate yolk is absorbed. At this point the mouth is terminal and the young are pelagic. They remain pelagic until the mouth moves to the ventral position at a length of 0.5 to 0.75 inch (Scott and Crossman 1973). As the largescale sucker grows larger, it moves toward the bottom and into deeper water. It is usually in water only a few feet deep, but has been taken from water as deep as 80 feet. It is often present in large numbers in weedy shore areas of lakes or in backwaters and stream mouths.

Preservation of Species

Apparently this species needs no special protection.

Mountain sucker
***Catostomus platyrhynchus* (Cope)**

Importance

Because of its relatively small size, abundance, and widespread distribution, the mountain sucker is valuable as a forage fish. In many areas it inhabits the same waters as trout, and the young supply an important source of food for them. It is used in some areas as a bait fish.

Range

This species is native to the drainage basin of ancient Lake Bonneville and to the Snake River system above Shoshone Falls, Idaho. It also occurs in the Lahontan basin of Nevada and in British Columbia, Wyoming, and Montana east to the Black Hills of South Dakota. Introductions have established it in several streams that are tributary to the Colorado River.

Description

The color is dark greenish above with black speckling, white on the lower sides and belly. There is a very slight separation between the light underparts and the dark lateral stripe and also between that mark and the reddish stripe above it. The dorsal and caudal fins may be greenish; the lower lobe of the caudal is amber in some. The lower fins are yellowish. Breeding males have a deep orange to reddish lateral stripe on each side above a greenish-black stripe that runs from the tip of the snout to just below the middle of the caudal fin base. Breeding females are much more somber than males. The young are mottled on the back and sides.

There is a distinct notch on each side of the mouth where the upper and lower lips meet. The upper lip is smooth and curved upward and the lower lip has a comparatively shallow notch at the midline, but this is deeper than in other species of this genus. The edges of the jaws inside the lower lips have cartilaginous structures that are used for scraping algae from rocks while feeding. The fontanelle, an opening beneath the skin in the roof of the skull, is typically open rather than closed (grown over by bone) as in other species. There are usually 80 to 85 scales along the lateral series. The dorsal fin rays, numbering 9 to 11, are typically 10 (Sigler and Miller 1963).

Size and Longevity

The mountain sucker is slow-growing and not long-lived. The total yearly length in inches for Montana fish age 1 to 5 is 1.2, 2.2, 4.0, 5.0, and 6.0 (8.0 for 8 year olds) (Brown 1971). The oldest mountain sucker recorded for Montana was 9 years old.

Limiting Factors

The mountain sucker is preyed on heavily by trout, birds, and mammals in some areas. It suffers when water temperatures reach the mid to high 70s. Persistent water diversions may adversely affect its habitat. Hybridization with the Tahoe sucker occurs.

Food and Feeding

This species feeds largely on algae attached to rocks and other substrates. In Montana (Brown 1971) diatoms were the most abundant food item taken. The scraping ridges of the jaws and the very long intestine are adaptations for this diet. It has also been recorded as feeding on small aquatic insects, rotifers, and crustaceans, all of which were probably living in the algal community attached to rocks. It occasionally feeds on higher plants.

Breeding Habits

Males become sexually mature in 2 to 3 years when they are 5 to 6 inches long, and females in 4 to 5 years at 5 to 7 inches. Females produce between 900 and 4,000 eggs. Spawning occurs in June and July when water temperatures exceed 50° F. Fry first appear in mid June, so the incubation period is probably short (Brown 1971). Mountain suckers in the headwaters of the Sevier River, Utah were in spawning condition at the end of July 1942 (Sigler and Miller 1963).

Habitat

The mountain sucker dwells mainly in riffles, preferring the clear, cold waters of creeks or rivers that have gravel, rubble, sand, or boulders, although it may occur in turbid streams with mud, sand, or clay bottoms. It is only rarely encountered in lakes. Adult and half-grown mountain suckers seek out moderate to swift currents in water from 1 to 3 feet deep, but the young are in shallower, quieter waters. Aquatic vegetation sought typically includes heavy algal growth. It is also often associated with pondweeds and *Chara*. Preferred summer water temperatures are between 55° and 70° F. In northern Utah it is abundant in Blacksmith Fork River but is absent, for unknown reasons, from nearby and similar Logan River (Sigler and Miller 1963).

Preservation of Species

The mountain sucker prospers where there is an abundance of algae growing on fixed substrate and relatively cool water. It needs protection from habitat degradation.

Tahoe sucker
Catostomus tahoensis Gill and Jordan

Importance

The Tahoe sucker is important as a forage fish over much of its range. It forms part of the food base for the fish-eating birds on Anahoe Island in Pyramid Lake, Nevada. Although Tahoe suckers are good to eat (La Rivers 1962), they are seldom taken by sportsmen. Historically, the Paiute Indians around Pyramid Lake selected cui-ui over Tahoe suckers.

Range

The Tahoe sucker is native to the Lahontan drainage of Nevada and northeastern California. This drainage includes Walker, Carson, Truckee, Susan, and Humboldt rivers and Tahoe, Eagle, Pyramid, and Walker lakes (La Rivers 1962). It has also been introduced into the Sacramento River system. With the exception of Walker Lake, where it is now rare (presumably because of high TDS levels), the Tahoe sucker fares well within most of its original range.

Description

This species tends to be dark olive on the upper half of the sides, the dark contrasting sharply with the yellow of the belly and lower half of the sides. There is usually a well-defined lateral band on the sides. In breeding males this band becomes a bright red stripe running across brassy-colored sides. Breeding tubercles are well developed on the anal and caudal fins in males.

The head is large, going 4 times into standard length. The snout is long and there are 77 to 93 fine scales in the lateral series. The caudal peduncle is thick, the least depth going 12 times into the standard length. It has a subterminal large mouth with papillose lower lips, so deeply incised that only 1 row of papillae crosses completely. The dorsal fin has 10 to 11 rays, the anal 7, and the pectorals 14 to 16.

Size and Longevity

The Tahoe sucker is fast-growing and relatively short-lived. In a 3-year study on Pyramid Lake, Nevada, the yearly total length in inches of 286 fish age 1 to 5 was 6.0, 8.9, 11.4, 13.9, and 16.5. Females live longer and grow larger than the males; the oldest female in this study was 5 years and 16.8 inches, the oldest male was 4 years and 12.5 inches. The males in Pyramid Lake are somewhat heavier than the females. Tahoe suckers in Lake Tahoe grow slower and live longer than those in Pyramid Lake. Willsrud (1971) reports a sucker 15 years old from Lake Tahoe. He also reports a record 24-inch Tahoe sucker from Pyramid Lake, although none approaching this size was seen during our study (Sigler and Kennedy 1978). Vondracek, Brown, and Cech (1982) report suckers from three streams were no longer than 10 inches and lived to age 7.

Limiting Factors

The Tahoe sucker appears to have few enemies other than predatory fish and birds that, in total, do not substantially reduce the population. The suckers in Pyramid Lake are relatively free of parasites, including the body cavity tapeworm that sometimes heavily parasitizes the Utah sucker in Bear Lake. There appears to be a more or less constant mortality rate of about 60 percent annually from age 3 to 6 in Pyramid Lake. Tahoe suckers commonly hybridize with mountain suckers (Hubbs, Hubbs, and Johnson 1943).

Food and Feeding

Tahoe suckers in Pyramid Lake, Nevada feed largely at night on invertebrates, algae, and vascular plants. Midge larvae and pupae are the most common food taken by suckers of all sizes. Mid-water column invertebrates and terrestrial insects are taken occasionally. Interestingly, small suckers feed more heavily on vascular plants than do adults. Marrin (1983) reports that resource partitioning between adults and young occurs as a result of adult fish foraging in a greater number of habitats and feeding on different prey types from juveniles. All size classes feed solitarily in littoral bottom areas at night. Adults feed primarily on algae, indicating their more pronounced bottom-feeding habits as they grow older. This, in general, agrees with the feeding habits of the Tahoe sucker in Lake Tahoe (Miller 1951). Vondracek, Brown, and

Cech (1982) report algae, detritus, and chironomid larvae as the major dietary components of Tahoe suckers in streams and reservoirs.

Breeding Habits

This species spawns in spring in either lakes or streams when water temperatures approach 53° F. In Pyramid Lake, nuptial tubercles first appear on males in December and by January are very pronounced, forming definite rows along the rays of the anal and caudal fins. The females usually have no tubercles, but a few have them on the anal fin. Pyramid Lake spawning commences in April and is nearly complete by July, at water temperatures ranging from 53° to 73° F. Males are in spawning condition throughout the spring and summer to as late as September. River-spawning Tahoe suckers leave the lake when the surface temperature reaches 50° F and the river temperature varies from 48° to 53° F. The river-spawning run starts in March or April and is largely complete by early July (Kennedy and Kucera 1978). The average size of fish in the river run is smaller than those spawning in the lake (La Rivers 1962). The majority of male suckers mature at age 2 and all are mature when they are 3 years old. A few females mature at 2 and the majority are mature at 3. In Lake Tahoe they mature at age 4 or 5 (Willsrud 1971).

Lake spawning takes place over rocks and gravel bottoms at depths of 16 to 60 feet. In streams the preferred spawning grounds are gravel riffles with a few large rocks. The adhesive yellow eggs are 0.06 to 0.08 inch in diameter. In Pyramid Lake, females from age 2 to 5 years produce from 13,000 to 59,000 eggs. Spawning suckers are not as aggressive as many other species of fish. The female may be attended by a few or a dozen or more males during the spawning act.

Habitat

Tahoe sucker occurs in both large and small lakes and streams. It achieves its largest size in large lakes such as Tahoe and Pyramid. The young tend to stay in the weedy, shallow areas near shore in the lake or the stream, but the adults frequent deeper water. Marrin (1983) reports schooling to some extent in all age classes. Adults occupy a variety of habitats and have a daily migration from deep water in the daylight to near shore after dark. In Pyramid Lake few Tahoe suckers are ever captured at depths greater than 150 feet, although one was taken at 279 feet. Nets set on the bottom at 295 feet caught no Tahoe suckers (Vigg 1978, 1980). In contrast, it has been captured as deep as 984 feet in Lake Tahoe (Willsrud 1971). It prefers the warmer, inshore, shallow waters during the warm weather months, but tends to move offshore at the beginning of winter. Marrin (1983) notes that during the day Tahoe suckers moved around slightly above the substrate while at night they rested on the bottom on their pectoral fins. Sparse cover areas are used at night and areas with tall vegetation or shallow water during daylight. It is not nocturnally gregarious but schools for some part of each day.

Preservation of Species

The Tahoe sucker needs little or no protection. Its high fecundity and wide adaptability to habitat make it eminently able to cope.

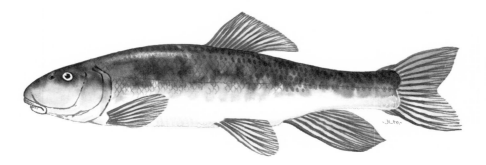

Warner sucker
Catostomus warnerensis Snyder

Importance

The Warner sucker is an important natural history entity. It has evolved in a restricted environment and is currently a threatened species (Carl Bond, personal communication, 1983).

Range

The Warner sucker occurs only in a relatively small area in the Warner Valley, Northwest system of the Great Basin (Coombs, Bond, and Drohan 1979).

Description

The Warner sucker and the Tahoe sucker are similar in appearance. The anal fins of male and female are noticeably different. There are 79 scales in the lateral series. The length of the base of the dorsal fin is equal to its height (Snyder 1908). Coombs, Bond, and Drohan (1979) report a distinctly rounded fin in the male while the female has a narrower fin with an angular distal edge that may be pointed. Fish in spawning condition, or those that have recently spawned, have a lateral band of spawning color. This band varies from slight color to pink to faint red to bright red. The width of coloration varies from the entire side to a very narrow band. Not all males develop the breeding colors. The smallest fish observed with a red breeding stripe was 4.5 inches long (Coombs, Bond, and Drohan 1979). The mouth is ventral with thick papillose lips, the notch separating the lobes of the lower lip is deep, and the snout is elongate and conical.

Size and Longevity

Only limited life history data are available for this species. It is fast-growing and medium-lived. Coombs, Bond, and Drohan (1979) report total lengths at the end of each year for fish age 1 to 8 in inches as 1.7, 3.3, 5.5, 6.7, 8.9, 10.5, 12.6, and 13.9. The largest recorded Warner sucker was 16.8 inches long.

Limiting Factors

The Warner sucker has been adversely affected by land development in the Warner Valley. Water diversions for agriculture and introduction of game fish have impacted its habitat and decimated the population through predation (Coombs, Bond, and Drohan 1979).

Food and Feeding

Specific food habit data are limited. It probably feeds on algae, invertebrates, and vascular plants.

Breeding Habits

It lives in lakes but spawns in creek beds. No spawning activity was observed by Coombs, Bond, and Drohan (1979). Fish in spawning condition or recently spent were collected from April 29 to June 24. Water temperatures in the area where they were captured ranged from 46° to 81° F. Spawning activities are probably similar to other suckers, the eggs being broadcast and fertilized but no parental care provided.

Habitat

The Warner sucker inhabits the remnants of what was once ancient pluvial Lake Warner. It is now confined largely to three permanent lakes and three perennial streams. These are small, shallow (less than 7 feet deep), marshy, weedy areas of fluctuating water levels and temperatures.

Juvenile Warner suckers are in streams in shallow backwater pools and on stream margins where there is no current. The substrate in these areas is generally mud with some emergent vegetation. Adults inhabit the lakes that are associated with the spawning streams (Coombs, Bond, and Drohan 1979).

Preservation of Species

The restricted habitat of the Warner sucker is at risk due to water-use patterns and livestock use of springs and streams. This habitat needs to be protected against further degradation and no more exotic fishes should be stocked where there are Warner suckers. The potential for habitat protection and improvement, including removal of barriers to migration, and further study of existing populations and habitats is needed to document appropriate measures (see chapter 4).

Cui-ui
Chasmistes cujus Cope

Importance

The cui-ui, an endangered fish, is endemic to Pyramid Lake. Once very abundant, its numbers declined drastically in the early 1930s. Historically, the cui-ui was an item of trade and a staple in the diet of Pyramid Lake Paiute Indians and was consumed by them both fresh and dried. The cui-ui is still a part of the Pyramid Lake Paiute Indian culture. Because it is listed as endangered by the U.S. Fish and Wildlife Service, it is not currently fished.

Range

The cui-ui is present only in Pyramid Lake and the lower Truckee River, Nevada. Adults move upriver to spawn; afterward they immediately return to the lake. The young remain in the river for a few days to 3 to 4 weeks before drifting down to the lake. The cui-ui was either living in ancient Lake Lahontan sometime between 11,000 and 21,000 years ago, or it evolved into the present species after Lake Lahontan dried enough to form 9 individual lakes, including Pyramid Lake (Koch 1972).

Description

The breeding male cui-ui has a brilliant red to brassy color on the sides. At other times it is black or brown above, fading into a flat white below. The female has a bluish-gray cast.

Unlike most other suckers, the cui-ui is relatively big-mouthed. The head is wide and somewhat rounded. The mouth is unsuckerlike with a ventro-terminal position. The lips are thin and obscurely papillose. The lower lip is somewhat pendant and divided by a very wide median notch. The cui-ui is coarse-scaled, with counts of 13 to 14 above the lateral line, 59 to 68 in the lateral series, and 10 to 12 below it. The total body length is about 9 times that of the dorsal fin base. Fin ray counts are: dorsal, 10 to 12; anal, 7; caudal, 8 or less. The caudal fin is weakly to moderately forked. The pharyngeal teeth are in a triangular section and delicate. The peritoneum is nearly black (La Rivers 1962).

Size and Longevity

The cui-ui is a slow-growing, long-lived fish. The growth in length up to 4 or 5 years is moderately fast, but quite slow thereafter. Cui-ui live 18 or more years. Scoppettone (1983), in a paper presented at the Desert Fishes Council, indicated he believes they live much longer. Yearly total length in inches for fish age 1 to 18 is 7.1, 11.9, 15.0, 17.7, 19.4, 20.2, 20.7, 21.3, 21.9, 22.6, 23.2, 23.9, 24.6, 25.0, 25.4, 26.0, 26.9, and 27.5 (Sigler, Vigg, and Bres 1986). It is interesting to note that scales are not reliable as a record of age after the cui-ui is 6 years old. A 15.6-inch fish weighs 1.2 pounds. A 24.3-inch fish weighs 3.9 pounds. Males and females grow in length at about the same rate; the female is slightly more robust than the male.

Limiting Factors

Predation on eggs and young is heavy from the time the eggs are laid until the young enter the lake. Even here the young must run a gauntlet of predators until they reach a length of 3 to 4 inches. Sub-optimal spawning conditions include high water temperatures, low flows, degraded substrate, and, in certain years, a lack of fresh water to initiate and sustain spawning. An inadequate number of mature fish and inadequate spawning grounds are the primary decimating factors of the cui-ui.

Food and Feeding

Larval, juvenile, and adult cui-ui feed primarily on zooplankton, less on aquatic insects, and occasionally on algae. Unlike other suckers, the cui-ui does not feed on the bottom but somewhat above the bottom in the water column in water 30 to 100 feet deep. It is not limited to feeding at certain depths because the small invertebrates on which it feeds are scattered throughout most of the lakes (Johnson 1958).

Breeding Habits

Spawning cui-ui move out of Pyramid Lake and up the Truckee River as early as April or as late as July. A surge of fresh water often triggers the spawning run and a lack of fresh water is apt to retard it. The cui-ui enjoys its greatest reproductive success when water temperatures are 57° F or less. Historically, cui-ui ran up the Truckee River, occasionally reaching downtown Reno, a distance of over 63 miles. Today they can run no further upstream than 38 miles (to Derby Dam) and generally the migration is much shorter. Spawning is usually at night in the vicinity of the head of gravel bars. Several males spawn with 1 or more females, which broadcast adhesive eggs over a large area. The spawning act lasts from 3 to 6 seconds and is repeated many times. Eggs are about 0.12 inch in diameter and are yellowish-white in color with a yellow yolk. Maturity is at age 5 or 6 years. One female may produce 40,000 eggs. Adults migrate back to the lake as soon as they have completed spawning; the young may remain a few days or weeks after emergence before they migrate downstream, often at night (Koch 1973). Cui-ui may also spawn with unknown success in springs or freshwater lake interfaces in the lake.

Habitat

Cui-ui prefers inshore areas with extensive shoals and shallow bars. It generally inhabits neither the deep-water areas of the lake nor the inshore areas with steep dropoffs, but Tom Trelease (personal communication, 1984) has observed large donut-shaped schools presumably feeding over deep water. The largest numbers are in the southeast section of the lake. It occurs just off the bottom at depths of less than 150 feet. Cui-ui activity is reduced when surface water temperatures approach 70° F. It is inclined to seek temperatures of about 60° F (Sigler, Vigg, and Bres 1986).

Preservation of Species

Two primary needs of cui-ui are an increase in number of mature fish and an improved spawning habitat. The ongoing artificial propagation program is producing millions of young fish and the Pyramid Lake fishway is providing the adults upstream access. An adequate supply of fresh water of 57° F or less is mandatory if maximum spawning success is to be attained. The bed of the lower Truckee River needs to be so manipulated that it is once again a meandering stable channel with secure banks and trees and shrubs for shading. Nothing should be done to discourage Tahoe suckers from spawning in the same general vicinity as the cui-ui. The sheer mass of large numbers of migrating fry provides a better chance of survival to the individual. The level of Pyramid Lake should not fluctuate more than plus or minus 10 feet except in high water years.

June sucker
***Chasmistes liorus* Jordan**

Importance

The June sucker is endemic to Utah Lake, Utah. In the mid 1800s it was an important food item for Mormon pioneers. David Starr Jordan (1891), a noted ichthyologist of the period, once proclaimed Utah Lake as "the greatest sucker pond in the universe." Due to drought in the 1930s the June sucker was believed to have been extirpated (Tanner 1936). It is currently listed as threatened by the Utah Division of Wildlife Resources.

Range

This species is restricted to Utah Lake, Utah and its tributaries.

Description

Coloration of the June sucker is black or brown above, fading to a flat white on the belly. Described in 1878, this large sucker is similar in appearance to the cui-ui of Pyramid Lake. The most distinguishing characteristics of adult fish are weakly developed lip papillae, with widely separated lower lobes and an oblique subterminal mouth.

The body is robust and the head is large. Scales are very large, numbering 55 to 62 in the lateral series. There are 10 to 12 rays in the dorsal fin and 7 rays in the anal fin. Breeding males may have a red lateral stripe (Baxter and Simon 1970).

Size and Longevity

Like other species of *Chasmistes*, the June sucker is probably slow-growing and long-lived. Size ranges of approximately 2 feet and weights of 6 pounds have been reported (Baxter and Simon 1970).

Limiting Factors

Between 1847 and the mid 1920s, adult June suckers were decimated by commercial fishing. During the same time, irrigation diversions and dewatering of the main stem of the Provo River, Utah adversely affected spawning success. In one instance in the late 1800s, an estimated 1,500 tons of spawning suckers (all species) were killed in a two-mile stretch of the Provo River due to dewatering (Carter 1969).

Food and Feeding

Data on the food habits of the June sucker are lacking. It is probably an opportunistic omnivore, feeding on zooplankton, aquatic insects, and algae.

Breeding Habits

The principal spawning area of the June sucker is the section of the Provo River below the Tanner Race diversion, a permanent upstream barrier. Shirley (1983) reports ripe females were captured in the Provo River on June 22. Peak spawning activity appears to be over a relatively brief period between June 15 and June 29. Spawning activity is greatest during midday from approximately 11:00 A.M. to 2:00 P.M.

Shirley (1983) observed suckers resting in the deeper pools of the lower Provo River and moving into shallow riffles to spawn. Spawning activity is typical for a river-spawning sucker. June suckers were observed in small groups of 3 to 6 individuals, a female accompanied by several males. Periodically, in a few seconds of intense activity, the female releases her eggs and the males fertilize them. The spawning activity subsides for a few moments and is then repeated. Water depth at the spawning sites ranges from 1 to 2.5 feet, with a mean depth of 1.7 feet. Substrate in the areas is a mixture of coarse gravel and cobble-sized material. The June sucker does not spawn in sand, silt, or calm backwater areas. The bottom velocity at one spawning site in the Provo River in 1982 was 0.6 foot per second. During the spawning period, mean daily water temperatures range from 53° to 55° F (Shirley 1983).

June sucker eggs are pale yellow and demersal, with a mean diameter of 0.13 inch. They hatch in 4 days at a mean temperature of 70° F. Newly hatched larvae remain on the bottom, entering the water column approximately 10 days after hatching. Larvae average 0.3 inch in length. Larvae and juvenile June suckers stay near the mouth of the Provo River during June and July. The most frequented areas are shallow, calm backwaters with a depth of 3 to 8 inches. Larvae form large schools of several hundred to several thousand. After metamorphosis, young begin to range into swifter, deeper water. They were observed in the river until January, indicating they remain there through the summer, fall, and winter months if adequate water flows are maintained (Shirley 1983).

Habitat

Adult June suckers remain in Utah Lake except when spawning. When great populations of these fish existed they probably inhabited the entire lake, feeding throughout the water column. In its reduced state the population of June suckers probably tends to inhabit more restricted areas of the lake that are shallower and more protected.

Preservation of Species

This unique endemic, whose habitat is restricted to Utah Lake, requires protection to increase the population. It is currently protected by the Utah Division of Wildlife Resources. The continued existence of this species requires maintenance of the habitat and water quality in Utah Lake necessary to sustain the adult population. Preservation of the limited spawning-rearing habitat in the Provo River and possibly other tributaries to Utah Lake is also essential (see chapter 4).

10

Siluriformes

BULLHEAD CATFISHES (ICTALURIDAE)

THE BULLHEAD CATFISHES are easily recognized by their large head and scaleless body and by the soft dorsal fin preceded by a sharp spine, by a small adipose fin, and the spines on the pectoral fins. There are four pairs of barbels on the mouth: the longest pair extends past the head; two pairs are flattened, wide barbels under the chin (the outer pair being twice as long as the inner pair); and the fourth pair, located just behind the posterior opening of the paired nostrils, is short.

This largely nocturnal family is native to the warm waters of North America east of the Rockies (Bond 1979). It has five genera and thirty-nine species (Robins et al. 1980); one genus and five species have been introduced and are prospering in the Great Basin. All of the catfishes guard their nest and to some extent the young. The five Great Basin species may be divided for identification into three groups: the white catfish has a squat body, a forked tail, and a short anal fin; the three bullheads have nearly square tails; and the channel catfish is generally spotted and has a forked tail and a long anal fin.

White catfish
Ictalurus catus (Linnaeus)

Importance

The white catfish is prized as a sport fish for its firm white flesh, its size, and the ease with which it may be caught either day or night. It is popular for these reasons in fee-fishing waters in several areas of the central and eastern United States (McClane 1965).

Range

Its native range is the Atlantic Coast from Chesapeake Bay and New Jersey south to Florida and Texas. In the Great Basin it is locally abundant in Lahontan Reservoir on the Carson River in west-central Nevada, in Indian Lakes and Stillwater Marsh, and in the Humboldt and Truckee River basins, Nevada.

Description

The white catfish is distinguished by its heavy body, moderately forked tail, and short, rounded anal fin, which generally has 19 to 23 rays. Young and nonbreeding adults are a bluish-black to silvery color above and whitish ventrally, giving them a bicolor appearance. The fins are lighter in color than adjacent body areas and the white catfish lacks the sharply defined dusky borders present in many young and subadult channel catfish. During the breeding season, the males and some of the females have a dark bluish-black head, the dorsal half of the body is dusky-blue, and the ventral area is a whitish-blue (Trautman 1981).

Size and Longevity

Adults are generally 10 to 18 inches long and weigh from 8 ounces to 4 pounds. Trautman (1981) reports the maximum size in Ohio as 24 inches.

Limiting Factors

Predation on eggs and young as well as hook and line fishing are the main causes of mortality. Habitat adaptability may be limiting since the white catfish has not prospered in a number of areas where it was stocked.

Food and Feeding

The white catfish, like the black bullhead, is omnivorous, feeding on insects, crustaceans, mollusks, or whatever is available. Larger individuals are sometimes piscivorous.

Breeding Habits

The male and the female combine efforts to build a nest up to 12 inches deep; eggs are fertilized, covered, and guarded by the parents. At an average water temperature of 79° F, the eggs hatch in 6 to 7 days (Miller 1966).

Habitat

La Rivers (1962) notes the white catfish is adapted to large rivers and stocking should be restricted to large reservoirs in Nevada. In its native range the white catfish inhabits the fresh and slightly brackish waters of streams, ponds, and bayous. The species is apparently somewhat migratory. It is tolerant of swiftly flowing waters, but seems to prefer currents more sluggish than those used by channel catfish. It also appears to be more tolerant of a heavily silted bottom than channel catfish. In dense beds of aquatic vegetation, the white catfish is not as abundant as the yellow bullhead, nor does it occur in as large numbers as the black bullhead in small, shallow ponds (Trautman 1981).

Preservation of Species

Where white catfish are abundant, liberal fishing regulations are in order. In areas where numbers are limited, regulations may be more restrictive.

Black bullhead
Ictalurus melas (Rafinesque)

Importance

The black bullhead is an ideal sport fish for youngsters and people who prefer minimum effort in their fishing. A cane pole functions about as well as more expensive gear. The black bullhead strikes slowly and without finesse; only a little patience is required to catch it. This, coupled with its widespread abundance, makes it one of the most popular pan fish in America. Purists may turn up their noses at the idea of angling for bullheads, but these fish provide many hours of fishing pleasure, some in waters where otherwise few fishing opportunities would exist. Almost any kind of live or prepared bait may be used, but worms are probably one of the best. Artificial lures rarely if ever catch bullheads. The only ground rule is to remember to fish on or close to the bottom. Ecologically it is near neutral; its nonselective feeding habits alter the environment very little, except occasionally when it feeds on eggs or young of game fish.

Range

The original range of the black bullhead is from western New York, the Great Lakes, and the St. Lawrence River west to North Dakota, then southeast to Alabama. It is now present in all contiguous forty-eight states. The black bullhead occurs throughout lower elevations (4,500 feet and less) of the Great Basin. Utah Lake and Willard Bay Reservoir in Utah and Lahontan Reservoir in Nevada have representative populations.

Description

The black bullhead has a truncate or very slightly emarginate caudal fin, with a distinct pale vertical bar at the base. The membrane of the anal fin is distinctly darker than the rays, which are usually 17 to 21. The chin barbels are black. Adults are blackish, dark olive, or dark brown on the back. The belly is greenish-white or occasionally bright yellow. Habitat very often dictates the shades of color of the black bullhead, which may be much brighter during the breeding season. Some authors recognize a southern population on the Gulf coast and in northern Mexico as a subspecies; other authors do not believe subspecies are recognizable (Smith 1979).

Size and Longevity

The black bullhead ordinarily does not reach a size of over 14 inches and 2 pounds. The average size is less than 1 pound. The all-tackle hook and line record is 8 pounds (Kutz 1982). Young of the year average 2 to 4 inches, but an abundance of food may produce 8- to 10-inch fish in one year. There are times when reproduction is so high that food is inadequate; the result is large numbers of small, stunted fish. Lost Island Lake in northwest Iowa at times produces large numbers of 7- to 9-inch bullheads that reproduce but grow no larger. Very few black bullheads live beyond 6 years of age.

Limiting Factors

Minnows and other fish feed on black bullhead eggs during spawning and egg incubation. Largemouth bass, frogs, and other predators decimate young even when they are schooled and guarded. One of the hazards the adults face is intensive fighting during the breeding season. Many are scarred; some die from fight-sustained injuries. In certain areas there is a tendency to produce dominant-year classes; this is followed by years of paucity of young. The reason(s) for this are not well understood.

Food and Feeding

The black bullhead is omnivorous and scavenging. It feeds on or near the bottom on plant material, snails, fish, and waste material or, in fact, on almost anything that is edible. When crustaceans are available they may make up as much as 75 percent of the diet. Although the black bullhead has a tendency to be nocturnal, it apparently very often feeds around the clock. An Iowa study shows them feeding heavily on midge larvae and mayfly nymphs along with other insects, small crayfish, worms, and small mollusks (Harlan and Speaker 1956). La Rivers (1962) reports that the black bullhead is omnivorous and shows no selectivity in prey choices. He states that as much as one-fourth of its food may consist of aquatic vegetation, along with fish, mollusks, snails, leeches, oligochaetes, and aquatic insects.

Breeding Habits

The black bullhead spawns from May to July. Eggs are laid in water from 6 inches to 4 feet deep when water temperatures reach 65° to 70° F. Nests are made under submerged logs, in abandoned muskrat dens, or under old stumps or rooted vegetation; even a hollow depression on the bottom is acceptable. The adhesive eggs, laid in a single gelatinous mass and numbering from 2,000 to 6,000, are incubated in about 15 days. At first either the male or female or both may guard the eggs and provide aeration, but the female may leave and the male may continue the vigil (Sigler and Miller 1963). When the young leave the nest they form a compact ball-like school. The conspicuous schools of coal-black youngsters are at times easily observed from shore. They are guarded by one or both parents until the young fish are about an inch long, then they are abandoned. Schooling persists throughout most of the summer but may be permanently disrupted by repeated attacks of predators.

Habitat

Black bullhead occurs in a wide variety of habitats, but is most abundant where there is turbid water, a silt bottom, no strong current, and often a lack of diversity of fish fauna. It may be the dominant fish in small ponds, quarries, small reservoirs, intermittent creeks, and muddy, inhospitable backwater areas. Its most common associates are minnows and sunfishes, although in Utah Lake the other dominant fish are white bass, common carp, walleye, and channel catfish. It is able to survive in areas of low oxygen (less than 2 ppm). Optimum temperatures are the low 70s but it can survive in waters as warm as the high 80s. It apparently prefers the weedy inshore areas of streams or lakes to open water, although if abundant it may be present throughout the area. In disturbed or polluted areas it is more apt to prosper than other catfishes.

Preservation of Species

Liberal fishing regulations are in order for the black bullhead in optimum habitat; generally there is no minimum size and no limit on numbers that may be taken. In a habitat barren of food and cover, structures for breeding such as three-sided containers may be introduced; brush piles or similar debris will increase food production. It may be undesirable to stock black bullhead in large bodies of water with populations of yellow or brown bullhead because the black may eventually dominate the other two species.

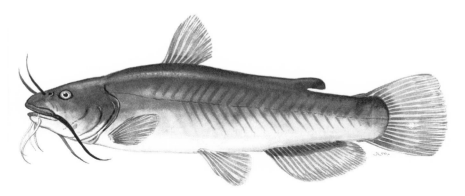

Yellow bullhead
Ictalurus natalis (Lesueur)

Importance

In some areas the yellow bullhead is the most important catfish in the creel. In Illinois, for example, where there are numerous small streams, it prospers and reaches a larger size than the black bullhead and is therefore more sought after. The same methods used for catching black bullhead are used for the yellow bullhead; however, Harlan and Speaker (1956) state that the yellow bullhead is more nocturnal than the other two bullheads and hence fewer are taken in an angler's daytime catch. Its very restricted occurrence in the Great Basin limits its importance as either a sport or a forage species.

Range

The original range of the yellow bullhead is the eastern and central United States, from the east coast and the Great Lakes west to the Dakotas, south to Mexico, Texas, and Florida (Lee et al. 1980). The range has been extended by a few plantings but it has not been planted as extensively as have some of the other catfishes. In the Great Basin it is present in Warner Valley, Oregon (Coombs, Bond, and Drohan 1979).

Description

The yellow bullhead is robust, olive or brown above and yellowish below. Immaculate white or yellow chin barbels and a long rounded caudal fin are its most distinctive features. It has 24 to 27 anal rays, with a vague dark stripe running through the middle of the anal fin. There is a finely serrated posterior edge on the pectoral spines. Young are distinctive because of the long anal fin and immaculate chin barbels (Smith 1979).

Size and Longevity

The yellow bullhead generally lives 5 to 6 years. It grows somewhat faster and larger than the black bullhead. Individuals weighing as much as 2 pounds are often taken from the Mississippi River and ones that weigh over a pound are not uncommon from Clear Lake and elsewhere in Iowa (Harlan and Speaker 1956). The all-tackle hook and line record is 3 pounds, 3 ounces (Kutz 1982).

Limiting Factors and Food and Feeding

Information under these headings is similar to that for the black bullhead.

Breeding Habits

The yellow bullhead spawns in May or June in waters from 18 inches to 4 feet deep. Nests are constructed and from 2,000 to 7,000 eggs are deposited; they hatch in 5 to 10 days. The fry are guarded by the parents until late July or August. They reach about 3 inches in size the first year and mature during the third year (Harlan and Speaker 1956).

Habitat

The yellow bullhead is a stream species, whereas the black bullhead is typical of ponds and lakes and the brown bullhead is present principally in lakes. The yellow bullhead is the most abundant and widespread catfish in Illinois, possibly because it is a creek species and has abundant habitats (Smith 1979).

In Ohio the largest populations occur in the shallow portions of large bays, lakes, ponds, and streams where the gradient is low, the water clear, and aquatic vegetation profuse. It apparently tolerates such diverse bottom types as gravel, sand, peat, and muck (Trautman 1981).

Preservation of Species

Degradation of habitat and competition from other catfishes are the two main limiting factors for the yellow bullhead.

Brown bullhead
Ictalurus nebulosus (Lesueur)

Importance

The brown bullhead is not as valuable to the sport fishery over its native range as the black or yellow bullhead, primarily because it is generally less abundant. It is more abundant than the yellow but not the black bullhead in the Great Basin. Where it is present in numbers it is popular and provides an important contribution to the sport fishery.

Range

The original range of the brown bullhead is from Maine and the Great Lakes south to Florida and Mexico and as far west as the Missouri River (Lee et al. 1980). In the Great Basin it was planted in the late 1870s in the Truckee, Carson, and Humboldt rivers as well as Washoe Lake. Recently, populations have been documented in the Carson River basin.

Description

The brown bullhead has 21 to 24 anal rays with large "teeth" on the posterior edge of the pectoral spines. It is yellowish brown or blue-black above and heavily mottled or marbled on the sides. The ventral surface is bright yellow to yellow or at times white. It has heavily pigmented chin barbels. The caudal fin, as in the yellow bullhead, is nearly square.

Size and Longevity

The size of the brown bullhead ranges from 7 to 15 inches and a weight of up to 2 pounds. A few reach a size of 16 to 18 inches and approximately 3 pounds. The all-tackle hook and line record is 5 pounds, 8 ounces (Kutz 1982). Limited data indicate that the brown bullhead lives 6 or 7 years.

Limiting Factors

The range of the brown bullhead has decreased since the turn of the century, presumably due to loss of habitat. It is apparently not as tolerant of polluted, silt-laden waters as the black bullhead. There are other indications that the brown bullhead cannot compete favorably with the black. Trautman (1981) states there is mass hybridization of black and brown bullheads in Ohio. Great Basin populations are adversely affected by interspecific competition and habitat destruction.

Food and Feeding

The food and feeding habits of the brown bullhead are similar to those of the black bullhead, but it may forage less in the daytime than the black bullhead. It feeds largely on insect larvae, crustaceans, snails, small crayfish, worms, and small fish (Harlan and Speaker 1956).

Breeding Habits

The brown bullhead spawns in the spring, fanning out a saucer-shaped nest and depositing 2,000 to 10,000 cream-colored adhesive eggs. These are guarded by one or both parents. The adults, or generally the male, guard the young through part of the summer, after which they are on their own. They mature when they are age 3.

Habitat

In Illinois the brown bullhead occurs in clear, well-vegetated lakes (Smith 1979). In Ohio the brown bullhead was once abundant only in clear waters of Lake Erie and its adjacent bays, harbors, and marshes. It was also present in widely separated postglacial lakes and impoundments of the northern end of the state. Only strays were present in flowing waters, except in one small northeast section, where small populations were found in small, clear, weedy, low-gradient streams (Trautman 1981). Trautman states he has never seen one that was taken from the Ohio River. The brown bullhead can live in stagnant waters and shallow ponds where most other species cannot survive.

Preservation of Species

Decimation of habitat rather than fishing pressure has apparently reduced the brown bullhead over much of its native range. Rehabilitation of habitat and stocking in clearwater lakes with heavy vegetation would appear to be the best management techniques.

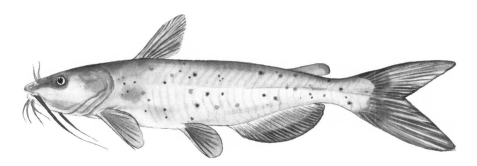

Channel catfish
Ictalurus punctatus (Rafinesque)

Importance

The channel catfish is one of the most important warmwater fish in the United States. It is sought by anglers of all ages with many diverse types of gear, most of which it is amenable to taking (Sigler and Miller 1963). In recent years the channel catfish has become more popular with western fishermen because it provides a fishery in waters that will not support trout. Channel catfish's customary bottom-feeding characteristic should be considered when fishing for it. Bait should be fished either on or just off the bottom and be as odiferous as possible. Surface baits also take channel catfish at night. La Rivers (1962) notes the channel cat is the most abundant game fish in the lower Colorado drainage below Nevada and the one most often caught. It is ranked second after largemouth bass in Lake Mead (La Rivers 1962). From a management point of view, catfishes have the additional benefit of feeding consistently on substances such as organic debris, plants, and other bottom material avoided by most other game fish. Fee-fishing catfish ponds are an important industry in the United States, with channel catfish providing an important segment of the total harvest (Tave et al. 1981). Sport fishing for channel catfish in swift water with light tackle provides some of the superior sport fishing in Arizona (Minckley 1973).

Fee fishing for channel catfish has not been developed in the Great Basin, possibly due to the preference of the populace for salmonids and the general availability of public waters, but the potential for increased recreational fishing and protein production is present. The commercial production of channel catfish exceeds that of any other fish in the United States.

Channel catfish has tremendous potential for aquaculture in the Great Basin. Tolerance of brackish water enables rearing it in such waters as geothermal energy production overflows, irrigation return flows, treated sewage waters, and others. Because of its omnivorous nature, channel catfish adapts well to commercial food rations in captivity, thereby making it a relatively easy species for pond culture.

Range

The original range of the channel catfish extends from the St. Lawrence River in Quebec, Canada, south on the western side of the Appalachian Mountains to southern Georgia and central Florida, west through the Gulf states to eastern Texas and northern Mexico, and then northwest through New Mexico to Montana. It has been widely introduced throughout the eastern and western United States and is probably present wherever there is suitable habitat (Scott and Crossman 1973). Channel catfish is not native to the Great Basin but was successfully introduced in the late 1800s. It is now widely distributed in warmwater lakes, reservoirs, and streams throughout the Great Basin.

Description

The channel catfish is distinguishable from other catfishes by its long anal fin and its deeply forked tail. The upper lobe may be slightly longer than the lower lobe; both lobes are sharply pointed. The body is pale bluish-olive above and bluish-white below. Spots may be present over much or none of the body; older fish are often without spots. The males at breeding time are often brightly colored and have enlarged heads, thickened lips, and fatty pads around the eyes. Both the dorsal and pectoral fins have strong, sharp spines. The dorsal fin has 5 to 6 soft rays; each pectoral fin has 4 to 5 rays; the adipose is soft and fatty.

Work by Wolters (1981) on polyploidy of channel catfish demonstrated that offspring from fish artificially spawned in the normal fashion were diploid (2n = 58 chromosomes) while cold-shocked fertilized eggs had 100 percent incidence of triploidy (3n = 87). Diploid and triploid fish reared for 8 months were significantly different in size (triploid fish were larger). Triploid male and female catfish have small gonads with altered histological features, indicating sterility, a potential explanation for better feed efficiency and greater growth. Increased feed efficiency, resultant larger size, and no reproductive capability all have

applications in commercial rearing, fee fishing, or occasionally management enterprises.

Size and Longevity

Channel catfish occasionally reaches 36 inches and 25 pounds, but
the average is 2 to 4 pounds. The all-tackle North American hook and
line record is 58 pounds (Kutz 1982). Fish as large as 32 pounds have
been caught in the Great Basin. Moyle (1976) reports that channel catfish in California demonstrates highly variable rates of growth but is
one of the fastest growing species of catfish. Sigler and Miller (1963)
report that young catfish at the mouth of the Bear River, just inside the
Bear River Migratory Bird Refuge, are sometimes as long as 6 to 7 inches
when they are 1 year old. Lawler (1960) in a Utah Lake study reports
length at the end of each year for fish age 1 to 12 in inches as 3.1, 6.9,
9.4, 12.1, 14.5, 16.7, 17.9, 18.9, 19.7, 20.6, 21.2, and 21.6. Purkett (1958)
found that channel catfish in the Salt River, Missouri grew somewhat
slower and did not live as long.

Limiting Factors

Data from the 1960s in California (Calhoun 1966) indicate that for
a particular population the mean annual survival rate was 0.560 (44 percent would die annually), annual expectation of death from fishing was
0.304 (30.4 percent would be caught by fishermen), and annual expectation of death from natural causes was 0.136 (13.6 percent would die
naturally). New Mexico reports annual returns of hatchery-reared
catchables of 18.5 percent, 17.3 percent, and 15 percent (Little 1963).
Arkansas estimates 75 percent of its stocked adult channel catfish are
harvested by anglers (Anonymous 1962). Age and growth studies have
documented the occurrences of individuals as old as 24 years, but most
members of the species probably live no more than 10 to 12 years.

Food and Feeding

Most authors agree the channel catfish is not particular about what
it eats. La Rivers (1962) notes channel catfish is a consumer of food materials such as organic debris and plants consistently avoided by other
game fishes and is therefore an efficient converter of vegetation to pro-
teins. In Iowa, when elm tree seeds are abundant, channel catfish in
some areas feeds on nothing else (Harlan and Speaker 1956). Channel
catfish in Utah eats clams, crayfish, earthworms, snails, fish, plant material, and seeds (Sigler and Miller 1963). It may feed during both
daylight and darkness. Bottom feeding is more characteristic, but it oc-

casionally feeds at the surface, particularly when young. During daylight hours in clear water, the channel catfish apparently relies more on sight than other senses for locating feed, a somewhat unique trait for a catfish.

Clady (1981) states that channel catfish in early spring (52° to 54° F) grows more rapidly in waters stocked with golden shiners and *Tilapia* sp. than it does when stocked alone. The other species seemed to stimulate the catfish to feed.

Work by Clady (1981) and Cannamela, Brader, and Johnson (1979) indicate the presence of other catfish may affect both food selection and the amount of feeding by channel catfish, particularly at the lower temperatures experienced in temperate climates, presumably by alternate food item selection and feeding behavior stimulation.

In two western Kentucky impoundments, Cannamela, Brader, and Johnson (1979) found that young catfish relied heavily on zooplankton and aquatic insects. Other food items that were seasonally important included trichopterans, bryozoans, and fish. Fish were the most important food of intermediate size (6- to 12-inch) catfish in both lakes.

Breeding Habits

Channel catfish is a secretive spawner. It will not spawn if the water is so transparent that it provides no shelter. Spawning is initiated in spring or early summer at water temperatures between 72° and 75° F. Semidark nests are built by the males in holes, undercut logs, banks, or rocky areas. Females spawn only once a year, but males may spawn several times (Scott and Crossman 1973). Females lay as many as 34,500 eggs, which are approximately 0.12 to 0.16 inch in diameter before laying. The male protects the nest after the eggs have been deposited and fertilized; the eggs hatch in 6 to 10 days. The young have a yolk sac for approximately 2 to 5 days, then they swim to the surface and begin to feed. The male may remain with the young for varying periods of time after hatching. Either the male or the female may devour the eggs if they are disturbed too often during incubation.

Moyle (1976) reports the age and size of channel catfish at first spawning is highly variable. Ages from 2 to 8 years have been recorded, corresponding to lengths of 7 to 22 inches. Most, however, probably mature at age 3, 4, or 5 years.

Habitat

Channel catfish, with its streamlined body and deeply forked tail, is adapted for living in large, moderately swift streams. It is more

adapted to stream life than most North American catfishes but it prospers in lakes. In rivers, adults typically spend the day in pools or beneath shelter such as logs or undercut banks, moving into riffle areas to
feed at dusk. Rising water levels, following a storm, tend to cause channel catfish to start feeding even in the daytime, possibly in response to
food washed in by rainfall or a slight chemical change in the water.
Young channel catfish remain in the riffles and utilize rocks or other
obstacles as barriers against the current.

If given an opportunity, channel catfish will seek clearwater lakes
and streams with a variety of bottom types. However, they live and
prosper in moderately muddy water if food is abundant. Large populations thrive in the lower Colorado, Bear, and Green rivers of Utah. They
prosper in numerous farm ponds across the country where they have
been planted.

Preservation of Species

Channel catfish, long popular in the Midwest and East, is rapidly
becoming one of the more popular sport fish in the western states. It is
easy to raise in hatcheries, reproduces readily in the wild, is relatively
easy to catch, and can provide a large sport fishery. Current management philosophies embrace the idea of maintaining population balance
through stocking, installation of spawning devices, thinning stunted
populations (always a costly effort), removing competing species, and
applying angling regulations. Legal limits on minimum size and number in the creel are generally in order.

ARMORED CATFISHES (LORICARIIDAE)

The armored catfishes, sometimes referred to as the suckermouth
catfishes in aquarium literature, are elongate, flattened fish with a full
coating of bony plates. These plates are roughened with a thick coating
of fine prickles. The mouth forms a sucking disc under the head. The
adipose fin is supported by a bony spine covered with fine prickles.
Members of this family inhabit South and Central America to Nica-
ragua. One species occurs in the Great Basin.

Suckermouth catfish
Hypostomus plecostomus (Linnaeus)

Importance

The suckermouth catfish is an important aquarium species because of its ability to provide "clean-up services" in aquaria. It is well equipped for eating algae, which it does industriously, even cleaning aquarium plants without injuring them. It has been introduced into waters of the Great Basin where it competes with native fishes.

Range

This species is ubiquitous in South America east of the Andes Mountains. It has been stocked in waters of the United States by accidental or intentional releases of aquarium fish and at least in one case for control of algae. It has been introduced in Florida, Texas, and Nevada. Within the Great Basin it exists in Indian Springs in the southeastern part of Nevada (Lee et al. 1980).

Description

The coloration of this species is generally brown with darkened spots on the dorsal and caudal fins and a mottled or dotlike pattern on the sides and head. The dot pattern on the head is smaller than elsewhere on the body (Innis 1979).

Size and Longevity

This fish generally grows to a length of no more than 10 inches. However, in the United States most are smaller (Innis 1979). Lee et al. (1980) report Florida populations ranging in size from 7 to 16 inches, with a maximum of 24 inches. Where food is abundant and water temperatures suitable, it probably grows rapidly and is relatively long-lived.

Limiting Factors

In the Great Basin where there are small native fishes, the suckermouth catfish is a negative ecological factor.

Food and Feeding

This species will eat almost anything, but it is mainly an algal grazer, primarily a nocturnal feeder, and somewhat timid.

Breeding Habits

The suckermouth catfish lays its eggs in holes and provides parental care for them (Innis 1979).

Habitat

In its native range the suckermouth catfish occupies lakes, streams, and rivers. It is able to live in deoxygenated water and may possibly make short migrations over land assisted by accessory respiratory organs in its stomach. In the United States adults are mainly in rocky habitats while juveniles are in areas of heavy vegetation. Temperature preferences are in the 62° to 80° F range, making the thermal springs and their outflows in Nevada optimum habitat (Lee et al. 1980).

Preservation of Species

No particular considerations should be given to this species. Additional stocking is discouraged. Eradication of existing populations may be desirable where it is detrimental to native species.

11

Atheriniformes

KILLIFISHES (CYPRINODONTIDAE)

KILLIFISHES RESEMBLE minnows in having soft-rayed fins, abdominal pelvic fins, and cycloid scales. Minnows and killifishes, however, are not closely related. The rounded or squared caudal fin (forked in minnows), the toothed jaws, and the presence of scales on the head readily provide means for distinguishing killifishes from minnows. The killifishes are small, often highly colorful little fish, about 2 to 4 inches long. The head is flattened on top with the mouth opening near or along its upper surface. These adaptations aid all these species in their surface-feeding habits. Killifishes are aggressive, usually with strong sexual dimorphism.

Members of this family are present in temperate and tropical regions over most of the world, including Africa, Spain, the Mediterranean Sea, southern Asia, and the East Indies. They are absent from Australia. Species inhabit salt, brackish, mineralized, and fresh waters, occurring in such desolate regions as Death Valley and around the Dead Sea. Some have even adapted to temporary ponds, laying eggs that survive in bottom soil after the pond water evaporates and the adults die. These eggs hatch quickly upon the return of seasonal rains. Perhaps the most remarkable of these fishes is the Devils Hole pupfish, a tiny species that occupies the smallest known range of any vertebrate animal, approximately 23 square yards, in Devil's Hole, Death Valley National Monument, Nevada (Sigler and Miller 1963; Moyle 1976).

Forty-eight species in ten genera are listed for this family in the American Fisheries Society's *List of Common and Scientific Names of Fishes from the United States and Canada* (Robins et al. 1980). Nine species in five genera occur in the Great Basin; seven species are native. Habitats occupied by members of this family in the Great Basin are generally restricted and subject to disruption.

Members of this family live in a variety of habitats in the Great Basin; many are springs or spring-fed. The ecological concept of springs or spring areas as "islands" is valid here. Many if not all of these species have evolved with little or no competition from other species and in habitats that have been ecologically stable for hundreds or thousands of years. Disruption or alteration of these islands will invariably result in changes to which the native species may not be capable of adapting.

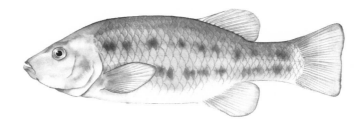

White River springfish
Crenichthys baileyi (Gilbert)

Importance

This species, along with other members of this genus, is a unique natural history entity. At least three subspecies exist, all of which are presently listed as threatened or of special concern (Williams 1981). The preservation of biological information that is potentially useful to mankind should be of sufficient import to prevent the subspecies' loss. This species' unique genetic makeup allows it to exist in high-temperature, low dissolved oxygen environments (Hubbs and Hettler 1964; see chapter 4).

Range

The White River springfish is present in suitable warm springs and their effluents, at intervals along the now disrupted pluvial White River drainage of extreme eastern and southeastern Nevada, from the vicinity of Preston and Lund in the north, to Warm Springs near Moapa in the south (La Rivers 1962).

Description

This species is olivaceous above and bright silvery on the lower half of the sides and below. It has 2 lengthwise series of coarse black spots, one along the midline of the body and the other on a level with the lower edge of the caudal peduncle. The anal fin is large. The dorsal and anal fins are set far back and have 11 and 14 rays, respectively. The dorsal fin is set exactly over the anal fin. The pectoral fins have about 16 rays; the pelvic fins are lacking (La Rivers 1962).

Size and Longevity

The maximum size of the White River springfish is about 2.5 inches. It probably lives 3 or 4 years.

Limiting Factors

Introduced exotic fishes have had adverse effects on the populations in Ash and Crystal springs in Pahranagat Valley as well as the populations in the warm springs of the Moapa Valley, Nevada. One population in Hiko Springs is now apparently extinct, presumably through interaction with introduced species (Deacon and Williams 1984; see chapter 4). Additional losses of local populations have been observed and attributed to habitat alterations in the warm springs of Moapa Valley.

Food and Feeding

Deacon et al. (1980) report that this species is omnivorous in June. By volume, plant material constitutes 37 percent of the food and animal matter 21 percent. Filamentous algae is the most important food in June, occurring in over 60 percent of the fish. In July, August, and September the fish are primarily herbivorous. Caddisfly larvae are the most important animal food item. Overall analyses strongly suggest it is primarily herbivorous (Williams and Williams 1982).

Breeding Habits

The male exhibits courtship characteristics that induce the female to extrude eggs. The eggs are fertilized singly as they appear. From 10 to 17 eggs seem to constitute a spawning. The eggs are about 0.07 inch in diameter. The incubation period is from 5 to 7 days. The spawning period extends over the warm summer months.

Habitat

The White River springfish lives in warm springs that range in temperature from 70° to 98.5° F, but it prefers the spring heads and quiet waters along the outflows (Deacon et al. 1980). Individuals in warm springs have a higher oxygen demand than those in the cool springs (La Rivers 1962). High temperatures of 70° to 98.6° F and low minimum dissolved oxygen concentrations (0.7 to 5.8 ppm) are typical in habitats occupied by this species (Hubbs and Hettler 1964; Williams and Wilde 1981).

Preservation of Species

This species needs to be protected from introduced species and their associated predation, competition, and parasites as well as from continued habitat alterations. Where it currently exists, consideration should be given to establishing the area as a refuge (see chapter 4).

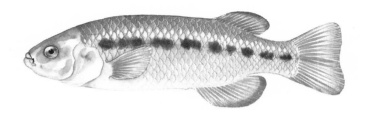

Railroad Valley springfish
Crenichthys nevadae Hubbs

Importance

The Railroad Valley springfish is ecologically important because it has evolved over thousands of years in a highly specialized habitat. It is considered threatened (Don Sada, personal communication, 1983).

Range

The Railroad Valley springfish is native to 7 thermal springs in the Railroad Valley, Nye County, Nevada (Williams and Williams 1981). This area is just west of the White River. It has been introduced into Chimney Hot Springs, Nye County and springs at Sodaville in nearby Mineral County (Deacon and Williams 1984).

Description

The dark spots along the sides of this species are in a single row. There are pale bars between the dark splotches. The body is massive, two-thirds as wide as deep, and especially heavy forward. The head is very heavy, almost as wide as it is deep. The lateral series has 30 scales. The dorsal fin has 12 rays and the anal fin 13 (La Rivers 1962).

Size and Longevity

Williams (1983) reports Railroad Valley springfish from Big Warm Spring have a mean total length of 1.4 inches with a range of 0.5 to 2.8 inches. It probably lives to an age of 3 to 4 years.

Limiting Factors

This species is threatened by destruction and/or alteration of habitat (Deacon et al. 1979). Introduction of predators and species that compete for resources (channel catfish and mollies, respectively) have also adversely affected this species (Peter Moyle, personal communication 1983; see chapter 4).

Food and Feeding

Deacon et al. (1980) report the Railroad Valley springfish was predominantly carnivorous in all months of a study. Animal foods constituted 64, 88, 68, and 65 mean percent volume in June, July, August, and September, respectively. Plant material was important in June, contributing 26 percent by volume. Gastropods were the most important foods in June, constituting 54 percent of the total volume. Most of the plant material eaten was filamentous algae. Intestine length indicates an omnivorous species; high water temperatures in its habitat may require consumption of higher-energy animal foods.

Breeding Habits

The breeding habits of the Railroad Valley springfish are presumably similar to those of the White River springfish. Williams (1983) reports high numbers of eggs in females with 264.5, 224.8, and 210.5 being averages for spring, summer, and fall, respectively. The average number fell to 53.8 in winter. The number of eggs per female was correlated with habitat type (Williams 1983). Females in warm lotic environments have more eggs than those in standing warm springs. Because most females carried several classes of eggs simultaneously, Williams (1983) postulates that it is probable that females may spawn two or more times annually in some habitats. Highest levels of reproductive activity are reached at temperatures of 86° F.

Habitat

Two springs that are inhabited by Railroad Valley springfish were investigated by Williams (1983). Big Warm Spring has a main headpool with a maximum width of 77 feet and a length of 78 feet. The substrate is a soft, easily disturbed mud. Aquatic vegetation in both the spring and the outflow is sparse. Little Warm Spring is similar to Big Warm Spring but supports a larger area (18.5 acres) of marsh. Reported temperatures range from 77° to 102° F for these springs. In controlled experiments, fish exhibited stress and swam poorly at 102° F. The critical maximum was 101° F. La Rivers (1962) reports that the temperature in Duckwater Spring ranges up to 88° F and the pH is 8.0.

Preservation of Species

During 1982 and 1983, this species was nearly eliminated from Duckwater Spring because of predation by introduced channel catfish. Modification of the spring has also allowed expansion of the exotic molly populations, resulting in increased competition for available resources (Peter Moyle, personal communication, 1983). Steps to eliminate or reduce both predation and competition are necessary to preserve this species. A stable, constant habitat is necessary so that minimum energy is expended for reproduction (Williams 1983). Provisions for these considerations will help ensure its continued existence (see chapter 4).

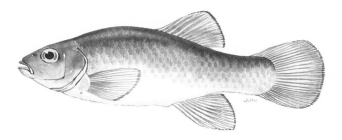

Devils Hole pupfish
***Cyprinodon diabolis* Wales**

Importance

No known species of animal is more unique than the Devils Hole pupfish. It survives in a single native habitat in a very restricted area (although two transplated populations have been established). The entire life cycle of this species, particularly reproduction, is tied to water levels in Devil's Hole, Nevada. This species has occupied this single habitat for more than 20,000 years (James 1969). The total population of Devils Hole pupfish is said to range from 200 to 700 individuals (Miller 1961). This species is listed as endangered by the U.S. Fish and Wildlife Service (see chapter 4).

Range

Devil's Hole, Ash Meadows, Nevada, a disjunct segment of Death Valley National Monument, constitutes the entire native range of this species. Approximately 60 individuals were transplanted to an artificial habitat below Hoover Dam in 1980 and 25 individuals were transplanted into an artificial habitat at the Amargosa Pupfish Station, Ash Meadows in 1983.

Description

The sides of the male have a metallic, bluish iridescence that changes to a metallic green or golden in a different light. The overall color is dark brown. All fins are edged with black. The dorsal has a golden iridescence. The anal is whitish toward its base. The opercles are especially iridescent with a violet sheen on the posterior portion. The iris is an iridescent blue. The general color of the female is more yellowish than that of the male. The back is yellowish-brown; the caudal and pectoral fins are yellowish on the basal half; the dorsal is edged with a black band. There is an indication of a lateral dark bar through the middle of the caudal peduncle. The opercles are metallic green; the eyes faint metallic blue. The young are much the same color as the female, with a faint vertical bar on the sides. There is no pelvic fin. The lateral series has 27 ctenoid scales. The pectoral fins have 17 rays; the dorsal fin 12 rays, the first 2 of which are simple, while the others are branched. The caudal fin, with 28 rays, is convex (La Rivers 1962; Baugh and Deacon 1983).

Size and Longevity

La Rivers (1962) lists the total length from the original description as approximately 1 inch. These little fish are reported to live less than 1 year (Baugh and Deacon 1983).

Limiting Factors

The single most important factor influencing the continued existence of this species is the water level in Devil's Hole. If water levels drop severely, the tiny area of shelf where reproduction occurs will be lost to the species. Earlier pumping of aquifers in the surrounding area threatened to accomplish this feat and seal the fate of the Devils Hole pupfish, something 20,000 years of natural activity failed to do. Negotiations for the purchase of a large portion of Ash Meadows from private holders has recently been completed. It is anticipated that several additional key holdings will be acquired. This will lead the way to the establishment of a new federal refuge and more stable water levels in Ash Meadows.

Food and Feeding

The Devils Hole pupfish is apparently largely an algal feeder, preferring diatoms except for occasional animal organisms such as beetles, amphipods, and less frequently snails.

Breeding Habits

Breeding behavior has been described by Baugh and Deacon (1983) and is moderately involved. As actual spawning occurs, both fish bend their bodies into an S shape and eggs and sperm are released. It is an opportunistic breeder and spawns on a variety of substrate materials on the shelf in Devil's Hole. Spawning activity can occur all year round but is concentrated in April and May.

Habitat

The original habitat of the Devils Hole pupfish is unique among vertebrate species. Devil's Hole is a rock-bound pool in Ash Meadows, Nevada. The area is characteristic of the arid southwestern desert. The hole itself is about 23 by 9 feet but is connected to a largely unexplored subterranean reservoir (Baugh and Deacon 1983).

This species lives in water up to 80 feet deep, but spends much of the time along the shallow south shelf of Devil's Hole in a total habitat of about 23 square yards. The limnological characteristics of this limestone habitat are briefly described as temperature 91° to 93° F, pH 7.3, dissolved oxygen 1.8 to 3.3 ppm, bicarbonate 256 ppm, and carbon dioxide 18 ppm (La Rivers 1962).

Preservation of Species

Continued existence of this species in its native habitat is contingent upon continued stability of the water level in Devil's Hole and the associated aquifer that supplies it. Close monitoring of the water level and quality should be continued and research into the ecological requirements of this species should be pursued.

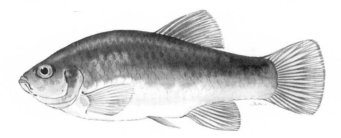

Amargosa pupfish
Cyprinodon nevadensis **Eigenmann and Eigenmann**

Importance

Some subspecies of this species are of special concern or endangered. Because of the wide genetic variability expressed in subspecific populations and their being established in a wide range of habitats, this fish should be protected at the subspecific level. They are effective predators on mosquito larvae.

Range

The Amargosa pupfish is confined to the Amargosa River basin in the California-Nevada area of the western Great Basin. This species, in which six subspecies are currently recognized, exists in a number of isolated populations. Individual populations usually consist of only one subspecies. It is the most widespread of the Death Valley pupfishes, with subspecies and population adapted to a wide variety of aquatic environments (Moyle 1976).

Description

Breeding males are blue over the entire body, including the caudal peduncle. They have a black band at the end of the tail. The vertical bars on the female are variable, ranging from 6 to 10 distinct bands to a lesser number of faint bars. It is a deep-bodied fish and males in particular show this trait (Miller 1948). This is the most variable species of pupfish. There are 23 to 28, usually 25 to 26, large scales in the lateral series. The scales before the dorsal fin are 14 to 24, usually 16 to 18. Anal rays are 8 to 11, usually 10, and pectoral rays are 11 to 18, usually 15 to 17. Gill rakers are 14 to 22, usually 15 to 17.

Size and Longevity

This species reaches a length of more than an inch in 4 to 6 weeks;

the maximum size is about 2.5 inches (Miller 1948). It probably lives 2 to 3 years.

Limiting Factors

Several subspecies of the Amargosa pupfish are currently threatened by habitat destruction and/or alteration, hybridization and competition with exotics, and the fact that some of the native ranges are restricted to small geographic areas. It is not threatened at the species level.

Food and Feeding

The main food of the Amargosa pupfish is algae, especially blue-green algae. However, small invertebrates are also an important item in the diet. It feeds heavily on mosquito larvae. The larval fish start feeding on small invertebrates within a day after hatching (Danielsen 1968).

Breeding Habits

The Amargosa pupfish matures at slightly over an inch in 4 to 6 weeks. It may have 8 to 10 generations per year in springs, but stream populations have only 2 to 3 (Miller 1948). The following describes breeding behavior of the desert pupfish, which is similar to the Amargosa pupfish (Liu 1969). Spawning is from April to October when water temperatures exceed 68° F. The brightly colored male patrols his territory seeking females in water about 3 feet deep. Spawning centers on some small object or bump on the bottom. Normally the male defends his territory of 11 to 22 square feet, although it may be a much larger area. When a female is ready to spawn she approaches a male, then tilts her head toward the bottom and nips at it, usually taking a small piece of substrate in her mouth. When she renews her horizontal position, she spits the piece out. This may occur several times. She lays, and the male fertilizes, a single egg at a time (Barlow 1961). The number of eggs laid per female ranges from 50 to 800 or more during a season. The eggs hatch in 10 days at 68° F.

Habitat

The populations in the Ash Meadows area, Nye County, Nevada inhabit freshwater springs that range in temperature from 70° to 91° F. These springs generally do not vary more than 4 to 13 degrees. In contrast, the Amargosa River varies from close to freezing in winter to nearly 104° F in summer, with substantial daily fluctuations. The maximum temperature the Amargosa pupfish can stand for any length of time is about 107° F. One of the more remarkable habitats occupied by this species is the Tecopa Bore, an outflow of an artesian well drilled in 1967. The temperature at the well head is 117.5° F but cools considerably before reaching the nearby marsh. Its coldest temperatures may be near freezing (Moyle 1976).

Preservation of Species

This species needs protection from habitat degradation, exotic species predation, competition, and disease. Efforts should be made to prevent habitat degradation and to remove and also prevent the introduction of exotic species.

Owens pupfish
***Cyprinodon radiosus* Miller**

Importance

This species is listed by the U.S. Fish and Wildlife Service as endangered and is also fully protected by California law. It has been used for mosquito control in Owens Valley, California.

Range

Originally Owens pupfish was present in the Owens River system from Lone Pine, California to Fish Slough and its springs, Mono County, California. It was once abundant in the Owens River and adjacent waters. Now warm springs near Lone Pine and refuges constructed around springs at Fish Slough contain the only surviving populations (Miller and Pister 1971).

Description

Breeding males are bright blue with purplish lateral bars and the dorsal may be pinkish-tan to orange, either black-bordered or not. These bars do not narrow ventrally as in other pupfishes. Females are similar to other female pupfishes. The large scales in the lateral series number 26 to 27. The dorsal rays number 10 to 12, usually 11; anal rays 9 to 12, usually 10; pectoral rays 13 to 17, usually 14 to 15; pelvic rays 6 to 8, usually 7; and caudal rays 16 to 19. The head is more slender and the caudal peduncle is longer than in other pupfishes from Death Valley (Miller 1948; Miller and Pister 1971).

Size and Longevity

Presumably this species reaches a length of something less than 2 inches during the first growing season. Maximum length is about 2.4 inches. Owens pupfish probably lives no more than 2 or 3 years.

Limiting Factors

Owens pupfish has been threatened by habitat destruction and the fact that its native range is severely restricted. Alterations in any part of this restricted habitat could have far-reaching consequences for this species (Deacon et al. 1979).

Food and Feeding

This species feeds mostly on aquatic insects, primarily midge larvae, and, to a lesser extent, mayfly larvae and beetle larvae and adults. It also feeds on mosquito larvae (Kennedy 1916).

Breeding Habits

The breeding habits of the Owens pupfish are similar to those of the Amargosa pupfish.

Habitat

This species, once thought to be extinct, is now protected by law. The sanctuaries where it is confined have large, clear pools with extensive shallow areas as well as holes up to 7 feet deep. It prefers warm, clear water, with heavy stands of emergent bulrushes in shallow water and dense mats of *Chara* on the bottom of the pools. Water temperatures range from 50° to 75° F.

Preservation of Species

This species was at one time (1948) thought to be extinct. Tremendous efforts were made by a number of individuals, agencies, and private groups to reestablish it in sanctuaries in the Owens Valley, California. Sanctuaries that attempt to exclude exotics and fences that reduce nonaquatic impact have restored this species to reasonable numbers. It is necessary to continue to maintain this area and to research the possibilities of reestablishing the species over more of its native habitat (Miller and Pister 1971).

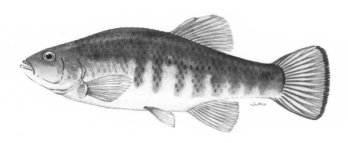

Salt Creek pupfish
Cyprinodon salinus **Miller**

Importance

The Salt Creek pupfish is unique even among pupfishes because of its ability to survive the high salinity and temperatures in one of the harshest environments in Death Valley.

Range

The Salt Creek pupfish is confined to a 1.5-mile stretch of Salt Creek, which originates in seepage on Mesquite Flat in the north part of Death Valley, and to Cottonball Marsh near the Salt Creek sink (Miller 1943). Additional populations have been established by transplant at Soda Lake, San Bernardino County and at River Springs, Mono County, California (Miller 1968).

Description

During the breeding season the male becomes deep blue on the sides and iridescent purple on the back. There is a conspicuous black terminal band on the caudal peduncle. There are 5 to 8 broad vertical bands that may be either continuous or interrupted on the sides of spawning males. The female is not as deep-bodied as the male and usually has 4 to 8 continuous vertical bars on the sides that narrow ventrally. The ventral bars are more conspicuous in younger fish. The Salt Creek pupfish is the most slender of all Death Valley pupfishes. It has 27 to 34 scales in the lateral series that have reticulated inner spaces between the circuli. The dorsal fin has 8 to 11 rays, usually 9 or 10. It is closer to the base of the caudal fin than to the snout. The anal rays are 9 to 11, usually 10; pectoral rays 14 to 17, usually 15 to 16; caudal rays 15 to 19, usually 16 to 17. The pelvic fins are small and occasionally absent. Gill rakers number 18 to 22 and are shorter and more compressed than in other pupfishes (LaBounty and Deacon 1972; Miller 1943).

Size and Longevity

Maximum length of the Salt Creek pupfish is about 1.5 inches. Many of them may live only 1 year or even less.

Limiting Factors

Because Salt Creek pupfish is the only fish species occupying Salt Creek and Cottonball Marsh, and the entire area is within the Death Valley National Monument, it is not presently affected by many negative factors impacting other species. Barring a natural disaster, these little fish should survive and prosper.

Food and Feeding

The Salt Creek pupfish presumably feeds on algae, aquatic insect larvae, amphipods, ostracods, and snails.

Breeding Habits

One of the most remarkable aspects of the Salt Creek pupfish in Salt Creek is its rapid population fluctuations. When water flows are high, the population increases rapidly, spreading beyond the limits of normal water flow. The peak population has been estimated to be in the millions. The rapid growth indicates a generation time of 2 to 3 months. As water temperatures rise and the stream shrinks, fish die by the thousands. Breeding behavior is presumably like that of other pupfishes (Miller 1943). Spawning habits in Cottonball Marsh probably do not differ markedly from those in Salt Creek, except the extremes in numbers are most likely lacking in Cottonball Marsh.

Habitat

Salt Creek, one of two habitats of the Salt Creek pupfish, starts from seeps about 200 feet below sea level and ends at approximately 300 feet below sea level. The upper part of the stream has water only in winter and spring, but further down the narrow canyon has water all year round. It has a series of rather large pools, edged with heavy growth of salt grass, pickleweed, and salt brush. These plants sometimes completely cover the interconnecting channels and provide shelter for the fish. Water temperatures range from close to freezing in winter to nearly 104° F in summer, although the deep pools probably seldom exceed 82° F. Total dissolved solids are as high as 23,600 ppm (Miller 1943). In the laboratory the fish tolerate temperatures of 108° F (Brown and Feldmeth 1971). In Cottonball Marsh, 262 feet below sea level, the Salt Creek pupfish lives in exposed pools that are from a few to more than 32 inches deep. Surface water temperatures in the two areas that total about a square mile range from near freezing to 104° F. Total dissolved solids range from 0.4 to 4.57 times that of seawater. The soil is so salty in most areas that there are only a few terrestrial plants growing high on alluvial fans and near the water source. In the water there are algae and emergent rushes (LaBounty and Deacon 1972).

Preservation of Species

The safety provided by being the only fish in Salt Creek and Cottonball Marsh and the fact that the habitats of this species are inside the Death Valley National Monument are probably adequate protection.

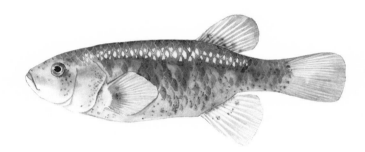

Pahrump killifish
Empetrichthys latos latos **Miller**

Importance

As in other genera of this family, economic importance is difficult and perhaps undesirable to assign to this subspecies. Original populations were once identified from three separate springs in the Pahrump Valley, Nevada, indicating that evolution of this subspecies was associated with restricted and unique habitat (Hubbs 1932). Subspecific considerations and the uniqueness of this subspecies as a whole are important. Two of the three original subspecies are considered to be extinct (Deacon and Williams 1984). The Pahrump killifish is listed by the U.S. Fish and Wildlife Service as endangered.

Range

The original populations of this subspecies were confined to three springs in Pahrump Valley, Nevada (La Rivers 1962). These populations have now been extirpated. It presently exists as a transplanted population in Shoshone Pond near Ely, Nevada (Deacon et al. 1980) and in Corn Creek Springs, southeastern Nevada (Deacon et al. 1979).

Description

The Pahrump killifish is dark brown to green above, lighter below. It may be streaked on the sides. It is rather slender with a gently sloping to convex profile forward of the single dorsal fin, which is set far back. The mouth is broad with a weak mandible. The scales number 29 to 33 in the lateral series. No pelvic fins are present and the pectoral fins have 16 to 18 rays. The caudal peduncle is stout and the caudal fin is rounded, not forked.

Size and Longevity

This small fish rarely exceeds 2 inches in length (La Rivers 1962). It probably lives 2 to 4 years.

Limiting Factors

This subspecies has been adversely affected by habitat destruction, competition with stocked exotics, and its initial limited natural range.

Food and Feeding

Deacon et al. (1980) report that the diet of this subspecies in what is now a dry pool at Manse Ranch was a mixture of insects, snails, and other invertebrates, accounting for 32 percent of the total volume. Debris was 56 percent of the mean volume.

Breeding Habits

Little is known about the reproductive mechanism of this subspecies. It probably produces few eggs per spawning but may, because of its existence in warm springs, reproduce much of the year. Most spawning probably occurs in March or April (Deacon et al. 1980).

Habitat

This subspecies originally inhabited warm springs, 74° to 77° F, which fluctuated little in daily temperature or on an annual basis. La Rivers (1962) reported it from spring-fed pools and ponds that were restricted in size (40 feet long and 5 to 25 feet wide). Deacon et al. (1980) provide information on Shoshone North Pond, where a transplanted population of Pahrump killifish exists. This pond is an artificially constructed and enclosed system. It is approximately 4 feet deep. No strong depth preferences have been noted for Pahrump killifish in either its native habitat or the artificial pond, although some evidence suggests a preference for deeper water. Young of transplanted populations are more active during daylight and adults are more active at night.

Preservation of Species

Continued support for the transplanted populations of Pahrump killifish is essential. Additional habitats where it could be established should be investigated. Efforts should be made to reestablish this subspecies in its native range.

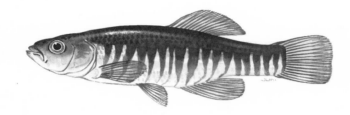

Plains killifish
Fundulus zebrinus Jordan and Gilbert

Importance

Plains killifish is not native to the Great Basin. This introduced species has been used as a bait fish in both its native and introduced range. Its effect on native species has not been studied. Plains killifish probably serves as forage for some game species.

Range

Plains killifish is native to the Pecos, Brazos, and Colorado rivers of New Mexico and Texas (Koster 1957). It is native over portions of Wyoming, Montana, and Missouri. It has been introduced in Arizona and Utah. In the Great Basin the plains killifish occurs in Juab County, Utah near Mona Reservoir (Lee et al. 1980; Sigler and Miller 1963; Randy Radant, personal communication, 1984).

Description

Numerous vertical bars give rise to the common name of zebra killifish in portions of the plains killifish's range. Several subspecies were at one time hypothesized. A dozen or more dark bars may occur on the sides of this species and are narrower in the female than the male. During breeding, males have red to orange coloration on the sides and lower fins (Sigler and Miller 1963). The body is compressed and slender, the head large. The mouth is nearly superior. There are 52 to 70 scales in a series from the head to the base of the caudal fin, and there is no lateral line. Dorsal fin rays number from 14 to 16 and anal fin rays 14.

Size and Longevity

Plains killifish does not generally reach lengths over 3 inches, although a few specimens of 6 inches have been reported. Most adults are between 1.5 and 2 inches in total length. It does not live more than 3 years.

Limiting Factors

Plains killifish is probably fed on by predatory fishes and birds. It may also be parasitized in some areas.

Food and Feeding

Plains killifish is an omnivore. The superior mouth is adapted for feeding at the surface. Its food is comprised largely of surface insects and floating matter, although it may feed on bottom organisms if other food is scarce (Sigler and Miller 1963). Diatoms and other plant material may be eaten when invertebrate food is scarce (Lee et al. 1980).

Breeding Habits

Plains killifish spawn in summer months, usually over sand or gravel in the shallow water of small pools. Eggs are laid and fertilized but no care is provided. Males are not strictly territorial but are aggressive during spawning. Males court receptive females by swimming a sinuous course ahead of the female. When a female is attracted, the male moves laterally and spawning occurs (Lee et al. 1980; Sigler and Miller 1963; Minckley 1973).

Habitat

Plains killifish is generally found in small, shallow, open streams with only moderate to slow currents. It may also occur in reservoirs, lakes, and springs. Tolerance to alkalinity and salinity is high (Sigler and Miller 1963).

Preservation of Species

No documentation exists on the ecological requirements of this species in Great Basin waters. The transplanted populations are reproducing and were noted as abundant as of 1977–78. No information has been developed that documents the effect of this species on native fish species. Its range within the Great Basin should not be extended without comprehensive ecological studies.

Rainwater killifish
***Lucania parva* (Baird)**

Importance

The rainwater killifish is important in mosquito control in marshes along the Atlantic slope; its value may be somewhat less in water that has high salinity. It is also used as an aquarium fish. It is a potential competitor of several small native fishes in the Great Basin.

Range

This species has a wide distribution on the Atlantic slope of North America, from Massachusetts to Tampico, Mexico. It is also present in the Rio Grande and Pecos rivers, Texas and New Mexico. In the Great Basin it is established in Timpie Springs near Timpie, Tooele County, Utah and in Blue Lake on the Utah-Nevada border. Presumably it was introduced there along with a shipment of largemouth bass from the vicinity of Dexter, New Mexico. It also exists in Irving Lake, southern California (Hubbs and Miller 1965; Sigler and Miller 1963).

Description

The rainwater killifish is dark olive to greenish-yellow on the back and sides, paler below. The scale outlines are brought out by underlying black pigments, producing a rhomboidal pattern. On the anterior sides of the scales there is a bluish and silver reflection. There is a dark streak along the midline in advance of the dorsal fin. The breeding male is deep yellow with black markings on the dorsal, anal, and caudal fins; the anal and pelvic fins may also be orange to red and the pectorals yellow. The rainwater killifish can be confused with the mosquitofish, but the killifish is of chunkier build, without distinctive markings, and the dorsal fin originates well in advance of the anal fin. The dorsal fin has 10 to 12 rays, rarely 9, and the anal fin 9 or 10, uncommonly 8 or 11. There are 26 to 28 scales in the lateral series. The lower jaw projects slightly. The upper and lower jaws have an outer row of well-developed teeth, but an inner row may be absent or represented by 1 or 2 strong teeth in the upper jaw (Sigler and Miller 1963).

Size and Longevity

The rainwater killifish attains a maximum size of slightly over 2 inches; females grow a little larger than males. It probably lives no more than 2 or occasionally 3 years.

Limiting Factors

The same factors that affect other killifishes affect the rainwater killifish; however, it may be more adaptable and resistant to adverse conditions, particularly high salt content, than some killifishes.

Food and Feeding

The rainwater killifish eats mosquito larvae, copepods, and miscellaneous crustaceans and aquatic insects. The small fish, about 0.5 inch long, feed almost exclusively on mosquito larvae, while larger fish feed mostly on crustaceans.

Breeding Habits

Sexual maturity is reached at 3 to 5 months at a length of 1 inch. Spawning takes place in late spring and summer. The female spawns more than once during a season. Once breeding begins, the male sets up a territory over or near beds of aquatic vegetation. He develops a cross-hatched breeding pattern on his sides and displays vigorously to males holding nearby territories. When a female approaches, the male rapidly circles her. If she is interested in spawning, she stops and he moves quickly beneath her. In this position they swim to the surface near suitable substrate and spawn. Eggs are fertilized as they are released. They hatch in about 6 days at 75° F. The larvae settle to the bottom and begin an active existence in about a week and after the yolk sac is absorbed. The eggs are about 0.04 inch in diameter and as many as 104 have been reported for 1 female (Foster 1967; Sigler and Miller 1963).

Habitat

This species occurs in quiet water, especially small pools that are abundantly supplied with plants. In its native range it is chiefly an inhabitant of brackish water, being plentiful in bays, ponds, creeks, and open flats where vegetation is present. In California it inhabits both brackish stretches of coastal streams and freshwater lakes. There is some evidence it migrates into fresh water, breeds, and then goes back into brackish water (Moyle 1976; Sigler and Miller 1963).

Preservation of Species

The rainwater killifish apparently prospers over a wide range of aquatic habitats. It is recommended there be no extension of its present range and no protection offered it in the Great Basin.

LIVEBEARERS (POECILIIDAE)

Members of this family resemble killifishes in size and general appearance, but bring forth their young alive and hence are termed ovoviviparous. They are easily distinguished from the killifishes by their small posteriorly placed dorsal fin, the occurrence of embryos in gravid females, and the development of the anal fin into a highly specialized, rodlike organ that lies beneath the tip of the pectoral fin in the male. This structure, the gonopodium, is used for internal fertilization, guiding the spermatozoa into the female. All other fishes inhabiting the Great Basin are oviparous; that is, they produce eggs that are fertilized after leaving the body of the female. This family is best known for the popular aquarium tropical species, especially the guppy. The family is found only in North and South America, ranging from the upper Mississippi Valley to Argentina. The greatest number of species occurs in Mexico and Central America.

In addition to its value as pet fish the group is well known for its habit of eating mosquitos. The mosquitofish has become widely established over the world as a means of combating malaria. Other species have been used in studying genetics and the production and mode of inheritance of cancers (Sigler and Miller 1963).

Twenty species in six genera exist in North America. Five species in three genera occur in the Great Basin (Robins et al. 1980). None is native to the Great Basin.

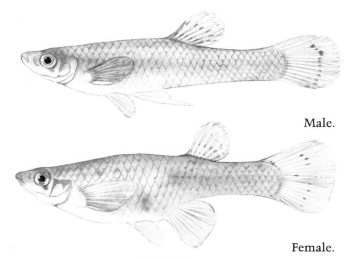

Male.

Female.

Mosquitofish
Gambusia affinis (Baird and Girard)

Importance

This species has been stocked throughout the world for mosquito control, particularly to combat malaria. Its appetite for mosquito larvae is well known and is used extensively in ornamental pools and small ponds. It is not considered effective for mosquito control in extensive freshwater marshes. It serves, to a limited extent, as a bait and forage fish.

The mosquitofish also has negative value in certain waters. In some small warmwater ponds or springs in Nevada that contain threatened or endangered native fishes, it outcompetes, preys on, and in general becomes a hazard for these generally smaller and less aggressive fishes, primarily the killifishes (Sigler and Miller 1963). Schoenherr (1981) points out that the mosquitofish has caused the near-extirpation of some species, not through direct competition for a common resource but by predation by mosquitofish females on young of native fishes. Aggressive actions on the part of the mosquitofish also have been cited as a negative factor in interactions with native species.

Range

The mosquitofish is native to the central United States from southern Illinois and southern Indiana to Alabama and the mouth of the Rio Grande River, Texas. Because of its reputation as a mosquito control agent, it has been introduced into suitable habitat over most of the world. In the Great Basin it is widely established in warm springs throughout the Bonneville system. In Nevada, stocking has been discouraged because of the hazards it presents to native fishes but it is widely established.

Description

The mosquitofish is olive or dull silvery, darkest on the head and back and lightest on the belly. The scales are outlined by dark pigment and there are usually 1 or several rows of black spots across the caudal fin (this is more prominent in females). Frequently there is a wedge-shaped bar below the eye and a very narrow dark line running along the midside from the head to the base of the caudal fin. Pregnant females are potbellied and have a black spot just above the anus.

The rounded caudal fin, large scales on the head as well as the body, superior position of the mouth, posteriorly placed dorsal fin (originating behind the origin of the anal fin), and a modification of the anal of the male into a spikelike reproductive organ all serve to identify this species. The dorsal fin usually has 6 rays, sometimes 7. There are about 30 scales in the lateral series and a true lateral line is lacking (Sigler and Miller 1963).

Size and Longevity

The female mosquitofish reaches a larger size than the male because she keeps growing throughout life, whereas the male ceases to grow when maturity is reached, usually in 4 to 6 weeks. The size attained by males is not more than 1.75 inches whereas large females may be 2.5 inches or more long. The newborn young are usually a little more than 0.33 inch and are able to fend for themselves at birth. Most fish die the same summer they reach maturity, although a few may live 15 months or more.

Limiting Factors

Mosquitofish cannot tolerate sustained water temperatures much below 40° F, although in northern Utah it lives in ponds that frequently form a thin layer of ice in winter. Presumably it is able to find warmer water in some of the springs or it adjusts to the colder water. It is heavily preyed upon by fish and birds.

Food and Feeding

In addition to mosquito larvae, the mosquitofish feeds chiefly on such small animals as crustaceans and various insects, but it is able to

readily adapt to diatoms and algae when other food is absent. It may
also feed on small fish. It lives and feeds at or near the surface, rarely
invading deep water (Sigler and Miller 1963). Mosquitofish was found
to be the least specialized fish living in a Florida marsh. There it fed
voraciously on mosquito larvae and pupae when abundant, but otherwise lived on a mixed diet of algae, zooplankton, fish, terrestrial insects, and miscellaneous invertebrates (Harrington and Harrington
1961). The diet is about the same throughout life except larger fish eat
larger items.

Breeding Habits

The female mosquitofish reaches maturity at about 1 inch. A mature male is somewhat smaller. A female may become gravid as early as
6 weeks of age. The gestation period is 3 to 4 weeks; therefore, 3 to 4
generations a year are possible in warm water. The potential of a rapid
increase in a mosquitofish population is very high. A female may contain as many as 315 embryos, the number usually increasing with the
size of the fish. However, it may also decrease as the female nears the
end of her life (Krumholtz 1948). Courtship and copulation are constant among mosquitofish. The male swims in front of the female, ori-
enting his body at a ninety-degree angle to hers, partially folds his dorsal and anal fins over her, bends his body into an S, then quickly swims
around behind the female and attempts to shove his gonopodium into
the female's genital opening. The more frequent lateral display is similar to frontal display, except it is performed alongside the female and
close to her head. In aquaria, receptive females are quickly surrounded
by males. Females that have previously been bred tend to be nonreceptive but will breed again as little as 30 minutes after giving birth
(Itzkowitz 1971). In the wild many attempts at copulation fail because
the female is nonreceptive.

Habitat

This species inhabits lakes, rivers, creeks, ponds, springs,
ditches—anywhere there is quiet shallow water and dense vegetation.
In a spring in southeastern Idaho, where an artesian well had a temperature of 120° F in the center and 108° F in a band about 4 feet wide
around the edge, mosquitofish were living and prospering in the 108° F
water. But if they were caught and tossed out into the center of the pool
they died instantly. However, it has been demonstrated that mosquitofish can be acclimated to the fairly severe climate of northern Illinois.
It is not inhibited by low oxygen levels since it skims along just at the

surface, using the very thin layer of surface water oxygen. A population of mosquitofish was observed in a dump in northern Utah. The puddle in which mosquitofish were evidently reproducing was small (3.5 feet across), shallow, and partially covered by a discarded door.

Preservation of Species

The mosquitofish needs little protection in warm waters with an abundance of food, but it cannot survive in open waters under heavy predation. It is doubtful that it should be protected in Great Basin waters where there are small native fishes.

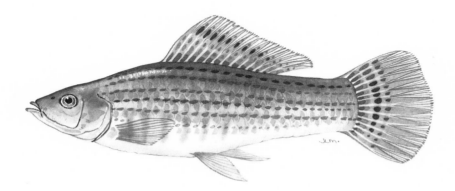

Sailfin molly
Poecilia latipinna (Lesueur)

Importance

The sailfin molly, an exotic in the Great Basin, is an important aquarium species. Its color and breeding habits make it popular. In the wild it is a negative factor when it competes with native species.

Range

The native range of the sailfin molly is from South Carolina to Florida and west into Mexico. The first specimen was identified from New Orleans, Louisiana (Axelrod 1968). It was introduced in California (Moyle 1976) and Indian Springs and the Pahranagat Valley, Nevada (Thom Hardy, personal communication, 1983).

Description

The sailfin molly is brightly colored. It may have a red tinge along the upper edge of the dorsal fin, particularly in the male. The back, especially in the female, is black, shading to purple iridescence in both sexes but somewhat higher on the male. The breast is red-orange to red or yellow and the fins are colored with green, blue, or red. The male has a spot pattern on the sides.

In salt water it has 13 to 14 dorsal rays while freshwater populations have 12 to 13 dorsal rays. The large saillike dorsal fin is present only on saltwater populations; it is much reduced on freshwater individuals (Axelrod 1968).

Size and Longevity

Freshwater individuals achieve only 70 percent of the size of saltwater populations. The adult female reaches a size of about 2 inches; the male is slightly larger. The largest individuals may reach 6 inches (Lee et al. 1980). It lives to an age of 2 years or less in the wild.

Limiting Factors

It is probably preyed upon by piscivorous species where habitats overlap. Severe cold probably limits its spread.

Food and Feeding

Algae, vascular plants, organic detritus, and mosquito larvae are the principal foods of sailfin molly (Lee et al. 1980). Harrington and Harrington (1961) report that specimens near the Salton Sea, California feed on 86 percent detritus and 14 percent algae.

Breeding Habits

As with other members of this family, it gives birth to live young. Courtship and copulation are relatively rapid and simple. Females can store sperm and give birth to several batches of young. A large female may produce 140 young at one time. The young are large, up to 0.5 inch, and self-sufficient at birth (Lee et al. 1980; Sterba 1959).

Habitat

Warm, brackish, coastal waters are the native habitat of this species. It does well in temperatures to 82° F and can tolerate salinities of almost 2.5 times that of seawater. It survives in irrigation ditches, lakes, ponds, streams, and salt marshes (Lee et al. 1980).

Preservation of Species

No special consideration need be given this species in the Great Basin. It is considered a nuisance in many locations and has probably impacted native species adversely.

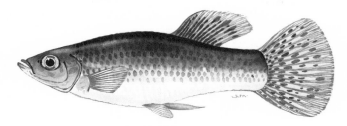

Shortfin molly
Poecilia mexicana Steindachner

Importance

The shortfin mollies as a group are not as popular in aquaria as the sailfin molly. This species was described relatively recently. Axelrod (1968) reports it will not be a popular aquarium species because of its lack of color. It is part of a species complex, the taxonomy of which is uncertain (Lee et al. 1980). It has had a negative impact on certain small native fish species in the Great Basin.

Range

The native range of the shortfin molly is from northern Mexico to South America (Migdalski and Fichter 1983). It has been stocked without authorization in certain waters in Nevada and elsewhere in the Great Basin (Tom Trelease, personal communication, 1983). It was introduced in Ash Springs, Nevada between March 1963 and June 1964 (Hardy 1982) and has established itself as the most abundant species in this system. It is also established in warm springs in Moapa Valley, Nevada.

Description

The shortfin molly lacks the high dorsal fin of the sailfin molly and has a much reduced tail. It lacks the distinctive coloration of other members of this complex.

Size and Longevity

Adult sizes range from 1.2 to 2 inches with a maximum size of 4 inches (Lee et al. 1980). It lives 2 years or less in the wild.

Limiting Factors

It is probably affected by the same adverse factors that distress other members of this family in the Great Basin. Where food is adequate and water temperatures are warm, it will do well.

Food and Feeding

Detritus, filamentous algae, diatoms, desmids, and bits of vascular plants constitute the food of the shortfin molly in its native habitat (Lee et al. 1980). Hardy (1982) reports the shortfin molly is herbivorous, an observation supported by the intestine length. Foods utilized by mollies in Ash Springs, Nevada include *Spirogyra*, which was the primary food, constituting up to 36 percent of the volume. Detritus was also a significant ingested component.

Breeding Habits

The shortfin molly produces live young. Breeding habits and courtship activity are probably similar to the sailfin molly and the mosquitofish (Migdalski and Fichter 1983).

Habitat

In its native range it occupies fresh and brackish waters. In the Great Basin it inhabits small thermal springs and their outflows. Hardy (1982) reports the occurrence of shortfin molly in Ash Springs, Nevada, where mud and silt substrates occur but sand and gravel dominate. Pools and riffles each occupy about 5 percent of the area while intermediate waters occupy about 90 percent.

Preservation of Species

No special consideration need be given this species in the Great Basin. Additional introductions into native fish habitat are strongly discouraged.

Guppy
***Poecilia reticulata* Peters**

Importance

The guppy has questionable value in the wild, even though it feeds on mosquito larvae, but it is a much admired aquarium fish. It is considered a hazard to native minnows and killifishes in the Great Basin.

Range

The native range of this species is Venezuela, Barbados, Trinidad, northern Brazil, and Guyana. Since it is widely used as a pet fish, it has been inadvertently stocked and is established in the wild in many parts of the world (Lee et al. 1980). In the Great Basin it is present in the Sheldon National Wildlife Refuge, Nevada (Williams, Williams, and Bond 1980) and in certain other waters (Deacon and Williams 1984).

Description

The female guppy is gray to greenish-brown with some rows of scales shining bluish in reflective light. The color of the male is highly variable, especially in aquarium specimens, but generally with red, green, or blue dominating. The male has large "high spots" on the sides in the vicinity of the caudal peduncle. The body of the female is somewhat elongated. The dorsal profile is slightly curved. The body of the male is highly variable. His dorsal profile is straight. In both sexes the head is small, the mouth is dorsal, and the upturned lower jaw projects beyond the upper. The dorsal fin has 7 to 8 rays, the caudal fin is rounded, and the anal fin has 8 or 9 rays (Simpson and Wallace 1978; Williams, Williams, and Bond 1980).

The mosquitofish may be confused with the guppy. However, many characteristics such as the lateral series scale count, color, and spotting characteristics of the male, the presence of a prominent fleshy palp on the gonopodium of the male, the filamentous dorsal fin of the male, and microstriations in the caudal fin of the female identify the guppy (Williams, Williams, and Bond 1980).

Size and Longevity

Growth is fairly rapid. The female seldom exceeds 1 inch in length; the male is no more than 0.5 to 0.75 of an inch. The life span is 1 year or less.

Limiting Factors

Factors that limit the guppy are probably similar to those affecting the mosquitofish.

Food and Feeding

The guppy is an opportunisitic omnivorous feeder much like the mosquitofish.

Breeding Habits

Maturity is reached in a few weeks. Displays and copulation are similar to that of the mosquitofish.

Habitat

The guppy prefers warm springs or ponds where temperatures range in the 70s to low 80s. It apparently adjusts to a wide range of habitats since it has been established, via accidental introduction and pet farms, in many places throughout the world.

This species is very adaptable, as demonstrated by the fact that it is present in the outflow creek from the bathhouse pool, Sheldon National Wildlife Refuge, Nevada. It is even found in soapy waters of the Virginia Valley Campground shower outflow. It is abundant in the bathhouse pool and outflow in the Thousand Creek spring, where there are swarms of adults and juveniles (Williams, Williams, and Bond 1980).

Preservation of Species

In the Great Basin the guppy is an unwanted species. It, and other pet fishes, should be kept in aquaria and not released into the wild.

Green swordtail
***Xiphophorus helleri* Heckel**

Importance

Green swordtail is one of the most popular aquarium species. It has been widely introduced and established in the southern and western United States, to the detriment of the native fishes.

Range

It is native on the Atlantic slope from Rio Nautla, Veracruz, Mexico to northwestern Honduras (Lee et al. 1980). It has been introduced in the Great Basin in Indian Springs, Nevada.

Description

The green swordtail has a flash of red and yellow on the sides along the lateral line. The caudal fin of the male may or may not be colored red; the female's is not. The male may also show color in the dorsal and may have a black margin on the caudal fin (Axelrod and Schultz 1955). The dorsal fin has 12 to 14 rays, the anal 8 to 10, the pectoral fins 12 or 13, and the pelvic fins 6. There are 26 to 30 scales in the lateral series (Axelrod and Schultz 1955).

Size and Longevity

Green swordtail reaches a size of about 5 inches (Axelrod and Schultz 1955). It is probably relatively short-lived (2 to 3 years).

Limiting Factors

Factors that limit the green swordtail are probably similar to those affecting the mosquitofish.

Food and Feeding

The food habits of this species are probably similar to those of other Great Basin livebearers, being generally omnivorous or herbivorous.

Breeding Habits

Breeding occurs at a length of about 2 inches. Breeding habits are similar to mollies. The young are born alive and are immediately able to sustain themselves. In warmwater habitats it may breed more than once a year.

Habitat

Fresh water is required for the green swordtail; it does not do well in brackish waters. Other habitat requirements are similar to those for other species of live-bearers. Optimum temperatures are 68° to 80° F (Axelrod and Schultz 1955).

Preservation of Species

No special considerations are needed. Additional introductions of this species into habitats of native species in the Great Basin are discouraged.

12

Gasterosteiformes

STICKLEBACKS (GASTEROSTEIDAE)

THE STICKLEBACKS ARE small, laterally compressed fishes with slender caudal peduncles. The head is moderate, the skull elongate, the mouth small with tiny, well-developed teeth. They have 3 branchiostegal rays and well-developed dorsal and pelvic fins. The soft dorsal fin is preceded by 3 to 16 separated, well-developed spines, each having a triangular membrane. There is usually a short spine closely associated with a soft dorsal fin of 6 to 14 rays. The caudal fin, either rounded or slightly forked, is usually about as long as the soft dorsal fin. The pelvic fins are thoracic in position, usually posterior to the pectoral fin base of a single strong, well-developed spine and 0 to 3 soft rays (Scott and Crossman 1973). This family is represented in the Great Basin by a single species, the threespine stickleback, in the Mojave River basin, California.

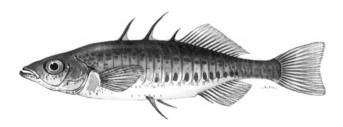

Threespine stickleback
***Gasterosteus aculeatus* Linnaeus**

Importance

The threespine stickleback is prized as an aquarium fish because of its pugnacious behavior and its colorful predictability while breeding. In the wild it provides a limited amount of forage for fish and surface-feeding birds.

Range

The threespine stickleback is nearly circumpolar in distribution; it is absent from the Arctic Siberian coast and most of the Arctic North American coast. It is widely distributed in the northern hemisphere in salt, brackish, and fresh water. It is present in Europe from southern Greenland, Novaya Zemlya, Norway, and Iceland south to Spain, the Mediterranean, and the Black Sea. In North America it ranges from Chesapeake Bay north to the Hudson Bay region and Baffin Island, then down the Alaskan and British Columbian Pacific coast to lower California (Scott and Crossman 1973). The population that exists in Holcomb Creek in the Mojave River drainage of the Great Basin may be native or may have been introduced with trout in the late 1800s (Bell 1982). Based on its probable evolution without predators, we have elected to list it as native.

Description

During breeding season, the male has bright blue eyes and becomes brilliantly colored with red on the belly and flanks, whereas the female assumes pink tints on the throat and belly. The body of the newly hatched larvae is yellowish. Young fish are bright silver. The color of nonbreeding adults is variable above. It can be silvery green, gray, olive, greenish-brown, or sometimes mottled with dark markings. Adults in fresh water are not as gaudy as ones in saltwater, but are usually olive to dark green on the back and sides with white to golden bellies (Migdalski and Fichter 1983; Scott and Crossman 1973). Bell (1982) has described a melanistic population in the Mojave River drainage of California. This is the first record of a population of this type outside of the Pacific Northwest and at such a high elevation (6,430 feet above sea level).

Size and Longevity

Most threespine sticklebacks probably live no more than 1 year with a few living 2 or even 3 years. Its maximum size is less than 2.5 inches.

Limiting Factors

Predation, parasites, and drainage or alteration of habitat are the negative factors affecting the threespine stickleback. The short spines of the Mojave River basin population indicate lack of coevolution with predatory fishes (Bell 1982), so it is assumed it is more vulnerable to fish predation than other populations.

Food and Feeding

This species feeds on small aquatic invertebrates, including insects and crustaceans, and on fry and eggs of fish (Hynes 1950). According to Moyle (1976), it tends to specialize in feeding on rather limited numbers of organisms such as midge larvae and ostracods; it is rather slow to learn to exploit new sources of food. Schooling appears to be related to finding usable concentrations of food.

Breeding Habits

This species spawns from April through July in shallow, weedy areas. As spawning season approaches, the male begins to assume breeding colors and moves away from the school to set up a territory on beds of aquatic plants. Once this is done he constructs a nest on the bottom by excavating a shallow pit with his mouth. The male then gathers strands of algae and other aquatic plants and deposits them in the pit. The material is pasted together with a sticky kidney secretion. The male wriggles through it until a tunnel is formed in each end of the barrel-shaped nest. He then rounds up a gravid female that is willing to spawn. The female enters the nest, lays eggs, and leaves. The male then goes in and fertilizes the eggs. Usually several females are courted in this fashion by each male and each female lays 50 to 300 eggs. When the male has finished courting, there are perhaps 600 eggs in the nest. The top of the nest is loosened and the male guards the eggs, which hatch in 6 to 8 days at 64° to 68° F. After the fry leave the nest, the male watches over them until they become too difficult to manage (Moyle 1976; Scott and Crossman 1973).

Habitat

Threespine stickleback lives in quiet waters with weedy pools and backwaters or among emergent plants at stream edges over sand or mud bottom. The Mojave River basin population occupies pools at 6,430 feet above sea level in which a gentle water flow is maintained.

Water temperatures are 60° to 71° F. Water depths are around 28 inches and willows grow near the pools (Bell 1982).

Preservation of Species

Protection of habitat from human activities is probably the only needed and feasible protection for this species.

13

Perciformes

TEMPERATE BASSES (PERCICHTHYIDAE)

MEMBERS OF this family have spines in the dorsal, anal, and pelvic fins; the latter lie beneath the pectoral fins and have a single sharp spine followed by 5 soft rays. The scales are ctenoid and there is a spine on the opercle. These are laterally compressed, deep-bodied fishes with well-developed jaws armored with numerous teeth. They have 7 branchiostegal rays. There are four species in the fresh waters of North America, one of which has both landlocked and anadromous populations (Sigler and Miller 1963; Scott and Crossman 1973). There are seven species in four genera of this family. A single introduced species is present in the Great Basin.

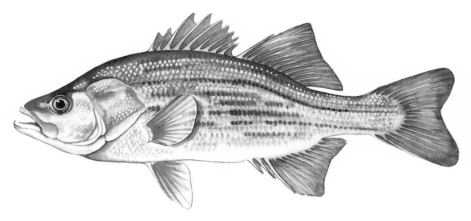

White bass
***Morone chrysops* (Rafinesque)**

Importance

The white bass is a fast-growing fish capable of producing a substantial amount of sport. In many areas in the South, where a few years ago it was unknown, it is now an important sport fish. When it is in large schools fishermen find that it is relatively easy to catch more than one, provided the fisherman quickly retrieves the catch and casts again into the school before it moves beyond range. The white bass fights well when hooked and has good table qualities. In areas where there is an abundance of small fish, either game or forage, it is able to effectively reduce them to a large poundage of sport fish. It is popular with fishermen of all ages (Sigler and Miller 1963). However, large populations of stunted white bass, too small to be acceptable to most sportsmen, may prove of little or negative value.

Range

The native range of the white bass is from Minnesota, Wisconsin, and Michigan south in the Mississippi drainage to the Gulf states of Alabama, Mississippi, and part of Texas. Originally one of the greatest concentrations was in the Great Lakes, primarily Lake Erie. It has been introduced widely in the United States. Some of the most dense populations today are in impoundments in Texas, Oklahoma, and other south-central states. In the Great Basin the most concentrated population is in Utah Lake, Utah, where the white bass literally dominates all other fish. It is present in Lahontan and Ryepatch reservoirs, Washoe Lake, and the Humboldt River, Nevada.

Description

The white bass has a silvery color with 5 to 7 generally unbroken, longitudinal stripes on each side. The back is dark green or gray, shading to silver on the sides and becoming white below. The eye is tinted with yellow. The scales are ctenoid; the mouth is moderately large with conical teeth in bands on the jaws. The gill rakers are usually stiff and armed with teeth. The pseudobranchiae are large and conspicuous. Superficially the white bass resembles the largemouth bass, but there are several distinct differences, color being the most notable (Sigler and Miller 1963).

Size and Longevity

The white bass is fast-growing and relatively short-lived in the southern part of its range; in the north it grows slower and lives longer.

It does not attain as large a size in the northern as it does in the southern part of its range. The yearly length for white bass age 1 to 6 in Oklahoma in inches is 7.5, 12.2, 14.4, 16.1, 17.1, and 17.8. In northern Iowa the yearly size for fish age 1 to 8 in inches is 5.2, 9.7, 12.8, 14.6, 15.3, 15.8, 16.0, and 16.6. In northern Iowa, 7- and 8-year-old fish are not uncommon. It weighs 0.5 pound when it is 10 inches long, 1 pound when it is 13 inches long, and 2 pounds when it is 16 inches long. Generally females weigh slightly more than males at the same length and they grow somewhat faster. In Spirit Lake, Iowa the growing season starts the latter part of May and continues to the middle of October. However, a high percentage of the growth is from June to late July or early August, when small yellow perch appear in greatest abundance. After the population of juvenile perch has been reduced, the rate of growth drops sharply (Sigler 1949). In Oneida Lake, New York bass live to 9 years and a length of 17.4 inches. The all-tackle hook and line record weighed 5 pounds, 9 ounces (Kutz 1982). Specimens in excess of 4 pounds from Utah and just over 3 pounds from Nevada have been recorded.

Limiting Factors

The life of white bass in the southernmost part of its range is so short (6 years) that old age may be considered, from a management standpoint, a limiting factor. The eggs and fry are fed on by minnows, suckers, and other fish. In Spirit Lake, Iowa the juveniles are preyed on by largemouth bass and walleye. Since the eggs are not cared for, as they are in the sunfish family, there is probably a higher mortality.

Food and Feeding

White bass are carnivorous. The young fish feed on small crustaceans, insect larvae, and fish. The diet of the adult white bass is fish, insects, and crustaceans, but fish is preferred. However, the adult switches easily to invertebrates when fish become scarce. Vertebrate animals other than fish are rarely taken. In Spirit Lake, Iowa most of the insects taken belong to two orders, the trueflies and the mayflies. Crustaceans eaten are mostly small individuals. *Leptodora kindti* was taken more than any other invertebrate. It was so abundant that at times it gave the water a milky appearance (Sigler 1949). As a rule, adult white bass consume more fish than all other foods combined.

Large schools of feeding adult white bass, swimming with the tip of the dorsal fin out of the water, can be quite a sight. Schools in open water drive small fish to the surface, where the little fish can be seen skipping about trying to avoid the many open mouths awaiting them.

At other times schools as large as 200 to 300 yards across swim parallel to shore until they detect small fish between themselves and shore. They then turn toward shore and literally drive some of the small fish out onto the beach. These large schools feed so effectively that few small fish escape them. As an indication of how they behave when feeding, on occasion schools were decoyed close inshore by throwing gravel into the water just short of the school and then, as they turned and moved shoreward, more gravel was splashed shoreward of them until some of them were so close to shore their backs were partly out of the water (Sigler 1949). The adults often feed in the shore areas where waves are lashing the beach. The young, on the other hand, feed in the quiet waters on the lee side of the lake.

Breeding Habits

In northern Iowa most white bass mature in their second year of life, a few in the third year, none the first year. White bass spawns in the spring when water temperatures reach approximately 62° F (58° to 66° F). It apparently prefers to spawn over sandy to rocky shoal areas in lakes, or in the vicinity of running water, or in streams. In Spirit Lake, Iowa it spawns at the inlet in water 3 to 4 feet deep and in deeper water away from the inlet. It spawns in daylight with little or no fear of humans. On one occasion, when the senior author was standing in 3 feet of water, a male white bass moved close to him and swam back and forth repeatedly while rubbing the leg of his rubber boot.

The males move into the spawning area ahead of females by as much as 2 or more days. Some of these males were observed going through the spawning ritual with each other. A seine haul early in the spawning season may net only males. The adhesive eggs, measuring about 0.03 inch, are distributed at random over the bottom. The number of eggs per female ranges from 240,000 to 933,000. No parental care is given the eggs or young. The eggs hatch in 45 hours at 62° F. The bass spawn in large schools, with no apparent tendency to establish territories. White bass are definitely big-water fish, demonstrated by the fact that they do not reproduce in small ponds. White bass stocked in a series of 2- to 3-acre ponds in northern Iowa did not reproduce. Although no absolute figure has been established, it is suggested that lakes of less than 300 to 500 acres may be too small for white bass reproduction (Sigler and Miller 1963).

Habitat

White bass prosper best in large streams, lakes, and impoundments. An example of this is the large population in Lake Erie and the almost explosive population in Lake Texoma, Texas-Oklahoma when it was newly formed. Previous to the impoundment, white bass had occurred naturally in the Red River, but only after it was impounded did the angling become famous. It is quite generally believed that shallow lakes are less acceptable than deeper ones. However, Utah Lake, Utah has a very large population of white bass and much of the lake is only 12 to 14 feet deep in normal water years. In Spirit Lake, Iowa, just before twilight, large schools of white bass move inshore and swim parallel to shore for several miles, often at a distance of no more than 50 feet from shore. Even when fishermen cause them to move out, they often move back and continue downshore.

In Utah Lake the very large population of white bass, which matures at a length of 7 to 8 inches, averages only 8 to 10 inches with a rare individual reaching a size of 2 or more pounds. In 1956 189 individuals were stocked in the lake. It was least abundant in gill net catches in 1958 and the most abundant of any fish in 1978 (Heckmann, Thompson, and White 1981). It is so voracious and so abundant that it dominates all other fish in the lake through its feeding habits and sheer numbers.

It was observed that dominant-year classes were frequently produced in Spirit Lake, Iowa; that is, such a large number of young fish were spawned in one year that this particular age group prospered and dominated the population for several years. This is not an unusual phenomenon of animals on the periphery or outside of their native range (Paul Errington, personal communication, 1946). In Utah Lake, on the other hand, white bass apparently dominate the lake by successfully spawning most years.

Preservation of Species

Once a population of white bass becomes established and reproduces successfully most years, it needs little or no protection from fishermen. Moyle (1976) points out that one of the main justifications for widespread stocking of white bass was that it would be able to utilize and ideally control large threadfin shad populations that have developed in many western reservoirs. Although white bass has shown excellent growth in two California waters where it was planted, it has otherwise not lived up to its reputation. It has failed to reproduce in the lower Colorado and has reproduced irregularly elsewhere. Further, according to Moyle, it has failed to have much effect on the superabundant threadfin shad populations and there is some evidence that in

Nacimiento Reservoir, California threadfin shad may control the white bass population rather than the reverse. This, Moyle believes, should give well-intentioned fishermen a pause before they make an unauthorized transfer of fish from one body of water to another.

In Utah Lake, Utah it has become so abundant it has severely depleted the food supply and adversely affected several species, including itself. Resultant numbers are high but the fish remain small in size.

SUNFISHES (CENTRARCHIDAE)

Sunfishes are a strictly North American family containing nine genera and thirty-two species. Nine species occur in four genera in the Great Basin. It is an important family in recreational fishing and contributes significantly to the sport fishery in areas wherever warmwater habitat exists. The sunfishes are prolific spawners and with rare exceptions protect the nest and/or the young (Pflieger 1975). The habits and life histories of all members of this family are similar, differing only in details. Populations of sunfish in situations where few predators (including humans) exist may become stunted, producing numerous small, mature fish. Members of this family are often stocked together (for example, bass with bluegill) in ponds or reservoirs in an attempt to produce diverse fishing opportunities, creating a high-yield fishery with one large and one small species.

The sunfishes are generally small to moderate-sized, with spiny rayed fins and laterally compressed bodies. The mouth is small to large; the eyes are large. Bands of villiform teeth are present on the jaws, vomer, palatines, and tongue of most species. The dorsal fin consists of a spinous portion of 6 to 13 spines and a soft-rayed portion, joined in varying degrees. Pectoral fins are moderately high on the body; pelvic fins, with 1 spine and 5 rays, are thoracic. The anal fin is preceded by 3 spines and may be as long as the dorsal fin. The caudal fin is forked to some extent (Scott and Crossman 1973).

The sunfishes are native to the United States east of the Mississippi River to the Atlantic coast, extending north into Canada. Prior to the Miocene epoch, sunfishes occupied waters over much of the United States. Changing geology and increasing dryness in the interior basins eliminated all species west of the Rocky Mountains except the Sacramento perch (Miller 1958). Several species have been widely introduced in the western states and the Great Basin. Sunfish populations are established in many suitable habitats throughout the Great Basin.

Sacramento perch
***Archoplites interruptus* (Girard)**

Importance

Sacramento perch is the only member of this family that is native west of the Rocky Mountains. Because of its isolation, the Sacramento perch has retained the high number of fin spines and centrarchid body shape that is more characteristic of fossil sunfishes (Moyle 1976). For this reason it is important from a natural history aspect.

In simple fish communities where it is the numerically dominant species, where it does not have to compete with other sunfishes (particularly bluegill), and where habitat and food are available it will grow rapidly, achieving larger size than introduced sunfishes. Under these circumstances it provides an exciting sport fishery. In Pyramid Lake, Nevada, where there is no other warmwater game fish, it is of limited importance. Its sports value there is somewhat reduced because it can generally be caught easiest on spawning grounds, which in Pyramid Lake are widely dispersed and not readily defined. The best Sacramento perch fishery in the Great Basin is probably Lake Crowley, California.

Range

The original range of this species is the Sacramento–San Joaquin drainage, San Francisco Bay tributaries, the Russian River, the Paharo-Salinus drainage, and Clear Lake in California (Sigler and Miller 1963). In the Great Basin it was introduced in Pyramid Lake, Walker Lake, and Lahontan waters about 1880 (Jim Curran, personal communication

1983), but is no longer in Walker Lake. It was introduced in western Utah in Gunnison Reservoir and in an impoundment of the lower Bear River in northern Utah.

Description

Adult Sacramento perch are blackish on the back, mottled black-brown and white on the sides, and white to silvery on the belly. There are 6 to 7 irregular, dark vertical bars on the sides and black spots on the opercle. It has a metallic sheen of green to purple on the sides (La Rivers 1962).

This species has more spines (11 to 12) in the dorsal fin than any other centrarchid. The spiny portion of the dorsal is continuous with the soft posterior portion, which has 10 rays. The anal fin has 6 to 7 spines and 10 rays and is prominent. The caudal fin is weakly emarginate.

This fish is deep-bodied, the body length about three times body depth. The mouth is large and oblique; the maxillary is broad and long, reaching back to about the middle of the eye. There are 38 to 48 scales in the lateral series and 25 to 30 long gill rakers and teeth on the jaws, vomer, tongue, and palatines. There are 2 groups of lingual teeth and the pharyngeal teeth are pointed.

Size and Longevity

Sacramento perch generally grow more rapidly than other centrarchids that have a similar diet. Vigg and Kucera (1981) report lengths at the end of each year in inches for fish age 1 to 5 as 6.8, 9.0, 10.8, 12.1, and 12.7 for Pyramid Lake, Nevada fish. In a composite of five California lake studies, the yearly length in inches was 3.4, 5.7, 7.0, 7.9, 8.6, and 9.9 for fish age 1 to 6. A maximum length of 24 inches has been reported (Jordan and Evermann 1896) while La Rivers (1962) reports a fish weighing nearly 8 pounds from Walker Lake. The recorded all-tackle hook and line record fish, weighing 4 pounds, 9 ounces, was caught in Pyramid Lake, Nevada (Kutz 1982). Overcrowding, diet, and sex of the fish affect growth rate. Stunted populations can occur in underharvested populations in ponds, while populations of large, fast-growing fish can occur in lakes with adequate food. Vigg and Kucera (1981) report that females live longer and grow faster than males.

Limiting Factors

Habitat destruction, egg predation, and interspecific competition (primarily with stocked centrarchids) have contributed to the decline of Sacramento perch in its native range. Draining of lakes and sloughs and the subsequent reduction of aquatic wetlands needed for spawning and nursery areas have impacted many populations. Egg predation by other sunfishes, carp, and catfish was originally thought to be a decimating factor. Further study led to the conclusion that this species may defend its nest and young. It is unlikely that egg predation is a primary cause of population decline. The most likely cause of decline of a particular population is interspecific competition for food and space, primarily with other sunfishes. Introduced centrarchids, particularly bluegill, dominate Sacramento perch in aquaria and small ponds and may force small perch into areas where they are vulnerable to predation. Sacramento perch may also be prevented from spawning by other sunfishes, further reducing populations (Moyle 1976). A very high level of TDS may have eliminated it from Walker Lake, Nevada, although it is very tolerant of moderately high TDS levels.

Food and Feeding

Like many temperate-zone fish, Sacramento perch is an opportunistic feeder. Prey size is dependent on body size of the predator in relation to the prey. Young fish feed on small crustaceans associated with the bottom or aquatic plants. Larger fish take aquatic insect larvae and pupae, especially midges. Fish over 3.5 inches feed primarily on other fish, particularly minnows. In large bodies of water such as Pyramid Lake, where prey species are abundant, fish are the most important food of Sacramento perch over 3.5 inches (Vigg and Kucera 1981). In smaller bodies of water lacking adequate prey, aquatic insects are important in the diet of large perch.

Because Sacramento perch is a rather sluggish and sedentary fish, spending most of its time close to the bottom, it stalks its prey slowly. It takes prey with a sudden rush by "inhaling" with a rapid expansion of the buccal cavity and then closing its mouth. Feeding occurs at any time of day or night but peaks of activity occur at dusk and dawn (Moyle 1976). La Rivers (1962) reports it takes worms, live bait, spinners, and wet flies at all times of the year. In Walker Lake, fishing was good only during the six-week to two-month spawning period, the fish evidently striking almost anything dragged through the spawning area. There was some indication they were not feeding during the spawning period.

Breeding Habits

Sacramento perch breed for the first time at age 2 or 3 years.

Spawning occurs from the end of March to early August but late May and early June are the peaks. Water temperatures of 70° to 84° F are required for spawning, according to Murphy (1948). In Pyramid Lake spawning is initiated at 68° F (Vigg and Kucera 1981). Surface water temperatures in Pyramid Lake rarely exceed 73° F. During spawning, perch congregate in shallow waters (8 to 20 inches deep) where there are heavy growths of aquatic macrophytes or filamentous algae. Rock piles, boulders, tufa, and submerged sticks or logs may also be used for egg deposition. Nests are not generally built but the male vigorously defends a selected territory. When the female is ready to spawn, she becomes restless and approaches a territorial male who promptly chases her away one or more times. Following this brief courtship, the male allows the female to enter the territory and spawning begins. The eggs are deposited on submerged objects and are either fertilized simultaneously with or immediately after deposition. The male remains near the territory for several days and defends it against both perch and other species. The male may guard the eggs for the 2 days required for hatching and for an additional 2 days until the larval fish are able to swim (La Rivers 1962). Some observers have noted both parents abandoning the eggs shortly after spawning, leaving the eggs and fry unprotected and subject to predation (Murphy 1948). Spawning has been observed from about 9:00 A.M. to 4:00 P.M., ceasing abruptly in late afternoon. Young remain in schools among the aquatic plants near the spawning area or congregate in shallow waters.

The fecundity of females is higher than most centrarchids but is still size-related. The average number of eggs produced by females in Lake Anza, California was 11,439 (Mathews 1962). In Pyramid Lake, females averaged 84,203 eggs in a 1976–77 study (Vigg and Kucera 1981).

Habitat

Originally, this species inhabited sloughs, sluggish rivers, and lakes of the Central Valley, California. Historic water quality fluctuations in which it evolved allow it to tolerate high turbidities, temperatures, salinities, and alkalinities (Moyle 1976). It is a bottom-dwelling species, both in its native range and where it has been stocked. Beds of rooted and emergent aquatic vegetation, serving as spawning beds and nursery areas, are important. It is a rather inactive fish and may remain near submerged objects or the bottom, moving only the opercles and paired fins. Like most centrarchids, it may be heavily infested with internal and external parasites. Other species in the same environment (for example, tui chub in Pyramid Lake) that are more free-roaming do not develop the same infestations, giving credibility to the hypothesized sedentary nature of the perch.

Preservation of Species

Preservation of habitat and the absence of other centrarchids as well as such egg and small fish predators as carp and catfishes will help preserve the species. Other centrarchids should not be stocked with populations of Sacramento perch. It may become overpopulated and stunted if populations are not controlled by harvest or predation. It is harder to catch than other centrarchids but is larger, so liberal catch regulations, including possibly identifying potential spawning areas in which it can be fished, may be in order.

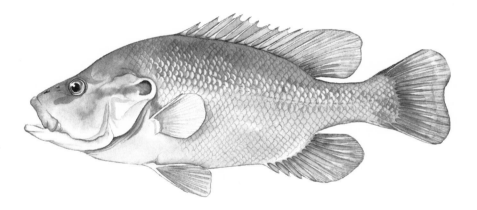

Green sunfish
***Lepomis cyanellus* Rafinesque**

Importance

Green sunfish is an important game fish in some areas of the United States. In Canada it is not sought after except by youngsters. In the eastern United States it is the most common sunfish in smaller streams and lakes. It is a palatable pan fish but its small size lessens adult fishing effort. Children are provided with much sport by this fish. It strikes hard but fights very little after being hooked. It is regarded as a nuisance or worse in many areas because of its abundance and its ability to compete with more desirable species (La Rivers 1962; Scott and Crossman 1973).

Range

The native range of the green sunfish is restricted to fresh waters of east-central North America. It occurs from southwestern New York, west of the Appalachian Mountains, south to Georgia and Alabama (west of the Escambia River), west and south to Texas and northeastern Mexico, north from New Mexico to Wyoming and eastern North Dakota, and finally east below the Red River system (except the Hudson Bay drainage of western Ontario) to Michigan and Ontario. It has been stocked in the panhandle of Florida and the western states (Lee et al. 1980). The green sunfish has been introduced extensively in the warmwater habitats of the Great Basin, occurring in most lower-elevation waters in drainages in Utah, Nevada, and California where suitable habitat and temperatures exist.

Description

The body is generally brown to olive with an emerald sheen and is darker on the dorsal surfaces and upper sides. The sides are light yellow-green, the upper sides with 7 to 12 dark but vague vertical bars. The belly is yellow to white and the breast is not conspicuously colored. The head has emerald spots and, at times, wavy, radiating emerald lines. In spawning males, the dorsal, caudal, and anal fins are dusky to olive; the membranes are darker and edged with a white, yellow, or orange border. Young do not have the emerald coloring, dark bars, or fin spots (Scott and Crossman 1973; Simpson and Wallace 1978).

This deep-bodied fish is laterally compressed. Its body is short and robust. The head is rather large and has a depression over the eyes. The opercle is stiff and long and is black in the center with a pale red, pink, or yellow margin. The mouth is large, terminal, and oblique with jaws of equal length. It has fine teeth on the palatines, vomer, and both jaws but not the tongue. Gill rakers in the center of the arch are long and thin, numbering 14 on the lower limb and 4 or 5 on the upper limb. Branchiostegal rays are usually 6, rarely 7.

The 2 dorsal fins are broadly joined, appearing as 1. The first is long with 9 to 10 spines. The second dorsal is soft with 10 to 12 rays and a rounded to slightly pointed edge in breeding males. The caudal is broad and slightly forked with rounded tips. The anal fin has 3 sharp spines and 9 to 10 soft rays and is round to slightly pointed in breeding males. Pelvic fins are thoracic and rather long with 1 spine and 5 rays. The pectorals are moderately high and not long but broad with generally 13 rays. The ctenoid scales number 45 to 50 in the lateral series.

The peritoneum is white to silvery, the intestine long and well differentiated. It has 6 to 8 pyloric caeca (Sigler and Miller 1963).

Size and Longevity

Growth of most green sunfish is slow and ultimate size is small, generally less than other sunfishes. In a northern Utah artesian-fed pond, length in inches of green sunfish at the end of each year was 2.0, 3.0, 4.0, 4.8, 5.4, and 6.4 for fish age 1 to 6. Out of the 351 fish examined only 4 were more than 6 inches long. Lengths at the end of each year in inches for Michigan green sunfish age 1 to 8 were approximately 1.0, 2.0, 3.0, 4.1, 4.9, 6.0, 6.3, and 7.3 (Hubbs and Cooper 1935). It may reach lengths of over 11 inches in California waters (Moyle 1976). In Ohio the largest fish was 10.8 inches long and weighed 14.5 ounces (Trautman 1981). Green sunfish may rarely reach an age of 10 or 11. Stunting occurs in many populations. The all-tackle hook and line record weighed 2 pounds, 2 ounces (Kutz 1982).

Limiting Factors

Predation by other warmwater species, parasites, and stunting may affect local populations of green sunfish. It freely hybridizes with other species of the genus *Lepomis*.

Food and Feeding

Green sunfish feeds on insects, mollusks, and small fish. The large, heavy mouth suggests the ability to eat large, hard-bodied organisms and, to some extent, fairly large fish. It is an opportunistic predator on large, active invertebrates. As it increases in size, it depends more on crayfish, fish, and large aquatic or terrestrial insects. Green sunfish in northern Utah ponds commonly feed on insects in early winter, crustaceans and fish in midwinter, and freshwater shrimp in late winter (Sigler and Miller 1963).

Breeding Habits

The green sunfish spawns in the spring in water from 2 to 8 feet deep when the temperature reaches about 66° F. The male constructs an oval nest that is from 6 to 15 inches in diameter. Nests are constructed in areas sheltered by rocks, logs, and clumps of grass or other debris. Males establish and defend territories during the breeding season. Precocious males have been observed defending territories and displaying a full range of fighting movements. Females enter the nest with the male and the eggs and sperm are deposited. The eggs are yellow, adhesive, and hatch within 3 to 5 days. Spawning for a pair takes place over a 1- to 2-day period. The male guards the nest and fans the embryos until hatching, then guards the young for varying periods of time (Sigler and Miller 1963).

In aquarium studies, males set up and guarded areas so precisely that their territories could be defined by making marks on the sides of the aquaria. Attacking males met intruders head-on, sometimes grasping them by the jaws. Even though there is considerable fighting, as many as 25 nests have been observed in a 50-square-foot area. Once the eggs are laid and boundaries accepted there is little disturbance. Maturity is at age 2 or 3, when the fish is usually 3 to 4 inches long, although in stunted populations it may be smaller (Sigler and Miller 1963).

Habitat

Perhaps the best ecological description of a green sunfish is that it is a miniature adult largemouth bass. It frequents the same areas, eats the same food, and is as aggressive as adult largemouth. It prospers in ponds inhabited with largemouth, bluegill, and bullhead catfishes. Although its preference is moderately warm water, it can easily survive in water in the high 80s or in the borderline trout waters of the mid to high 60s.

Green sunfish inhabits small, warm streams, ponds, and lake edges generally at low elevations (4,500 feet or less in the Great Basin). It is not generally abundant in ecosystems with more than three or four other fish species. It may be locally abundant in shallow or weedy areas of reservoirs that are not inhabited by other species. Green sunfish occurs with other species in turbid or muddy streams but is evidently able to take over physically disrupted areas only when native species have been depleted (Sigler and Miller 1963).

Preservation of Species

Stable, suitable habitats, with weedy areas for spawning and nursery areas, are necessary. Green sunfish suffers predation from other warmwater fish. Since it rarely qualifies as a valuable game fish, its welfare should not be an area of concern. In some locations where it has been introduced it may disrupt native species.

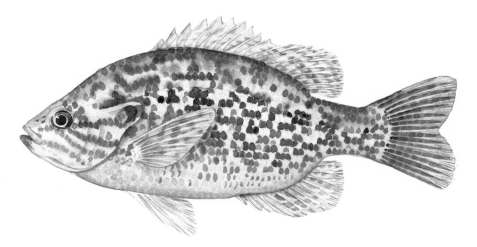

Pumpkinseed
Lepomis gibbosus (Linnaeus)

Importance

Pumpkinseed is the northern counterpart of the redear sunfish and is replaced by the redear in some locations (Pflieger 1975). It is well established in the Lahontan system and contributes to the fishery there, but Moyle (1976) discourages its spread because of its slow growth rate and tendency to stunt. In Canada it is a common sunfish and contributes significantly to panfishing, especially for youngsters. It occurs in large numbers in shallow, sheltered situations close to shore and attacks live bait viciously, providing a strong but erratic fight when hooked. It may be available to anglers when other fish are not. It is commercially fished in parts of Ontario and Quebec, providing an important contribution (Scott and Crossman 1973).

Range

The native distribution of the pumpkinseed is restricted to the fresh waters of North America. The species occurred from New Brunswick south along the Atlantic seaboard to northeastern Georgia. West of the Appalachian Mountains it was present from southern Quebec to southern Ohio, west to northern Missouri, north through eastern South Dakota to eastern Manitoba, east through western Ontario, Minnesota, and Michigan, and across southern Ontario. It has been introduced in California, Wyoming, Montana, Washington, and Oregon (Scott and Crossman 1973). It has also been widely introduced elsewhere in North America and in England, France, the Low Countries,

Germany, and the Danube River basin. It is present in Sheldon National Wildlife Refuge, northwest Nevada, in Suffurrena Ponds, and possibly in other Lahontan waters.

Description

The dorsal surface of the head and body and the upper sides are golden-brown to greenish-olive; lower sides are golden with irregular, wavy, interconnected blue-green lines. The ventral surface is bronze to red-orange. The sides of the body and head are flecked with spots of olive, orange, or red with blue, emerald, or green reflections and may have 7 to 10 indistinct vertical bars. Females are paler with the vertical bars more prominent. All colors are intensified in the breeding season. The young have a much less intense color pattern with a green to olive background color (Scott and Crossman 1973; Simpson and Wallace 1978).

Pumpkinseed is a deep-bodied fish, laterally compressed and almost disclike, usually 7 to 9 inches in length. The back is humped more than in other sunfishes. The head is quite deep and rather long with a pronounced hollow over the eyes. The opercle flap is flexible only at the tip and is black at the center with a narrow colored border and a red spot. The mouth is terminal, only slightly oblique and small. It has no palatine teeth but brushlike teeth occur in patches on the jaws with a single row on the vomer. Gill rakers are short and stubby and number about 8 on the lower limb, 4 on the upper.

The 2 dorsal fins are broadly joined and appear as 1. The first dorsal is long and spinous, usually with 10 spines. The soft portion of the dorsal fin is higher than the first with 10 to 12 rays and the edge shallowly rounded. The anal fin has 3 spines and 8 to 11 rays. The pelvic fins are thoracic and moderately long with 1 spine and 5 soft rays. The ctenoid scales number 35 to 47 in the lateral series. The peritoneum is silvery (Scott and Crossman 1973; Simpson and Wallace 1978).

Size and Longevity

Growth is slow to moderate and extreme longevity is 10 to 12 years in pumpkinseed. The estimated yearly total lengths in inches for pumpkinseed age 1 to 9 in some Canadian lakes are 3.6, 5.2, 6.0, 6.7, 7.3, 8.0, 8.4, 9.1, and 9.2 (Scott and Crossman 1973). Weights in Lake Simcoe, Ontario increased from 1 to 2 ounces at age 3 to 8 to 12 ounces at age 7. In small, productive bodies of water with large populations, stunting occurs and maximum lengths may not exceed 4 to 5 inches. Maximum size and age in Canada are 10 inches, 17 ounces and 8 to 10 years. In Idaho it seldom exceeds 5 inches and 4 to 5 ounces. Elsewhere it lives 12 years but rarely exceeds 11 inches (Simpson and Wallace 1978).

Limiting Factors

Populations that are not heavily harvested or not heavily preyed upon may become stunted. Egg and fry predation may decimate local populations. Pumpkinseed is eaten by other pumpkinseeds, bass, walleye, yellow perch, northern pike, and muskellunge. Parasites affect some populations. It hybridizes readily with other sunfishes.

Food and Feeding

Food is mainly a variety of insects and secondarily other invertebrates with some shifts due to season and size of fish. Food taken by pumpkinseed in Welch Lake, New Brunswick, Canada in descending order of frequency is dragonfly nymphs, ants, larval salamanders, amphipods, mayfly nymphs, midge larvae, roundworms, snails, water boatmen, and vertebrates (Reid 1930). Small pumpkinseed may contribute significantly to the diet of adult fish. Food is taken at the surface, off the bottom, or in the water column. Snails are the most important item of diet in some waters, but aquatic insects are apparently preferred.

Breeding Habits

Pumpkinseeds mature in their second or third year. Maturity is only partially size-related since stunted populations, the majority of which are under 4 inches, reproduce. Spawning takes place in late spring and early summer as water temperatures reach 68° F. The male constructs his nest in a colony with others but each defends his separate nest. Nests are shallow depressions 4 to 16 inches in diameter and constructed in areas of submerged vegetation over bottoms of clay, sand, gravel, or rock, generally in 6 to 12 inches of water. There is considerable display associated with prespawning activity. Mutual butting, nipping, and swimming in a circular pattern near the nest precede actual spawning. Egg deposition takes place during these circular swimming motions. Small quantities of eggs and sperm are emitted at irregular intervals. Each male may spawn with several females. The number of eggs varies from 600 to 3,000; the fecundity increases with size and age. Adhesive pale amber eggs, about 0.04 inch in diameter, stick to soil particles, roots, sticks, and other debris. The male guards the embryos and larvae for a few days, and when the minute young stray from the nest the male returns them in his mouth. The larvae are transparent and for a time visible only because of the eye spots. The male may guard the young for as long as 11 days. After the young depart, the male cleans the nest in preparation for a second spawning (Breder and Rosen 1966; Hubbell 1966), although not all males will spawn again.

Habitat

Pumpkinseed prefers clearwater lakes, sloughs, or sluggish streams with beds of aquatic vegetation. It is often in large schools and near or at the surface of areas exposed to direct sunlight. Pumpkinseed ranges over various bottom types. In lakes it generally stays close to shore in shallow waters where weed beds occur.

Preservation of Species

In populations that are not harvested or preyed upon, pumpkinseed may become stunted, reducing its desirability as a sport fish. High mortality, which may be principally from fishing, is necessary to prevent stunting. Liberal fishing regulations are therefore in order.

Bluegill
Lepomis macrochirus **Rafinesque**

Importance

The bluegill is probably one of the best known of the sunfishes.

Many people enjoy observing this active, colorful fish, which is inquisitive and fearless enough to be fed from shore. In North America it is an important pan fish. It can be taken with a very light fly rod and wet or dry flies, small lures, or worms. A large bluegill on light tackle provides great fishing pleasure and youngsters are delighted with its antics. Its edibility is good enough that most people rank it equivalent to most warmwater fish (Sigler and Miller 1963). Bluegill is one of the most common forage fish, providing food for the larger and more actively sought sport fish such as largemouth bass. It is stocked with bass and other piscivorous fish in managed waters (Pflieger 1975). Bluegill provides only a moderate fishery in the Great Basin with a few locations, including Railroad Valley, Nevada and central Utah, providing the majority of good to excellent fishing. It does well in a wide variety of environmental conditions, thriving in many waters that will not support other kinds of hook and line fishing.

Range

The native range of the bluegill includes the fresh waters of eastern and central North America. It occurs from the St. Lawrence River west of the Appalachian Mountains south to the region of the Chattahoochee River in Georgia to west Texas and into northeastern Mexico. The western edge of the range is eastern New Mexico to eastern Minnesota and western Ontario (Lee et al. 1980).

In waters of the Great Basin it, along with green sunfish and pumpkinseed, has been stocked extensively. It is present in low elevation, warmwater ponds and streams throughout the area.

Description

The bluegill is highly colorful. In the breeding season the breast of the male is red and the opercles are often blue with a black spot on the posterior margin of the ear flap, a characteristic that separates it from other sunfishes. Copper coloring on the heads of spawning males has led to the name "copperhead" in parts of Florida. It has a black spot at the back of the soft-rayed portion of the dorsal fin. Adults are yellowish-olive to dark olive green above with a bluish luster; the sides are bluish and the breast and belly yellowish. It has 5 to 10 vertical bars on the sides that are generally more prominent below the lateral line (Sigler and Miller 1963; Simpson and Wallace 1978).

The body is compressed laterally and is very short and deep; the greatest depth is at the third dorsal spine. The head is deep and narrow, the mouth terminal and slightly oblique with the lower jaw longer than the upper jaw. There are brushlike teeth on the jaws and vomer.

The pectoral fins are long and pointed and located fairly low on the body; the pelvic fins are thoracic. Bluegill has 3 anal spines; the ctenoid scales number 38 to 44 in the lateral series and the spinous dorsal has 10 spines with the soft portion attached (Sigler and Miller 1963; Simpson and Wallace 1978).

Size and Longevity

Although growth of bluegill in the Great Basin is slow to moderate, it is not long-lived. A newly hatched bluegill is approximately 0.25 inch long. By the end of its first year it has reached a length of 2 inches and may grow approximately 1 inch per year thereafter. It may live to 9 years. Bluegill grow best in areas where water temperatures range from 59° to 77° F. Pflieger (1975) gives the yearly size in inches as 1.5, 3.1, 4.4, 5.4, and 6.2 for fish age 1 to 5 years in Missouri streams and 2.8, 4.2, 5.6, and 6.6 for fish age 1 to 4 years in new reservoirs. The more rapid growth in the new reservoirs reflects the abundance of food available in newly inundated areas. Bennett et al. (1983) report mean total lengths in inches as 1.4, 2.8, 4.8, 5.9, 6.9, 7.6, and 8.3 for fish age 1 through 7 in lower Snake River reservoirs. Utah bluegill grow slowly and rarely reach lengths over 7 or 8 inches (Sigler and Miller 1963). The exception to this is Pelican Lake (not Great Basin) in east central Utah, where large bluegill have been the rule. In 1979, a 2-pound, 2-ounce one was caught there. The all-tackle record is 4 pounds, 12 ounces (Kutz 1982).

Limiting Factors

Overcrowded and stunted populations often result when total mortality is low. This is due in part to underharvesting. There is often heavy predation on eggs, fry, and young from other sunfishes and catfishes. The well-known bass/bluegill stocking combination is used with great success in the southeastern United States and with fair to poor success elsewhere. The bluegill population is kept in check but not decimated by the bass predation. Because of the high reproductive potential of bluegill, where populations are well established overfishing is not common.

Food and Feeding

Bluegill feeds day and night but to a lesser extent at night. Peaks of feeding may occur in the early morning and late evening or midafternoon and just after dark. It is affected to some extent by geographic location (Moyle 1976; Pflieger 1975). Throughout its life, bluegill feeds on small plants and animals but the size of food item taken increases with increasing fish size (the mouth size limits the size of the prey). It will feed anywhere—in shallow waters, on the bottom or at the surface, hovering at any depth through the use of its paired fins and then darting forward to capture prey. Adults may take insects or small fish, crayfish, and snails. Feeding is primarily by sight and occurs at all water depths. When mayflies and other aquatic insects are emerging, it will feed at the surface (Pflieger 1975; Sigler and Miller 1963).

Breeding Habits

Bluegill are extremely prolific; a female lays 2,000 to 50,000 eggs, depending on her size. Several females may spawn in the same nest, which is guarded by 1 male. One nest contained 61,000 eggs and a group of Michigan nests had an average of 18,000 eggs (Sigler and Miller 1963). Spawning begins in the spring when water temperatures approach 64° F. Some biologists believe that temperatures of 80° F are required for continuous spawning. Mature fish may be only 1 or 2 years old but usually are 2 to 3 (Sigler and Miller 1963). The male constructs a nest in shallow water (12 to 40 inches) by vigorously fanning his fins. This creates a depression 8 to 12 inches or more in diameter, 2 to 6 inches deep, and generally 1.5 times the body length. Nests are constructed on bottoms of gravel, sand, or even mud containing pieces of debris such as twigs or leaves. The males build nests in close proximity to one another, but each defends its own territory (Breder and Rosen 1966). Females stay in the general area of the nests in schools. When she is ready to spawn, a female approaches a nest area and is in turn approached by a male, generally the largest in the vicinity. The male attracts the female to his nest and the two spawn side by side. Courtship movements are accompanied by distinctive grunting sounds (Gerald 1971). The adhesive eggs attach to debris on the bottom of the nest and hatch in 2 to 3 days in 68° F water. The male guards the nest, but bluegill are more tolerant of other bluegill in close proximity than are other species of sunfishes during spawning. The fry are guarded to various degrees after hatching and soon move away from the nests to nearby aquatic plant beds or other cover. Evidence of a pelagic life stage for a period of 1 month or more from swimup also exists (Sigler and Miller 1963).

Habitat

The bluegill is gregarious, often moving about in loosely associated groups of 20 to 30. During midday, it remains in somewhat deeper waters or in the shade of trees or docks, moving into shallower water in early morning and evening to feed, although it may feed all day. It is frequently close to beds of aquatic vegetation. Individual bluegill spend most of their lives in rather restricted areas, even in large bodies of water. It does well in most clean waters of creeks, ponds, lakes, and reservoirs where the bottom is sand or gravel, where there is abundant vegetation, and where summer water temperatures reach 70° to 80° F. The latter temperature, although not required for successful spawning, evidently promotes higher success. It has been stocked extensively in small, relatively shallow farm ponds where it prospers and grows to a large size if harvested or fed on intensively by predators.

Preservation of Species

Bluegill will successfully reproduce and grow to fishable sizes if not allowed to overpopulate or if not too severely cropped by predators in the egg or fry stage. An established population is difficult to overfish (but it can be done) and liberal harvest regulations are in order.

Smallmouth bass
Micropterus dolomieui **Lacepède**

Importance

Smallmouth bass is one of the more sought-after game fish in North America. It is a highly prized sport fish in coolwater fisheries over all of its range. The magnitude, antiquity, and intensity of interest in this fish are reflected in the fact that angling results were mentioned in Fothergills' 1816 to 1836 "account of the natural history of eastern Canada" (Scott and Crossman 1973). It has been stocked throughout North America, with introductions beginning as early as the 1850s and culture practices as early as 1884 in Canada. It was commercially fished in Canada until 1936, selling for as little as six to eight cents per pound. Protests against the depletion of the species by the commercial fishery were reported as early as 1893 in Canada (Scott and Crossman 1973).

Its attraction for anglers and its sporting quality are almost legendary. Angler success, enjoyment, and harvest have been extensively studied (Budd 1961). Techniques for capture and the thrill of catching this species are the subject of many popular books and articles. Unfortunately, its scarcity in many areas of the United States, including the Great Basin, reduces its popularity.

Range

Originally smallmouth bass was restricted to fresh waters of central and eastern North America. Its original range was limited to the Great Lakes–St. Lawrence system and the Ohio, Tennessee, and upper Mississippi river systems (Lee et al. 1980). It did not originally occur east of the Allegheny Mountains (La Rivers 1962). Jordan, Evermann, and Clark (1930) suggest the type locality (where the original specimen was described) as South Carolina but Hubbs and Bailey (1940) report that Lake Champlain is more reasonable. Its range has been expanded by stocking so that it now occurs in suitable habitats over much of the United States. It has been successfully introduced in England, Europe, Russia, and Africa. Smallmouth bass has been stocked in the Great Basin in the Humboldt and Carson river drainages, Nevada.

Description

The color of smallmouth bass is variable with habitat, but it is normally dark olive to brown on the back with the sides lighter and yellowish and the belly yellowish-white. Most scales have golden flecks. It usually has 9 (8 to 15) or more dark vertical bars on the sides, a characteristic that distinguishes it from the largemouth bass (Simpson and Wallace 1978). In clear or stained waters it is darker with pronounced, contrasting markings. In turbid waters it is much lighter with vague markings. The head has dark bars radiating backward from the red or orange eyes. The caudal fin has a band of dark pigment near the caudal peduncle.

The body is moderately compressed and is more elongate than other sunfishes except the largemouth bass and the spotted bass, which have a similar robust body form. The head is large and deep with a shallow depression over the eyes. The snout is long and bluntly pointed and the mouth terminal with the lower jaw slightly longer than the upper jaw. The maxillary normally does not extend beyond the middle of the eye, a characteristic that distinguishes it from the largemouth bass. The jaws, palatine, and vomer are covered with fine, brushlike teeth.

The spinous portion of the dorsal fin (10 spines) is low and joined broadly to the soft portion, another characteristic that distinguishes it from the largemouth bass. The pelvic fins are thoracic with 1 spine and 5 rays. The pectoral fins are broad, short, and rounded; the anal fin has 3 graduated spines and 13 to 15 soft rays and a rounded edge. The ctenoid scales number 68 to 76 in the lateral series (Simpson and Wallace 1978; La Rivers 1962; Scott and Crossman 1973).

Young fish appear much as adults but have prominent vertical bars or rows of spots. The caudal fin has an unmistakably orange and then black band at the base and white to yellow tips (Scott and Crossman 1973).

Size and Longevity

The smallmouth bass is larger than other species in the sunfish family, except the largemouth bass. Most individuals in Canada measure 8 to 15 inches (Scott and Crossman 1973). The young are approximately 0.25 inch long at hatching, and in 12 days, after absorption of the yolk sac, they are 0.33 inch long. In a Lake Michigan–Green Bay study, the length in inches at the end of the year for fish age 1 to 13 was 3.1, 6.3, 9.2, 10.4, 11.9, 13.1, 15.0, 15.9, 16.3, 17.5, 17.8, 18.5, and 19.9 (Becker 1983). Few live longer than 15 years. Growth for smallmouth bass appears to be less variable than for largemouth, presumably because smallmouth are more restricted by habitat requirements. In the Central Valley of California, growth is excellent; a 4-year-old fish is typically 14.5 inches long and an older fish of almost 16 inches is not uncommon (Moyle 1976). The all-tackle hook and line record weighed 11 pounds, 15 ounces (Kutz 1982). The Great Basin record is 2 pounds, 15 ounces, from the Lahontan Reservoir, Nevada.

Limiting Factors

Much preferred habitat of the smallmouth has been reduced through inundation of streams by impoundments. Factors such as summer temperatures, fluctuating water levels, high winds, nest desertion, predation on eggs and fry, angling, and the bass tapeworm can greatly reduce reproduction and fry survival. This results in varying year class strengths, which are reflected in the harvest. The smallmouth competes well in suitable habitats and can be fished rather liberally when an established population exists. In some locations it is threatened by domestic, industrial, and possibly thermal pollution (Scott and Crossman 1973). It is prosperous but not abundant in the Great Basin.

Food and Feeding

Smallmouth fry feed largely on microcrustaceans and aquatic insects until they are about 2 inches long, when they start feeding on fish. It is often cannibalistic at almost any size, though less so than the largemouth bass. Crayfish, fish, and insects, in that order, are dominant food items in Little Goose Reservoir on the lower Snake River (Bennett et al. 1983). As an adult it takes a variety of food from the surface, in the water column, and off the bottom. For adults in most habitats, crayfish make up 60 to 90 percent of the food volume, fishes 10 to 30 percent, and aquatic and terrestrial insects 0 to 10 percent. Frogs, tadpoles, and fish eggs are often eaten also (Scott and Crossman 1973).

Breeding Habits

Sexual maturity is attained by females in their fourth to sixth year and by males in their third to fifth year. Females probably spawn every year; males may not (Scott and Crossman 1973). Smallmouth bass spawn usually over a period of 6 to 10 days (or longer in the northern part of their range) in late spring and early summer in water temperatures of 61° to 65° F. The male, as with most other centrarchids, builds a nest, usually 1 to 6 feet in diameter in 2 to 20 feet of water on sand, gravel, or rocky bottoms of lakes and rivers. Nests are usually constructed in areas where protective logs, brush, or rocks are present. Some males return to the same nest in subsequent years and over 85 percent of them return to within 150 yards of a previous nest (Scott and Crossman 1973). A ripe female evidently convinces the nest-defending male of her identity by persistence in returning to the nest area, by behavioral changes, and by changing colors so that the mottled markings on her sides are very distinct. Prior to spawning, there is considerable prespawning activity such as display, rubbing, and nipping. The male and female swim around the nest and eventually come to rest on the bottom. Egg deposition and fertilization take place for about 5 seconds but may be repeated over a period of 2 hours. A female, depending on size, produces from 2,000 to 25,000 eggs; approximately 7,000 per pound of female is average. The embryos are light amber to pale yellow in color, 0.05 to 0.09 inch in diameter and demersal. After spawning, the female leaves the nest and may spawn with another male in another nest. The male guards the nest, fans the eggs, and guards the young for several days to weeks after they hatch. The male stays with the brood until they disperse. The hatching period ranges from 9.5 days at 55° F to 2.25 days at 75° F (Becker 1983).

Habitat

In the spring adult smallmouth bass congregate on the spawning grounds. Later it is usually found in rocky and sandy areas of large clear lakes, streams, and rivers in moderately shallow water. In the heat of summer it retreats to greater depths and cooler water. Smallmouth bass is found in areas with abundant cover such as rocks, shoals, or submerged logs. It does not associate with dense growths of aquatic vegetation to the degree that the largemouth does. Preferred temperatures are between 66° and 80° F. It may do well at lower temperatures but requires at least 1,000 degree-days (days times degrees above freezing) with temperatures over 50° F for population stability. It begins to feed in the spring when water temperatures reach 47° F. The smallmouth bass is gregarious, tending to wander less than the largemouth and to be less solitary (Scott and Crossman 1973).

Preservation of Species

Stabilization of water levels during spawning and rearing of fry tends to ensure a strong year class. Wide temperature fluctuations during spawning or egg incubation may lead to nest abandonment. The smallmouth is not always competitive with largemouth bass, green sunfish, and bullheads. In ponds it should generally be stocked alone. Often there is no minimum size limit, but creel limits frequently are in order.

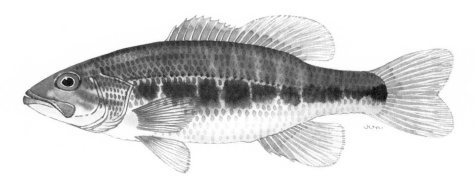

Spotted bass
Micropterus punctulatus (**Rafinesque**)

Importance

Spotted bass was ignored by taxonomists and confused by sports-men with largemouth bass for more than 100 years after it was origi-nally described. In 1931 interest was revived in this species, which is in many ways intermediate between the largemouth and smallmouth bass. It does not grow as fast as the largemouth and generally lives only 7 years. Its confusion with the largemouth bass has held it in some obscurity. It does well, even outside its native range, in habitat in-termediate between that required by the largemouth and smallmouth bass, providing a fair sport fishery. The distribution of spotted bass is so limited in the Great Basin that it is of little importance as a sport fish.

Range

The spotted bass occurs naturally in the Ohio River basin west from West Virginia, North Carolina, and Ohio through Indiana, Illinois, Kentucky, and Tennessee. It occurs naturally in the central Mississippi River drainage and in parts of the Gulf coast drainages of Georgia, Flor-ida, Alabama, and Texas. Within this area the native range has been ex-tended by stocking (Vogele 1975; MacCrimmon and Robbins 1975). Spotted bass has also been stocked in Arizona, California, Iowa, Nebraska, New Mexico, South Carolina, and Virginia. In the Great Basin it has been stocked in Eagle Valley Creek and Eagle Valley Reser-voir, Nevada (Cal Allan, personal communication, 1983).

Description

The spotted bass is distinctively marked with horizontal rows of regularly arranged spots below the lateral line, giving rise to its com-mon name. It has a lateral band of dark blotches that tend to merge and form an irregular, longitudinal stripe similar to the largemouth bass. It has dark olive, variegated markings above the lateral band of blotches, a creamy-white ground color below the lateral band, and a prominent dark spot on the top of the opercle and at the base of the caudal fin.

The dorsal fins are not deeply separated. The first fin has 9 to 11 spines and the second fin has 9 to 12 rays. The anal fins have 3 spines and 9 to 11 rays, the pectoral fins 14 to 17 rays. The lateral series has 59 to 65 scales. Scales on the cheeks are in 12 to 17 rows. It is somewhat laterally compressed and shaped generally like the largemouth bass.

Size and Longevity

Growth of spotted bass is generally slower than largemouth bass in the same environment. The maximum age is 7 years and it apparently does not reach that age in all populations. Growth is somewhat faster in reservoirs than in streams, probably as a result of food availability. It may grow for a longer period of time each year than the largemouth bass. Average yearly length in inches of a Texas population is 5.1, 7.7, 9.9, 12.5, 14.6, 16.9, and 17.9 for fish age 1 to 7 (Vogele 1975). The all-tackle hook and line record weighed 8 pounds, 10 ounces (Kutz 1982).

Limiting Factors

Spotted bass embryos and fry are probably preyed upon by piscivorous fish, particularly other sunfishes that occur in the same habitat. It is affected by a wide range of parasites, and in some populations infestation may be 100 percent. Habitat destruction and modification also affect it. Males may desert the nest if disturbed by such factors as temperature drops, human interference, and dropping water levels (Carlander 1977).

Food and Feeding

Food of the spotted bass varies widely with size of fish, habitat, season, and locality. It is popularly known to prefer a diet of crayfish. In lower gradient streams the fry subsist on zooplankton; larger fish take crayfish, insects, and fish. In most populations fish such as gizzard shad, carp, crappies, and bluegill are an important part of its diet. It apparently feeds both day and night, with peaks of activity immediately before sunset and soon after sunrise, the lowest activity being between midnight and sunrise (Vogele 1975).

Breeding Habits

Over half of the 1-year-old females and one-third of the 1-year-old males in Mississippi reservoirs were mature. Other populations mature as late as the third or fourth year (Vogele 1975). Moyle (1976) reports that California populations mature in the second or third year. The males prepare the nest with vigorous sweeping of the tail and may guard it for as long as 3 days before spawning. Spawning begins when temperatures range from 57° to 74° F and is more dependent on temperature than calendar date. The nests are usually circular depressions about 3 feet in diameter. Once a female is attracted to the nest area, the male guides her in circular motions, repeatedly biting her opercle and vent. After 20 minutes to 1 hour, egg deposition begins. The female lies on her side at a 45-degree angle and deposits eggs for a few seconds, although the entire spawning act may require several hours. More than 1 female may attempt to spawn with a single male. The number of eggs deposited varies from 763 to 18,995 and averages 5,000 in eastern populations and from 2,000 to 2,500 in California populations. Males defend the nest from prior to spawning through the larval development stage (Vogele 1975).

Habitat

The spotted bass lives in both low-gradient streams and reservoirs. In Oklahoma it occurs in small, clear, rocky streams but in Alabama it is abundant in larger streams (Vogele 1975). It is established in only two streams in California in areas that are intermediate habitat between that utilized by the largemouth and smallmouth bass (Moyle 1976).

Preservation of Species

Where established it can be fished with a limited creel. Preservation of habitat for spawning and nursery areas is important. It is extremely tolerant of high turbidity. Its intermediate ecological requirements between largemouth and smallmouth bass will most likely restrict its spread in the Great Basin. However, it is adaptable and existing populations should remain stable if not displaced by habitat disruption.

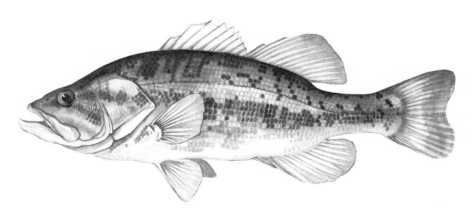

Largemouth bass
Micropterus salmoides (Lacepède)

Importance

The largemouth bass is the most important warmwater sport fish in the United States. Over all of its natural and introduced range it is highly prized by sportsmen, more than making up in size what it may questionably have to give up to the smallmouth in sport quality. It provides a quality fishery in many waters of the Great Basin. It was, along with the smallmouth, an important commercial species in Canada until 1936 when harvesting was restricted to sport fishing. It tolerates high temperatures and slight turbidity and prospers in a wide range of habitats from large reservoirs to warmwater farm ponds.

Range

The native range of the largemouth bass includes most of the eastern half of the United States and north to southern Quebec and Ontario. This includes the lower Great Lakes states and the central part of the Mississippi River system south to the Gulf of Mexico. It was originally in Florida and north on the Atlantic coast to Virginia. Through extensive stocking it now occurs over virtually the entire Atlantic coast in fresh waters from Maine to Florida, west to Texas and northern Mexico, north through the eastern parts of New Mexico to North Dakota, and east across southern Canada to western New York. It has been introduced in England, Scotland, Germany, France, South Africa, Hong Kong, the Philippines, and Brazil (Lee et al. 1980). It has been introduced in many parts of the West, including the Great Basin, where it now occurs in the large river reservoirs of the Lahontan and Bonneville basins as well as numerous natural ponds and lakes.

Description

The dorsal surface of the body and head of largemouth bass is bright green to olive, and the sides are almost as dark in large fish. The ventral surface is milk white to yellow. A pronounced, wide, solid black lateral band sometimes extends continuously from snout to the posterior edge of the opercle in young; it is broken or inconspicuous in adults. The sides of the head are olive to golden-green with some scattered black pigment. The belly and the inside of the mouth are milk white. The eye is brownish. The dorsal and caudal fins are opaque and green to olive. The anal and pelvic fins are green to olive with some white and the pectoral fins are amber and clear (Scott and Crossman 1973; Sigler and Miller 1963; Simpson and Wallace 1978). The young are pale green after yolk sac absorption, in contrast to the young of smallmouth bass, which are black. The caudal fin of the young is like that of the adults—bright colors are absent.

The largemouth is a moderately large, robust fish with an ovate body that is less laterally compressed and deeper than the smallmouth bass. The head is large, long, and deep, its length 26.6 to 31.7 percent of total body length (Scott and Crossman 1973). It has a long, deep notch over the eyes. The opercle is bony to the edge and pointed. The mouth is large, terminal, and wide with the lower jaw reaching past the center of the eye in adults, a characteristic that distinguishes it from the smallmouth bass. Fine brushlike teeth occur on both jaws, palatines, vomers, and sometimes the tongue.

The first dorsal has 10 spines and is deeply separated from the soft ray portion, another characteristic that distinguishes it from the smallmouth. The pelvic fins are thoracic with 1 spine and have their origin under that of the first dorsal fin. The pectoral fins are rather short and broad with the tip rounded; they have 13 to 15 rays. The anal fin has 3 spines. The caudal fin is slightly forked and not long, but broad with rounded tips. The ctenoid scales are larger than those of smallmouth bass with 8 rows from the lateral line to the dorsal origin and 14 to 18 rows from the lateral line to the anal fin insertion. The lateral line is complete, high, and only slightly arched. There are 55 to 69 scales in the lateral series. The peritoneum is silvery and the intestine well differentiated (La Rivers 1962; Scott and Crossman 1973; Sigler and Miller 1963). It may be confused with the spotted bass as well as the smallmouth.

Size and Longevity

The largemouth bass is fast-growing and long-lived. It is by far the largest of the sunfishes. Yearly growth rates vary with locale, being higher in warmer, southern areas. Cold waters may produce interruptions in growth. Growth is rapid immediately after hatching from the initial size of 0.1 inch. Young in Ohio are 2 to 5 inches long (Trautman 1981). The availability of invertebrate food of appropriate size and water temperature affect the size during early August of the first year and have an effect upon the final size and overwinter survival of young. In the southern edge of its range it may grow year-round. The length at the end of each year for Lake Simcoe, Ontario largemouth in inches is 4.0, 8.0, 10.0, 12.0, 13.5, 14.5, 16.0, 17.0, 17.5, 18.0, 19.0, 19.8, 20.4, 21.0, and 21.4 for fish age 1 to 15 (MacCrimmon and Skobe 1970). Largemouth bass in lower Snake River reservoirs (Bennett et al. 1983) have mean total lengths in inches of 3.3, 5.8, 9.1, 11.5, 14.1, 16.5, and 17.4 for fish age 1 to 7. Fish in colder climates grow slower and live longer. La Rivers (1962) states that fish age 3, 4, 5, and 6 years from Ruby Marsh, Nevada measure 7.0, 8.8, 12.8, and 15.8 inches. Moyle (1976) states the maximum size is 30 inches and the maximum age is 16 years. In Cache Valley, northern Utah the length in inches at the end of each year is 3.0, 5.6, 7.6, 10.4, 13.4, 15.5, 16.9, and 18.6 for fish age 1 to 8 (Sigler and Miller 1963). The all-tackle hook and line record weighed 22 pounds, 4 ounces (Kutz 1982).

Limiting Factors

Largemouth bass embryos and fry are doubtless part of the food of other predaceous fish such as other sunfishes, yellow perch, walleye, northern pike, and about any other species that share a particular habitat. It is also preyed upon by such birds as heron, bittern, and kingfisher. Crayfish, dragonfly larvae, and predaceous diving beetle larvae prey on the young. Adverse water temperatures at spawning time, intense wave action, nest desertion, fluctuating water levels, parasite-caused sterility, and food availability for new fry are probably the most important decimating factors (Scott and Crossman 1973). Food availability for fry is probably the most important factor, creating strong and weak year classes that are eventually reflected in the harvest.

Food and Feeding

Adult largemouth bass are largely fish-eating predators. Food changes from primarily zooplankton to insects, fish, crayfish, and frogs as size increases. In Lake Opinicon, Ontario, Keast and Webb (1966) report largemouth at a size of 1.2 to 2 inches eat cladocerans, mayfly nymphs, amphipods, chironomid larvae, and other items such as copepods, waterbugs, and caddisfly nymphs. Fish 2 to 3.8 inches long eat 40 percent mayfly nymphs, 20 percent dragonfly and damselfly nymphs, 20 percent crayfish nymphs, and small quantities of amphipods, chironomid larvae, and small fish. Over 3 inches its diet is 50 to 90 percent small fish and 10 to 40 percent crayfish.

Food is taken at the surface morning and evening and during midday in the water column and from the bottom. It is a sight-feeder and often moves in schools near shore and close to vegetation. Feeding is reduced at water temperatures below 50° F and decreases during spawning and in winter. It requires about 4 pounds of food to produce 1 pound of fish flesh. Largemouth bass eats such fish as gizzard shad, carp, bluntnose minnow, golden shiner, yellow perch, pumpkinseed, bluegill, and, to a lesser extent, largemouth bass. In short, it doubtless eats whatever species is available (Scott and Crossman 1973). It readily eats small mammals that fall into the water and has been known to consume ducklings.

Breeding Habits

Largemouth bass spawn from late spring to midsummer (occasionally as late as August) with the peak of spawning in early to mid June in Canada (Scott and Crossman 1973). In California, Moyle (1976) reports spawning activity in April when water temperatures reach approximately 59° F; Sigler and Miller (1963) report 62° F. It spawns for the first time in its second or third spring at 7 to 10 inches in some populations. Nests are generally shallow depressions fanned out by the male in sand, gravel, or debris-littered bottoms at depths of 3 to 7 feet. Nests are often built next to cover. Spawning activity is similar to that of the smallmouth bass but the male is less vigorous in his defense of the nest area. Each female lays eggs in 1 or more nests, the total number being dependent on fish size but ranging from 2,000 to 90,000. The eggs adhere to the substrate and hatch in 2 to 10 days. Sac fry spend 5 to 8 days in the nest or close proximity and are guarded to varying degrees by the male. Broods formed by fry from several nests will be protected by a male for about 2 weeks beyond the swimup stage.

Habitat

Largemouth bass inhabits the upper levels of warm water of small, shallow lakes and ponds, shallow bays of large lakes, and, in some cases, large, slow rivers. It occurs in reservoirs over much of its range. It is almost universally found in association with soft bottoms, stumps, and extensive growths of a variety of emergent and submergent vegetation. Largemouth bass is rarely found in the rocky situations that smallmouth bass inhabits. Movement is not extensive, usually less than 5 miles, and summer territories are small. It generally moves to the bottom of the habitat in winter but is more active than the smallmouth bass, providing an under-ice fishery in many areas. In the spring it may return to previous spawning areas and summer territories. Largemouth bass can tolerate higher water temperatures than smallmouth bass, preferring temperatures near 80° F. At temperatures in excess of 80° F it becomes inactive, resting in shaded areas of aquatic or shore vegetation. It does not tolerate low oxygen concentrations well (Scott and Crossman 1973; Sigler and Miller 1963).

Preservation of Species

Stable water levels during spawning and reduction of fish competing with young largemouth will improve yearly production. Since it is an aggressive feeder, it is subject to overfishing and may on occasion need the protection of minimum size and, more often, creel limits.

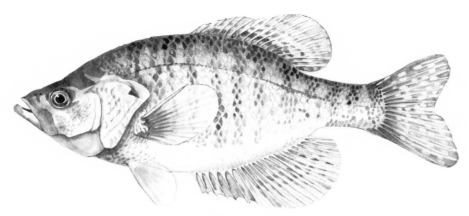

White crappie
***Pomoxis annularis* Rafinesque**

Importance

White crappie is an important game fish over much of its native and introduced range, contributing significantly to the warmwater pan fishery. In some locations it is caught in greater numbers than largemouth bass and contributes greater weight to the creel than do the smaller sunfishes. It is viewed with disfavor in some locations due to the often-held notion that it outcompetes bass and may decimate their populations through predation on fry and young. In both the creel data and many published fishing statistics it is not separated from the black crappie, making exact catch data impossible to record. Its flesh is white, flaky, and quite palatable (La Rivers 1962).

Range

The native range of the white crappie is restricted to the fresh waters of east-central North America. This includes from southwestern New York, south (west of the Appalachian Mountains) to the Gulf coast area of Alabama, then west to eastern Texas, north to South Dakota and southern Minnesota, then east across lower Michigan into southern Ontario. It has been widely introduced in the states of Washington, Oregon, California, and Connecticut. Early stockings were sometimes labeled as "crappies" and may have been both white and black crappies (La Rivers 1962; Scott and Crossman 1973). In Nevada the planting of white crappies was recent (1956) and it is now established in the lower Humboldt and Carson rivers in Ryepatch, Lahontan, and Echo reservoirs and Indian Lakes. White crappie is not known to occur elsewhere in the Great Basin.

Description

The back and top of the head is a darkish green to olive or brownish; it may have a blue-green or silver cast. The upper sides are a lighter and more iridescent green and may shade to silver. There are generally 5 to 10 vague, vertical blotches of black, sometimes extending down to the anal fin but becoming indistinct on the lower back and upper sides. The belly is silvery to milky white. The eye is yellow to green. The opercular bone may have iridescent pink or green pigment. The dorsal, caudal, and anal fins are heavily vermiculated, contrasting with light-colored spots and opaque pelvic fins. The paired fins are lightly colored or unpigmented. The dark pigment and iridescent colors on head, chin, and breast are intensified on breeding males, which may be as heavily spotted as the male black crappie. The young have much less black pigment.

White crappie is a moderately large, slab-sided, deep-bodied fish, more elongate than the black crappie. The back is somewhat flattened and the caudal peduncle rather longer and somewhat narrower than the black crappie. The head length into total length is 3.2 to 4.0. The snout is short, rather sharply pointed, and not as deep as that of the black crappie. The mouth is terminal, somewhat oblique and large. The lower jaw is large and longer than the upper jaw. There are fine teeth on both jaws and palatines. The gill rakers are close-set, long, and slender, numbering 22 to 24 on the lower limb and 6 to 8 on the upper limb. There are 7 branchiostegal rays.

The 2 dorsal fins are closely joined. The first usually has 6 (4 to 7) spines of graduated length; the second dorsal fin is longer and higher with 12 to 16 soft rays and a rounded edge. The caudal fin is moderately long and shallowly forked with rounded tips. The anal fin has a long base with 6 graduated spines followed by 17 to 18 soft rays and a squarish to rounded edge. The pelvic fins are thoracic with the origin under the pectoral fins and far in advance of the dorsal fin with 1 spine and 5 rays. The pectoral fins are high and not long but rounded with 13 rays. The ctenoid scales are rather large but markedly smaller and crowded on the anterior dorsal surface. The lateral line is complete and shallowly arched over the pectoral fin with 39 to 46 scales in the lateral series. There are no nuptial tubercles (Becker 1983).

Size and Longevity

Growth of white crappie in areas where it has been stocked (such as California) is somewhat slower than where it is native. In California it reaches 2 to 4 inches its first year, 4 to 7 inches the second year, 6 to 8 inches the third year, and 8 to 10.5 inches the fourth year. It seldom reaches lengths in excess of 14 inches or lives longer than 7 or 8 years (Moyle 1976). White crappie in lower Snake River reservoirs (Bennett et al. 1983) have mean total lengths in inches of 2.7, 6.0, 8.6, 9.6, 10.2, and 10.6 for fish age 1 to 6. In Ohio, Roach and Evans (1948) report lengths in inches as 2.6, 5.4, 7.6, 9.0, 10.4, 11.8, 13.7, and 15.7 for fish age 2 to 9. The all-tackle record is 5 pounds, 3 ounces (Kutz 1982). A 2-pound, 8-ounce white crappie was caught in Lahontan Reservoir, Nevada.

Limiting Factors

Embryos and small white crappie are preyed on by other sunfishes. It is parasitized by protozoans, trematodes, cestodes, and leeches over all of its range. It hybridizes with the black crappie. Populations that are fished can sustain heavy pressure in areas where reproduction is high.

Food and Feeding

The white crappie is basically an opportunistic feeder that takes whatever is available. The food of the young is zooplankton crustaceans but adults eat aquatic insects, some crustaceans, and a large number of small fish (La Rivers 1962). Hansen (1951) gives the following percentage of volume for white crappies' food in Illinois: fish 58, aquatic insects 35, unidentified animal matter 5, other aquatic invertebrates 1. White crappie in lower Snake River reservoirs eats cladocerans, fish, and aquatic insects. Cladocerans constitute 43 percent of the total and are eaten by 83 percent of the fish. Fish represent 46 percent of total food volume and 13 percent of the identifiable species are suckers (Bennett et al. 1983). The feeding mechanism of white crappie is unusual in that it has long, fine gill rakers, suitable for straining small zooplankters from the water, combined with a large, protrusible mouth that is suitable for ingesting large prey, including fish.

Breeding Habits

Sexual maturity is reached in the second to fourth year and fish on nests are usually 6 to 8 inches long. White crappie spawning takes place for approximately one month in late spring to early summer at water temperatures of 57° to 73° F, but it is most active at temperatures of 61° to 68° F. The aggressive, territorial males arrive at the spawning grounds first and clean out nests. These nests are not well defined but are approximately 5 to 12 inches in diameter with little depression and are constructed in 8 inches to 5 feet of water. Nests are often constructed in areas of rooted plants or algae and near the protection of undercut banks. Crappies generally nest in colonies of 35 to 50, 2 to 4 feet apart. Spawning takes place in the mornings with little of the active, circular swimming characteristic of some other sunfishes. Each spawning act is from 2 to 5 seconds, with the same pair taking part in as many as 50 acts, usually with 1 to 50 minutes between them. Only a small portion of the eggs is released at any one time and the same females may spawn in the nests of several males. Egg numbers vary; one 6-inch female had 1,908 eggs, one 13-inch female had 325,677 eggs (Morgan 1954). The eggs are 0.03 inch in diameter, colorless, adhesive, and demersal. The male guards the nest and fans the eggs. He does not abandon the nest when water temperatures drop. Eggs hatch in 17.5 to 24 hours at a temperature of 70° to 74° F (Morgan 1954). The tiny, transparent young remain on the nest only a short period and may leave the nest as soon as 4 days after hatching (Becker 1983; Scott and Crossman 1973).

Habitat

White crappie is most abundant in warm, somewhat turbid lakes, reservoirs, and stream backwaters. In Ontario, Canada it is found in rather silted streams, lakes, and ponds and in muddy, slow-moving areas of larger rivers. In the Great Lakes it is present in the mouths of tributary streams and in warm, weedy, sheltered bays. The white crappie appears to have greater tolerance than the black crappie for high turbidities, alkaline waters, current, high temperatures, and lack of aquatic vegetation or other cover. It tends to school and is often localized in its distribution. Individuals may move considerable distances within a water body, but most do not. Optimum temperatures appear to be 80° to 84° F. During the day it tends to congregate around submerged logs or boulders in quiet water 6 to 13 feet deep. The white crappie may move out into open water to feed during evening and early morning; it is more nocturnal than diurnal (Becker 1983).

Preservation of Species

Young white crappies probably fall prey to the same predators that other sunfishes do. The larger individuals with their deep bodies may escape all but the largest predators. Stocking of other sunfishes in waters with established populations of white crappies should probably be avoided. White crappie has potential for other Great Basin waters. Stocking should be based on individual water studies that identify both habitat and prey base as well as desirability to the fishing public.

Black crappie
Pomoxis nigromaculatus (Lesueur)

Importance

Black crappie draws its importance from its popularity as a fair-sized pan fish. It is relatively easy to hook and it fights well. Catch rates in some midwestern waters may be as high as 1.2 fish per hour for acceptable-size fish, making it desirable for casual fishermen and youngsters. In Canada it is fished both for sport and commercially. The flesh is white, flaky, and very palatable (Scott and Crossman 1973; Sigler and Miller 1963).

Range

The native range of black crappie is restricted to the fresh waters (rarely brackish waters) of eastern and central North America. It occurs naturally from Quebec south through western New York (west of the mountains) to the Gulf coast in Alabama, east through Florida, and north along the Atlantic coast to Virginia. It occurs west from Alabama to central Texas, north from Oklahoma to South Dakota, most of North Dakota, and in eastern Montana, east through southern Manitoba, Ontario, and Quebec. Black crappie has been so widely introduced in warmwater habitats throughout the United States that it is now virtually impossible to define its limits (Lee et al. 1980). It has been stocked in the western states of California, Nevada, and Utah. It occurs in the Great Basin in warm waters such as the Bear and Logan rivers, Willard Bay, Utah and the Humboldt River system, Nevada.

Description

The color of the black crappie is silver olive with numerous black or dark green splotches on the sides. Vertical bars, which are prominent in the young, are not present in adults. The sides are light, iridescent green to silvery. The head and sides have an irregular mosaic of black blotches. The belly is silvery to white. The dorsal, caudal, and anal fins are strikingly vermiculated with black, forming round or oblong yellow to pale green spots in the center of the vermiculations. The pelvic fins are opaque with some black on the tips of the membranes. The pectoral fins are dusky and transparent. When it is in clear, vegetated water it is darker with a contrasting color pattern; individuals from turbid water have a bleached look. In breeding males the black, particularly on the head, becomes darker, more intense, and velvety in color (Sigler and Miller 1963; Simpson and Wallace 1978). The young have less pigment and pattern.

It is a deep-bodied fish, less elongate than the white crappie and extremely compressed laterally. The head is long, almost one-third the body length. There is a very narrow, marked depression over the eyes, the back is rounded, and the snout is upturned, producing an S-shaped profile. The snout is short and somewhat deeper than that of the white crappie. The mouth is terminal, large, and oblique; the large lower jaw is somewhat longer than the upper jaw. The maxillary is long and reaches to the posterior edge of the pupil. It has fine teeth on both jaws and the palatines. There are 7 branchiostegal rays.

The black crappie has 2 dorsal fins but they are so joined as to appear as 1. The first dorsal has 7 or 8 spines of graduated length. The second dorsal is higher than the first with 14 to 16 soft rays and a rounded edge. The caudal fin is long, broad, and shallowly forked with rounded tips. The anal fin has a long base with 5 or more spines, 16 to 18 rays, and a rounded to squarish edge. The pelvic fins are thoracic with 5 rays and 1 spine and the tips are rounded. The base of the dorsal fin is about the same length as the base of the anal fin. The pectoral fins are moderately high on the body and long, broad, and rounded with 13 to 15 rays. The scales are ctenoid and large but smaller and crowded on the anterior dorsal surface and the breast. The lateral line is complete and high, shallowly arched over the pectoral fin with 36 to 41 scales in the lateral series. There are no nuptial tubercles (Sigler and Miller 1963; Simpson and Wallace 1978).

Size and Longevity

Growth of young is rapid at first. In northern Wisconsin populations the length at the end of each year in inches is 2.4, 4.9, 6.8, 8.0, 9.0, 9.8, and 10.7 for fish age 1 to 7 (Snow 1969). Growth varies tremendously with size of the population and productivity of the habitat. Mantua and Willard reservoirs in northern Utah in the late 1970s had vast populations of 7- to 8-inch black crappie that were caught at times at the rate of 8 to 10 fish per hour. Beckman (1949) gives the following size in inches for fish age 2 to 8 years as 5.9, 8.0, 9.0, 9.9, 10.7, 11.3, and 11.6. California populations grow somewhat slower than their eastern counterparts. Moyle (1976) reports age 1 to 4 fish at sizes in inches from 1.6 to 3.2, 4.7 to 8.3, 6.0 to 11.0, and 6.7 to 13.0. The largest fish reported from California weighed 3.9 pounds. Bennett et al. (1983) report that age 1 to 4 fish from lower Snake River reservoirs have mean total lengths in inches of 2.9, 5.7, 7.7, and 8.6. The all-tackle hook and line record is 6 pounds (Kutz 1982). The Great Basin record is 3 pounds, 2 ounces.

Limiting Factors

Young black crappie are preyed upon by a variety of warmwater predaceous fish such as largemouth bass, smallmouth bass, crappies, and others. The spines and long body of an adult protect it from all but the large predators. It is parasitized by protozoans, trematodes, cestodes, nematodes, and others over most or all of its range. Black and white crappies hybridize.

Food and Feeding

Feeding mechanisms of black crappie are almost identical to those of white crappie and its diet is similar. It is primarily a mid-water feeder, eating zooplankton and small diptera larvae predominantly when it is small and fish and aquatic insects when larger (Keast and Webb 1966). It is not uncommon to find planktonic crustaceans in the stomachs of fish up to about 6 inches. Black crappie will feed at temperatures as low as 44° F and therefore feed year-round in many areas. It will feed at any time of the day or night but feeding generally peaks at noon, midnight, and early morning (Keast 1968). Cladocerans are the single most important food item for black crappie in lower Snake River reservoirs, constituting 65.8 percent of total food eaten. Aquatic insects represent 16 percent of total volume and occur 43.9 percent of the time (Bennett et al. 1983).

Breeding Habits

Black crappie matures in the second or third year at about 4 to 8 inches. Spawning is initiated in March or April as temperatures approach 58° to 64° F and may continue until July. Nests built by the male are shallow depressions on bottoms ranging from mud to gravel to debris. Nests are usually built in water less than 3 feet deep near or in beds of aquatic plants. Males construct nests 6 to 10 feet from the nearest neighbor. Groups of spawning fish appear in loose colonial association. A female may spawn with more than 1 male and produce eggs several times during the summer. A female lays between 10,000 and 200,000 eggs, the number being related to her size and age. Eggs measure slightly less than 0.04 inch in diameter and are whitish, demersal, and adhesive. Eggs hatch in 3 to 5 days and are guarded by the male for a short time, but the fry soon rise from the nests and spend the next few weeks drifting in open water, presumably feeding on zooplankton (Moyle 1976; Sigler and Miller 1963).

Habitat

Black crappie does well in large, warm, clear lakes or reservoirs that have large beds of aquatic plants. It is usually found in clear, quiet, warm waters of large ponds, small lakes, and bays, shallow areas of larger lakes, and backwater areas in large rivers. It is almost always found in areas of abundant aquatic vegetation over sandy to muddy bottoms. It is less tolerant of turbidity than the white crappie. It grows and prospers best in water temperatures of about 75° F. When temperatures become excessive it tends to move to deeper water. It is highly localized in schools and spends its days around large, submerged objects, moving offshore to feed in open waters in the evenings and early mornings or, in case of heavy competition, all hours of the day.

Preservation of Species

Fishing regulations can be very liberal on established populations. Numbers tend to fluctuate greatly in some reservoirs. Dominant-year classes may reduce subsequent year class reproduction.

PERCHES (PERCIDAE)

This family consists of 2 subfamilies, the perches and the darters, with 5 genera and 130 species. The subfamily Percinae has 2 genera and 4 species, only 2 of which occur in the Great Basin.

The members of this family are usually elongate, terete, and somewhat laterally compressed. The mouth varies from species to species and may be large or small and terminal or inferior. There are villiform teeth on the jaws, vomer, and palatines in bands and the lower pharyngeals bear sharp teeth.

The 2 dorsal fins are well separated, in contrast to sunfishes. The first dorsal has 6 to 15 spines. The pectoral fins are moderately long and the pelvic fins are thoracic with 1 spine and 5 rays. The anal fin is small with 1 or 2 spines and the caudal fin is lunate, truncate, or rounded.

This family is circumpolar in distribution but most species are restricted to North America. The perches inhabit warm, temperate, to cold subarctic streams and lakes. Four members of this family are important sport and commercial species, providing both economic and recreational benefits. Most members of this family are darters (small colorful fishes), none of which is established in the Great Basin.

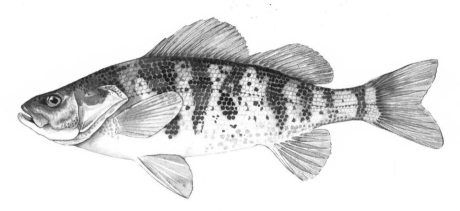

Yellow perch
Perca flavescens **(Mitchill)**

Importance

The yellow perch inhabits a vast territory and a wide variety of habitats, occurs in schools, and congregates near shore in the spring. All of these factors tend to make it a valuable sport fish and, in some areas, a commercial fish. It it taken commercially from Ohio to Alberta, Canada (Scott and Crossman 1973). It is an active feeder all year and can be caught by sportsmen both summer and winter, adding to its importance as a game fish. It takes most lures readily and produces a good sport fishery. Yellow perch rates very high in edibility. Conversely, underfished populations that are not cropped heavily may produce numerous small fish, reducing its appeal to sportsmen. In the Great Basin it provides a sport fishery in a few areas but in many locations the populations have become so abundant that fish of desirable size are rare (Sigler and Miller 1963).

Range

Yellow perch is not native to the Great Basin. The native range in North America is from Nova Scotia south along the Atlantic coast to the Florida panhandle and Alabama, west of the Appalachian Mountains from Pennsylvania to upper Missouri and from eastern Kansas northwest to Montana, then north to Great Slave Lake, Alberta, Canada and southeast to James Bay, Quebec, Canada and New Brunswick, Canada. It has been introduced into all of the states to the west and south of this general area, including Washington, Oregon, California, Utah, Nevada, New Mexico, and Texas (Scott and Crossman 1973; Sigler and Miller 1963; La Rivers 1962). It occurs in Deer Creek Reservoir and many other waters in Utah and in the West Carson and Humboldt rivers, Lahontan and Rye Patch reservoirs, and Washoe Lake in Nevada.

Description

It is dark olive green on the back and the sides are rich yellow to brassy, reflective of the species name, which means yellowish. The belly is light to whitish. It is distinguished by 6 to 8 dark vertical bars that extend across the back and down the sides.

The body is elongate and oval rather than cylindrical and is somewhat laterally compressed. The mouth is moderately large and terminal. The maxillary extends at least to the midpoint of the eye. Teeth are small and in brushlike bands on the jaws, palatines, and vomer.

The 2 dorsal fins are distinctly separated. The first dorsal is high and slightly rounded with 12 to 14 spines; the second dorsal is smaller with 12 to 13 soft rays. The caudal fin is slightly forked; the anal fin is square to rounded with 2 spines and 6 to 8 rays. The pelvic fins are thoracic; the pectoral fins are broad and rounded with 13 to 15 rays. The ctenoid scales number 51 to 67 in the lateral series, which is complete and slightly arched. Yellow perch has no nuptial tubercles (Sigler and Miller 1963).

Size and Longevity

Growth of yellow perch is extremely variable with habitat productivity, size of fish, and numbers in the population. Northern populations grow more slowly and live longer than those at the southern end of the range. Where stunting occurs in crowded populations, adults may never exceed 6 to 7 inches in length. The yearly size in inches for Klamath River, California yellow perch age 1 to 5 is 3.5, 5.9, 7.9, 9.1, and 10.6 (Coots 1956). In northern Wisconsin drainage lakes, the yearly size in inches for fish age 1 to 6 is 2.7, 4.3, 5.5, 7.1, 7.9, and 9.3 (Snow 1969). Yellow perch may live to be 9 or more years old. Females grow faster than males even at age 1 and achieve a larger size. The all-tackle record weighed 4 pounds, 3 ounces (Kutz 1982). The Great Basin record is 1 pound, 2 ounces.

Limiting Factors

The yellow perch is preyed upon by almost all other warm- to cool-water predatory fishes such as basses, small sunfishes, crappies, walleye, northern pike, yellow perch, and, to some extent, lake trout. A wide variety of parasites afflict this species. Yellow perch suffers from a number of fish diseases and such pathological conditions as tumors. Only a few fish diseases are harmful to humans when the flesh is eaten raw (Scott and Crossman 1973).

Food and Feeding

The yellow perch is chiefly carnivorous. It changes its feeding habits as it grows and with the seasons. It feeds largely on immature insects, larger invertebrates, and fishes, generally taken in the open water or off the bottom. It also feeds at the surface, as attested to by fly fishermen. Adult yellow perch browse methodically among aquatic plants, selecting the larger invertebrates such as crayfish, dragonfly larvae, and snails. Most feeding takes place during the day, with peaks of activity in the morning and at dusk, when they may move close to shore and then travel parallel to it. Large perch prefer fish but readily shift to invertebrates.

Breeding Habits

Males generally mature at 3 years or earlier and females at 4 years or less. Yellow perch spawns in the spring, usually at night. Spawning takes place over submerged beds of aquatic plants in quiet water at temperatures ranging from 44° to 50° F. When she is ready to spawn, the female makes a series of rapid turns or other quick movements, attracting 2 or 3 males. The female then swims rapidly, releasing a long string of eggs encased in a gelatinous sheath that may be as long as 5 or 6 feet. The total number of eggs deposited may be as high as 76,000, but is general 4,000 to 40,000 and is proportional to the size and age of the female. The males follow the female and release sperm, which envelops the eggs. These sticky bands of eggs are draped across vegetation. The eggs hatch in 10 to 20 days and the larvae, which are 0.02 inch long, start to feed on zooplankton soon after hatching. Some reserve food is available in the yolk sac (Scott and Crossman 1973; Sigler and Miller 1963).

Habitat

Yellow perch is very adaptable and able to utilize a wide variety of warm- to coolwater habitats from large lakes to reservoirs or quiet rivers. It may move into brackish waters where rivers flow to the sea. Yellow perch is most abundant not far from shore or sometimes in open-water lakes with moderate vegetation and clear water over bottoms that range from muck to sand and gravel. Schools of 50 to 200 are typical and aggressive actions are rare.

Preservation of Species

Stable habitat is probably the most important requirement of this species. Yellow perch will decline in areas where aquatic weed beds are reduced or removed. Spawning success may be minimal if there is a protracted drop in water temperature just when spawning is about to begin. Since the yellow perch is intensely competitive and populations tend to stunt, it is of somewhat questionable value as either forage or sport in some waters of the Great Basin.

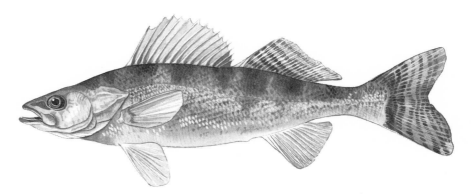

Walleye
Stizostedion vitreum vitreum **(Mitchill)**

Importance

The walleye is economically valuable over most of its range. It is taken commercially by gill, pound, and trap nets in the Great Lakes region and is probably the most economically valuable species in inland Canadian waters. It is often reluctant to take a hook, is not a spectacular fighter, and is difficult for novices to hook, thereby somewhat reducing its sport value, but it rates very high in palatability. It can be caught in summer and in winter through the ice; in some areas it is the most eagerly sought sport fish (Scott and Crossman 1973; Sigler and Miller 1963). Walleye populations provide keen sport fishing in the Great Basin.

Range

The walleye is restricted to fresh waters of North America, occurring only rarely in brackish water. Its native range is from Quebec, Canada, south to New Hampshire, and southwest to Pennsylvania; it occurs west of the Appalachian Mountains to the Gulf coast of Alabama, northwest to eastern Oklahoma, north through the eastern half of the states from Kansas to North Dakota, then north to near the Arctic coast in the McKenzie River, Canada, and finally southeast across James Bay to Quebec. It has been widely introduced on the Atlantic coast and in virtually all of the western states. It was introduced into Utah in 1951. It now occurs in the Great Basin in Willard Bay and Yuba reservoirs, Utah Lake, and Weber River, Utah. It is in Rye Patch, Lahontan, and Chimney reservoirs and Little Humboldt River, Nevada (Jim Curran, personal communication, 1983; Lee et al. 1980; Sigler and Miller 1963).

Description

Walleye color is highly variable with both habitat and fish size. In turbid water it is paler with a less obvious black pattern and in clear water colors are more vivid. Its background color is usually olive brown to golden-brown to yellow. Adults may be dark silver to dark olive brown mottled with brassy spots. This sometimes shades into yellow or milk white on the belly. In smaller fish, 4 to 14 inches, 6 to 7 vague to obvious dark, vertical bands occur across the back and down the sides. These bars are usually absent in adult fish. The fins are variously spotted.

The body is elongate and subcylindrical in young; adults are more laterally compressed. The head has a blunt point at its front and the snout is long and bluntly pointed; the jaws are equal in length. The mouth is large, terminal, and almost horizontal; the maxillary is very long, extending to the posterior edge of the eye. Walleye have strong teeth on the premaxillaries, jaws, and head of the vomer and palatines.

Canine teeth on the head of the vomer are often large, sharp, and re-curved and serve to distinguish the walleye from yellow perch.

The dorsal fins are well separated; the first dorsal has 12 to 16 spines and is high and rounded. The second, nearly square dorsal is about as high as the first with 1 fine spine and 18 to 22 rays. The caudal is long and broadly forked with rounded tips. The anal fin has 2 spines and 11 to 14 rays. The pelvic fins are thoracic with 1 spine and 5 rays; the pectoral fins have 13 to 16 rays and rounded tips. Ctenoid scales number 86 to 92 in the lateral series. The cheeks are scaleless. There is no nuptial tubercle and external differentiation of the sexes is difficult.

Size and Longevity

The walleye is relatively fast-growing and moderately long-lived. Growth is more rapid in the southern part of its range than in northern locations. Females grow faster than males from age 7 on in some Canadian populations. The difference in size is approximately 6 percent, re-sulting in females being 2 to 4 inches longer than males at a given age. In Utah Lake, Utah walleye size in inches is 6.7, 11.6, 13.4, 15.2, 16.6, and 17.0 for fish age 1 to 6 (Arnold 1960). A Canadian population reached the following approximate total length in inches: 8.7, 13.2, 16.4, 19.0, 21.2, 22.8, 23.9, 25.2, 26.0, 26.6, 28.0, and 28.9 for fish age 1 to 12 (Payne 1964). Walleye may weigh less than 3.5 ounces the first year. The average is probably 5 to 6 pounds. The all-tackle hook and line record weighed 25 pounds (Kutz 1982). The record for the Great Basin, caught in Utah Lake, Utah, is 11 pounds, 12 ounces.

Limiting Factors

Northern pike are probably the most decimating predators of wall-eye where their ranges overlap. Walleye is probably preyed upon by a wide variety of predatory fishes and is eaten by fish-eating birds and mammals. Water temperature, streamflow, and wind at spawning time are important factors in controlling population levels. Fry mortality, in-cluding natural death and cannibalism, may be as high as 99 percent in some populations. A wide variety of parasites, including protozoans, trematodes, cestodes, nematodes, and others, affect it over most of its range.

Food and Feeding

As the walleye grows, its food shifts very quickly from inverte-brates to fish. Young fish eat primarily copepods, cladocerans, and small fish. It is highly cannibalistic if other prey are not available. Hatchery-men sort young walleyes by size frequently during rearing to reduce cannibalism. When it becomes piscivorous, the relative amounts of prey depend upon availability. It eats those species present in greatest numbers, but appears to select yellow perch and freshwater drum when they are present. It takes crayfish, snails, frogs, and occasionally small mammals. In northern Iowa feeding in shallow water was at night.

Breeding Habits

Walleye do not build nests and the males are not territorial. The males move onto the spawning grounds first. There is much prespawn-ing activity that includes pursuit, pushing, circular swimming, and fin erection. One large female and 1 or 2 generally smaller males partici-pate in this activity and then rush to the spawning area, which is fre-quently over boulder or coarse gravel shoals in lakes or streams. The female rolls on her side near the males and egg and sperm are deposited; the eggs fall into crevices in the substrate and are sticky until water-hardened. Spawning occurs in the spring or shortly after the ice goes out in water temperatures of 38° to 48° F. A year may be skipped if tem-peratures are not appropriate. The probable reason for this is that water temperatures reach near-spawning levels and then drop for an extended time. Prespawning activity may occur at temperatures as low as 34° F. Fish often move into tributary streams immediately after ice breakup when the lakes are still ice-covered. There is evidence that it homes to the same stream for spawning year after year. Males generally mature at 2 or 3 years of age; females at age 3 to 4 in northern Utah. One 12-pound female produced 388,000 eggs and the number of eggs may be as high as 612,000 in very large females. The eggs are 0.05 inch in diame-ter and hatch in 12 to 18 days. Newly hatched fry are 0.2 to 0.3 inch in length and disperse into the upper levels of open water in 10 to 15 days after hatching (Scott and Crossman 1973; Sigler and Miller 1963).

Habitat

Walleye is tolerant of a great range of environmental conditions. The most favorable conditions appear to exist in large, shallow, turbid lakes such as Spirit Lake, Iowa or large streams or rivers, provided they are deep or turbid enough to afford cover. It uses logs, boulders, shoals, and weed beds for cover. Walleye moves up and down in depth in re-sponse to light intensity and moves seasonally or daily in response to temperature or food availability. It is not reluctant to migrate many miles. One individual in northern Utah migrated from Hyrum Reservoir to the mouth of the Bear River, a distance of about 40 miles (Sigler and Miller 1963).

Preservation of Species

Historically, many populations were overfished commercially, resulting in rapid population decline. Environmental degradation, including destruction of spawning areas, can affect local populations. Where it is well established it can be fished liberally by sportsmen.

Walleye in Great Basin waters can provide sport-fishing opportunities in habitats where salmonid species do not prosper. In some cases it is useful as a management tool to control other species. Evidence of negative impacts on established populations (for example, in Columbia River reservoirs on juvenile salmon) requires that careful investigation precede stocking.

CICHLIDS (CICHLIDAE)

These fishes enjoy great popularity as pets. Their intense coloration and unusual breeding habits make them interesting to observe. They are extremely hardy and easy to raise, but are also predaceous and somewhat vicious. Members of this family are found in Africa, South Amerca, Central America, and the southwestern United States and one genus occurs in Asia (Axelrod and Schultz 1955).

They will tolerate a wide range of water quality from brackish to fresh waters and several species move freely from oceans to fresh waters. They are spiny-rayed fish and prefer live foods but will accept many substitutes. Males are generally more colorful and have more pointed dorsal and anal fins than females (Axelrod and Schultz 1955).

In some areas of the United States members of this family have been promoted as a game fish and for aquatic weed control. Consequently, they have been released throughout the southern United States, often without due consideration of the long-term effects (Moyle 1976). Two species occur in the Great Basin.

Convict cichlid
Cichlasoma nigrofasciatum (Günther)

Importance

The convict cichlid is an important aquarium fish in North America. A negative importance, however, must be associated with its unwarranted stocking in desert waters where it competes with native species, often to their detriment.

Range

Native range includes Guatemala, El Salvador, Costa Rica, Panama, and other areas in Central America (Frank 1969; Axelrod and Schultz 1955). It has been extensively imported into the United States as an aquarium fish and has been stocked in many U.S. waters. It occurs in Ash and Crystal springs in the Pahranagat Valley, Nevada in the Great Basin (Deacon and Williams 1984).

Description

The convict cichlid gets it name from its visibly distinctive color pattern. It is dark brown to bluish on the back and mouse gray on the sides. It has 8 or 9 vertical stripes, the intensity of which vary with habitat. The fins are metallic green. The dorsal fin is placed just anterior to the caudal fin and has 6 spines and 7 or 8 rays. The anal fin is located far back on the ventral surface and has 8 or 9 spines and 6 rays. Both of these fins are larger in the male than the female. The pectoral fins appear as 13 or 14 separate rays. The female has more rounded fins and more reddish color than the male; this is extraordinary among cichlids. It has 29 or 30 scales in the lateral series (Frank 1969; Axelrod and Schultz 1955).

Size and Longevity

It reaches a maximum size of about 6 inches and probably 4 or 5 years of age. Deacon et al. (1980) report mean size of fish observed in Ash Springs as 1.6 inches.

Limiting Factors

It may be preyed upon by piscivorous fish with which it shares habitats but is more likely to infringe on the habitat requirements of native species. It does well in areas of suitable habitat and temperature. Since its introduction in 1963 it has become the second most abundant fish species in Ash Springs, Nevada.

Food and Feeding

This species feeds on aquatic plants in aquaria, often destroying them in the process. In captivity it may also be fed lettuce leaves and algae (Frank 1969). Intestine lengths indicate it is on the borderline between carnivorous and omnivorous (Hardy 1982). Food habits of convict cichlids in Ash Springs, Nevada consist of algae (55 percent), copepods, dragonfly nymphs, chironomids (11 percent), and other insect larvae and adults. Snails were also eaten (Hardy 1982; Deacon et al. 1980).

Breeding Habits

Convict cichlid breeds, like most other cichlids, by laying its eggs on a flat rock or other material near the bottom. It is an extremely secretive spawner and will go to considerable lengths to maintain that concealment, moving the young if the nest is disturbed. Both adults guard the nest and the young, but the female assumes most of the effort. Young may remain with the adults for an extended period. Optimum breeding temperature is 75° F. Hardy (1982) states that convict cichlids in Ash Springs, Nevada had an average number of young per nest of 18 and most were less than 0.8 inch long. Nests were within definite territories and vigorously defended. Most breeding occurred in two areas of the spring where substrates were firm silt, gravel, and sand. Riparian habitat is well developed and gradient is low.

Habitat

The convict cichlid occurs in the wild in ponds and lakes and probably inhabits warm waters with slow to moderate currents or the shallow to moderate depths of lakes and ponds. Ash Springs in Pahranagat Valley, Nevada is the southernmost spring system contributing water to the pluvial White River channel. Spring water temperature in the area averages approximately 92° F at the source. Temperatures in various sections of the spring area range from 59° to 86° F. Ash Springs has a definite riparian zone dominated by ash, willow, grape, cottonwood, and mesquite. The substrate is firm sand and gravel or mud and silt in areas of slower current velocity. Convict cichlids were found in all habitat types within Ash Springs (Hardy 1982).

Preservation of Species

No special considerations are necessary to preserve this species and additional stockings are discouraged because of its documented adverse impact on native desert fishes.

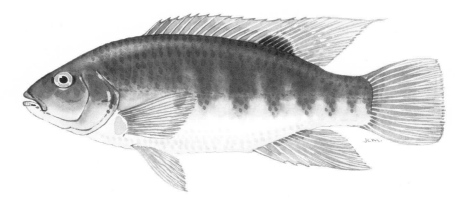

Redbelly tilapia
Tilapia zilli (Gervais)

Importance

Outside its native range, the redbelly tilapia has been introduced to control aquatic vegetation. Where it has been stocked in the wild it may adversely affect native species by destroying aquatic vegetation required by them.

Range

Redbelly tilapia is native to rivers and lakes in north and central Africa to Jordan (Lee et al. 1980). It has been successfully established in irrigation canals in the Imperial Valley, California and in the Salton Sea and lower Colorado River. In the Great Basin it has been introduced in a manmade pond in Cottonwood Park, Pahrump Valley, Nevada.

Description

The body is elongate but laterally compressed with a long dorsal fin. During spawning, the fish becomes shiny dark green on the back and sides and red and black on the throat and belly. Distinct vertical bands are present on the sides. The male is more intensely colored than the female. When they are not in spawning condition, coloration is dark olive green on the back, a lighter olive green to yellow-brown on the sides. The anal fin has 3 spines and 7 to 10 branched rays. There are 28 to 30 cycloid scales in the lateral series (Minckley 1973; Moyle 1976).

Size and Longevity

Males grow faster than females and both sexes live to be 6 or more years of age in their native range. It is not a fast-growing species. In its native range the redbelly tilapia may reach 2 to 4.7 inches its first year and 5.5 to 10 inches by the end of the third year. Where food supply is abundant it may reach 7 inches the first year and 10 inches its second year (Lee et al. 1980). At one time the Cottonwood Park population consisted of numerous small fish and one pair of 10-inch fish (Courtney and Deacon 1982).

Limiting Factors

Redbelly tilapia is affected by food supply and seasonal low temperatures. Temperatures as low as 46° F may not affect all members of a population, but Courtney and Deacon (1982) report high mortalities at water temperatures of 58° F in the Cottonwood Park population.

Food and Feeding

Redbelly tilapia is evidently omnivorous, despite its adaptations for feeding on vegetation. Aquatic plants are an important part of the adult diet but it also feeds on algae, invertebrates, and other fish.

Breeding Habits

Redbelly tilapia normally breeds for the first time at 5.5 inches but may breed at smaller sizes under crowded conditions. This species is unusual in the genus because eggs are not incubated in the mouth of the female, as is true of most other species of tilapia. They are deposited on sandy or muddy bottoms in a nest that resembles that of sunfishes. Courtship behavior begins when water temperature reaches 68° F. Eggs are laid in strips of 50 to 100 and fertilized. A total of 1,000 to

6,000 eggs is laid in a territory that is vigorously defended (Fryer and Iles 1972).

Habitat

The native habitat of redbelly tilapia includes large lakes and streams. It does well in artifical habitats such as ponds and irrigation ditches. It can survive in salinities to 45,000 ppm and over a wide range of temperatures. It is generally found where established aquatic vegetation exists (Lee et al. 1980).

Preservation of Species

Because of its potential undesirable effects on native species, the redbelly tilapia should not be introduced in waters before specific interactive ecological studies are performed.

SCULPINS (COTTIDAE)

Most members of this large and diverse family are marine, but sculpins of the genus *Cottus* have invaded fresh water, where there are numerous species, especially in the northwestern United States. There are 111 species in 36 genera in North America. Only 3 species occur in the Great Basin.

Sculpins are distinguished by large flattened heads, fanlike pectoral fins, and absence of true scales. The ctenii, or hooks, remnants of ctenoid scales, remain in some species as patches of prickles. They have 2 dorsal fins, the first composed of feeble dorsal spines. The anal fin lacks spines. The thoracic-placed pelvic fins have 1 imbedded spine and 3 or 4 soft rays, which are characteristic of the family. Sculpins are large-headed fishes. The body tapers from the head to a relatively narrow caudal peduncle. The skull is low, generally broad, and composed of thin bones. The preopercular bone is often variously armed with spines; the eyes are in a dorsal position, high on the head and prominent. The jaws are strong with well-developed teeth. There are 5 to 7 branchiostegal rays. Sculpins are bottom-dwelling, primarily marine fishes of Arctic and temperate seas. Freshwater sculpins are small, generally 7 inches or less, but some marine species reach a length of 24 inches or more. They have existed from the Oligocene epoch to Recent.

Mottled sculpin
Cottus bairdi Girard

Importance

The mottled sculpin provides a considerable amount of food for trout and other game fish. Contrary to earlier opinions, it rarely feeds on viable trout eggs. Its presence is considered an indicator of trout waters.

Range

The mottled sculpin ranges widely but discontinuously through North America from the Tennessee River system of Georgia and Alabama to Labrador on the north to west of the Great Lakes basin. It is present in parts of the Missouri River and the Columbia River system in southern Canada. It is present in the Bonneville system of the Great Basin (Lee et al. 1980; Sigler and Miller 1963).

Description

The first dorsal fin is marginated with reddish, brownish, or cream in adults, particularly in breeding males. Females rarely show such coloration and none exists in young and half-grown fish. The body is olivaceous to slaty, barred and spotted. The lower sides may be tinged with greenish gold. The caudal fin is more or less randomly speckled, the anal fin usually darkly speckled, and the pectoral fins banded.

The broad, flattened head, expansive pectoral fins, and scaleless body readily distinguish the bottom-dwelling sculpin. The first dorsal fin is composed of slender spines. It is joined at the base to the second, or soft dorsal fin. The dorsal spines and the single spine in each pelvic fin are so feeble as to pass unnoticed compared with those of other spiny-rayed fishes (Sigler and Miller 1963).

Size and Longevity

The mottled sculpin attains an age of 5 years and occasionally a total length of 6 inches. Adults in Logan River, Utah are usually between 3 and 4 inches long.

Limiting Factors

Clear, well-oxygenated water is required by the mottled sculpin. It is preyed upon heavily by piscivorous fish. At times it may be parasitized by protozoans, trematodes, cestodes, nematodes, acanthocephalans, mollusks, and crustaceans.

Food and Feeding

The food of this sculpin in Logan River, Utah consists almost entirely of aquatic insects, with plant material and fish a minor part of the diet. The fish eaten are generally small sculpin. Only 3 trout eggs had been eaten by 275 sculpins (Zarbock 1952). In another study in Montana, bottom-dwelling aquatic insects made up nearly 100 percent of the food (Bailey 1952).

Breeding Habits

Reproductive activity takes place in either rapid or slow-moving clear water during late winter and early spring, generally February to May. As spawning time approaches, the male becomes dark-headed. He selects a spawning site under a rock or ledge. The female enters the nest after suitable courtship, deposits her salmon-colored adhesive eggs in a mass on the ceiling of the nest while upside down, and departs or is driven off. More than one female usually deposits eggs in one nest. The male fertilizes the eggs and guards against predation. He fans them with his pectoral fins to maintain a current and keep the eggs supplied with oxygen. Spawning males are larger than females and ripen in advance of them. An average of 629 eggs per female has been observed in the Logan River sculpin. Maturity for both sexes is achieved at age 2 or 3 (Sigler and Miller 1963).

Habitat

Clear, cool mountain streams of rapid to moderate current are the preferred habitat of the mottled sculpin. The bottom typically consists of coarse gravel, small loose rocks, or rubble, but individuals are found over sand, clay, or mud bottoms and around lake margins. Preferred summer temperatures vary from 55° to 65° F with a few records of capture in water over 70° F. Water depths are commonly 2 feet or less. These fish associate with vegetation and live under stones or in moderately swift riffles (Sigler and Miller 1963).

Preservation of Species

The maintenance of a habitat of clear, cold, well-oxygenated water is the prime requisite of the mottled sculpin. If all cover provided by both plants and rocks were absent, predation would be heavy.

Paiute sculpin
***Cottus beldingi* Eigenmann and Eigenmann**

Importance

The Paiute sculpin is one of the most abundant fish in the Lahontan system and certainly the most abundant strictly bottom-dwelling fish in cold waters. In Sagehen Creek, California population densities are as high as six adults per square meter of bottom. Like the mottled sculpin, it does not deserve the reputation as a trout egg predator. On the other hand, it serves as a substantial prey item in the diet of game fish and converts bottom material to a form available to predatory species such as trout (Moyle 1976).

Range

The Paiute sculpin is the only sculpin found in the Lahontan system of California and Nevada, including Lake Tahoe and its tributaries. It also occurs in portions of the Columbia River drainage in Oregon and Washington and in the Bear River of the Bonneville system in Utah and the Upper Colorado system in Colorado (Lee et al. 1980).

Description

The color of the Paiute sculpin is brownish to brownish-black on the back and upper sides but somewhat paler below. The body is heavily mottled with 5 to 7 crossbars on the back. There may be lateral banding present; fins are flecked with black (Simpson and Wallace 1978).

The head is strongly typical of the genus. The lateral line may be complete or incomplete. Prickles on the body are absent. The head is moderately robust with a preopercle, which usually has a single spine.

The large mouth has palatine teeth, which are much reduced or absent. The dorsal fin has 15 to 18 rays, the anal fin 11 to 13. The caudal is rounded.

Size and Longevity

The Paiute sculpin is slow-growing and short-lived. In a California study, fish from Lake Tahoe and Sagehen Creek grew at about the same rate. Their yearly size in inches is 2.1, 2.7, 3.3, and 3.7 for fish age 1 to 4. The largest sculpin recorded was from Lake Tahoe and measured 5 inches. Sculpins of this size are rare and generally males (Ebert and Summerfelt 1969; Miller 1951).

Limiting Factors

As with the mottled sculpin, the Paiute sculpin suffers from degraded habitat, which may affect reproduction. Populations may suffer from excessive predation.

Food and Feeding

The Paiute sculpin feeds by ambushing bottom-dwelling aquatic invertebrates. When a prey organism nears the concealed sculpin, it lunges out suddenly and engulfs it. In Sagehen Creek of the Truckee River drainage 63 percent of the sculpin's diet by volume is aquatic insect larvae, especially those of mayflies, stoneflies, and caddisflies. The remainder of the diet consists of miscellaneous bottom organisms such as snails, water mites, aquatic beetles, and algae. In Lake Tahoe 65 percent of the Paiute sculpin diet is bottom organisms, especially midge larvae. Snails are the most commonly taken food at depths of 100 to 200 feet, while oligochaetes are the most abundant food for sculpins feeding in still deeper water. As with most fish, the diet of the Paiute sculpin varies with availability. The sculpins feed year-round but feeding is diminished in fall and winter. There is little or no evidence of Paiute sculpin preying on trout eggs (Ebert and Summerfelt 1969; Miller 1951).

Breeding Habits

In Lake Tahoe Paiute sculpin spawn in May or June in shallow water in windswept littoral areas or just off the mouth of streams. The eggs are laid in clusters on the underside of a rock and the nest is tended by a male, who defends it against other males. The Paiute sculpin selects crevices under rocks that are located on gravel bottoms, apparently avoiding otherwise suitable sites on bedrock or mud bottom. Some spawning in deep water may take place in Lake Tahoe since no dramatic inshore movement of sculpin has been observed during the spawning season. In streams most spawning sites are located in riffles. The number of eggs in each nest is usually 100 to 200, which is the number of eggs produced by 1 female, indicating multiple spawning is not common. Maturity is generally at age 2. After the fry hatch, at a length of less than 0.5 inch, they drop down into the gravel and remain there for 1 or 2 weeks until the yolk sac is absorbed (Ebert and Summerfelt 1969; Miller 1951).

Habitat

The Paiute sculpin prefers bottom habitat of rubble and gravel, although it is not unusual to find it living on other substrates. Its typical stream habitat is rocky riffle sections with clear, cold water, where it is almost always associated with trout. Like other sculpins the Paiute sculpin spends the daylight hours in comparative inactivity, hiding under rocks and in aquatic weeds. It forages at night, but there is no evidence of territoriality or of schooling behavior. There are two pronounced times of drift of young sculpin: one immediately following yolk sac absorption and the other in slightly larger individuals about two weeks later. These young move off the bottom into the currents and drift downstream, presumably populating new areas (Miller 1951).

Preservation of Species

A stable unpolluted habitat, including spawning areas, is the prime need of the Paiute sculpin.

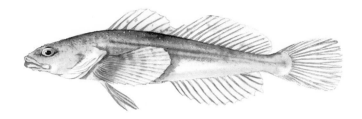

Bear Lake sculpin
***Cottus extensus* Bailey and Bond**

Importance

The Bear Lake sculpin is probably the second most numerically abundant fish in Bear Lake, Utah-Idaho. It is therefore very important as a forage fish for large predators such as cutthroat trout and lake trout.

Range

The Bear Lake sculpin is known only from Bear Lake, Utah-Idaho, although it has been planted in Flaming Gorge Reservoir, Utah-Wyoming on the Green River. Its fate there is unknown.

Description

The color is tan or brownish above, lighter below, with a few large splotches sometimes visible on the sides. The body has the general shape of other sculpins. The lateral line is straight but incomplete, terminating below the dorsal fin. The Bear Lake sculpin has no true scales, but prickles, remnants of ctenoid scales, are well developed on the upper part of the body and sides. The head is short, going 29 to 32 percent into standard length. The preopercle has 3 spines, the principal one directed backward and slightly upward. The middle spine is directed downward and backward. The dorsal fin is in 2 parts; the first is short and spiny, the second with rays of 16 to 19. The anal fin has 13 rays, the pectoral 16. The caudal fin is rounded (Bailey and Bond, 1963).

Size and Longevity

One hundred twenty Bear Lake sculpins taken in gill nets averaged 3 inches in length. It probably lives 4 to 5 years and grows at about the same rate as the Paiute sculpin (McConnell, Clark, and Sigler 1957).

Limiting Factors

A change in water quality in Bear Lake or a drop in water levels so that the best spawning habitats were exposed would function as limiting factors.

Food and Feeding

A 1985 study of Bear Lake sculpin found stomach contents to be 68 percent ostracods, 5 percent chironomids, and 14 percent copepods (Darcie Devroy, personal communication, 1986).

Breeding Habits

The Bear Lake sculpin spawns in 40° F temperature and above near shore in April to May on the underside of rocks. Spawning behavior is similar to that of the Paiute and mottled sculpins. After spawning it migrates to deeper water.

Habitat

Except when it moves into the shallow water in the spring to spawn, the Bear Lake sculpin lives in water from 50 to 175 feet deep. This is an area of few plants (*Chara*) and no cover other than the soft marl bottom (McConnell, Clark, and Sigler 1957). The fact that no hard substrate exists in deep water indicates it burrows in the soft marl for cover. Lake trout with sculpin and mud in their stomachs have been captured from Bear Lake.

Preservation of Species

Maintenance of suitable water quality, water levels, and cover conducive to spawning is required by this species.

14

Annotated Checklist of Fishes of the Great Basin

TROUTS (SALMONIDAE)
Sockeye salmon (Kokanee)   *Oncorhynchus nerka* **(Walbaum)**

This small landlocked sockeye salmon is present in tributaries of Lake Tahoe during spawning runs and the lake at other times; it is not abundant. Elsewhere in the Great Basin there are smaller populations. Although it has been stocked for forage and sport in many Great Basin areas, it has not always prospered. For example, the population in Bear Lake, first introduced in 1923, dwindled to a few fish by the early 1950s. Individuals larger than 2 to 3 pounds are rarely taken, and the average length is 12 to 16 inches. The life cycle generally lasts no more than 3 years. It dies after spawning.

Bear Lake whitefish*   *Prosopium abyssicola* **(Snyder)**

The Bear Lake whitefish is one of three species of whitefishes that occur only in Bear Lake. This is a small fish rarely reaching a length of more than 10.5 inches and ordinarily not venturing inshore except to spawn. It is frequently confused with the Bonneville whitefish, which is similar in appearance but grows much larger.

(* = native, e = endangered, t = threatened, sc = special concern)

Bonneville cisco*   *Prosopium gemmiferum* (Synder)

This small pelagic species rarely reaches a length greater than 8.5 inches, but it is the most numerous fish in Bear Lake. It is one of three whitefishes endemic to Bear Lake. Hundreds of thousands of these little fish move inshore each mid January and spawn in water between 6 inches and 40 feet deep. Dip-netting is allowed at this time. Considering the wide variety of activities on the east shore of Bear Lake at that time, the area resembles a circus more than a remote, high desert lakeshore. During the spawning run, between 60 and 75 percent of the fish netted are males. This offers an interesting management option; if the population during the summer is approximately half male and half female, then the cisco is not being overfished and the current level of fishing pressure can be maintained without depleting the fishery.

Bonneville whitefish*   *Prosopium spilonotus* (Snyder)

This, the third whitefish endemic to Bear Lake, is much larger than the other two. It reaches lengths of 18 to 22 inches and is sought by hook and line fishermen. It occurs more in shallow water than the other two endemic whitefish, spawning and remaining inshore throughout the cold months from November to late May or June.

Mountain whitefish*   *Prosopium williamsoni* (Girard)

This whitefish ranges throughout many of the cold waters of the Great Basin. This moderate size fish is sought by sportsmen but with less relish than trout or salmon; it is less sporting to catch and is judged by many to be less palatable. In some areas it competes with trouts for food and space.

Golden trout   *Salmo aguabonita* Jordan

This relatively small, very cold water trout is sought by fishermen because of its rare beauty and its scarcity. It is too scarce in the Great Basin to provide much fishing. Golden trout have been stocked mostly from the Kern River drainage, California. It is not an able competitor with other trouts and is easily caught, hence the populations can easily suffer heavy losses. It is recommended that it be stocked in areas that are otherwise fishless and have ingoing or outgoing streams in which it can spawn. It is primarily a downstream spawner.

Cutthroat trout*   *Salmo clarki* Richardson

This species, the only trout native to most of the Great Basin, was once widespread and abundant in all suitable waters throughout the basin. Because of the remarkable variations in color, spotting, scale number, and body form, populations of this species have received many different scientific names in different parts of the native range. It is not presently as abundant as some of the introduced trouts, but it is highly prized by anglers. Most subspecies of cutthroat trout are small to medium size, generally 2 to 3 pounds, with individuals occasionally reaching 8 to 10 pounds. The number of cutthroat today is only a small fraction of the original population, largely due to habitat destruction. It is locally stocked throughout the Great Basin.

Yellowstone cutthroat trout   *S. c. bouvieri* Bendire

The Yellowstone cutthroat was at one time stocked extensively in the Great Basin from eggs produced in Yellowstone National Park, Wyoming. The young from these eggs were planted more or less indiscriminately in habitats varying from small streams to large lakes. It seems reasonable that a remnant of the gene pool of the Yellowstone cutthroat exists in many Great Basin locations today, but it is doubtful if it should be identified as a distinct subspecies.

Lahontan cutthroat trout*   *S. c. henshawi* Gill and Jordan[1]

The Lahontan is the largest of all cutthroat trout. The world record is 41 pounds, caught in Pyramid Lake, Nevada. There it is fast-growing and relatively short-lived (8 to 9 years). Elsewhere it lives longer (10 or more years), but does not reach the size it does in Pyramid Lake. The largest one caught in Pyramid Lake in recent years weighed 28 pounds; however, 5 to 6 pounds is the average. Pyramid Lake, entirely in the Pyramid Lake Paiute Indian Reservation, is the terminus of the Truckee River, the main stem of which originates at the outflow of Lake Tahoe. This drainage system has most of the Lahontan cutthroat trout. The Pyramid Lake population is maintained by stocking; there is little or no natural reproduction at present.

Alvord cutthroat trout*   *S. c. alvordensis* (undescribed)[sc]

The Alvord cutthroat trout, thought to be extinct since 1934, has recently been discovered in a remote canyon in northern Humboldt County, Nevada. Specimens of this cutthroat, which is close to the Lahontan subspecies, were collected in 1985 and measured 15, 17, and 20 inches. These trout are differentiated from Lahontans primarily by the presence of fewer and finer spots, most of which occur above the lateral line. The discovered population is extremely limited and exists in a restricted habitat. Efforts to transplant pure Alvord cutthroat trout to a protected habitat are planned for 1986 (Behnke 1981; Robert Behnke, personal communication, 1986).

Paiute cutthroat trout*   *S. c. seleniris* Snyder[1]

This small, unspotted, lightly colored trout is native only to Silver King Lake, California but has been transplanted to Cottonwood Lake, California.

Unnamed species*   *S. c. smithi* (undescribed)[sc]

An undescribed subspecies of cutthroat trout exists in Whitehorse Basin, northern Humboldt County, Nevada. Its habitat is well protected and, though undescribed, this subspecies appears to be prospering (R. Behnke, personal communication, 1986).

Bonneville cutthroat trout*   *S. c. utah* Suckley[1]

This subspecies was once thought to be extinct. Small populations exist in the upper Bear River drainage, Wyoming and in western Utah–eastern Nevada. Additional small populations exist in other parts of the Bonneville basin. The size, probably determined by habitat, is relatively small.

Rainbow trout*   *Salmo gairdneri* Richardson

This is probably the most sought after coldwater sport fish in the United States and the Great Basin, primarily because it is heavily and continuously stocked. It is easier to raise in hatcheries than other trouts, hence its popularity with hatcherymen. When it feeds on invertebrates it increases in size rapidly to about 2 pounds; after that it generally needs to shift its diet and feed on fish to continue rapid growth. It is native to Eagle Lake in the Great Basin.

Brown trout   *Salmo trutta* Linnaeus

This fast-growing, long-lived species (10 to 12 years) is present in many of the cold waters of the Great Basin. It often attains a large size where there are ample forage fish. It is a remarkably successful fall spawner that rarely needs supplemental stocking once a breeding population is established. Because of this, it is an important component in today's fishery management options. It inhabits deep river pools but is also present in lakes and impoundments. Novices sometimes find it hard to catch but some experts prefer to fish for it because of its elusiveness.

Brook trout *Salvelinus fontinalis* (Mitchill)

The brook trout is present in higher elevation streams and small lakes. It grows slowly and tends to stunt where there is a scarcity of food and lack of fishing pressure. Small ones are easy to catch, making them a favorite of youngsters. Large individuals are rare and difficult to catch. Species of the genus *Salvelinus* are known as chars.

Lake trout *Salvelinus namaycush* (Walbaum)

There are populations of large lake trout in Bear Lake, Utah-Idaho, Lake Tahoe, Nevada-California, and Donner Lake, Nevada. This slow-growing, long-lived fish (15 to 20 years) thrives in deep, cold, infertile lakes; outside the Great Basin it occasionally lives in streams. Many individuals reach a weight of 20 pounds and a few 30 or more. It does not strike a lure or a lure with bait readily or hard and is relatively easy to land, but this is outweighed, in the eyes of many sportsmen, by its large size.

Arctic grayling *Thymallus arcticus* (Pallas)

Within its native range in northern latitudes, arctic grayling thrives in very cold streams and to some extent in lakes. It has a high, saillike, colorful dorsal fin that often has an iridescent purple sheen. It rarely reaches a length over 18 inches. It strikes lures readily and is easy to catch, therefore a population may be readily overfished. Populations in the Great Basin are all introduced and too limited to provide much sport fishing.

SMELTS (OSMERIDAE)
Delta smelt *Hypomesus transpacificus* McAllister

The delta smelt was stocked as forage from California in Willard Bay Reservoir, northern Utah in 1982. Its present status is undetermined.

PIKES (ESOCIDAE)
Northern pike *Esox lucius* Linnaeus

The pike is a fast-growing, long-lived fish (20 or more years) that reaches a large size. It is a carnivore that begins eating fish at a very early age. Individuals weighing 20 pounds or more are common and many are much larger. Its aggressive method of feeding makes it generally easy to catch since it strikes lures readily, although in the Fernley Wildlife Management Area this is not true (Tom Trelease, personal communication, 1983). It fights savagely when hooked and is highly prized by sportsmen. Northern pike is a long, slender fish with a large snout and heavily toothed jaws. It thrives in either warm or cold water and large or small streams and lakes, generally in the vicinity of weed beds. Few populations exist in the Great Basin.

CARPS AND MINNOWS (CYPRINIDAE)
Chiselmouth* *Acrocheilus alutaceus* Agassiz and Pickering

This species is largely a Columbia River drainage fish, but its native range extends into northwest Great Basin. The chiselmouth reaches a length of 12 inches and an age of 6 years. It uses its chisellike mouth (a hard, cartilaginous sheath) to scrape algae off rocks. Chiselmouth provides forage and was used by Indians as food at one time.

Goldfish *Carassius auratus* (Linnaeus)

This species, normally a pet fish, has been planted sporadically in the Great Basin but is not anywhere abundant. Valuable as a pet and in research, it is a nuisance in the wild. Here it may be a few inches to a foot long and live 5 to 8 years. It competes successfully with small native fishes to their detriment.

Grass carp *Ctenopharyngodon idella* (Valenciennes)

This Asian species has been introduced in the United States to control aquatic weeds and is now established in several midwestern major waterways. Only limited, isolated populations exist in the Great Basin. Its impact on natural waters and its ultimate value are unknown, but its ecological effects on native species are of great concern.

Common carp *Cyprinus carpio* Linnaeus

This well-known native of Asia is established and abundant in most of the warm waters of the contiguous forty-eight states. It is very common in Great Basin warm waters and even in cold Bear Lake, Utah-Idaho. Introduced in the late 1880s as a table delicacy, its success in adapting has far exceeded its table value. It is harvested lightly in the Great Basin but is more popular in several other regions of the United States. When abundant, the carp typically disrupts fish and water bird habitats and outcompetes other fish for food. Its low palatability results from the fact that in many waters it picks up a "muddy" flavor in the spring. In most areas this flavor disappears in winter. Carp is used for human consumption, smoked and fresh, and for domestic animal feed. It fights well when hooked and is difficult to land. It is a fast-growing, medium-lived fish (8 to 10 years), often reaching 10 to 12 and sometimes 35 or more pounds in the Great Basin.

Desert dace*   *Eremichthys acros* **Hubbs and Miller**[t]

The desert dace is a small, short-lived minnow (2 to 4 years) that inhabits warm springs and creeks in Soldier Meadows, northwestern Nevada. The habitat is almost 5,000 feet above sea level, with water temperatures of 67° to 100° F. This species suffers from habitat degradation caused by agricultural development and overgrazing.

Alvord chub*   *Gila alvordensis* **Hubbs and Miller**[sc]

The Alvord chub is indigenous to a small area in the Northwest system of the Great Basin. It lives in both cool and warm springs in a limited area and grows to a length of 5 inches.

Utah chub*   *Gila atraria* **(Girard)**

The Utah chub is abundant in most waters within the Bonneville system of the Great Basin. There is a lesser number in Nevada. Growth is rapid to 8 to 10 inches and it often grows much larger. The Utah chub lives 8 to 10 or rarely 11 years and provides forage for fish and birds, but it sometimes competes with game fish for food and space. It adapts easily to high, cold lakes or low, warm streams and lakes.

Tui chub*   *Gila bicolor* **(Girard)**

The tui chub is a western ecological counterpart of the Utah chub in the Great Basin. It lives in habitats ranging from deep, cold lakes to warm, shallow springs. The tui chub's adaptability to a wide variety of habitats is demonstrated by the large number of subspecies and forms. Its morphological and ecological adaptability is of interest to scientists. The chub is forage for fish over much of its range, particularly in Pyramid Lake, Nevada, where it is an important component of the food base for Lahontan cutthroat trout. It is also an important food base for the nesting birds on Anahoe Island, Pyramid Lake. The average size is 8 to 10 inches. It lives 5 to 8 years.

Borax Lake chub*   *Gila boraxobius* **Williams and Bond**[e]

The Borax Lake chub lives only in Borax Lake, Oregon and the other water courses in the immediate vicinity in the Northwest system of the Great Basin. It is typically about 2 inches long and lives 1 to 3 years. Borax Lake is a small, clear, shallow lake with temperatures ranging from 62 ° to 95° F.

Leatherside chub*   *Gila copei* **(Jordan and Gilbert)**

The leatherside chub is present in cool to cold creeks over much of the Bonneville system. The skin has a fine leathery texture, hence the common name. The average size is 3 to 5 inches, with a few reaching 6 inches. It has some importance as a forage fish.

Arroyo chub   *Gila orcutti* (Eigenmann and Eigenmann)

This small chub was introduced into the Mojave River system of the Great Basin from its native habitat in the Los Angeles Plain, California. Originally it lived in torrential streams in winter and clear brooks in summer. It has adversely affected the Mojave tui chub in the Mojave River system.

Pahranagat roundtail chub*   *Gila robusta jordani* Tanner[e]

This small chub is present only in the outflow of Ash Springs, Nevada, where it occurs in a small pool, 16 by 10 feet, with depths to 8 feet. The pool has a sand bottom and overhanging banks. Speckled dace is a common associate. This subspecies is the most endangered native fish in the Great Basin. Fewer than forty adults exist in the only known population.

California roach   *Hesperoleucus symmetricus* (Baird and Girard)

In the Great Basin the California roach occurs in Warner Valley, Oregon. It survives in higher levels of pollution than most other species. Green sunfish that have been introduced in its range often outcompete it. It is a small, short-lived species.

Least chub*   *Iotichthys phlegethontis* (Cope)[ʟ]

The least chub is locally abundant in Leland Harris Spring in Snake Valley, western Utah. The original range has been much reduced by habitat degradation, predation, and competition. This species suffers from the effects of introduction of such species as Utah chub and largemouth bass. Efforts to transplant it in other suitable habitats are too recent to evaluate. It is 1 to 2.5 inches long and lives 1 to rarely 3 years. Leland Harris Spring varies widely in temperature and water chemistry. The chub is of some use for mosquito control.

White River spinedace*   *Lepidomeda albivallis* Miller and Hubbs[ʟ]

The White River spinedace is native to the relict White River drainage, eastern Nevada. It lives in springs and their outflows where water temperatures are 65° to 71° F. There is moderate to swift current in some areas. It reaches a length of 4 inches.

Big Spring spinedace* *Lepidomeda mollispinis pratensis* Miller and Hubbs[e]

This subspecies lives in only one small creek. It frequents pools and avoids the swiftest riffles. It is scarce in areas of muddy water with shifting sand bottoms and no vegetation, preferring clear water that contains algae and pond weeds. Temperatures of 80° to 85° F are tolerated. The Big Spring spinedace reaches a length of 4 to 4.5 inches and probably lives 3 to 4 years. It was thought to be extinct but a remnant population has been discovered in Meadow Valley Wash, southeastern Nevada. It is the only surviving subspecies of this species in the Great Basin.

Hornyhead chub *Nocomis biguttatus* (Kirtland)

The hornyhead chub was introduced in Willard Bay Reservoir, Utah in 1982. It is widely distributed in previously glaciated areas in the midwestern United States. It is native to the Great Lakes area west to Wyoming (Lee et al. 1980).

Golden shiner *Notemigonus crysoleucas* (Mitchill)

The golden shiner has been introduced in the Great Basin as a forage fish. It grows rapidly to a length of 4 to 5 inches, may reach 10 inches, and lives to 4 to 5 years. The presence of this species may be an indication of pollution, since it survives pollution levels that eliminate most other species.

Emerald shiner *Notropis atherinoides* Rafinesque

The emerald shiner was introduced in Willard Bay Reservoir and Utah Lake, Utah in 1983. It is native to the Mississippi River basin into Canada and across the Great Lakes area to the east coast.

Common shiner *Notropis cornutus* (Mitchill)

The common shiner is native to the upper United States from the east coast across the Great Lakes area into Canada and to the upper Mississippi drainage. It was introduced in Willard Bay Reservoir, Utah in 1982.

Spottail shiner *Notropis hudsonius* (Clinton)

The spottail shiner was introduced into Willard Bay Reservoir, northern Utah, in 1982 and Utah Lake, Utah in 1983 as a forage fish. It is reportedly reproducing and prospering. Its native range is the Atlantic slope, including the Great Lakes, the St. Lawrence River, the eastern Mississippi River, and Canada north to the mouth of the Mackenzie River.

Sand shiner   *Notropis stramineus* (Cope)

The sand shiner is native to the Gulf slope drainages in Texas into the upper Mississippi River basin and the Great Lakes area. It was introduced in Willard Bay Reservoir, Utah in 1982.

Sacramento blackfish   *Orthodon microlepidotus* (Ayres)

The Sacramento blackfish was introduced in the Carson River drainage, Nevada. It is sufficiently abundant in Lahontan Reservoir, Nevada to possibly support a small commercial fishery. It is heavily preyed on by game fish such as white bass.

Bluntnose minnow   *Pimephales notatus* (Rafinesque)

The bluntnose minnow is native to central North America in Mississippi and to the Great Lakes basins from southern Canada to the Gulf slope (Lee et al. 1980). It was introduced in Willard Bay Reservoir, Utah in 1982.

Fathead minnow   *Pimephales promelas* Rafinesque

The fathead is native to the eastern and midwestern United States and was introduced in Utah Lake as forage in 1969. It may occur in other Great Basin locations. It grows to a length of 3.5 inches and lives about 2 years. The female has the interesting habit of laying her eggs on the underside of floating objects such as boards and leaves of submerged aquatic vegetation.

Bullhead minnow   *Pimephales vigilax* (Baird and Girard)

This species was introduced in Utah Lake in 1969. It may be reproducing in small inlet streams but its presence has not been reported recently.

Northern squawfish   *Ptychocheilus oregonensis* (Richardson)

The northern squawfish is representative of Columbia River fauna. It was introduced in the Harney system of the Great Basin.

Relict dace*   *Relictus solitarius* Hubbs and Miller[sc]

The relict dace lives in a variety of habitats in northeastern Nevada, ranging from thermal springs to large marshes. Temperatures of water in these areas vary greatly. It experiences medium to high mortality at 87° F.

Blacknose dace *Rhinichthys atratulus* (Hermann)

The blacknose dace is native to the New England states and Nova Scotia, south to Georgia, and west past the Great Lakes to the lower Missouri River drainages. It was introduced in Willard Bay Reservoir and Utah Lake, Utah in 1983.

Longnose dace* *Rhinichthys cataractae* (Valenciennes)

The longnose dace lives in small to large streams where temperatures range from 55° to 70° F. It is common in the northeast Bonneville system. This species reaches a size of 2.5 to 3.5 inches and lives 4 to 5 years. It is important forage.

Speckled dace* *Rhinichthys osculus* (Girard)

This omnipresent species lives in a wide variety of habitats from swift, cold riffles of mountain streams and strong currents to low-altitude, warm rivers. It is also present in quiet, isolated, cool, or warm springs and their overflow ditches, but is rarely present in water over 3 feet deep. Speckled dace occurs in the major drainages and many desert springs of the Bonneville and Lahontan systems. The speckled dace reaches a length of 2 to occasionally 4 inches and probably lives 4 to 5 years. It is important as a forage fish. Deacon and Williams (1984) list five undescribed and ten described subspecies.

Redside shiner* *Richardsonius balteatus* (Richardson)

The redside shiner is native to and widespread in all habitable waters of the Bonneville system. It is present but not native in the Harney basin of the Great Basin. This species reaches a length of 2.5 to 3 inches; a few reach 5 inches. It lives 5 to 6 years. It is important as a forage fish but may also prey on larval game fish and eggs.

Lahontan redside* *Richardsonius egregius* (Girard)

The Lahontan redside is the western Great Basin counterpart of the redside shiner. It lives in a wide variety of habitats and is locally abundant in much of its range. Size and longevity are similar to that of the redside shiner. It provides forage for game fish. In the lower Truckee River, Nevada it preys on the eggs and young of cui-ui and probably other species.

Creek chub   *Semotilus atromaculatus* (Mitchill)

The creek chub is native throughout most of eastern North America, west to Montana and New Mexico. It was introduced into Willard Bay Reservoir and Utah Lake, Utah in 1983.

SUCKERS (CATOSTOMIDAE)
Utah sucker*   *Catostomus ardens* (Jordan and Gilbert)

This is the second largest sucker in the Great Basin. It is abundant in the Bonneville system. It adapts to deep, cold lakes and shallow, warm streams. Early pioneers in Utah used it as a staple in their diet when crops failed. The young provide forage for game fish.

Desert sucker*   *Catostomus clarki* Baird and Girard

This small sucker is not abundant over any of its limited range throughout the lower Colorado River basin. The range of habitat, however, is highly varied. In the Great Basin it is present in the lower part of the relict White and Carpenter river drainages in southeastern Nevada.

Bridgelip sucker*   *Catostomus columbianus* (Eigenmann and Eigenmann)

This medium size sucker is locally abundant in the Harney drainage, northwestern Great Basin. It is of value as a forage fish for introduced game species.

White sucker   *Catostomus commersoni* (Lacepède)

This species was introduced in Willard Bay Reservoir, northern Utah in 1982. Its present status there is unknown. Native range is from the Arctic Circle south to New Mexico and Georgia. Ecological impact on native species, if it survives, is probably neutral.

Bluehead sucker*   *Catostomus discobolus* Cope

This species is abundant in the high, cold mountain streams in the eastern Great Basin, especially in the Bear and Weber rivers. The green sucker, *Catostomus (Pantosteus) virescens* (Cope) is considered to be synonymous with the bluehead sucker.

Webug sucker   *Catostomus fecundus* Cope and Yarrow

Taxonomic information on this sucker suggests that it may represent a hybrid between the Utah and June suckers. It is assumed that it does not represent a true species in Utah.

Owens sucker* *Catostomus fumeiventris* Miller

This newly described species is present in the Owens River, Death Valley area, California. It was described by R. R. Miller in 1973.

Largescale sucker* *Catostomus macrocheilus* Girard

This medium-sized sucker is present in the Harney drainage, north-western Great Basin. It is not abundant.

Mountain sucker* *Catostomus platyrhynchus* (Cope)

This species is abundant in cold mountain streams over much of the Great Basin. It is small thoughout its life, which makes it valuable as a forage fish.

Tahoe sucker* *Catostomus tahoensis* Gill and Jordan

This medium-sized sucker is very abundant in Lake Tahoe and Pyramid Lake and several Lahontan basin streams. It was abundant at one time in Walker Lake, but it is still common (Tom Trelease, personal communication, 1983). It thrives in deep, cold lakes and in relatively small, warm streams.

Warner sucker* *Catostomus warnerensis* Snyder[1]

The Warner sucker is confined to a small area in the Warner Valley of the Great Basin. There are four breeding populations (Carl Bond, personal communication, 1983). It reaches a size of about 16 inches and lives 8 or more years. This species lives in streams and ponds where temperatures reach 81° F.

Cui-ui* *Chasmistes cujus* Cope[c]

This large, slow-growing, long-lived species (18 years or much more) is endemic to Pyramid Lake. It is the largest of the Great Basin suckers. Cui-ui may or may not reproduce in Pyramid Lake water, which has a high level of total dissolved solids. It is possible that it can reproduce at the lake-river interface or other freshwater sources within the lake. Normally it moves into the fresh water of the Truckee River to reproduce. Certainly most of the natural reproduction is in the river. Numbers have declined dramatically since 1930. It was historically valued by the Pyramid Lake Paiute Indians as food.

June sucker* *Chasmistes liorus* Jordan[1]

Endemic to Utah Lake and thought to be extinct about 1930. A small population now breeds in the Provo River, a tributary to Utah Lake, Utah. It is listed as threatened by the Utah Division of Wildlife Resources.

BULLHEAD CATFISHES (ICTALURIDAE)
White catfish   *Ictalurus catus* (Linnaeus)

This small to medium size catfish is present in Lahontan Reservoir, Carson River, Indian Lakes, and Stillwater National Wildlife Refuge, Nevada. It reaches a larger size than other members of the family in the Great Basin except the channel catfish, but it is less willing to take a lure during the daytime. In areas where it is abundant and not stunted it is a relatively important sport fish.

Black bullhead   *Ictalurus melas* (Rafinesque)

The black bullhead is a small, prolific catfish, generally 12 to 14 inches long. The ease and frequency with which this species may be caught make it popular with youngsters and casual fishermen. It lives in a wide variety of habitats, including small streams, sloughs, intermittent streams, ponds, and gravel pits. Except locally, it is not abundant in the Great Basin.

Yellow bullhead   *Ictalurus natalis* (Lesueur)

The yellow bullhead primarily inhabits small, warm streams and shallow areas of lakes with clear water and abundant vegetation. It is primarily a stream species. It lives 5 to 6 years and reaches a size of 2 pounds. It is present in northwestern Great Basin.

Brown bullhead   *Ictalurus nebulosus* (Lesueur)

The brown bullhead is larger than the black bullhead but is generally less abundant. It is primarily a lake species that thrives with an abundance of aquatic vegetation and invertebrates.

Channel catfish   *Ictalurus punctatus* (Rafinesque)

Channel catfish farms in the United States produce more pounds of fish than those of any other cultured fish. This species grows more rapidly and larger than any of the other catfishes in the Great Basin and is more sporting to catch. It is stocked for sport fishing in cool streams of the Great Basin.

ARMORED CATFISHES (LORICARIIDAE)
Suckermouth catfish *Hypostomus plecostomus* (Linnaeus)

This species has been introduced in Indian Springs, southeastern Nevada and is a threat to native species. It probably reaches a length of 6 to 8 inches. Some members of this genus are able to make short overland migrations, using the vascularized stomach as a lung. It is a South American species and further introductions are strongly discouraged.

TROUT-PERCHES (PERCOPSIDAE)
Trout-perch *Percopsis omiscomaycus* (Walbaum)

The trout-perch was introduced in Willard Bay Reservoir and Utah Lake, Utah in 1983. It is native to the central Atlantic slope west to Ohio and the lower Missouri River basin and north over much of northern Canada and Alaska. It is typically a lake-dwelling species.

KILLIFISHES (CYPRINODONTIDAE)
White River springfish* *Crenichthys baileyi* (Gilbert)[1]

This native species lives in springs in eastern Nevada that range in temperature from 70° to 98° F. It reaches a size of 2.5 inches and probably lives 3 or 4 years. There is considerable genetic divergence at the subspecies level.

Railroad Valley springfish* *Crenichthys nevadae* Hubbs[1]

The Railroad Valley springfish is native to Railroad Valley, just west of the White River system in eastern Nevada. It has been established in springs at Sodaville, near Mina, Nevada. It is a small, heavy-bodied fish that lives in water with temperatures up to 88° F.

Devils Hole pupfish* *Cyprinodon diabolis* Wales[e]

The Devils Hole pupfish lives in Devil's Hole, Death Valley National Monument and two areas where it has been transplanted. The few hundred individuals in the natural habitat live in water to 80 feet deep, but spawn and feed on a shallow shelf. It is a small, short-lived species that hangs on precariously in this tiny habitat, which is said to be the smallest for any known vertebrate.

Amargosa pupfish* *Cyprinodon nevadensis* Eigenmann and Eigenmann

The Amargosa pupfish adapts to extremes of temperature in the Ash Meadows area it inhabits. It matures in 4 to 6 weeks and those living in springs may produce 8 to 10 generations a year. Stream-dwellers produce only 2 to 3 generations per year. It is the most widespread of the Death Valley pupfishes. The temperature extremes tolerated by this species are better evidenced in Amargosa Gorge below Tecopa, where water temperatures can get down to 40° F, and in the Tecopa Bore, where water temperatures exceed 90° F. The habitats in Ash Meadows range from 83° to 87° F.

Owens pupfish*   *Cyprinodon radiosus* Miller[e]

Originally this pupfish was present in many parts of the Owens River system but is now only in warm springs near Lone Pine and in refuges constructed around springs at Fish Slough, between Bishop and Big Pine, California. This species, once thought to be extinct, now lives in sanctuaries that have large, warm, clear pools with extensive shallow areas and emergent vegetation as well as one large 7-foot-deep pool.

Salt Creek pupfish*   *Cyprinodon salinus* Miller

The Salt Creek pupfish is unique even among pupfishes because it survives in the harshest environment of Death Valley, California, 200 to 300 feet below sea level. One of the remarkable aspects of it in Salt Creek is its rapid population fluctuations. Peak numbers have been estimated in the millions. Then, as water temperatures rise and the stream shrinks, most die. It probably lives only 1 year and is 1.5 inches long.

Pahrump killifish*   *Empetrichthys latos latos* Miller[e]

Two of the three subspecies of this species are extinct. This surviving subspecies presently exists as transplanted populations in two Nevada locations.

Plains killifish   *Fundulus zebrinus* Jordan and Gilbert

The plains killifish has been introduced in Juab County, Utah near Mona Reservoir. It is native to the Pecos, Brazos, and Colorado rivers of New Mexico and Texas as well as portions of Wyoming, Montana, and Missouri.

Rainwater killifish   *Lucania parva* (Baird)

This species is widely distributed in its native habitat on the Atlantic coast of the United States. It was apparently transported to Timpie Springs, Utah in the Great Basin along with a load of largemouth bass. It reportedly feeds heavily on mosquito larvae.

LIVEBEARERS (POECILIIDAE)
Mosquitofish   *Gambusia affinis* (Baird and Girard)

This species is stocked worldwide to control mosquitos. It is present throughout the Bonneville and Lahontan systems. It is a hazard to native fishes when stocked with them, especially certain minnows and killifishes. The mosquitofish survives very high temperatures (108° F) but is not tolerant of temperatures much below 40° F.

Sailfin molly   *Poecilia latipinna* (Lesueur)

The sailfin molly is an aquarium species that has been stocked in the wild much to the consternation of fishery biologists and undoubtedly the distress of small native fishes. It is present in Indian Springs west of Las Vegas, Nevada.

Shortfin molly   *Poecilia mexicana* Steindachner

The native range of the shortfin molly, which has been stocked in Nevada, is from northern Mexico to South America. It lacks the high dorsal fin of the sailfin molly, has a much reduced tail, and is less popular as an aquarium fish than the sailfin.

Guppy   *Poecilia reticulata* Peters

This small aquarium fish has been stocked by well-meaning pet owners and probably dealers in warm springs in southern Nevada and the Sheldon National Wildlife Refuge in northwestern Nevada. It outcompetes and at times preys on small native fishes. The species is able to survive high temperatures and intense pollution; for example, the soapy bath waters in one of the Sheldon camp areas.

Green swordtail   *Xiphophorus helleri* Heckel

The green swordtail is one of the most popular aquarium species. It has been introduced in the Great Basin in Indian Springs, Nevada. As with other exotic livebearers, it is an unwelcome addition to the limited areas inhabited by small native species. It does not do well in brackish water.

STICKLEBACKS (GASTEROSTEIDAE)
Brook stickleback   *Culaea inconstans* (Kirtland)

The brook stickleback is native from Nova Scotia west to Montana and north into Canada to Great Slave Lake. A relict population exists in northeastern New Mexico (Lee et al. 1980). It was introduced in Willard Bay Reservoir and Utah Lake in 1983.

Threespine stickleback*   *Gasterosteus aculeatus* Linnaeus

The threespine stickleback is a small, pugnacious, colorful little fish that lives in shallow, heavily vegetated waters. It builds a nest of aquatic vegetation and the male guards the eggs and young. The stickleback provides limited forage for fish and surface-feeding birds. It is native in the Great Basin in the Mojave River, California.

TEMPERATE BASSES (PERCICHTHYIDAE)
White bass   *Morone chrysops* (Rafinesque)

The white bass is a fast-growing, warmwater fish that prospers in large lakes and reservoirs. Reaching a size of 3 pounds, it provides fast and furious fishing when a school moves within range of the fisherman's cast. It is noted for producing very large, dominant populations. The largest numbers of white bass in the Great Basin are in Utah Lake, Utah and Lahontan Reservoir, Nevada.

SUNFISHES (CENTRARCHIDAE)
Rock bass   *Ambloplites rupestris* (Rafinesque)

The rock bass is native to the eastern United States west of the Appalachian Divide and west to the Mississippi drainage (Lee et al. 1980). It was introduced in Utah Lake, Utah in 1983.

Sacramento perch   *Archoplites interruptus* (Girard)

This species is the only sunfish native to the west coast, but it is not native to the Great Basin. The population in Pyramid Lake provides a very limited summer fishery. It is also present in Garrison Lake and Cutler Reservoir, Utah and in Rye Patch Reservoir, Humboldt River, Nevada. The Sacramento perch reaches a size of 2.5 pounds. The most productive Great Basin population is probably in Lake Crowley in the Owens River drainage. It lives in medium-depth water, generally near cover.

Green sunfish   *Lepomis cyanellus* Rafinesque

The small, pugnacious green sunfish generally does not reach a large enough size to provide sport. It competes very ably with other fish for food and space. The green sunfish was probably introduced in Utah in 1890, when a railroad carload of several species of fish was brought from the Illinois River, Illinois. It occurs in many of the warm, weedy waters of the Great Basin, generally not far from shore.

Pumpkinseed   *Lepomis gibbosus* (Linnaeus)

This small to medium size species provides limited fishing in the Great Basin. It generally reaches a length of 8 to 9 inches and lives 7 or 8 years. It inhabits both small and large lakes but stays near shallow, weedy areas or other cover.

Bluegill   *Lepomis macrochirus* Rafinesque

The bluegill is the most popular of the smaller sunfishes. It grows rapidly to 0.5 pound or more, is highly palatable, and is sporting to catch with ultralight tackle. The bluegill schools in the vicinity of weed beds in large numbers where it is easy to find and still easier to catch. It was probably brought into the Great Basin shortly after the turn of the century, when the popular belief was that midwestern warmwater species should be stocked in the warm waters of the Great Basin. The bluegill prospers in large, warm to cool lakes and in small, warm farm ponds, where it is often stocked in combination with largemouth bass. The theory is that the largemouth bass will eat enough young bluegills so they will not stunt while the largemouth bass are also prospering. This combination has worked better in the deep South than it has in the Midwest or far West.

Redear sunfish   *Lepomis microlophus* (Günther)

The redear is a small to medium size fish. It is also known as the "shellcracker," a name earned because it often feeds on snails and other mollusks. The redear seems to prosper in warm lakes, reservoirs, and large ponds. It may or may not be present in the Great Basin.

Smallmouth bass   *Micropterus dolomieui* Lacepède

The smallmouth bass is a coolwater stream fish highly prized by fishermen. It also inhabits deep, cold lakes. Second in size of the sunfishes only to the largemouth bass, the smallmouth is known for its fighting ability and table qualities. It is not abundant in the Great Basin, although it has been stocked widely. The smallmouth reaches a size of 5 pounds and lives 14 years.

Spotted bass   *Micropterus punctulatus* (Rafinesque)

This medium size black bass (*Micropterus* spp.) provides a limited fishery in some reservoirs in Nevada.

Largemouth bass   *Micropterus salmoides* (Lacepède)

The largemouth is the largest member of the sunfish family. It inhabits both warm and cold lakes, ponds, and streams. It grows to its largest size in large lakes but prospers in small farm ponds. It is the most sought after warmwater fish. Its popularity is attested to by the fact that boats are built especially to be used for largemouth bass fishing. Bass tournaments are frequent throughout the year and there is a large number of bass clubs. Probably more money is spent preparing and fishing for largemouth bass than any other species in the United States. It commonly reaches a size to 8 pounds but is frequently much larger. It lives 12 to 15 years.

White crappie   *Pomoxis annularis* Rafinesque

The white crappie and the black crappie are generally larger than the smaller sunfishes (*Lepomis* spp.) but smaller than the black basses (*Micropterus* spp.). They are prized because they are highly palatable, relatively easy to catch when a large school is found, and offer a brave, if limited, fight.

Black crappie   *Pomoxis nigromaculatus* (Lesueur)

This species was first planted in Utah in 1890 in a carload shipment of mixed fish from the bottomlands of the Illinois River, Illinois, a common practice of stocking fish in western states at that time. The black crappie has been planted throughout the Great Basin. Generally smaller than the white crappie, it provides good fishing unless it becomes stunted. It is subject to extreme fluctuation in population numbers in some Great Basin areas. For example, in Willard and Mantua reservoirs, northern Utah, populations have ranged from a few thousand to hundreds of thousands, then back to a few, in a matter of five to six years. It provides forage for other game fish and probably for larger members of its own species.

PERCHES (PERCIDAE)
Yellow perch   *Perca flavescens* (Mitchill)

The yellow perch is present in many areas of the Great Basin, primarily because it has been stocked so extensively. In most of these areas it has prospered. This pan-sized, highly palatable fish is especially appreciated by youngsters and fly fishermen. The yellow perch is primarily a lake fish, where it loafs and feeds near weed beds or other cover. In prime habitat it tends to stunt unless fished or preyed upon heavily. In many areas juvenile yellow perch are the mainstay in the diet of game species. This is true because the yellow perch are hatched earlier and are first on the food line, so to speak.

Logperch   *Percina caprodes* (Rafinesque)

This species is the most widespread of all darters. It occurs in midwestern states from eastern Texas north into Canada. It was introduced in Willard Bay Reservoir, Utah in 1983.

Walleye   *Stizostedion vitreum vitreum* (Mitchill)

The walleye, the largest member of the perch family, often reaches weights of 5 pounds and not infrequently much more. It lives on or near the bottom of both coldwater and warmwater lakes and streams. It is considered tops as a table delicacy, but it is often difficult to catch except by experienced anglers. There are three moderate populations of walleye in Utah: one in Yuba Reservoir, one in Utah Lake, and the third in Willard Bay Reservoir. There are several populations in Nevada.

CICHLIDS (CICHLIDAE)
Convict cichlid   *Cichlasoma nigrofasciatum* (Günther)

The convict cichlid was introduced into Pahranagat Valley, Nevada where it is a hazard to native fishes. This species, normally an aquarium fish, reaches a length of about 6 inches. It feeds heavily on aquatic algae and other plants. The distinctive color pattern suggests the common name.

Redbelly tilapia   *Tilapia zilli* (Gervais)

This species was introduced in the Great Basin to control aquatic vegetation. It occurs in Cottonwood Park, southeastern Nevada. Additional introductions are discouraged.

SCULPINS (COTTIDAE)
Mottled sculpin*   *Cottus bairdi* Girard

This species, usually living within a few inches of the bottom, is abundant in the Bonneville system. This cold-stream inhabitant is rarely more than 4 inches long. It has a large head and a tapered body. The adhesive eggs are deposited on the undersides of rocks near fast-running water. The body is covered with modified ctenoid scales that are no more than hooks. It lives 3 to 5 years, is valued as forage for trout, and its presence is considered an indicator of trout waters.

Paiute sculpin*   *Cottus beldingi* Eigenmann and Eigenmann

This species is abundant in upper cold reaches of lakes and streams in the Lahontan basin of Nevada and California where there is no other sculpin. It does not occur in Pyramid Lake, Nevada. Paiute sculpin is similar in habitat, description, and value to the mottled sculpin.

Utah Lake sculpin*   *Cottus echinatus* Bailey and Bond

This species is known from seven specimens collected in Utah Lake, Utah between 1880 and 1928. When originally described by Bailey and Bond in 1963, the survival of the species was questioned because of the low lake levels between 1932 and 1935. Subsequent collectors have failed to find the Utah Lake sculpin. It is considered to be extinct.

Bear Lake sculpin*   *Cottus extensus* Bailey and Bond

The Bear Lake sculpin, indigenous to Bear Lake, is the second most numerous species in the lake. It is important as forage. It lives in deep water except in the spring when it migrates inshore to spawn. The Bear Lake sculpin is small, rarely reaching a length of over 3.5 inches.

APPENDIX 1
Established Fishes of the Great Basin

ORDER SALMONIFORMES
Trouts (Salmonidae)

Sockeye salmon (Kokanee)	*Oncorhynchus nerka* (Walbaum)
Bear Lake whitefish*	*Prosopium abyssicola* (Snyder)
Bonneville cisco*	*Prosopium gemmiferum* (Snyder)
Bonneville whitefish*	*Prosopium spilonotus* (Snyder)
Mountain whitefish*	*Prosopium williamsoni* (Girard)
Golden trout	*Salmo aguabonita* Jordan
Cutthroat trout*	*Salmo clarki* Richardson
Lahontan cutthroat trout*	*S. c. henshawi* Gill and Jordan
Paiute cutthroat trout*	*S. c. seleniris* Snyder'
Bonneville cutthroat trout*	*S. c. utah* Suckley'
Rainbow trout*	*Salmos gairdneri* Richardson
Brown trout	*Salmo trutta* Linnaeus
Brook trout	*Salvelinus fontinalis* (Mitchill)
Lake trout	*Salvelinus namaycush* (Walbaum)
Arctic grayling	*Thymallus arcticus* (Pallas)

Pikes (Esocidae)

Northern pike	*Esox lucius* Linnaeus

ORDER CYPRINIFORMES
Carps and Minnows (Cyprinidae)

Chiselmouth*	*Acrocheilus alutaceus* Agassiz and Pickering
Goldfish	*Carassius auratus* (Linnaeus)

---

* = native; e = endangered; t = threatened; sc = special concern

Grass carp	*Ctenopharyngodon idella* (Valenciennes)
Common carp	*Cyprinus carpio* Linnaeus
Desert dace*	*Eremichthys acros* Hubbs and Miller[1]
Alvord chub*	*Gila alvordensis* Hubbs and Miller[sc]
Utah chub*	*Gila atraria* (Girard)
Tui chub*	*Gila bicolor* (Girard)
Borax Lake chub*	*Gila boraxobius* Williams and Bond[e]
Leatherside chub*	*Gila copei* (Jordan and Gilbert)
Arroyo chub	*Gila orcutti* (Eigenmann and Eigenmann)
Pahranagat roundtail chub*	*Gila robusta jordani* Tanner[e]
California roach	*Hesperoleucus symmetricus* (Baird and Girard)
Least chub*	*Iotichthys phlegethontis* (Cope)[1]
White River spinedace*	*Lepidomeda albivallis* Miller and Hubbs[1]
Big Spring spinedace*	*Lepidomeda mollispinis pratensis* Miller and Hubbs[e]
Golden shiner	*Notemigonus crysoleucas* (Mitchill)
Spottail shiner	*Notropis hudsonius* (Clinton)
Sacramento blackfish	*Orthodon microlepidotus* (Ayres)
Fathead minnow	*Pimephales promelas* Rafinesque
Northern squawfish	*Ptychocheilus oregonensis* (Richardson)
Relict dace*	*Relictus solitarius* Hubbs and Miller[sc]
Longnose dace*	*Rhinichthys cataractae* (Valenciennes)
Speckled dace*	*Rhinichthys osculus* (Girard)
Redside shiner*	*Richardsonius balteatus* (Richardson)
Lahontan redside*	*Richardsonius egregius* (Girard)

Suckers (Catostomidae)

Utah sucker*	*Catostomus ardens* Jordan and Gilbert
Desert sucker*	*Catostomus clarki* Baird and Girard
Bridgelip sucker*	*Catostomus columbianus* (Eigenmann and Eigenmann)
Bluehead sucker*	*Catostomus discobolus* Cope
Owens sucker*	*Catostomus fumeiventris* Miller
Largescale sucker*	*Catostomus macrocheilus* Girard
Mountain sucker*	*Catostomus platyrhynchus* (Cope)
Tahoe sucker*	*Catostomus tahoensis* Gill and Jordan
Warner sucker*	*Catostomus warnerensis* Snyder[1]
Cui-ui*	*Chasmistes cujus* Cope[e]
June sucker*	*Chasmistes liorus* Jordan[1]

ORDER SILURIFORMES
Bullhead Catfishes (Ictaluridae)

White catfish	*Ictalurus catus* (Linnaeus)
Black bullhead	*Ictalurus melas* (Rafinesque)
Yellow bullhead	*Ictalurus natalis* (Lesueur)
Brown bullhead	*Ictalurus nebulosus* (Lesueur)
Channel catfish	*Ictalurus punctatus* (Rafinesque)

Armored Catfishes (Loricariidae)

Suckermouth catfish   *Hypostomus plecostomus* (Linnaeus)

ORDER ATHERINIFORMES
Killifishes (Cyprinodontidae)

White River springfish*   *Crenichthys baileyi* (Gilbert)[ᶜ]
Railroad Valley springfish*   *Crenichthys nevadae* Hubbs[ᶜ]
Devils Hole pupfish*   *Cyprinodon diabolis* Wales[ᵉ]
Amargosa pupfish*   *Cyprinodon nevadensis* Eigenmann and
                                    Eigenmann
Owens pupfish*   *Cyprinodon radiosus* Miller[ᵉ]
Salt Creek pupfish*   *Cyprinodon salinus* Miller
Pahrump killifish*   *Empetrichthys latos latos* Miller[ᵉ]
Plains killifish   *Fundulus zebrinus* Jordan and Gilbert
Rainwater killifish   *Lucania parva* (Baird)

Livebearers (Poeciliidae)

Mosquitofish   *Gambusia affinis* (Baird and Girard)
Sailfin molly   *Poecilia latipinna* (Lesueur)
Shortfin molly   *Poecilia mexicana* Steindachner
Guppy   *Poecilia reticulata* Peters
Green swordtail   *Xiphophorus helleri* Heckel

ORDER GASTEROSTEIFORMES
Sticklebacks (Gasterosteidae)

Threespine stickleback*   *Gasterosteus aculeatus* Linnaeus

ORDER PERCIFORMES
Temperate Basses (Percichthyidae)

White bass   *Morone chrysops* (Rafinesque)

Sunfishes (Centrarchidae)

Sacramento perch   *Archoplites interruptus* (Girard)
Green sunfish   *Lepomis cyanellus* Rafinesque
Pumpkinseed   *Lepomis gibbosus* (Linnaeus)
Bluegill   *Lepomis macrochirus* Rafinesque
Smallmouth bass   *Micropterus dolomieui* Lacepède
Spotted bass   *Micropterus punctulatus* (Rafinesque)
Largemouth bass   *Micropterus salmoides* (Lacepède)
White crappie   *Pomoxis annularis* Rafinesque
Black crappie   *Pomoxis nigromaculatus* (Lesueur)

Perches (Percidae)

Yellow perch   *Perca flavescens* (Mitchill)
Walleye   *Stizostedion vitreum vitreum* (Mitchill)

Cichlids (Cichlidae)

Convict cichlid   *Cichlasoma nigrofasciatum* (Günther)
Redbelly tilapia   *Tilapia zilli* (Gervais)

Sculpins (Cottidae)

Mottled sculpin*   *Cottus bairdi* Girard
Paiute sculpin*   *Cottus beldingi* Eigenmann and
                         Eigenmann
Bear Lake sculpin*   *Cottus extensus* Bailey and Bond

APPENDIX 2

Fishes Mentioned in the Text that Do Not Appear in Appendix 1 or the Annotated Checklist of Fishes

Australian lungfish (Ceratodidae)
    Australian lungfish *Neoceratodus forsteri* (Krefft)
Coelacanths (Latimeriidae)
    Coelacanth *Latimeria chalumnae* Smith
South American lungfishes (Lepidosirenidae)
    Lepidosirena *Lepidosirena paradoxa* Fitzinger
Four-eyed fishes (Anablepidae)
    Anableps *Anableps anableps* Linnaeus
Archer fishes (Toxotidae)
    Archerfish *Toxotes juculator* (Pallas)
Electric eels and knifefishes (Gymnotidae)
    Electric eel *Electrophorus electricus* (Linnaeus)
Whale sharks (Rhincodontidae)
    Whale shark *Rhincodon typus* Smith
Mackerel sharks (Lamnidae)
    White shark *Carcharodon carcharias* (Linnaeus)
Sturgeons (Acipenseridae)
    Beluga *Huso huso* Linnaeus
Paddlefishes (Polyodontidae)
    Paddlefish *Polyodon spathula* (Walbaum)
Gars (Lepisosteidae)
    Shortnose gar *Lepisosteus platostomus* Rafinesque
    Alligator gar *Lepisosteus spatula* Lacepède
Bowfins (Amiidae)
    Bowfin *Amia calva* Linnaeus
Tarpons (Elopidae)
    Tarpon *Megalops atlanticus* Valenciennes
Freshwater eels (Anguillidae)
    American eel *Anguilla rostrata* (Lesueur)

Herrings (Clupeidae)
     American shad *Alosa sapidissima* (Wilson)
     Gizzard shad *Dorosoma cepedianum* (Lesueur)
     Threadfin shad *Dorosoma petenense* (Günther)
Trouts (Salmonidae)
     Lake whitefish *Coregonus clupeaformis* (Mitchill)
     Chum salmon *Oncorhynchus keta* (Walbaum)
     Chinook salmon *Oncorhynchus tshawytscha* (Walbaum)
     Atlantic salmon *Salmo salar* (Linnaeus)
     (Sebago salmon),
     Dolly Varden *Salvelinus malma* (Walbaum)
Mudminnows (Umbridae)
     Alaska blackfish *Dallia pectoralis* Bean
Pikes (Esocidae)
     Muskellunge *Esox masquinongy* Mitchill
Carps and Minnows (Cyprinidae)
     Hitch *Lavinia exilicauda* Baird and Girard
     Umpqua dace *Rhinichthys evermanni* Snyder
Suckers (Catostomidae)
     Santa Ana sucker *Catostomus santaanae* (Snyder)
     Blue sucker *Cycleptus elongatus* (Lesueur)
Piranha (Serrasalmidae)
     Palometa *Serrasalmus marginatus* (Valenciennes)
Bullhead catfishes (Ictaluridae)
     Blue catfish *Ictalurus furcatus* (Lesueur)
     Flathead catfish *Pylodictis olivaris* (Rafinesque)
Labyrinth catfishes (Clariidae)
     Walking catfish *Clarias batrachus* (Linnaeus)
Cavefishes (Amblyopsidae)
     Northern cavefish *Amblyopsis spelaea* DeKay
Goosefishes (Lophiidae)
     Anglerfish (Goosefish) *Lophius americanus* Valenciennes
Killifishes (Cyprinodontidae)
     Desert pupfish *Cyprinodon macularius* Baird and Girard
Silversides (Atherinidae)
     California grunion *Leuresthes tenuis* (Ayres)
Temperate basses (Percichthyidae)
     Striped bass *Morone saxatilis* (Walbaum)
Sunfishes (Centrarchidae)
     Rock bass *Ambloplites rupestris* (Rafinesque)
Jacks (Carangidae)
     Palometa *Trachinatus goodei* Jordan and Everman
Drums (Sciaenidae)
     Freshwater drum *Aplodinotus grunniens* Rafinesque
Gobies (Gobiidae)
     Pygmy goby *Pandaka pygmaea* Herre
Righteye flounders (Pleuronectidae)
     Atlantic halibut *Hippoglossus hippoglossus* (Linnaeus)
Molas (Molidae)
     Ocean sunfish *Mola mola* (Linnaeus)

GLOSSARY

Abdominal: Of the belly. Fins are abdominal when they are located on the belly far behind the pectoral fins.

Acanthocephalan: A parasitic worm family that infests vertebrates. It has a proboscis covered with recurved hooks and no digestive tract.

Adipose fin: A fleshy, finlike, but usually rayless structure lying on the back between the dorsal and caudal fins of certain fishes such as trouts and catfishes.

Aeration: The process of supplying with air.

Algae: Mostly small, one-celled aquatic plants that give water a green or brown color.

Alluvial: Pertaining to a deposit of sand, mud, etc. formed by flowing water and deposited in recent times.

Anadromous: Fishes that are hatched in fresh water, run to sea to obtain growth, then return to fresh water to spawn, as do shad and Pacific salmon.

Anal fin: The fin on the ventral median line behind the anus.

Anion: A negatively charged particle attracted to the anode in electrolysis.

Anterior: In the front of, preceding. Opposite of posterior.

Aquifer: A geological formation containing water, especially one that supports wells or springs.

Areal: Involving a particular area. An area of particular extent.

Autochthonous: Produced within the system.

Axils: The regions under or behind the base of the pectoral or pelvic fins.

Barbel: An elongate thin fleshy projection usually on the head. Catfishes have barbels.

Basibranchials: The three median bones on the floor of the gill chamber.

Benthic: Living on or near the bottom.

Binomial nomenclature: A taxonomic name consisting of a genus name and a species name. An artificial key in which steps are in paired choices.

Bony fishes: Fishes having a hard, calcified skeleton as opposed to a cartilaginous one.

Brachial artery: Belonging to the pectoral fins or other forelimbs of a vertebrate.

Branchiostegals: The bony rays supporting the branchiostegal membrane under the head of fishes, below the opercular bones, behind the lower jaw, and attached to the hyoid arch.

Breast: An area with indefinite boundaries between the pelvic fins and the isthmus; sometimes called chest.

Bryozoan: A sessile marine or freshwater animal belonging to the phylum Bryozoa.

Buccal: Pertaining to the mouth, or mouthlike.

Caecum, caeca: A blind sac or cavity connected to the alimentary canal.

Cardiform: Teeth of some fishes that are arranged like a series of combs.

Carnivorous: Meat-eating. Feeding or preying on living animals.

Cation: A positively charged particle that is attracted to the cathode in electrolysis.

Caudal fin: The tail fin.

Caudal peduncle: The tapering or slender portion of the body behind the base of the last ray of the anal fin. Its length is measured from the base of the last anal ray to the mid base of the caudal fin. The least depth of caudal peduncle is taken as its slenderest part dorsoventrally.

Cestode: A parasitic flatworm of the class Cestoda, or tapeworms.

Charr: Fishes of the genus *Salvelinus*.

Cheek: The area between the eye and preopercular.

Chironomid: A genus of trueflies, midges.

Circulus: A growth ring on the scales or other bony parts of a fish.

Circumpolar: Around or near one of the earth's poles.

Cloaca: A chamber in the lower part of the gut into which empty the ducts from the kidney and reproductive organs. It has one external opening (the cloacal aperture) instead of separate anal (vent) and urogenital openings.

Coelacanth: A crossopterygian fish (*Latimeria chalumnae*) thought to be extinct but found off the coast of southern Africa in 1938.

Compressed: Flattened from side to side.

Convoluted: Twisted or coiled.

Copepods: Small crustaceans.

Crania: The part of the skull enclosing the brain.

Creel: The number and kinds of fish caught in a day. Also a basketlike container.

Cretaceous ichthyofauna: Fish of a period of the Mesozoic era, which occurred from 70,000,000 to 135,000,000 years ago when the extinction of giant dinosaurs occurred.

Ctenoid scales: Scales with a comblike margin of tiny prickles or ctenii, on their exposed, posterior field, as in sunfishes.

Cycloid scales: Scales having a smooth, evenly curved posterior margin, as in suckers.

Decimate: To destroy a great number or proportion of something.

Decurved: Curved downward or ventrally.

Degree-day: Used to define fish embryological development time. One degree-day is a twenty-four-hour period in which the temperature is one degree above freezing (32° F).

Demersal: Eggs that are heavier than water and thus sink.

Desiccation: The drying up of a body of water.

Desmid: Any of the freshwater unicellular algae belonging to the family Desmidiaceae.

Detritus: Debris material (generally plant) that has been deposited on the bottom of an aquatic habitat or is suspended in the water column.

Diatomaceous: Consisting of or abounding in diatoms or their siliceous remains.

Dimorphism: The occurrence of two forms distinct in structure among animals of the same species.

Diploid: Having two similar complements of chromosomes.

Dorsal: Pertaining to the back.

Dorsal fin: The single or double fin lying on the midline of the back; it may consist of soft rays only or of both spines and soft rays. The fin on the back or dorsal side in front of the adipose fin if it is present.

Effluent: The outflow of a stream, reservoir, or other body of water.

Elasmobranch: The group of cartilaginous fishes to which sharks and rays belong.

Emarginate: Weakly crescent-shaped as opposed to definitely forked, as in the outline of a fin.

Endemic: Occurring only at a specific or particular location.

Endoparasite: A parasite that occurs internally.

Epilimnion: The uppermost zone of summer circulating water in a lake. It is separated from the hypolimnion by the thermocline.

Escarpment: A long, precipitous clifflike ridge, land, or rock.

Estivate: To spend the summer (or other period) in relative inactivity.

Estuary: The part of a river where its current meets the sea.

Exoskeleton: Having a hard outer shell that supports internal organs, as in insects.

Extirpate: To destroy totally.

Eyed eggs: Unhatched fish eggs in which the eyes are formed and visible.

Faunal: Pertaining to animals.

Fecundity: The potential reproductive capacity as measured by the individual production of mature eggs.

Filamentous: Consisting of or bearing threadlike rays; applied to fins of fishes and some algal forms.

Fish: A vertebrate adapted for aquatic respiration by means of gills. When used in the plural, fishes refers to two or more species.

Forage: Food for certain animals. The act of seeking for food.

Fork length: Distance from the anteriormost margin of the head to the tip of the middle ray (fork) of the caudal fin.

Form: A division of subspecies with no taxonomic standing.

Fry: Newly hatched fish.

Ganoid scales: The platelike scales of gars.

Gastropod: The group of mollusks to which all snails belong.

Gills: Highly vascular fleshy filaments used in aquatic respiration.

Gonopodium: Literally, a sexual foot. An organ adapted for sexual use.

Gradient: A progression from one level or form to another across many similar but slightly differing types.

Gravid: Said of a female swollen with eggs or embryos.

Herbivorous: Plant-eating.

Heterocercal: Unequally lobed; said of the tail or caudal fin of a fish where the upper lobe is larger than the lower and in which the last few vertebrae of the vertebral column are bent upward.

Holarctic: Pertaining to the Palaearctic and Nearctic; the two biogeographical regions of the Arctic.

Homocercal: Equally lobed; said of the tail or caudal fin when upper and lower lobes are more or less equal and the backbone or vertebral column ends at the middle of the base of the fin.

Hybrid: A cross between two different genera or species.

Hypocercal: A fish's caudal fin that has dissimilar halves, its lower lobe larger (generally used in reference to fossils).

Hypolimnion: The summer stagnating lower levels of lake water lying below the thermocline.

Ichthyology: The (scientific) study of fishes.

Immaculate: Without spots or pigment pattern.

Inferior: Used in reference to the mouth when the snout is longer than the lower jaw.

Insertion of fin: A term applied to the point where the paired fins arise from the body.

Interspecific: Between two species (for example, competition), as opposed to intraspecific, which means between two individuals of the same species.

Landlocked: A term applied to fishes that normally run to sea, then return from the ocean to fresh water to spawn, but are unable, because of land barriers, to do so (for example, Kokanee salmon).

Lateral: Pertaining to the side.

Lateral line: The line formed by a series of tubes with openings (pores) to the exterior that extends backward from the head along the side of the body.

Lateral scale series: Scales occurring in a lateral row or line. Generally the location is designated for a particular species.

Length: Standard length is measured from the tip of the snout to the last vertebrae, which can be located by flexing the caudal fin. Fork length is from the tip of the snout to the fork in the tail. Total length is measured from the tip of the snout to the end of the tail.

Littoral: Pertaining to the near-shore region of a lake, sea, or ocean; shallow water.

Lotic: Moving water, as a stream.

Lunate: Crescent-shaped, referring to the tail fin.

Melanistic: Black-colored.

Melanophore: Literally, bearing black. A set of pigment-bearing structures that variously provide black coloration.

Metalimnion: The stratum between the epilimnion and the hypolimnion that exhibits a marked thermal discontinuity. Used synonymously with thermocline.

Monoploid: Having or being a chromosome set comprising a single genome.

Morphology: Form shape; the study of form.

Mottled: Blotched; color spots running together.

Mouth inferior: The mouth located ventrally and a little behind the tip of the projecting snout.

Mouth oblique: The mouth lying at an angle to the horizontal axis of the body.

Mouth ventral: The mouth notably located on the ventral side of the head.

Nematode: A class of unsegmented, cylindrical worms; roundworms.

Notochord: The rodlike, primitive backbone of vertebrates.

Nuptial tubercles: Sometimes called pearl organs. Small hornlike projections on the skin of some fishes during the breeding season.

Odiferous: Producing a strong, distinct odor.

Oligochaete: A group of worms that includes earthworms and certain small, freshwater species.

Oligotrophic: Poor in nutrients. A lake or other body of water that has a small amount of dissolved nutrients, generally few species, and high oxygen content. Opposite of eutrophic.

Omnivorous: Eating all kinds of food, somewhat indiscriminately.

Opercle: A large, nearly flat, thin bone on each side of the head covering the gills; also called operculum or gill cover.

Opercular flap: The fleshy prolongation of the upper posterior angle of the opercle.

Operculum: The bony covering of the gill cavity composed of opercular bones (preopercle, interopercle, subopercle, opercle).

Origin of the fin: The term applied to the anterior point where a fin begins.

Otolith: The bones of the inner ear of vertebrates.

Oviparous: Said of fishes that lay and fertilize eggs outside of the body cavity.

Ovipositor: A male organ in live-bearing fishes for depositing sperm in the female. Synonymous with gonopodium.

Ovoviviparous: Livebearers. Said of fishes whose eggs are fertilized, developed, and hatched within the body. The eggs may or may not derive nourishment from the female.

Palatine: On or in the palate (for example, teeth).

Paleontologist: A person who studies life forms that existed in former geological times.

Papilla, papillose: Small fleshy nobs or ridges.

Parr: Young fish, primarily salmonids, that have developed parr markings.

Parr markings: Vertical dark bands, typical of juvenile fish in some species, that may persist in adults of a few species.

Pectoral fins: Normally the anterior or dorsalmost paired fins in fish, corresponding to the anterior limbs of the higher vertebrates.

Pelagic: Living in deep, open waters away from shore.

Pelvic fins: Paired fins corresponding to the posterior limbs of the higher vertebrates (sometimes called the ventral fins).

Peritoneum: The membrane that lines the inside of the body cavity.

Pharyngeal: On or near the pharynx (for example, teeth).

Photoperiod: The interval in a twenty-four-hour period during which an organism is exposed to sunlight (or artifical light).

Physoclistous: Having a swim bladder isolated from the esophagus (cannot swallow air).

Physostomous: Having a swim bladder connected to the esophagus by a duct (can swallow air).

Pineal: Pertaining to a vestigial sense organ in vertebrates.

Piscivorous: Fish-eating.

Placoid: A type of scale that resembles a tooth; found on the skin of sharks.

Plerocercoid: The solid elongate infective larva of some tapeworms usually occurring in the muscles of fishes.

Pluvial: Having much rain.

Polyploidy: The condition of having a chromosome number that is a multiple greater than two of the monoploid number.

Portage: The carrying, transportation, or passage around obstacles in a water course.

Posterior: Behind or at the rear of. Opposite of anterior.

PPM: Parts per million.

Pseudobranchiae: The small gills on the opercle inner side near its union with the preopercle.

Race: A division of subspecies that breeds true when isolated from other subspecies. It has no taxonomic standing.

Redd: A nest prepared by salmonid fishes.

Reservoir: A body of water created by a manmade obstruction, often with a river flowing through it.

Rhomboidal: Formed as a rhomboid (i.e., slanted rectangle).

Riffle: An area in a stream that has surface disturbance, generally caused by underlying obstacles.

Riparian: Of, situated on, or dwelling on the bank of a water body.

Scales in the lateral line: The number of scales bearing tubes in the lateral line.

Scute: The armorlike scales of sturgeon.

Second dorsal: The posterior of two fins, usually the soft-rayed dorsal fin of spiny-rayed fishes.

Serrated: Notched on the edge, like a saw.

Smolt: A salmonid physiologically ready to migrate to sea.

Snout: The nose or part of the head anterior to the eye but not including the lower jaw.

Soft dorsal: The part of the dorsal fin, sometimes all of it, composed of soft or articulated rays.

Species: A scientific classification or biological unit subordinate to the genus, the members of which differ among themselves only in the most minor details of structure, color, physiology, and behavior; they are capable of producing fertile offspring like the parents indefinitely.

Spine: A sharp projecting bony point; of fin rays, technically inarticulated, unpaired median rays, regardless of whether or not they are stiff and sharply pointed.

Spinous dorsal: Anterior part of the dorsal fin of spiny-rayed fishes; any dorsal fin composed of inarticulated rays.

Spiny rays: Sharply pointed or non-cross-striated fin rays.

Spiral valve: A continuous spiral ridge of mucous membrane in the large intestine of the more primitive groups of fishes. It makes a number of complete turns, increasing the surface for absorption and retarding the passage of food.

Stock: Used to differentiate between members of the same species that inhabit slightly different areas: that is, the stocks of anadromous salmonids (for instance, chinook salmon) in the Columbia River drainage. It has no taxonomic status.

Strain: Most often refers to a subspecies group with special characteristics. Often developed in hatcheries. It has no taxonomic status.

Stratification: The arrangement of the waters of a lake into hypolimnion and epilimnion separated by a thermocline as a result especially of differences in specific gravity brought about by natural warming of the waters above the thermocline.

Subspecies: A group of local populations of a species that inhabit a geographic subdivision of the range of the species and that differ taxonomically from other populations of the species. A division of species.

Substrate: Pertaining to the bottom or bottom type in aquatic habitats (mud, rock, or gravel).

Swimup: Phase or life stage when embryonic fish emerge from the nest or spawning deposition area and "swim up" into the water column.

Tail: Caudal fin of fish.

TDS: Total dissolved solids.

Teleost: Most living species of fish are in this group. The skeleton is fully ossified or "bony."

Terete: Cylindrical but tapering, usually at both ends.

Terminal: Lips of lower and upper jaws foremost and equal or nearly so.

Terrestrial: Of the land; not aquatic.

Tertiary: Third (final) level of an organization or treatment or ecosystem. May denote final consumer in a food web.

Thermocline: The intermediate summer zone in lakes between overlying epilimnion and underlying hypolimnion, defined as that region in which the temperature decrease reaches one degree C or more for each meter of descent (= 0.55 degrees F per foot). Synonymous with metalimnion.

Thoracic: Pertaining to the thorax or chest. Pelvic fins are thoracic when attached immediately below or a little behind the pectoral fin base.

Trematode: Any parasitic flatworm of this class that has one or more external suckers.

Trichoptera: Members of the caddisfly order of aquatic insects.

Triploid: Having a chromosome number that is three times the monoploid number.

Trophic: Levels of nutrient status or nutrient richness, as algae, invertebrates, and fish are representative of varying trophic levels.

Truncate: Having a square or broad end.

Tubercle: A small round projection usually on the fins.

Turbid: Clouded. Water that is unclear (muddy) due to sediment or other material suspended in the water column.

Variety: A term of no real merit in ichthyology. Sometimes loosely used as divisions of species or subspecies.

Ventral: On the lower surface (the belly).

Ventral fins: This term, when applied to fishes, is the same as pelvic fins.

Vermiculate: Marked with irregular wavy impressed lines like worm tracks.

Villiform: In the form of villi (fingerlike projections); said of teeth that are slender and crowded closely together in bands.

Vomer: The anterior bone on the roof of the mouth.

Vomerine: Pertaining to the vomer (such as vomerine teeth).

Voracious: Consuming large quantities of food. Insatiable appetite.

Zooplankton: Small aquatic invertebrates with feeble swimming ability.

LITERATURE CITED

Anonymous. 1962. Fish stocking policy—small lakes, ponds, streams. Nebraska Game, Forests and Parks Commission, Fish Division. Mimeo. 5 pp.

Arnold, B. B. 1960. Life history notes on the walleye, *Stizostedion vitreum vitreum* (Mitchill) in a turbid water, Utah Lake, Utah. M.S. thesis, Utah State University, Logan. 107 pp.

Axelrod, H. R. 1968. *Mollies . . . in color*. Neptune, N.J.: TFH Publications. 32 pp.

Axelrod, H. R., and L. P. Schultz. 1955. *Handbook of tropical aquarium fishes*. New York: McGraw-Hill. 718 pp.

Bailey, J. E. 1952. Life history and ecology of the sculpin, *Cottus bairdi punctulatus* in southwestern Montana. *Copeia* 1952(4):243–255.

Bailey, R. M., and C. E. Bond. 1963. Four new species of freshwater sculpins, genus *Cottus*, from western North America. *Occasional Papers of the Museum of Zoology of the University of Michigan, Ann Arbor* 634. 27 pp.

Barlow, G. W. 1961. Social behavior of the desert pupfish. *Cyprinodon macularius*, in the field and in the aquarium. *American Midland Naturalist* 65(2):330–359.

Barnes, R. N. 1957. A study of the life history of the western roach, *Hesperoleucus symmetricus*. M.A. thesis, University of California, Davis. 25 pp.

Baugh, T. M., and J. E. Deacon. 1983. The most endangered pupfish. *Freshwater and Marine Aquarium* 6(6):22–26, 78–79.

Baxter, G. T., and J. R. Simon. 1970. Wyoming fishes. Cheyenne: Wyoming Game and Fish Department, Bulletin 4. 168 pp.

Becker, G. C. 1983. *Fishes of Wisconsin*. Madison: University of Wisconsin Press. 1,052 pp.

Beckman, W. C. 1949. The rate of growth and sex ratio for seven Michigan fishes. *Transactions of the American Fisheries Society* 76(1946):63–81.

Behnke, R. J. 1974. The effects of the Newlands project on the Pyramid Lake fishery. File Report. 15 pp.

———. 1979. Monograph of the native trouts of the genus *Salmo* of western North America. Washington, D.C.: U.S. Forest Service, U.S. Fish and Wildlife Service, U.S. Bureau of Land Management. 163 pp.

———. 1981. Systematic and zoogeographical interpretation of Great Basin trouts. Pp. 95–124 in R. J. Naiman and D. L. Soltz (eds.), *Fishes in North American deserts* New York: John Wiley and Sons.

Bell, M. A. 1982. Melanism in a high elevation population of *Gasterosteus aculeatus. Copeia* 1982(4):829–835.

Bennett, D. H., P. M. Bratovich, W. Knox, D. Palmer, and H. Hansel. 1983. Status of the warmwater fishery and the potential of improving warmwater fish habitat in lower Snake reservoirs. Completion report. Contract no. DACW68-79-0057. Walla Walla, Wash.: U.S. Army Corps of Engineers. 451 pp.

Benson, L. V. 1978. Fluctuation in the level of Pluvial Lake Lahontan during the last 40,000 years. *Quaternary Research* 9:300–318. University of Washington.

Bisson, P. A., and C. E. Bond. 1971. Origin and distribution of the fishes of Harney Basin, Oregon. *Copeia* 1971(2):268–281.

Black, E. C. 1953. Upper lethal temperatures of some British Columbia freshwater fishes. *Journal of the Fisheries Research Board of Canada* 10(4):196–210.

Bond, C. E. 1979. *Biology of fishes.* New York: Holt, Rinehart and Winston, CBS College Publishing. 514 pp.

Bradley, C., S. de la Plain, S. Garrett, S. L. Mayer, J. MacLennan, T. A. Siefring, and R. Swink. 1980. *Rand McNally encyclopedia of world rivers.* Bison Books. 352 pp.

Breder, C. M., and D. E. Rosen. 1966. *Modes of reproduction in fishes.* New York: Natural History Press. 941 pp.

Broecker, W. S., and A. Kaufman. 1965. Radiocarbon chronology of Lake Lahontan and Lake Bonneville II, Great Basin. *Geological Society of America Bulletin* 76:537–566.

Brown, C. J. D. 1971. *Fishes of Montana.* Bozeman: Agricultural Experiment Station, Montana State University. 207 pp.

Brown, J. H., and C. R. Feldmeth. 1971. Evolution in constant and fluctuating environments: Thermal tolerances of desert pupfish, *Cyprinodon. Evolution* 25(2):390–398.

Brown, L. R., and P. B. Moyle. 1981. The impact of squawfish on salmonid populations: A review. *North American Journal of Fisheries Management* 1(1):104–111.

Budd, J. 1961. *The use of the South Bay creel census in understanding the smallmouth bass fishery and predicting its course.* South Bay Mouth, Ontario, Can.: Ontario Department of Lands, Forestry Resources Branch. 9 pp.

Bulkley, R. V. 1961. Fluctuations in age composition and growth rate of cutthroat in Yellowstone Lake. Wildlife Resources Report 54. U.S. Fish and Wildlife Service, Bureau of Sport Fisheries. 31 pp.

Busack, C. A., and G. A. E. Gall. 1981. Introgressive hybridization in populations of Paiute cutthroat trout (*Salmo clarki seleniris*). *Canadian Journal of Fisheries and Aquatic Sciences* 38(8):939–951.

Busack, C. A., G. H. Thorgaard, M. P. Bannon, and G. A. E. Gall. 1980. An electrophoretic, karyotypic and meristic characterization of the Eagle Lake trout, *Salmo gairdneri aquilorum. Copeia* 1980(3):418–424.

Calhoun, A. (ed.). 1966. *Inland fisheries management*. Sacramento: Resources Agency, California Department of Fish and Game. 546 pp.

Cannamela, D. A., J. D. Brader, and D. W. Johnson. 1979. Feeding habits of catfish in Barkley and Kentucky lakes. *Proceedings of the Annual Conference of the Southeastern Association of Fish and Wildlife Resource Agencies* 32:686–691.

Carbine, W. F. 1936. The life history of the chub *Tigoma atraria* Girard, of the Great Basin area of Utah. M.S. thesis, University of Utah, Salt Lake City. 107 pp.

Carey, F. G. 1973. Fishes with warm bodies. *Scientific American* 228(2):36–44.

Carl, G. C., W. A. Clemens, and C. C. Lindsey. 1967. The fresh-water fishes of British Columbia. B.C. Provincial Museum Handbook 5. 192 pp.

Carlander, K. D. 1969. *Handbook of freshwater fishery biology, vol. I*. Ames: Iowa State University Press. 752 pp.

———. 1977. *Handbook of freshwater fishery biology, vol. II*. Ames: Iowa State University Press. 431 pp.

Carter, D. R. 1969. A history of commercial fishing on Utah Lake. M.S. thesis, Brigham Young University, Provo, Utah. 140 pp.

Cavender, T. M. 1968. Freshwater fish remains from the Clarno Formation Ochoco Mountains of north-central Oregon. *Ore Bin* (Oregon Department of Geology and Mineral Industries) 30:125–141.

Cavender, T. M., J. G. Lundberg, and R. I. Wilson. 1970. Two new fossil records of the genus *Esox* (Teleostei, Salmoniformes) in North America. *Northwest Science* 44:176–183.

Clady, M. D. 1981. Cool-weather growth of channel catfish held in pens alone and with other species. *Progressive Fish Culturist* 43(2):92–95.

Clemens, W. A. 1939. The fishes of Okanagan Lake and nearby waters. Pp. 27–38 in A biological survey of Okanagan Lake, British Columbia. *Fisheries Research Board of Canada Bulletin* 56. 70 pp.

Coffin, P. 1981. Distribution and life history of the Lahontan/Humboldt cutthroat trout, Humboldt River drainage basin. Nevada Department of Wildlife Species Management Plan. 69 pp.

Constantz, G. D. 1981. Life history patterns of desert fishes. Pp. 237–290 in R. J. Naiman and D. L. Soltz (eds.), *Fishes in North American deserts*. New York: John Wiley and Sons.

Coombs, C. I., C. E. Bond, and S. F. Drohan. 1979. Spawning and early life history of the Warner sucker *Catostomus warnerensis*. Final Report for Order no. 10181-0294.

Cooper, S. D., and C. R. Goldman. 1980. Oppossum [*sic*] shrimp (*Mysis relicta*) predation on zooplankton. *Canadian Journal of Fisheries and Aquatic Sciences* 37(6):909–919.

Coots, M. 1956. The yellow perch, *Perca flavescens* (Mitchill), in the Klamath

River. *California Fish and Game* 42(7):219–228.

Cope, O. B. 1955. The future of the cutthroat trout in Utah. *Utah Academy Proceedings* 32:89–93.

Cordone, A., S. Nicola, P. Baker, and T. Frantz. 1971. The Kokanee salmon in Lake Tahoe. *California Fish and Game* 57(1):28–43.

Courtney, W. R., and J. E. Deacon. 1982. Status of introduced fishes in certain spring systems in southern Nevada. *Great Basin Naturalist* 42(3): 361–366.

Crawford, M. 1979. Reproductive modes of the least chub *Iotichthys phlegethontis* (Cope). M.S. thesis, Utah State University, Logan. 80 pp.

Danielsen, T. L. 1968. Differential predation on *Culex pipiens* and *Anopheles albimanus* mosquito larvae by two species of fish (*Gambusia affinis* and *Cyprinodon nevadensis*) and the effects of simulated reeds on predation. Ph.D. dissertation, University of California, Riverside. 129 pp.

Deacon, J. E., T. B. Hardy, J. Pollard, W. Taylor, J. Landye, J. Williams, C. Williams, P. Greger, and M. Conrad. 1980. Environmental analysis of four aquatic habitats in east-central Nevada, June–September, 1980. Environmental Consultants Inc., Report for Henningson, Durham, and Richardson. 123 pp., appendixes.

Deacon, J. E., G. Kobetich, J. D. Williams, and S. Contreras. 1979. Fishes of North America, endangered, threatened, or of special concern: 1979. *Fisheries* 4(2):29–44.

Deacon, J. E., and J. E. Williams. 1984. Annotated list of the fishes of Nevada. *Proceedings of the Biological Society of Washington* 97(1):103–118.

Dees, L. T. 1967. Rains of fishes. Washington, D.C.: U.S. Department of the Interior, Fishery Leaflet 513. 5 pp.

———. 1969. Sea horses. Washington, D.C.: U.S. Department of the Interior, Fishery Leaflet 495. 9 pp.

Ebert, V. W., and R. C. Summerfelt. 1969. Contributions to the life history of the Paiute sculpin, *Cottus beldingii* Eigenmann and Eigenmann, in Lake Tahoe. *California Fish and Game* 55(2):100–120.

Eckholm, E. 1981. Disappearing species: The social challenge. *National Forum* (Summer):31–32.

Ellison, J. P. 1980. Diets of mountain whitefish, *Prosopium williamsoni* (Girard), and brook trout, *Salvelinus fontinalis* (Mitchill), in the Little Walker River, Mono County, California. *California Fish and Game* 66(2): 96–104.

Eschmeyer, P. H., and T. G. Scott (eds.). 1983. Fisheries and wildlife research 1982. U.S. Fish and Wildlife Service. 2 pp.

Estes, R. 1970. Origin of the recent North American lower vertebrate fauna: An inquiry into the fossil record. *Forma et Function* 3:139–163.

Evans, D. H. 1969. Life history studies of the Lahontan redside, *Richardsonius egregius*, in Lake Tahoe. *California Fish and Game* 55(3):197–222.

Fite, K. R. 1973. Feeding overlap between roach and juvenile steelhead in the Eel River. M.S. thesis, California State University, Humboldt. 38 pp.

Follett, W. I. 1977. Fish remains from Thea Heye Cave, NV-Wa-385, Washoe County, Nevada. *Contributions of the University of California Archeological Research Faculty* 35:59–80.

Foster, N. R. 1967. Comparative studies on the biology of killifishes (Pices, Cyprinodontidae). Ph.D. dissertation, Cornell University, Ithaca, N.Y. 388 pp.

Frank, S. 1969. *The pictorial encyclopedia of fishes.* New York: Hamlyn. 552 pp.

Fritz, E. C. 1983. Saving species is not enough. *BioScience* 33(5):301.

Fry, D. H. 1936. Life history of *Hesperoleucas venustus* Snyder. *California Fish and Game* 22(2):65–98.

Fryer, G., and T. D. Iles. 1972. *The cichlid fishes of the Great Lakes of Africa.* Hong Kong: TFH Publications. 610 pp.

Gerald, J. W. 1971. Sound production during courtship in six species of sunfishes (Centrarchidae). *Evolution* 25(1):75–87.

Graham, R. J. 1961. Biology of the Utah chub in Hebgen Lake, Montana. *Transactions of the American Fisheries Society* 90(3):269–276.

Grande, L. 1980. Paleontology of the Green River Formation, with a review of the fish fauna. *Geological Survey of Wyoming Bulletin* 63:1–133.

Grande, L., J. T. Eastman, and T. M. Cavender. 1982. *Amyzon gosiutensis,* a new catostomid fish from the Green River Formation. *Copeia* 1982(3): 523–532.

Greenfield, D. W., and G. W. Deckert. 1973. Introgressive hybridization between *Gila orcutti* and *Hesperoleucus symmetricus* (Pisces: Cyprinidae) in the Cuyama River basin, California. II. Ecological aspects. *Copeia* 1973(3): 417–427.

Greenwood, P. H. 1975. *A history of fishes.* 3rd ed.; 1st ed. by J. R. Norman. London: Ernst Benn Limited. 467 pp.

Hansen, D. F. 1951. Biology of the white crappie in Illinois. *Bulletin of the Illinois State Natural History Survey* 25(4):211–265.

Hardy, T. B. 1980. The inter-basin area report—1979. *Proceedings of the Desert Fishes Council* 11:5–21.

———. 1982. Ecological interactions of the introduced and native fishes in the outflow of Ash Springs, Lincoln County, Nevada. M.S. thesis, University of Nevada, Las Vegas. 79 pp.

Hardy, T. B., and J. E. Deacon. 1986. Introduced fishes of the Southwest. *Southwestern Naturalist* (in press).

Harlan, J. R., and E. B. Speaker. 1956. *Iowa fish and fishing.* Illus. M. F. Reece. Des Moines: Iowa State Conservation Commission. 377 pp.

Harrington, R. W., and E. S. Harrington. 1961. Food selection among fishes invading a high subtropical salt marsh from onset of flooding through the progress of a mosquito brood. *Ecology* 42(4):646–656.

Heckmann, R. A., C. W. Thompson, and D. A. White. 1981. Fishes of Utah Lake. Pp. 107–127 in S. L. Wood (ed.), *Great Basin naturalist memoirs.* Utah Lake Monograph. Provo, Utah: Brigham Young University.

Herald, E. S. 1961. *Living fishes of the world.* Garden City, N.Y.: Doubleday and Co. 304 pp.

Hessel, R. 1878. Carp and its culture in rivers and lakes; and its introduction in America. Pp. 865–900 in United States Fish Commission Report 1875–1876.

Hickman, T. J. 1978. Systematic study of the native trout of the Bonneville Basin. M.S. thesis, Colorado State University, Fort Collins. 122 pp.

Hickman, T. J., and R. F. Raleigh. 1982. Habitat suitability index models: Cutthroat trout. U.S. Department of the Interior, U.S. Fish and Wildlife Service, FWS/OBS-82/10.5. 38 pp.

Hopkirk, J. D., and R. J. Behnke. 1966. Additions to the known native fish fauna of Nevada. *Copeia* 1966(1):134–136.

Houghton, S. G. 1976. *A trace of desert waters: The Great Basin story*. Glendale, Calif.: Arthur H. Clark Co. 287 pp.

Hubbell, P. M. 1966. Pumpkinseed sunfish. Pp. 402–404 in A. Calhoun (ed.), *Inland fisheries management*. California Department of Fish and Game.

Hubbs, C. L. 1932. Studies of the fishes of the order Cyprinodontes. XII. A new genus related to *Empetrichthys*. *Occasional Papers of the Museum of Zoology of the University of Michigan, Ann Arbor* 252. 5 pp.

Hubbs, C. L., and R. M. Bailey. 1940. A revision of the black basses (*Micropterus* and *Huro*) with descriptions of four new forms. *University of Michigan Museum of Zoology, Ann Arbor. Miscellaneous Publications* 48: 1–51.

Hubbs, C. L., and G. P. Cooper. 1935. Age and growth of the long-eared and green sunfishes in Michigan. *Papers of the Michigan Academy of Science, Arts and Letters* 20:669–696.

Hubbs, C. L., L. C. Hubbs, and R. E. Johnson. 1943. Hybridization in nature between species of catostomid fishes. Contributions Laboratory of Vertebrate Biology, University of Michigan 22. 76 pp.

Hubbs, C. L., and R. R. Miller. 1942. Mass hybridization between two genera of cyprinid fishes in the Mohave Desert, California. *Papers of the Michigan Academy of Science, Arts and Letters* 28:343–378.

———. 1948. The zoological evidence: Correlation between fish distribution and hydrographic history in the desert basins of western United States. In The Great Basin with emphasis on glacial and postglacial times. *Bulletin of the University of Utah* (Biological Series, vol. 10, no. 7) 38(20):17–166.

———. 1965. Studies of cyprinodont fishes. XXII. Variation in *Lucania parva*, its establishment in western United States and description of a new species from an interior basin in Coahuila, Mexico. University of Michigan, Museum of Zoology, Miscellaneous Publications 127. 104 pp.

Hubbs, C. L., R. R. Miller, and L. C. Hubbs. 1974. *Hydrographic history and relict fishes of the north-central Great Basin*. California Academy of Sciences, vol. 7. 259 pp.

Hubbs, Clark, and J. E. Deacon. 1964. Additional introductions of tropical fishes into southern Nevada. *Southwestern Naturalist* 9(4):249–251.

Hubbs, Clark, and W. F. Hettler. 1964. Observations on the toleration of high temperature and low dissolved oxygen in natural waters by *Crenichthys baileyi*. *Southwestern Naturalist* 9(4):245–248.

Hynes, H. B. N. 1950. The food of the fresh-water sticklebacks (*Gasterosteus aculeatus* and *Pygosteus pungitius*), with a review of methods used in studies of the food of fishes. *Journal of Animal Ecology* 19(1):36–58.

Innes, W. T. 1979. *Exotic aquarium fishes*. Elmwood Park, N.J.: Metaframe. 266 pp.

Inskip, P. D. 1982. Habitat suitability index models: Northern pike. U.S. Department of the Interior, U.S. Fish and Wildlife Service, FWS/OBS-82/10.17. 40 pp.

Itzkowitz, M. 1971. Preliminary study of the social behavior of male *Gambusia affinis* (Baird and Girard) (Pisces: Poeciliidae) in aquaria. *Chesapeake Science* 12(4):219–224.

James, C. J. 1969. Aspects of the ecology of the Devils Hole pupfish, *Cyprinodon diabolis* Wales. M.S. thesis, University of Nevada, Las Vegas. 62 pp.

Janssen, P. J. 1983. Investigation of selected aspects of Kokanee (*Oncorhynchus nerka*) ecology in Porcupine Reservoir, Utah, with management implications. M.S. thesis, Utah State University, Logan. 57 pp.

Johannes, R. E., and P. A. Larkin. 1961. Competition for food between redside shiners (*Richardsonius balteatus*) and rainbow trout (*Salmo gairdneri*) in two British Columbia lakes. *Journal of the Fisheries Research Board of Canada* 18(2):203–220.

Johnson, V. K. 1958. Fishery management report. Lakes—Pyramid, Walker and Tahoe. Reno: Nevada Fish and Game Department, Dingell-Johnson Completion Report, FAF-4-R. 47 pp.

Jordan, D. S. 1891. Report of exploration in Colorado and Utah during the summer of 1889, with an account of the fishes found in each of the river basins examined. *Bulletin of the United States Fish Commission* 9(1889):1–40.

Jordan, D. S., and B. W. Evermann. 1896. Fishes of North and Middle America. A descriptive catalogue of the species of fish-like vertebrates found in the waters of North America, north of the Isthmus of Panama. *Bulletin of the U.S. National Museum* 47. 3,705 pp. (Originally published in 4 volumes: 1, 1896; 2, 3, 1898; 4, 1900.)

————. 1904. *American food and game fishes, a popular account of all the species found in America north of the equator, with keys for ready identification, life histories and methods of capture.* New York: Doubleday, Page and Co. 572 pp.

Jordan, D. S., B. W. Evermann, and H. W. Clark. 1930. Checklist of the fishes and fish-like vertebrates of North and Middle America north of the northern boundary of Venezuela and Colombia. United States Commissioner Fisheries Report, fiscal year 1928. Part 2, appendix 10:1–670.

Juday, C. 1907. Notes on Lake Tahoe, its trout and trout-fishing. *Bulletin of the Bureau of Fisheries* (U.S. Department of Commerce and Labor) 26(1906):133–146.

Keast, A. 1968. Feeding biology of the black crappie, *Pomoxis nigromaculatus*. *Journal of the Fisheries Research Board of Canada* 24(1):285–297.

Keast, A., and D. Webb. 1966. Mouth and body form relative to feeding ecology in the fish fauna of a small lake, Lake Opinicon, Ontario. *Journal of the Fisheries Research Board of Canada* 23(12):1845–1867.

Kennedy, C. H. 1916. A possible enemy of the mosquito. *California Fish and Game* 2(4):179–182.

Kennedy, J. L., and P. A. Kucera. 1978. The reproductive ecology of the Tahoe sucker, *Catostomus tahoensis*, in Pyramid Lake, Nevada. *Great Basin Naturalist* 38(2):181–186.

King, G. Q. 1982. Morphometry of Great Basin playas. Ph.D. dissertation, University of Utah, Salt Lake City. 137 pp.

Koch, D. L. 1972. Life history information on the cui-ui lakesucker (*Chasmistes cujus* Cope, 1883) endemic to Pyramid Lake, Washoe County, Nevada. Ph.D. dissertation, University of Nevada, Reno. 343 pp.

————. 1973. Reproductive characteristics of the cui-ui lakesucker (*Chasmistes cujus* Cope, 1883) and its spawning behavior in Pyramid Lake, Nevada. *Transactions of the American Fisheries Society* 102(1):145–149.

Koster, W. J. 1957. *Guide to the fishes of New Mexico.* Albuquerque: University of New Mexico Press, in cooperation with the New Mexico Department of Game and Fish, Santa Fe. 116 pp.

Krumholtz, L. A. 1948. Reproduction in the western mosquitofish *Gambusia affinis affinis* (Baird and Girard) and its use in mosquito control. *Ecological Monographs* 18:1–43.

Kutz, R. 1982. *Freshwater angling records, official—world, USA, and state.* Hayward, Wisconsin: National Freshwater Fishing Hall of Fame. 57 pp.

LaBounty, J. F., and J. E. Deacon. 1972. *Cyprinodon milleri*, a new species of pupfish (family Cyprinodontidae) from Death Valley, California. *Copeia* 1972(4):769–780.

La Rivers, I. 1962. *Fishes and fisheries of Nevada.* Reno: Nevada State Fish and Game Commission. 782 pp.

————. 1964. A new trout from the Barsstovian (Miocene) of western Nevada. *Occasional Papers of the Biological Society of Nevada* 3:1–4.

————. 1966. Paleontological miscellanei. *Nevada Biological Society Occasional Papers* 11:1–8.

Lawler, R. E. 1960. Observations on the life history of channel catfish, *Ictalurus punctatus* (Rafinesque), in Utah Lake, Utah. M.S. thesis, Utah State University, Logan. 69 pp.

Lee, D. S., C. R. Gilbert, C. H. Hocutt, R. E. Jenkins, D. E. McAllister, and J. R. Stauffer, Jr. 1980. *Atlas of North American freshwater fishes.* Raleigh: North Carolina State Museum of Natural History. 854 pp.

Leitritz, E., and R. C. Lewis. 1980. Trout and salmon culture. Sacramento: California Department of Fish and Game, Bulletin 164. 197 pp.

Little, R. G. 1963. Evaluation of statewide channel catfish planting. Santa Fe: New Mexico Department of Game and Fish, Job Completion Report, Dingell-Johnson Federal Aid Project F-22-R-4. Mimeo. 7 pp.

Liu, R. K. 1969. The comparative behavior of allopatric species (Teleostei—Cyprinodontidae: *Cyprinodon*). Ph.D. dissertation, University of California, Los Angeles. 185 pp.

Lucas, F. A. 1900. A new fossil cyprinoid, *Leuciscus turneri*, from the Miocene of Nevada. *Proceedings of the U.S. Natural History Museum* 23:333–334.

Lugaski, T. 1977. Additional notes and discussion of the relationship of *Gila esmeralda* La Rivers 1966 from the "Esmeralda Formation." *Occasional Papers of the Biological Society of Nevada* 43:1–4.

————. 1979. *Gila traini*, a new Pliocene cyprinid fish from Jersey Valley, Nevada. *Journal of Paleontology* 53:1160–1164.

MacCrimmon, H. R., and W. R. Robbins. 1975. Distribution of the black bass in North America. Pp. 56–66 in R. H. Stroud and H. Clepper (eds.), *Black bass biology and management.* Washington, D.C.: Sport Fishing Institute.

MacCrimmon, H. R., and E. Skobe. 1970. *The fisheries of Lake Simcoe.* Toronto: Ontario Department of Lands and Forests. 140 pp.

MacPhee, C., and R. Ruelle. 1969. A chemical selectively lethal to squawfish (*Ptychocheilus oregonensis* and *P. umpquae*). *Transactions of the American Fisheries Society* 98(4):676–684.

Madsen, P. 1910. The grasshopper famine—the mullet and the trout. Pp. 516–521 in *The improvement era*. Salt Lake City: The Church of Jesus Christ of Latter-day Saints.

Mariner, R. H., J. B. Rapp, L. M. Willey, and T. S. Presser. 1974. The chemical composition and estimated minimum thermal reservoir temperatures of selected hot springs in Oregon, U.S. Geological Survey, Open-File Report.

Marrin, D. L. 1983. Ontogenetic changes and introspecific resource partitioning in the Tahoe sucker, *Catostomus tahoensis*. *Environmental Biology of Fishes* 8(1):39–47.

Marrin, D. L., and D. C. Erman. 1982. Evidence against competition between trout and nongame fishes in Stampede Reservoir, California. *North American Journal of Fisheries Management* 2(3):262–269.

Mathews, S. B. 1962. The ecology of the Sacramento perch, *Archoplites interruptus*, from selected areas of California and Nevada. M.A. thesis, University of California, Berkeley. 93 pp.

McClane, A. J. (ed.). 1965. *McClane's standard fishing encyclopedia*. New York: Holt, Rinehart and Winston. 1,057 pp.

McConnell, W. J., W. J. Clark, and W. F. Sigler. 1957. Bear Lake: Its fish and fishing. Utah Department of Fish and Game, Idaho Department of Fish and Game, Utah State Agricultural College, Logan. 76 pp.

Migdalski, E. C., and G. S. Fichter. 1983. *Fishes of the world*. New York: Greenwich House. 316 pp.

Miller, E. E. 1966. Channel catfish. Pp. 440–463 in A. Calhoun (ed.), *Inland fisheries management*. California Department of Fish and Game.

Miller, R. G. 1951. The natural history of Lake Tahoe fishes. Ph.D. dissertation, Stanford University, Stanford, California. 160 pp.

Miller, R. R. 1943. *Cyprinodon salinus*, a new species of fish from Death Valley, California. *Copeia* 1943(2):69–78.

———. 1945. Four new species of fossil cyprinodont fishes from eastern California. *Journal of the Washington Academy of Science* 35(10):315–321.

———. 1948. The cyprinodont fishes of the Death Valley system of eastern California and southwestern Nevada. *Miscellaneous Publications of the Museum of Zoology of the University of Michigan* 68:1–155.

———. 1958. Origin and affinities of the freshwater fish fauna of western North America. Pp. 187–222 in *Zoogeography, a symposium of the American Association for the Advancement of Science*. Publication 51. Washington, D.C.

———. 1961. Speciation rates in some freshwater fishes of western North America. Pp. 537–560 in F. Blair (ed.), *Vertebrate speciation*. Austin: University of Texas Press.

———. 1965. Quaternary freshwater fishes of North America. Pp. 569–581 in H. E. Wright, Jr., and D. G. Frey (eds.), *The quaternary of the United States*. Princeton, N.J.: Princeton University Press.

———. 1968. Records of some native freshwater fishes transplanted into various waters of California, Baja California, and Nevada. *California Fish and Game* 54(3):170–179.

————. 1973. Two new fishes, *Gila bicolor snyderi* and *Catostomus fumeiventris* from the Owens River Basin, California. *Occasional Papers of the Museum of Zoology of the University of Michigan, Ann Arbor* 667 : 1–19.

Miller, R. R., and J. R. Alcorn. 1946. The introduced fishes of Nevada, with a history of their introduction. *Transactions of the American Fisheries Society* 73 : 173–193.

Miller, R. R., and C. L. Hubbs. 1960. The spiny-rayed cyprinid fishes (Plagopterini) of the Colorado River system. *Miscellaneous Publications of the Museum of Zoology, Ann Arbor, Michigan* 115 : 1–39.

Miller, R. R., and E. P. Pister. 1971. Management of the Owens pupfish, *Cyprinodon radiosus*, in Mono County, California. *Transactions of the American Fisheries Society* 100(3) : 502–509.

Minckley, W. L. 1973. *Fishes of Arizona*. Phoenix: Arizona Game and Fish Department, Sims Printing Co. 293 pp.

Minckley, W. L., D. A. Hendrickson, and C. E. Bond. 1985. *Geography of western North American freshwater fishes: Description and relationships to intracontinental tectonism*. Chapter 15 in *Zoogeography of North American freshwater fishes*. Ed. E. O. Wiley and C. H. Hocutt. Wiley-Interscience.

Moodie, G. E. E. 1966. Some factors affecting the distribution and abundance of the chiselmouth (*Acrocheilus alutaceus*). M.S. thesis, University of British Columbia, Vancouver, B.C. 53 pp.

Morgan, G. D. 1954. The life history of the white crappie, *Pomoxis annularis*, of Buckeye Lake, Ohio. *Denison University Science Laboratory Journal* 43(618) : 113–114.

Morrison, R. B. 1964. Soil stratigraphy: Principles, applications to differentiation and correlation of quaternary deposits and landforms, and applications to soil science. Ph.D. dissertation, University of Nevada, Reno. 181 pp.

————. 1965. New evidence on Lake Bonneville stratigraphy from southern Promontory Point, Utah. Pp. 110–119 in U.S. Geological Survey Professional Paper 525C.

Morrow, J. E. 1980. *The freshwater fishes of Alaska*. Illus. M. J. Dalen. Anchorage: Alaska Northwest Publishing Co. 248 pp.

Moyle, P. B. 1976. *Inland fishes of California*. Berkeley: University of California Press. 405 pp.

Murphy, G. I. 1948a. A contribution to the life history of the Sacramento perch (*Archoplites interruptus*) in Clear Lake, Lake County, California. *California Fish and Game* 34(3) : 93–100.

————. 1948b. Distribution and variation of the roach (*Hesperoleucus*) in the coastal region of California. M.A. thesis, University of California, Berkeley.

————. 1950. The life history of the greaser blackfish (*Orthodon microlepidotus*) of Clear Lake, Lake County, California. *California Fish and Game* 36(2) : 119–133.

Neuhold, J. M. 1957. Age and growth of the Utah chub, *Gila atraria* (Girard). *Transactions of the American Fisheries Society* 85(1955) : 217–233.

Nevada Wildlife Department. 1982. Job progress report, Lahontan Reservoir,

January 1, 1981 through December 31, 1981. Reno: Nevada Department of Wildlife. Unpublished report. 29 pp.

Nyquist, D. 1963. The ecology of *Eremichthys acros*, an endemic thermal species of cyprinid fish from northwestern Nevada. M.S. thesis, University of Nevada, Reno. 247 pp.

Olson, H. F. 1959. The biology of the Utah chub, *Gila atraria* (Girard), of Scofield Reservoir, Utah. M.S. thesis, Utah State University, Logan. 34 pp.

Patten, B. G., and D. T. Rodman. 1969. Reproductive behavior of northern squawfish (*Ptychocheilus oregonensis*). *Transactions of the American Fisheries Society* 98(1): 108–111.

Patterson, C. 1981. The development of the North American fish fauna—a problem of historical biogeography. Pp. 265–281 in P. L. Forey (ed.), *The evolving biosphere*. London: British Museum (Natural History).

Payne, N. R. 1964. The life history of the walleye, *Stizostedion vitreum vitreum* (Mitchill), in the Bay of Quinte. M.A. thesis, University of Toronto, Toronto, Ontario. 40 pp.

Pflieger, W. L. 1975. *The fishes of Missouri*. Jefferson City: Missouri Department of Conservation. 343 pp.

Pister, E. P. 1981. The conservation of desert fishes. Pp. 411–446 in R. J. Naiman and D. L. Soltz (eds.), *Fishes in North American deserts*. New York: John Wiley and Sons.

Popov, B. H., and J. B. Low. 1950. Game, fur animal and fish: Introductions into Utah. Salt Lake City: Utah Department of Fish and Game, Miscellaneous Publications 4. 85 pp.

Purkett, C. A. 1958. Growth of fishes in the Salt River, Missouri. *Transactions of the American Fisheries Society* 87(1957): 116–131.

Raleigh, R. F. 1982. Habitat suitability index models: Brook trout. U.S. Department of the Interior, Fish and Wildlife Service, FWS/OBS-82/10.24. 42 pp.

Reiber, R. W. 1983. Reproduction of Arctic grayling, *Thymallus arcticus*, in the Lobdell Lake system, California. *California Fish and Game* 69(3): 191–192.

Reid, H. 1930. A study of *Eupomotis gibbosus* (L.) as occurring in the Chamcook lakes, N.B. *Contributions to Canadian Biology and Fisheries* 5(16): 457–466.

Reimers, M. 1979. A history of a stunted brook trout population in an Alpine lake: A lifespan of 24 years. *California Fish and Game* 65(4): 196–215.

Ringuelet, R. A., R. H. Aramburu, and A. Alonso de Aramburu. 1967. *Los peces argentinos de agua dulce* [The freshwater fishes of Argentina]. La Plata, Argentina: Provincia de Buenos Aires. 602 pp.

Roach, L. S., and I. M. Evans. 1948. Growth of game and pan fish in Ohio. Two crappies. Columbus: Ohio Division of Conservation, Section of Fish Management, Fish Management Report. 29 pp.

Robins, C. R., R. M. Bailey, C. E. Bond, J. R. Brooker, E. A. Lachner, R. N. Lea, and W. B. Scott. 1980. *A list of common and scientific names of fishes from the United States and Canada*. 4th ed. Bethesda, Md.: American Fisheries Society, Special Publication 12. 174 pp.

Schoenherr, A. A. 1981. The role of competition in the replacement of native fishes by introduced species. Pp. 173–203 in R. J. Naiman and D. L. Soltz (eds.), *Fishes in North American deserts*. New York: John Wiley and Sons.

Schreck, C. B., and R. J. Behnke. 1971. Trouts of the upper Kern River Basin, California, with reference to systematics and evolution of western North American *Salmo*. *Journal of the Fisheries Research Board of Canada* 28(7):987–998.

Schultz, L. P., with E. M. Stearn. 1948. *The ways of fishes*. New York: D. Van Nostrand Co. 264 pp.

Scott, W. B., and E. J. Crossman. 1973. Freshwater fishes of Canada. Fisheries Research Board of Canada, Bulletin 184. 966 pp.

Seegrist, D. W., and R. Gard. 1972. Effects of floods on trout in Sagehen Creek, California. *Transactions of the American Fisheries Society* 101(3) 478–482.

Shirley, D. J. 1983. Spawning ecology and larval development of the June sucker. *Transactions of the Bonneville Chapter, American Fisheries Society*, pp. 18–36.

Sigler, W. F. 1949. Life history of the white bass, *Lepibema chrysops* (Rafinesque) of Spirit Lake, Iowa. Iowa Agricultural Experiment Station Bulletin 366. 22 pp.

———. 1951. The life history and management of the mountain whitefish *Prosopium williamsoni* (Girard) in Logan River, Logan, Utah. Utah State Agricultural College, Logan, Bulletin 347. 36 pp.

———. 1953. The rainbow trout in relation to other fish in Fish Lake. Utah Agricultural Experiment Station Bulletin 358. 26 pp.

———. 1958a. Fish life history series: The whitefishes of Bear Lake. *Utah Fish and Game Magazine* 14(12):20–21.

———. 1958b. The ecology and use of carp in Utah. Utah Agricultural Experiment Station, Logan, Bulletin 405. 63 pp.

———. 1962. Bear Lake and its future, twenty-sixth honor lecture. The Faculty Association, Utah State University, Logan. 25 pp.

Sigler, W. F., W. T. Helm, P. A. Kucera, S. Vigg, and G. W. Workman. 1983. Life history of the Lahontan cutthroat trout, *Salmo clarki henshawi*, in Pyramid Lake, Nevada. *Great Basin Naturalist* 43(1):1–29.

Sigler, W. F., and J. L. Kennedy (eds.). 1978. *Pyramid Lake ecological study*. Logan, Utah: W. F. Sigler & Associates. 545 pp.

Sigler, W. F., and R. R. Miller. 1963. *Fishes of Utah*. Salt Lake City: Utah Department of Fish and Game. 203 pp.

Sigler, W. F., S. Vigg, and M. Bres. 1986. Life history of the cui-ui, *Chasmistes cujus* Cope, in Pyramid Lake, Nevada. *Great Basin Naturalist* 45(4).

Sigler, W. F., and G. W. Workman. 1975. Studies on the least chub, *Iotichthys phlegethontis* (Cope), in geothermal activities of Snake and Tule valleys, Utah. In *Studies for wildlife on energy areas*. Washington, D.C.: U.S. Department of the Interior, Bureau of Land Management. 23 pp.

———. 1978. The Bonneville cisco of Bear Lake, Utah-Idaho. Logan: Utah Agricultural Experiment Station, Research Report 33. 34 pp.

Simpson, J. C., and R. C. Wallace. 1978. *Fishes of Idaho*. Moscow: University of Idaho Press. 237 pp.

Smith, G. R. 1975. Fishes of the Pliocene Glenns Ferry Formation, southwest Idaho. *University of Michigan Papers in Paleontology* 14:1–68.

————. 1978. Biogeography of intermountain fishes. Pp. 17–42 in K. T. Harper and J. L. Reveal (eds.), *Intermountain biogeography: A symposium*. Great Basin Naturalist Memoirs 2. Provo, Utah: Brigham Young University.

————. 1981. Late Cenozoic freshwater fishes of North America. *Annual Review of Ecology and Systematics* 12:163–193.

Smith, P. W. 1979. *The fishes of Illinois*. Published for the Illinois State Natural History Survey. Urbana: University of Illinois Press. 314 pp.

Smith-Vaniz, W. F. 1968. *Freshwater fishes of Alabama*. Auburn, Alabama: Auburn University Agricultural Experiment Station. 211 pp.

Snow, H. 1969. Comparative growth of eight species of fish in thirteen northern Wisconsin lakes. Wisconsin Department of Natural Resources Research Report 46. 23 pp.

Snyder, J. O. 1908. Relationships of the fish fauna of the lakes of southeastern Oregon. Bulletin of the U.S. Bureau of Fisheries, vol. 27, document 636. 103 pp.

————. 1918. The fishes of the Lahontan system of Nevada and northeastern California. *Bulletin of the United States Bureau of Fisheries* 35(1915–1916):31–86.

Sterba, G. 1959. *Freshwater fishes of the world*. London: Vista Books. 878 pp.

Sumner, F. H. 1940. The decline of the Pyramid Lake fishery. *Transactions of the American Fisheries Society* 69(1939):216–224.

Tanner, V. M. 1936. A study of the fishes of Utah. *Utah Academy of Sciences, Arts, and Letters* 13:155–183.

————. 1950. A new species of *Gila* from Nevada (Cyprinidae). *Great Basin Naturalist* 10:31–35.

Tave, D. A., A. S. McGinty, J. A. Chappel, and R. O. Smitherman. 1981. Relative harvestability by angling of blue catfish, channel catfish and their reciprocal hybrids. *North American Journal of Fisheries Management* 1(1):73–76.

Taylor, D. W., and G. R. Smith. 1981. Pliocene molluscs and fishes from northeastern California and northwestern Nevada. *University of Michigan Museum of Paleontology Contributions* 25:339–413.

Townley, J. M. 1980. *The Truckee Basin fishery, 1844–1944*. Reno: University of Nevada, Nevada Historical Society and Water Resources Center. 88 pp.

Trautman, M. B. 1981. *The fishes of Ohio*. 2nd ed. Columbus: Ohio State University Press, in collaboration with the Ohio Sea Grant Program Center for Lake Erie Research. 782 pp.

Varley, J. D., and P. Schullery. 1983. *Freshwater wilderness Yellowstone fishes and their world*. Yellowstone National Park, Wyo.: Yellowstone Library and Museum Association. 132 pp.

Vigg, S. 1978. Vertical distribution of adult fish in Pyramid Lake, Nevada. *Great Basin Naturalist* 38(4):417–428.

————. 1980. Seasonal benthic distribution of adult fish in Pyramid Lake, Nevada. *California Fish and Game* 66(1):49–58.

————. 1982. Ecology of the Nevada relict dace, *Relictus solitarius* Hubbs and Miller. Reno: Desert Research Institute, Bioresources Publication 50019. 110 pp.

Vigg, S., and P. A. Kucera. 1981. Contributions to the life history of the Sacramento perch, *Archoplites interruptus* (Girard), in Pyramid Lake, Nevada. *Great Basin Naturalist* 41(3):278–289.

Vogele, L. E. 1975. The spotted bass. Pp. 34–45 in R. H. Stroud and H. Clepper (eds.). *Black bass biology and management.* Washington, D.C.: Sport Fishing Institute.

Vondracek, B., L. R. Brown, and J. J. Cech, Jr. 1982. Comparison of age, growth, and feeding of the Tahoe sucker from Sierra Nevada streams and a reservoir. *California Fish and Game* 68(1):36–46.

Warner, R. 1982. Metamorphosis. *Science* 82/83(10):43–46.

Wheeler, S. H. 1974. *The desert lake: The story of Nevada's Pyramid Lake.* Caldwell, Idaho: Caxton Printers Ltd. 133 pp.

Williams, C. D. 1983. Life history of the Railroad Valley springfish *Crenichthys nevadae* Hubbs (Cyprinodontidae) of central Nevada. M.S. thesis, California State University, Sacramento. 69 pp.

Williams, C. D., and J. E. Williams. 1981. Distribution and status of native fishes of the Railroad Valley system, Nevada. *California-Nevada Wildlife Transactions* 1981:48–51.

———. 1982. Summer food habits of fishes from two springs in west-central Nevada. *Southwestern Naturalist* 27(4):437–445.

Williams, J. D. 1981. Threatened desert fishes and the Endangered Species Act. Pp. 447–475 in R. J. Naiman and D. L. Soltz (eds.), *Fishes in North American deserts.* New York: John Wiley and Sons.

Williams, J. E. 1980. Systematics and ecology of chubs (*Gila*: Cyprinidae) of the Alvord Basin, Oregon and Nevada. Ph.D. dissertation, Oregon State University, Corvallis. 187 pp.

Williams, J. E., and C. E. Bond. 1980. *Gila boraxobius*, a new species of cyprinid fish from southeastern Oregon with a comparison to *G. alvordensis* Hubbs and Miller. *Proceedings of the Biological Society of Washington* 93(2):291–298.

———. 1983. Status and life history notes on the native fishes of the Alvord Basin, Oregon and Nevada. *Great Basin Naturalist* 43(3):409–420.

Williams, J. E., and G. R. Wilde. 1981. Taxonomic status and morphology of isolated populations of the White River springfish, *Crenichthys baileyi* (Cyprinodontidae). *Southwestern Naturalist* 25(4):485–503.

Williams, J. E., and C. D. Williams. 1980. Feeding ecology of *Gila boraxobius* (Osteichthyes: Cyprinidae) endemic to a thermal lake in southeastern Oregon. *Great Basin Naturalist* 40(2):101–114.

Williams, J. E., C. D. Williams, and C. E. Bond. 1980. Fishes of the Sheldon National Wildlife Refuge. In R. A. Tubb (principal investigator), *Survey of fishes, amphibians and reptiles on the Sheldon National Wildlife Refuge, Nevada.* Washington, D.C.: U.S. Fish and Wildlife Service. 58 pp.

Willsrud, T. 1971. A study of the Tahoe sucker, *Catostomus tahoensis* Gill and Jordan. M.S. thesis, San Jose State College, San Jose, California. 96 pp.

Wilson, M. V. H. 1977. Middle Eocene freshwater fishes from British Columbia. *Royal Ontario Museum Life Sciences Contributions* 113:1–61.

Wolters, W. R. 1981. Triploidy in channel catfish, *Ictalurus punctatus*. Ph.D. dissertation, Purdue University, Purdue, Indiana. 60 pp.

Workman, G. W., W. F. Sigler, and W. G. Workman. 1976. The least chub, *Iotich-thys phlegethontis* (Cope), in Juab County, Utah. *Utah Academy of Sciences, Arts and Letters Proceedings* 53(2):16–22.

Wydoski, R. S., and R. R. Whitney. 1979. *Inland fishes of Washington.* Seattle: University of Washington Press. 220 pp.

Yarrow, H. C. 1874. On the speckled trout of Utah, *Salmo virginalis* Girard. Pp. 363–368 in U.S. Fish Commission Report for 1872 and 1873, part XII.

Zarbock, W. M. 1952. Life history of the Utah sculpin, *Cottus bairdi semi-scaber* (Cope), in Logan River, Utah. *Transactions of the American Fisheries Society* 81(1951):249–259.

INDEX TO FISHES

Each fish species is discussed under nine life-history subheadings. These are: importance, range, description, size and longevity, limiting factors, food and feeding, breeding habits, habitat, and preservation of species. Boldface numbers in this index indicate pages where the life histories are discussed.

GENERAL INDEX